Wolfgang Obenaus · Josef Weidacher

Handbook of Business English

Keywords in Context

D1722387

SERVICE
Fachverlag an der
Wirtschaftsuniversität Wien

Englische Wirtschaftstermini
Auf Englisch erläutert – Ins Deutsche übersetzt

CIP-Kurztitelaufnahme der Deutschen Bibliothek

Obenaus,Wolfgang
Handbook of Business English: Keywords
in Context / Wolfgang Obenaus; Josef Weidacher. – 2. durchgesehene Aufl. – Wien:
Service, Fachverlag an der Wirtschaftsuniversität, 1986
ISBN 3-85428-050-5

NE: Weidacher, Josef; HST

Copyright: Service-Fachverlag an der Wirt-
schaftsuniversität Wien, 1986
Druck: Berger, Horn
Layout: Dipl.-Ing. Bengt Sprinzl
Printed in Austria

To Professor Helmut Haschka

PREFACE

This is the second of a planned series of books on Business English. While the first one* deals with the grammar of Business English, from a contrastive angle, the present volume is concerned with the more factual aspects of the subject. Its purpose is to give the reader a survey of what the authors in their long teaching careers have found to be useful and important topics in economics and business administration. These topics have been selected with special regard to the Business English courses taught at the Vienna University of Economics and Business Administration, and reflect the language needs of students and graduates in academic and occupational contexts. It is for this reason that the theory and practice of international trade have been given such prominence in this book.

To facilitate reference, the material is presented in encyclopaedic form, i.e., the entries are headed by keywords, indicating their main subjects, and arranged in alphabetical order. They range from simple, succinct definitions to fairly long essays. The authors have deliberately not aimed at achieving linguistic and stylistic uniformity, but have chosen a variety of styles and approaches. To enhance the usefulness of the book, it is planned to publish a supplement containing a detailed alphabetical English-German vocabulary as well as a list of all keywords classified according to subject-matter. Thus, for instance, somebody interested in the material on banking will find all banking terms under this heading in the supplement.

In conclusion, the authors wish to express their gratitude to all those who have helped to make this book possible: to Dr. Gernot Neuwirth, who prepared the entries dealing with the' Environment'; to Dr. Ursula Peter-Heinrich, who assisted in drafting the entries on 'Banking'; to Dr. Ingrid Markwitz and Mag. Renate Putz, who provided material for entries on 'Business Organisations' and 'Financial Management', respectively. Special thanks are due to Tony Smith, B.A. Honours, who painstakingly checked and rechecked the bulk of the entries from the language point of view. Help in this area was also provided by Keith Oliff, B.A. Honours, and Mag. Stuart Heaman-Dunn, M.A. However, responsibility for any inaccuracies that may exist lies with the authors. Last, but not least, thanks go to Miss Christine Beck and Miss Irene Siedl for their valued assistance and hard work in typing out the manuscript.

September 1985   *Wolfgang Obenaus*
                                                                   Josef Weidacher

---

* Obenaus, W., and Weidacher, J.: Englische Wirtschaftssprache – Übungen zur Grammatik: Angabenteil und Lösungsteil; 490 S.; SERVICE, Fachverlag an der Wirtschaftsuniversität Wien; Wien 1983.

BOOKS SPECIFICALLY MENTIONED IN THE TEXT:

Gartside, L.:
>   Commerce – A Guide to the Business World; MacDonald & Evans Ltd.; 1977.

Jowitt, Earl:
>   The Dictionary of English Law; Sweet & Maxwell Ltd., London 1959.

Kotler, Philip:
>   Marketing Management – Analysis, Planning and Control; 4th ed., Prentice-Hall International, Inc., Englewood Cliffs, 1980.

Schmitthoff, Clive M.:
>   The Export Trade – The Law and Practice of International Trade; 6th ed.; Stevens & Sons Ltd; London 1975.

The Concise Oxford Dictionary:
>   6th ed., edited by J.B. Sykes; Oxford University Press; Oxford 1976.

A

accelerator principle   Akzeleratorprinzip

The accelerator principle is a theory which tries to explain the level of investment expenditure in an economy. It states that, where an economy is operating at, or near, full capacity, expected changes in the output of consumer goods tend to produce more than proportionate changes in capital expenditure.

The basic idea of the accelerator principle is not difficult to grasp: when output is expected to remain constant, it will not be necessary to expand existing plant and equipment. Investment will be limited to replacing existing machinery as it wears out. If, however, income rises and an increase in consumer demand is forecast, it will be necessary to invest in new plant and equipment to produce the additional output. This is where the accelerator principle comes in: in order to produce, for instance, an additional one billion dollars' worth of consumer goods in a given period of time, a much larger investment in plant and equipment will be required, e.g., four billion dollars if the capital output ratio is four to one. An expected fall in consumer demand, on the other hand, means that there will be no new investment, and that business organisations may not even bother to replace existing capacity.

To sum up: expected changes in consumer demand tend to produce much more violent swings in capital expenditure, something that will obviously have a destabilising effect on the economy. It is for this reason that a more sophisticated version of the accelerator principle, taking account of construction lags and the cost of capital, plays an important role in explanations of the trade cycle.

acceptance (of a bill of exchange)   Annahme (eines Wechsels)

The drawee of a time bill is under no liability to holders of the bill until he has accepted it. Therefore, the bill is, as a rule, presented to the drawee for acceptance.

Acceptance generally means that the drawee writes the word 'Accepted' across the face of the bill, followed by his signature and, sometimes, by the date of acceptance and the place of payment (e.g., "Accepted. Payable at Barclay's Bank Ltd., High Street, S.W.4. George Brown"). In the case of a bill payable a specified period after sight - which, in practice, means payable a specified period after acceptance - the date of acceptance is imperative for the maturity of the bill to be determined. By accepting the bill the drawee becomes the 'acceptor' and incurs the obligation to pay it at maturity.

Finally, it should be noted that the term 'acceptance' is also applied to the accepted bill itself. For example, where payment has been arranged "against three months' acceptance", the seller (drawer and payee) sends a bill payable three months after sight to the buyer (drawee), who, after accepting it, returns the acceptance to the seller. The latter may either keep it and present it for payment at maturity, or pass it on in payment of a debt, or discount it with a bank.

acceptance (of an offer)   Annahme (eines Antrages)

The acceptance of an offer is the offeree's consent to the offer made by the offeror and a prerequisite for the conclusion of a contract. The acceptance may be oral, in writing, or implied from conduct (e.g., somebody receives goods which he has not ordered and remits the purchase price to the supplier; a supplier dispatches the goods ordered; etc.). As a general rule, silence on the part of the offeree is not an acceptance.

For a contract to become effective, the acceptance must be unqualified, i.e., it must correspond with all the terms of the offer. A qualified acceptance constitutes a rejection of the offer and causes it to lapse (for example, if a house is offered for sale at £1,000 and the offeree qualifies his acceptance by making a counter-offer at £950, the offer lapses).

Normally, an acceptance is not effective until it has been communicated to the offeror, i.e., until it has been received by him. The offeror, however, may expressly authorise the offeree to use a particular means of communication to communicate his acceptance (e.g., A sends an offer to B by mail for acceptance by return mail). In this case, the acceptance is effective when it is delivered to the agency of communication. (For example, since in most commercial contracts today the post is used as a means of communication, acceptance is effective as soon as it is posted. It does not matter if the letter of acceptance is lost in the post and never reaches the offeror: the contract is complete as soon as the letter of acceptance is posted). By contrast, in Austria, there are no exceptions to the rule that an acceptance becomes effective (thus resulting in a contract) only when it is received by the offeror.

acceptance (of goods)   Annahme (von Waren)

One important obligation of the buyer under a contract of sale is to accept the goods delivered to him by the seller. The acceptance of the goods should not be confused with their mere receipt. From the legal point of view, the buyer is deemed to have accepted the goods:
1. when he intimates to the seller, after he has inspected the goods, that he has accepted them;
2. when the goods have been delivered to him, and he acts as if he were the owner, e.g., if he resells the goods or pledges them as security; or
3. when, after the expiry of a reasonable time, he retains the goods without intimating to the seller that he has rejected them.

This shows that, from the legal point of view, there is a clear distinction between "to accept the goods" (die Waren annehmen) and "to take delivery of the goods" (die Waren übernehmen / abnehmen /). In the latter case, the buyer merely takes over the goods from the seller, carrier, etc., without indicating whether he wants to accept or reject them.

account[1]   Konto

In accounting, the term 'account' refers to a record of debit and credit entries posted to a ledger page from books of original entry to cover transactions of a particular type or of a particular person or concern. Accounts are usually T-accounts, so called because they are shaped like the capital letter T.

The left-hand side of an account is called the 'debit side', the right-hand side the 'credit side'. An entry on the debit side of an account is called a 'debit entry', or simply a 'debit'; an entry on the credit side is referred to as a 'credit entry', or a 'credit'. When an entry is made on the debit side, this is known as 'debiting the account'; 'crediting the account' is obviously the opposite. An account can be debited/credited with an amount, or, which comes to the same thing, an amount may be debited/credited to an account. The difference between the sum total of all debits and the sum total of all credits is known as the 'balance'. If the money total of the debit entries exceeds the money total of the credit entries, the account is said to have a debit balance. In the opposite case, the account has, or shows, a credit balance.

Accounts may be classified into 'real accounts' and 'nominal accounts'. Real accounts are the balance sheet accounts, i.e., they are used to record assets (asset accounts) and liabilities (liability accounts, including owners' equity accounts). In the Cash account, for instance, receipts and payments of cash are recorded, receipts on the debit side, and payments on the credit side. Other typical examples of asset accounts are: Land, Buildings, Machinery, Machinery and Equipment, Office Equipment, Furniture and Fixtures, Patents, Accounts Receivable, Notes Receivable, Merchandise Inventory. Accounts Payable, Notes Payable, Bonds Payable, Capital Stock, and Retained Earnings are commonly used liability accounts. On the balance sheet date, all real accounts must be closed to the balance sheet.

Nominal accounts are used to record income (or revenue) items (income accounts, or revenue accounts) and expense items (expense accounts), income being entered on the credit side and expense on the debit side. It should be noted that the term 'income accounts' may also be used in a broader sense, viz., as a synonym for 'nominal accounts', or, to put it slightly differently, as an all-inclusive term for both revenue and expense accounts. The following are some examples of expense accounts: Wages Expense, Salaries Expense, Wages and Salaries Expense, Office Expense, Rent Expense, Advertising Expense, Interest Expense, Insurance Expense, Depreciation Expense, Travel Expense, Freight Out, etc.. Sales, Interest Income, and Rent Income are some illustrative account titles for revenue accounts. In contrast to real accounts, nominal accounts are closed to the income statement.

account[2] (pl.)   Buchhaltung (im Sinne der Geschäftsbücher)

Especially in British English, the term 'account', when used in the plural, may refer to the bookkeeping records of any organisation, including journals, ledgers, vouchers, and other supporting documents.

account[3] (pl.)   (Rechnungs-)Abschluß, Jahresabschluß

In an accounting context, the term 'accounts' may be taken to mean the financial statements of an enterprise, i.e., basically the balance sheet and the profit and loss account (U.S.: income statement), drawn up at the end of an accounting period. Accounts may be prepared annually (annual accounts) or at shorter intervals (e.g., quarterly accounts).

account[4]   -bilanz (im Sinne der
                                                         volkswirtschaftlichen Gesamtrechnung)

Accounts are not only used in business accounting, but also in social (or national)
accounting. For instance, the subdivisions of the balance of payments, and
sometimes even the balance of payments itself, are referred to as 'accounts'. The
balance of trade may be called the 'visible account' or 'merchandise account'.
There is also an 'invisible account', a 'current account', and a 'capital account'.
The balance of payments may be referred to as 'external accounts', because it
comprises a number of 'accounts' recording transactions with non-residents.

account[5]   Rechnung

In addition to denoting an amount owed, the expression 'account' may also be
taken to mean a statement showing, frequently in great detail, how much is due.
'Account', therefore, can be used in many contexts as an alternative to 'bill' or
'invoice'.

Suppliers render accounts for the goods and services they sell, while their
customers have to settle, i.e., pay, these accounts.

account[6]   Kunde,
                                                         Klient

Especially in an advertising or marketing context, 'account' may be used instead
of 'client', 'customer', or 'patron'.

Part of the marketing resources of a company will be devoted to servicing
accounts, in particular key accounts. The accounts of an advertising agency are
looked after by special account executives.

account[7]   Werbeetat,
                                                         Kundenetat

The term 'account' may also be used to describe the product or products
entrusted by an advertiser to a particular advertising agency, and, by implication,
the funds allocated by the advertiser for this purpose.

account[8]   Geschäftsbeziehung,
                                                         Kundenbeziehung,
                                                         Kundschaft

Sometimes, 'account' refers not to the customer or client himself, but to the
relationship between supplier and customer or to the patronage received from a
person or organisation. "Reviving inactive accounts" is, therefore, equivalent to
"putting new life into old business relationships", while "to secure a firm's
account" is another way of saying "to win a firm's patronage or custom" or "to win
a firm as a customer".

account executive

Kundenbetreuer,
(Werbe-)Kontakter

An account executive is an employee in an advertising agency. As the name suggests, he is responsible for a designated account, i.e., for a particular product or brand for which his agency prepares advertising. He is charged with maintaining liaison with the client whose account he services, with developing and controlling the client's advertising programmes, and with related matters. In a large agency, an account executive may report to an account supervisor, while in a smaller agency, he may work directly under the head of the account management department.

The term can also be used in banking contexts to describe an employee responsible for a client or a group of clients.

accounting

Rechnungswesen

In principle, accounting is concerned with the recording in monetary terms of business transactions and of activities incidental to them. Its principal purpose is to provide relevant financial information to internal and external users, such as management, investors, government agencies, etc.. Management, for instance, will need cost data from the accounting system for setting product prices; investors may decide to buy, hold, or sell a particular share on the basis of accounting information; and a government agency's decision to give or withhold a subsidy will certainly be influenced by the shape of the potential recipient's accounts.

If used without any qualifying adjective, accounting usually means 'financial accounting', the oldest and most representative form of accounting. Financial accounting is basically concerned with recording a firm's transactions with its environment (e.g., with customers, banks, suppliers) and certain external and internal events affecting the firm's fortunes (e.g., earthquakes, depreciation); with preparing financial statements, summarising these transactions; and, finally, with designing the accounting systems required for this purpose. The simpler aspects of the accounting process, viz., the actual chores of collecting the relevant business documents and entering the information contained in them in the appropriate journals and ledgers, are referred to as 'bookkeeping', while 'accounting' tends to be used for the aspect dealing with financial statements and the design of accounting systems. The same distinction applies to the terms 'bookkeeper' and 'accountant'.

'Cost accounting', the second-most important variant of accounting, is concerned with identifying, classifying, recording, allocating, and reporting the current, projected, or planned costs of a business organisation.

'Auditing' is another important area of accounting. It involves a detailed examination of the accounts and procedures of an organisation, either by its own staff (internal audit) or by outside experts (external audit). Its main purpose is to detect error and fraud, as well as to ensure conformity with the generally accepted accounting principles and, increasingly, with certain broadly defined efficiency criteria.

'Corporate social accounting' is a new aspect of accounting and reflects the increasing sense of social responsibility in the corporate world. Social accounts supplement the information provided in the more traditional financial statements by focussing attention on such matters as staff welfare programmes, staff benefits, and environmental expenditures.

Sometimes budgeting and business statistics, or at least those aspects of budgeting and statistics that are concerned with accounting concepts, such as assets, liabilities, revenues, and expenses, are regarded as forming part of accounting.

In recent years, all these accounting tasks have been greatly facilitated by the use of computers. A wide range of standardised application programs is available in this field.

accounting cycle

Buchungszyklus (vom Beleg bis zum Jahresabschluss)

Financial accounting can be regarded as an information processing cycle, starting with the capture of business data and ending with the preparation of periodic financial statements.

Accounting data appears in the form of business documents either generated automatically by transactions (e.g., invoices, credit notes, bank statements, etc.) or prepared specially for accounting purposes, such as depreciation computations or schedules of assets lost in connection with an event insured against.

The information contained in many of these source documents is subsequently recorded chronologically in books of original entry, or journals. In most accounting systems, several books of original entry, such as cash books, sales day books, purchase books, bills books, are used. These specialised books introduce a systematic element into what is basically the chronological stage of the accounting cycle. The classification format, however, comes into its own in the next stage of the accounting cycle, viz., in the ledger, the centre-piece of every double-entry bookkeeping system.

A ledger is essentially a set of accounts designed to reflect, systematically and in accordance with accepted accounting rules, the thousands of transactions entered into by a business firm. The ledger accounts are usually divided into real accounts, which record assets and liabilities, or changes in assets and liabilities respectively, and nominal accounts, concerned with income and expense items. In some old-fashioned accounting systems, however, there are also mixed accounts, such as the mixed merchandise account, which contains both nominal and real elements (viz., stocks and sales revenue). More detailed information on the accounts used by a particular firm can be found in that firm's chart of accounts, i.e., a systematically arranged list of accounts, giving account names and numbers, if any.

Originally, ledgers were literally books of accounts, into which entries were made manually. Today, a ledger consists of a set of loose-leaf-type accounts (loose-leaf account sheets), or, increasingly, of a set of computer files. The process of transferring accounting information from the books of original entry to the ledger accounts is referred to as 'posting the ledger'.

It should be noted that there are bookkeeping systems under which the ledger is posted straight from the source documents, and the journals are either completely dispensed with (as, for instance, in many computerised accounting systems) or become a by-product of the basic posting process (as, for instance, in some duplicating systems).

At the end of an accounting period, the ledger accounts are balanced, and their respective debit or credit balances are listed in what is referred to as the 'unadjusted trial balance'.

The next step is to develop the adjusting entries, such as the annual depreciation charges; accrued and deferred items, meant to identify income and expense with their proper benefit period; estimated liabilities; etc.. This is usually done on a worksheet with separate columns for the unadjusted trial balance, the adjusting entries, the adjusted trial balance, and, finally, for the income statement, the statement of retained earnings, and the balance sheet. From these latter columns the financial statements are developed, a process which completes the accounting cycle described in this entry.

accounting principles

Grundsätze ordnungsgemäßer
Buchführung und Bilanzierung

Accounting principles are the doctrines underlying current accounting practices, conventions, and procedures. They may be classified into 'basic accounting principles' and 'generally accepted accounting principles'. The former are the broad standards or guidelines intended to achieve the primary objective of accounting, viz., to provide relevant information to internal and external decision-makers. The latter (often abbreviated as GAAP) are more specific: they include not only broad guidelines of general application, but also detailed principles and procedures. They prescribe how transactions and other events should be recorded, classified, summarised, and reported, and are the means of implementing the basic principles.

The following is a brief summary of the most important basic accounting principles:
1. Cost principle: under this principle, also known as the 'historical cost principle', all assets and liabilities (including owners' equity) have to be recorded initially at cost (i.e., the value at the date of the transaction).
2. Matching principle: the matching principle holds that the expenses incurred in generating the revenues realised in a particular period should be reported in that same period, i.e., revenues and expenses should be matched. This matching of expenses with revenues requires that the accrual basis of accounting, as opposed to the cash basis, be used to record and report expenses and revenues. According to the accrual basis, revenue is considered realised (i.e., earned), and is recognised in the accounts, in the period in which the transaction occurs (i.e., when a sale is completed or when a service is performed), regardless of when the related cash is collected. Similarly, expenses are recognised when they are incurred as a result of a transaction, regardless of when the cash payment is made.
3. Concept of conservatism, or concept of prudence: where acceptable accounting alternatives for recording events or transactions are available, the alternative having the least favourable immediate influence on owners' equity should be selected. In compliance with the concept of conservatism, assets

15

have to be valued at each balance sheet date at the lower of cost or market (lower-of-cost-or-market principle), and liabilities at the higher of cost or market (higher-of-cost-or-market principle). The basic idea underlying these two principles is that expected but unrealised losses have to be recognised in the accounts, whereas expected but unrealised gains must be ignored.

4. Consistency principle: for the financial statements of successive periods to be comparable, accounting concepts, standards, and procedures have to be consistently applied from one accounting period to the next. In other words, consistency means that transactions in the current period are treated in the same way as they were treated in previous periods, so that the financial statements for the current period can be compared with previous periods without erroneous conclusions being drawn from them. The emphasis on consistency does not mean that accounting methods, once adopted, can never be changed. The principle of fair presentation, however, requires that any inconsistency be disclosed.

5. Principle of fair presentation: this principle states that financial statements have to be presented in accordance with the generally accepted accounting principles.

accounts payable

Verbindlichkeiten aufgrund von Warenlieferungen und Leistungen

'Accounts payable' in the narrower sense of the term refers to amounts owing to creditors, generally on open account, in respect of goods supplied or services rendered. In other words, accounts payable are - usually short-term - liabilities on open account (i.e., they are not evidenced by a bill of exchange or promissory note) arising from purchases of goods or services used in the regular course of business. In this sense, the term is used as a synonym for 'trade accounts payable', 'accounts payable to trade creditors', or 'trade creditors'. The term 'account payable' is also applied to a ledger account for such a liability.

Occasionally, 'accounts payable' is also used in a wider sense, in which case it additionally includes amounts owed, for example, to partners, officers, shareholders, and employees. On the balance sheet, however, these amounts should be shown separately or as miscellaneous accounts payable.

According to the concept of conservatism, (trade) accounts payable, like all other debts , have to be valued at the higher of cost or market. This is particularly true of accounts payable denominated in a foreign currency. At the balance sheet date, they have to be entered on the books either at the historical (or original) rate of exchange (i.e., the rate in effect at the time a specific transaction occurred) or at the closing rate of exchange (i.e., the rate ruling at the balance sheet date), whichever is the higher.

accounts receivable[1] - general

Buchforderungen;
Forderungen aufgrund von Warenlieferungen und Leistungen - allgemein

In the narrower sense, 'accounts receivable' refers to a firm's short-term claims, generally on open account, against trade debtors. In other words, accounts receivable denote amounts due from customers which are collectible within one year, are not evidenced by a bill of exchange or promissory note, and arise from goods and/or services sold on credit in the ordinary course of business. In this sense, the term is used synonymously with 'trade accounts receivable' or 'trade debtors' (the term used in Britain). The term 'account receivable' is also applied to a ledger account for such a claim.

In the wider sense, 'accounts receivable' is applicable to all of a firm's short-term claims on open account. Consequently, it not only includes trade accounts receivable, but also claims arising from transactions other than normal trade transactions, such as claims against employees, claims against insurance companies for losses sustained, advances to subsidiaries, etc.. On the balance sheet, these amounts should be shown separately or as miscellaneous (or special) accounts receivable.

accounts receivable[2] - valuation   Forderungen aufgrund von Warenlieferungen und Leistungen - Bewertung

According to the concept of conservatism, accounts receivable, an important item of current assets, have to be valued at the balance sheet date at the lower of cost or market. 'Market' in this context means the expected net realisable value of the accounts, i.e., gross claims less estimated uncollectible accounts. Valuation of accounts receivable is a rather complicated matter and, therefore, requires some further comments.

Valuation of accounts receivable poses the problem of estimating the amount which will be actually realised by collection. When credit is extended on a regular basis, some accounts receivable will almost invariably prove uncollectible. These losses due to uncollectibility must, in compliance with the matching principle, be matched with the revenue of the period in which the sales transactions occurred, rather than in later periods when the specific accounts receivable turn out to be uncollectible. However, since these 'uncollectible accounts' (also known as 'uncollectibles' or 'bad debts') are not known until the periods in which they are determined to be uncollectible, the bad debt expense must be estimated in advance, recorded in the accounts, and reported in the current financial statements. The estimate for expected bad debt losses is most commonly expressed as a certain percentage of the current period's net credit sales. This percentage is based on past experience, i.e., on the relationship between sales in previous accounting periods and bad debt losses resulting from them.

The most widely known method of accounting for bad debts is the 'allowance method'. Under this method, the estimated loss from uncollectible accounts is debited to the expense account Bad Debt Expense and credited to the valuation account Allowance for Bad Debts (also designated as Allowance for Doubtful Accounts, Allowance for Uncollectible Accounts, Provision for Bad Debts, etc.). When, in a later period, a specific account receivable turns out to be uncollectible, it has to be written off by debiting Allowance for Bad Debts and crediting 'Accounts Receivable - name of debtor'. If an account receivable previously written off as uncollectible is collected, the account has to be reinstated, usually by debiting the customer's account ('Accounts Receivable - name of debtor') and crediting Allowance for Bad Debts. The cash collection will then be recorded by a debit to Cash and a credit to 'Accounts Receivable - name of debtor'. Collections made on accounts which have been written off as uncollectible are referred to as 'recoveries'.

It follows from the nature of the allowance method that it is particularly suitable for business firms with a large number of accounts receivable. Smaller firms, or business enterprises where experience has shown that the amount of loss from uncollectible accounts is minor in relation to the revenue, usually use the 'direct write-off method'. Under this method, bad debts are recognised in the accounts and statements in the period in which the accounts receivable are determined to be uncollectible. They are written off by the following entries: "debit Bad Debt Expense, and credit Accounts Receivable - name of debtor".

Accounts receivable denominated in a foreign currency have to be shown on the balance sheet either at the historical (or original) rate of exchange (i.e., the rate in effect at the time a specific transaction occurred) or at the closing rate of exchange (i.e., the rate ruling at the balance sheet date), whichever is the lower. This is in compliance with the concept of conservatism, according to which unrealised losses must be recognised and unrealised gains must be ignored. (In contrast to realised exchange gains and losses,which arise from settlement transactions, unrealised exchange gains and losses are the result of valuation practices at the balance sheet date.).

acid rain   saurer Regen

Acid rain, which has become increasingly prevalent in industrialised and neighbouring countries in the 1970s and 1980s, is precipitation (rain, snow, etc.) characterised by the formation of weak solutions of sulphuric acid (H_2SO_4) and nitric acid (HNO_3) when the water vapour in the air reacts with the air pollutants sulphur dioxide (SO_2) and nitrogen dioxide (NO_2) emitted from factories, fossil fuel power-stations, motor cars, and domestic heating. Estimates concerning the share for which each of these polluters is responsible vary, as do estimates of the percentages of "home-made" and "imported" acid rain. An official figure for Austria is 80 per cent home-made, and 20 per cent imported. Great Britain "exports" a large amount of acid rain to Scandinavia, as does the U.S.A. to Canada.

Acid rain is largely responsible for the destruction of the forests. Proposals to alleviate the effects of acid rain range from the breeding of resistant trees and from sprays providing protective plastic coating for ordinary trees, to speeding up the construction of nuclear and hydro-electric power-plants to replace fossil fuel power-stations. However, recent evidence suggests that nuclear power-plants may themselves contribute to the destruction of the forests, while large hydropower plants, such as the Hainburg project, purportedly save woods by destroying large areas of the most resistant woodlands of all, viz., wetland forests.

Feasible solutions include effective scrubbers for fossil fuel plants, reduction in the waste of materials and energy, increased energy efficiency, discouragement rather than promotion of electric resistance heating, and changes in life-style.

acid-test ratio   Liquidität 2. Grades

The acid-test ratio, or quick ratio, is a very important liquidity ratio, i.e., it is a useful indicator of a firm's ability to meet its short-term financial obligations when they fall due. It is computed by dividing a firm's quick (current) assets by its current liabilities. Quick (current) assets consist of cash, trade accounts receivable, short-term notes receivable, and temporary (i.e., short-term) investments in marketable securities. These assets are called 'quick' because either they are cash or can quickly be converted into cash to meet financial obligations. Quick assets do not include inventories, because the latter are not readily convertible into cash . This is why the acid-test ratio is a more appropriate indicator of a firm's liquidity than the current ratio.

Traditionally, an acid-test ratio of 1:1 (a rule-of-thumb standard) has been regarded as desirable. As is the case with the current ratio, the quick ratio for any particular firm has to be evaluated in the light of industry characteristics and other factors.

act of god   Naturereignis

An act of god is a force-majeure event caused by natural forces which no human power could prevent, e.g, earthquake, flood, lightning, storm, volcanic eruption.

ad valorem duty   Wertzoll

An ad valorem duty is any kind of import duty which is charged at a certain percentage of the value of the imported goods. Ad valorem duties are mainly used for motor cars, watches, cameras, and other manufactured goods. Whereas the United States uses both ad valorem and specific duties in roughly equal proportion, European countries use mainly ad valorem duties.

Ad valorem duties are considered to be more equitable than specific duties. A person, for example, importing a Rolls Royce pays more than a person importing a Citroen 2CV, which means that ad valorem duties are a form of proportional taxation. The value on which ad valorem duties are based is the value for customs purposes, which is approximately equivalent to the c.i.f. value of the goods or to their value at the frontier of the importing country.

advertisement   Werbemittel,
                                      Inserat,
                                      Annonce

An advertisement is a message or announcement presented in a medium (e.g., T.V., radio, magazine) at the expense of an identified person or organisation (the advertiser) to persuade the audience to accept an idea, buy a product or service, or take some other action desired by the advertiser. Examples are classified ads, posters, electric signs, commercials (either a radio commercial or a T.V. spot), sky-writing, full-page and double-spread ads in newpapers or magazines.

advertiser   Werbungtreibender

The advertiser is the person or organisation (usually a business firm) that arranges and pays for the production and placing of an advertisement with a view to persuading the target group to take some action desired by the advertiser (usually to buy a product or service).

An advertiser may have his own advertising department, headed by an advertising manager, but will almost invariably avail himself of the services offered by advertising agencies.

advertising   Werbung

Advertising is undoubtedly the most important and best-known of all promotional tools, and, as is the case with all other forms of promotion, its main purpose is to inform, persuade, and influence the general public or a selected target group with a view to modifying their behaviour in some way desirable for the advertiser, e.g., increasing their purchases of a particular product. In contrast to the other promotional tools, advertising involves the dissemination of messages over the mass media and is paid for directly by an identified sponsor. Product advertising, as the name suggests, is geared to the goods and services offered by the advertiser, while institutional advertising is intended to create a favourable attitude towards the advertiser and to build goodwill.

Advertising, because it is so much in the limelight, is, however, also a social issue. There are many who argue, quite convincingly, that advertising, because it operates in a buyers' market, puts too much emphasis on persuasion and attempts to influence people in ways that are not really beneficial to them. Since an outright ban on advertising would probably require a radical change in our socio-political system, most critics only advocate stricter regulations for this form of promotional activity.

advertising agency   Werbeagentur

The term 'advertising agency' is a misnomer in at least two respects: first, it is not an agency in the narrower legal sense of that word, but an independent commercial service organisation acting for its own account. Second, it offers not only advertising services - such as the planning and implementation of advertising campaigns, the creation of the actual advertisements and arrangements for placing them in appropriate media - but increasingly a much wider range of marketing services, including the carrying out of market research, the conducting of test campaigns, the preparation of sales manuals, etc..

A typical advertising agency will have a research department; a creative department, charged with conceiving, developing, and executing advertising ideas, and staffed by creative directors, copy-writers, commercial artists, etc.; a media selection department; and an account management department. This latter department is responsible for the individual accounts (i.e., for the brands or products for which the agency prepares advertising) and is charged with maintaining close contact with the clients of the agency. The agency executive with overall responsibility for an account is called the 'account executive'. Most agencies have, in addition, a separate internal service department, which is responsible for office management, finance, billing, accounting, and related matters.

advertising copy   Werbetext

Advertising copy is the text of an advertisement, in contrast to non-textual elements, such as pictures, drawings, layout. Persons specialising in producing copy are referred to as 'copy-writers'. Copy is an important element in advertising. Most advertisements include some copy, whether in the form of an advertising slogan (e.g., on a poster) or of a full page of text (e.g., in the case of a major newspaper advertisement).

advertising medium   Werbeträger

Advertising media are the means used to communicate advertisements to the chosen audience. Usually, the term refers to the major (or mass) media (radio, television, the press, and the outdoor media, such as hoardings). The lesser media include direct mail (e.g., sales letters), directories, fairs, exhibitions, and motion pictures.

The advertiser or his advertising agency has the task of selecting the advertising medium or media and, within each medium, the vehicle and advertising schedule suitable for a particular purpose or situation. For example, a decision may have to be made on whether to use radio or press advertising. Then it will be necessary to select a specific radio programme or journal (the vehicle) and the appropriate time or times for running the particular advertisements (advertising schedule). Factors to be allowed for in media selection include: the type of product to be advertised, the target group, and the cost involved.

One of the problems is to select the medium or combination of media (and, of course, the vehicle(s) and advertising schedule(s)) that will reach as many members of the target group as possible (optimum coverage) and as few people outside the target audience as possible (minimum loss of circulation). For this reason, the trade press would be a suitable medium for advertising capital goods (e.g., specialised industrial equipment), while advertising on T.V. would not.

advice of dispatch   Versandanzeige

An advice of dispatch, also called a 'shipping advice' or 'advice note', is a written notice sent by the consignor to the consignee informing the latter that the goods have already been, or will shortly be, dispatched. It is customary to specify the time of shipment, the method of transport, and, in many cases, to give a description and state the quantity of the goods concerned.

The main purpose of the dispatch advice is to notify the customer that the goods are, or will shortly be, on their way and to enable him to check the goods when they arrive or, if they have been delayed or gone astray, to make inquiries. The advice of dispatch is often dispensed with and replaced by an invoice sent on or before the day the goods are dispatched.

agenda   Tagesordnung

An agenda is a list of the items to be discussed at a meeting, such as a board meeting, an annual general meeting, or a meeting of a standing committee. The term is derived from the Latin verb "agere" and literally means "things that are to be done". Where meetings are conducted on the basis of formal rules of procedure, the latter contain detailed provisions concerning the agenda. They usually specify the person or persons responsible for drawing up the agenda (e.g., the person to chair the meeting), the rights of the other members to have items included, certain standard items to be included in any case (e.g., an item dealing with the minutes of the last meeting), the time limits to be observed when circulating the agenda to the members, etc..

agent

Vertreter,
Handlungsbevollmächtigter

In law, an agent is a person who acts on behalf of another person (the principal). The relationship between the agent and his principal is called the 'agency'. In general, it means any relationship in which one person acts for the benefit and under the control of another (e.g., the relationship between employer and employee, or between a firm and its commercial agents). In a narrower sense, the term 'agency' includes only the relationship between agent and principal under which the former is authorised to procure contracts from, or to enter into contracts with, third parties on/for the principal's account. He can enter into these contracts either in the principal's name (e.g., commercial agent) or in his own name (e.g., forwarding agent). In the first case, the parties to the contract are the principal and the third party, whereas in the second case, the contracting parties are the agent and the third party. A contract concluded by an agent within the scope of his authority binds the principal in the same manner as if the principal himself had concluded it.

As regards the extent of the agent's authority, he is either a general agent or a special agent. A general agent has authority to represent his principal in all business of a certain kind, e.g., in managing a branch office of a bank. A special agent has limited authority for a particular task, e.g., someone is authorised to purchase a particular house.

Finally, it should be mentioned that the term 'agent', as used in law, has a different meaning from that attributed to it in commercial practice: it is wider in so far as it covers, for instance, employees, and narrower in so far as it does not include persons who buy and sell on their own account, e.g., distributors.

aggregate

volkswirtschaftliche Globalziffer,
Aggregat,
Gesamtgröße

In economics, the term 'aggregate' refers to a macro-economic variable, i.e., to a variable related to the economy as a whole, and not to some lesser economic unit. Typical examples of aggregates are national income, gross national product, and money supply.

The term can also be used as an adjective, as in 'aggregate demand', i.e., the sum total of all goods and services demanded, or purchased, in a national economy at a given price level, in contrast to the demand for a particular commodity or service. If used as a verb, 'aggregate' means "to combine into a whole".

agribusiness

"Agribusiness",
industriell betriebene Landwirtschaft

Agribusiness is the name given to current methods of agriculture in industrialised countries. It is characterised by mechanisation and automation, and by the intensive use of chemicals in the form of artificial fertilisers and poisons (e.g., pesticides, herbicides, etc.). Agribusiness with its heavy machinery is extremely energy-intensive, and so is the manufacture of artificial fertiliser.

Agribusiness has helped to increase yields and to reduce considerably the number of agricultural workers. Some critics consider this a mixed blessing at a time of growing general unemployment. They also point out that agribusiness often leads to over-production: each year in the E.E.C. alone, about one million tons of agricultural products are deliberately destroyed in order to maintain predetermined price levels.

At the same time, agribusiness has done very little to help the hungry of the world, and attempts to transplant it to the Third World ("Green Revolution") have frequently failed and ended in soil erosion, the elimination of natural pest control (birds, etc.), an increase in resistant pests, increased social injustice, and impoverishment. About 500,000 people in the Third World are damaged by pesticides, etc., each year.

Critics further argue that even industrialised countries pay too dearly for whatever advantages they may get from agribusiness. Our rivers are now polluted by traces of artificial fertiliser, our food is poisoned by all-pervasive traces of agricultural herbicides, pesticides, fungicides, etc., the manufacture of which sometimes causes accidents, as in the case of the dioxin explosion at Seveso, Italy. (Dioxin is a by-product developed in the production of some herbicides. It is one of the most deadly substances known and is now prohibited in most civilised countries. In the Free West, the Austrian Chemie Linz AG was one of the last companies to insist on continuing production. Production was suspended only in 1983, after direct clashes between protesting members of GREENPEACE Austria and trade union functionaries at the Chemie Linz works.)

As an alternative to agribusiness, organic farming is now being proposed. Organic farms, though severely opposed by agribusiness from the beginning, are slowly but surely gaining ground in Austria and in other parts of the world.

all-risks cover

All-Gefahren-Deckung

In general, the term 'all-risks cover' means insurance protection against total or partial loss of, or damage to, the subject-matter insured arising from any fortuitous causes except those that are specifically excluded. 'All-risks policies' are in contrast to 'specified-perils policies' (also referred to as 'named-perils policies'), which cover only the risks specified in the policy. The all-risks form of coverage is the broadest insurance protection generally available.

All-risks policies are very common in marine insurance and aviation insurance (both cargo and hull insurance), but they are also used in other classes of insurance. In the case of cargo insurance, an all-risks cargo policy covers all risks of loss of, or damage to, the goods insured, subject only to specific exclusions. In (ocean) marine insurance, it also gives the insured full cover against general average. The following are some illustrative examples of risks covered: loss or damage due to fire; explosion; stranding or sinking of the vessel; collision; entry of sea, lake, or river water into the conveyance or container; overturning or derailment of land conveyance; theft and pilferage; acts of god (e.g., earthquake, flood, volcanic eruption, lightning); etc.. Excluded from coverage are, for example, wear and tear of the goods; natural deterioration of the goods, e.g., of perishable goods; loss, damage, or expense caused by insufficient or unsuitable packing, by inherent vice of the goods, by delay, etc.. Political risks, such as the risk of loss or damage caused by war, strikers, locked-out workmen, and so on, are usually also excluded, but may be covered for an extra premium.

alternative marketing organisation
alternative Vertriebsorganisation

Distribution is one major problem faced by less developed countries: how to get the goods from the producer to the consumer who may be thousands of miles away? This is particularly true of third-world co-operatives and similar socially-oriented ventures, which, in addition to being confronted with the basic logistical problems, may encounter a boycott from the local trading community. These difficulties make it impossible for them either to sell the products at remunerative prices or to sell them at all.

Alternative marketing organisations (AMOs), such as OXFAM in England or EZA in Austria, have tried to provide outlets for this type of third-world producer. Their efforts are based on the following principles: promotion of labour-intensive forms of production, fostering self-reliance, co-operation with non-exploitative enterprises, avoidance of the traditional trading channels (dominated by large multinational companies), prefinancing the producer (by paying in advance), stabilising prices as far as possible, maximising benefits to the third-world producer, encouraging voluntary groups (e.g., youth organisations) to distribute third-world products in industrialised countries, and setting up a separate distribution network (OXFAM, for instance, runs a mail-order operation).

analogue
analog

Analogue (American spelling: 'analog') refers to the representation of data by means of a continuously variable physical entity. In analogue computers, for instance, data may be represented by voltages. In broadcasting, data is transmitted by means of frequency modulation. Voice transmitted over telephone lines is in analogue form, and so is the music recorded on traditional disks or tapes. Analogue is contrasted with 'digital'.

antitrust law
etwa: U.S.-amerikanische Kartell- und Monopolgesetzgebung

American antitrust law is an elaborate and comprehensive body of law dealing not only with trusts in the widest sense of that term (see: trust[2]), but also with any other form of restraint of trade. The main purpose of the various antitrust laws (e.g., the Sherman Act of 1890, the Clayton Act and the Federal Trade Commission Act of 1914) is to safeguard competition. Although the American antitrust laws are perhaps unique in scope of content and rigour of enforcement, many other countries do, of course, have similar legislation: two examples in the United Kingdom are the Restrictive Practices Act and the Resale Prices Act of 1976.

appreciation   Wertsteigerung

Appreciation refers to an increase in the value of an asset, e.g., of property, of stocks held by merchants and manufacturers (stock appreciation), or in the value of a currency in relation to other currencies (especially under a system of floating exchange rates).

arbitrage   Arbitrage

Arbitrage is generally defined as the act of purchasing foreign exchange, commodities, etc., in one market and selling it/them simultaneously in another market at a higher price.

Applied to foreign exchange, arbitrage is a highly specialised form of foreign exchange dealing, carried out mainly by experts, especially by banks, for the purpose of taking advantage of differences in exchange rates ruling in different dealing centres at any given moment. The idea is to buy a currency in a particular (foreign exchange) market and sell it in another market at a higher price. Where only two markets are involved, the operation is one of 'simple' (or 'direct') arbitrage, and in the case of more than two markets, one of 'compound' (or 'indirect') arbitrage.

The following example is intended to illustrate the functioning of a direct arbitrage operation. Let us assume that, at a given moment, one British pound is trading for $1.82 in London, and that, at the same time, £1 is trading for $1.78 in New York. An arbitrager may benefit from the difference in the exchange rates/prices between the two markets by buying pounds in New York at $1.78 per pound and selling them in London for $1.82, thus making a profit of four cents per pound, or, for example, one of $40,000 on a purchase and sale of £1 million. To realise his anticipated profit, the arbitrager must carry out his buying and selling operations simultaneously, since exchange rates are constantly changing, and if he waits, the London rate may have moved against him.

Generally speaking, arbitrage operations tend to eliminate any exchange rate differential between the two markets. This is because, due to the increased demand for the currency, there is an upward pressure on its price in the market where it is bought, whereas the increased supply in the market where it is sold results in a downward pressure.

Arbitrage should be carefully distinguished fom speculation. Unlike a speculator (bull or bear), an arbitrager assumes no risk. He makes his profit by exploiting price differentials existing between geographical locations at any given time.

arbitration proceedings   Schiedsgerichtsverfahren

By arbitration proceedings is meant the settlement of disputes between parties to a contract by a person or persons chosen by the parties themselves or appointed by a court of arbitration.

If a dispute between a seller and a buyer (e.g., the buyer claims that the quality of the goods is not according to the contract, and the seller claims that it is) cannot be settled by the parties themselves, they have to refer the matter either to a court of arbitration or to a court of law. Usually, the contracting parties try to avoid litigation (i.e., law-suits), which is both costly and time-consuming. Therefore, they may agree in the contract that disputes arising from it are to be settled by arbitration, the decision rendered by the arbitrators (arbitration award) being final and binding on the parties.

It is advisable to include an arbitration clause in the contract, because, once the dispute has arisen, the parties, although basically willing to use arbitration, may find it difficult to agree on the details. For example, the arbitration clause of the International Chamber of Commerce reads as follows: "All disputes arising in connection with the present contract shall be finally settled under the Rules of Conciliation and Arbitration of the International Chamber of Commerce by one or more arbitrators appointed in accordance with the Rules."

assets   Aktiva

Generally speaking, assets are physical objects or rights which are owned by a business firm and which have economic value to their owner.

In the U.S.A. and in Austria, assets are listed on the debit (or left-hand) side of the balance sheet. This is in contrast to Great Britain, where they appear on the credit (or right-hand) side. For balance sheet purposes, the items on the asset side are broadly grouped into 'fixed assets' (tangible and intangible), 'current assets' (cash, receivables, inventories, temporary investments, prepaid expenses), and 'permanent investments'.

auction   Auktion

An auction is a method of selling under which the auctioneer invites the persons present to bid for the goods to be sold. The bidder is the offeror, and he can withdraw his bid at any time before the auctioneer has accepted it, which the latter usually does by knocking with a hammer. It must be clearly understood that there is no contract until the auctioneer has knocked down the item to the highest bidder. Property in the item passes to the buyer as soon as the hammer falls, i.e., as soon as the contract is made. Each item put up for sale becomes the subject of a separate contract.

Auctions are used for works of art, furniture, jewellery, but also for commodities that cannot be easily graded, such as tobacco, tea, wool, and livestock.

audio typist   Phonotypist(in)

In contrast to shorthand typists, who type letters and other documents from their own shorthand notes, audio typists work from material recorded on tape or a similar storage medium. The audio typist plays back the recording at any desired speed, using foot or hand controls for stopping and starting the machine. In large offices, the audio typists are usually centralised in a typing pool.

auditing   Rechnungsprüfung,
                                                   Buchprüfung

In the widest sense of the term, auditing refers to an independent, detailed examination of accounting records, procedures, and even of physical assets of organisations. Audits are carried out for the purpose of detecting and preventing errors, fraud, inconsistencies, inefficiencies, and lack of conformity with external and internal rules and standards.

Auditing may be performed either by outside experts ('external auditing') or by inside experts ('internal auditing').

In many countries, including the United Kingdom, the United States, Austria, and West Germany, external audits of the annual accounts of certain types of companies are prescribed by law (statutory audits) or by regulatory agencies, such as the Securities and Exchange Commission in the United States (regulatory audits).

In the case of statutory or regulatory audits, the relevant laws or regulations lay down who can be an official auditor. In the U.K., for instance, only members of accounting bodies recognised by the Department of Trade, such as members of the Institute of Chartered Accountants, can be auditors.

External audits serve only a limited purpose. External auditors are required to examine the books, vouchers, records, and accounts of a company with a view to ascertaining whether they represent a true and fair view of the company's affairs, whether they have been prepared in conformity with the generally accepted accounting principles, and whether these principles have been consistently applied over the years. External auditors are not supposed to detect waste, management inefficiencies, and similar shortcomings.

The results of an external audit are summarised in the auditor's report. Today, usually the short-form report, appended to the annual accounts of the company in question, is used. A more detailed report or letter may be addressed to the management or the directors. Auditors' reports are either unqualified, i.e., they accept the accounts as they stand, or qualified, which means that the auditor is of the opinion that the accounts do not give a true and fair view. An auditor may also state that he is unable to form an opinion (disclaimer of opinion).

Internal audits are carried out by the firm's own staff, who should, however, also be independent in the sense that they should not report to the organisational units whose affairs might have to be audited by them. An internal audit may cover the same things as an external audit and may, therefore, simplify the work for the external auditor. But in many cases the emphasis is not on ascertaining conformity or non-conformity with the generally accepted accounting rules, but on discovering inefficiencies and improving performance (operational auditing).

austerity   (drastisches) Sparprogramm,
                                                   Austerity

The term is typically applied to government policies that are deliberately deflationary and try to restrain public and/or private expenditure. Austerity programmes are usually meant to reduce inflation or government deficits, to solve balance-of-payments problems, to allocate more of a country's resources to new investment, or to achieve similar goals. The International Monetary Fund frequently makes the granting of loans to countries in financial difficulties conditional upon the introduction of austerity measures.

On a technical level, an austerity programme usually involves higher taxes, lower government expenditure, higher interest rates, and wage restraints, i.e., it may be implemented by fiscal, monetary, and incomes policy measures.

autarky   Autarkie

Autarky denotes self-sufficiency, i.e., the independence of an economic unit from exchanges with other economic units. In our modern world, complete autarky is not possible, since all economic units, whether they are households, firms, or countries, have to obtain at least some goods and services from outside in order to survive. Partial autarky, i.e., self-sufficiency in certain fields, is, however, possible, and also desirable, as it helps to make economic units less vulnerable to crises. Many countries, for instance, try to achieve self-sufficiency in food to prevent famine when external supplies are cut off, e.g., in times of war.

The benefits of autarky do not, however, come free. In most cases, autarky involves a loss of welfare, since the country concerned foregoes the advantages of the international division of labour, such as lower prices and a greater variety of goods and services.

automated teller machine   automatischer Bankschalter,
                                     erweiterter Geldausgabeautomat

An automated teller machine (ATM) is an unmanned customer-activated terminal (CAT), which consists of a keyboard, a display screen, a magnetic strip reader, a note dispenser, and optional features. ATMs may be installed on-site (i.e., at the main office or a branch of a bank) or off-premises, such as in shopping centres, governmental institutions, etc.

To get access to his account, the customer inserts a magnetically encoded plastic card (bank card, cash card) into a slot provided for this purpose and keys in his personal code. This enables him to initiate a range of basic teller functions, including cash withdrawals and deposits, account balance inquiries, and transfers between accounts.

automatic selling   Automatenverkauf

Coin-operated vending machines enable a retailer to sell, and consumers to buy, a limited range of convenience goods 24 hours a day, although there are units which are not accessible round the clock. For the retailer, the main attraction is the saving of labour, since, in contrast to conventional self-service methods, automatic vending dispenses with both sales personnel and cashiers. For the consumer, the principal advantage is the 24-hour service. Against this must be set the cost of buying or hiring, filling, maintaining, and servicing the machines, and, for the consumer, the limited range of goods, the frequent mechanical failures, empty machines, and, last but not least, the need to have the right coins (there are, however, sophisticated units which accept banknotes and return the small change).

28

Vending machines are most widely used in the sale of cigarettes and beverages, although a surprisingly wide range of consumer goods can be, and are being, sold by this method. They include: razor blades, batteries, books, postage stamps, ice cream, fresh flowers (sold from refrigerated units), cassettes, stationery, etc..

Because of its obvious limitations, automatic vending is probably never going to replace the more conventional forms of retailing, but will remain an interesting and useful supplementary method.

average[1]   Durchschnitt (arithmetisches Mittel)

If interpreted strictly, the term 'average' is synonymous with 'arithmetic mean'. It is calculated by adding up a set of items, dividing by the number of items. Simple unweighted indices are, therefore, often referred to as 'averages'. If used attributively, as in 'average quality' or 'below-average performance', the meaning of the term is often less precise and cannot be reduced to calculating an arithmetic mean.

average[2]   (ungewichteter) Index

In American English, the term 'average' can also be used to describe an 'index', especially an unweighted index of security prices. The best-known of these averages is the Dow-Jones industrial average, comprising thirty blue-chip stocks listed (quoted) on the New York Stock Exchange (NYSE, Wall Street).

average[3]   Havarie

When used in (ocean) marine insurance, the term 'average' is applied to a partial loss or damage, that is, a loss or damage which is not total. There are two kinds, 'general average' and 'particular average'.

aviation insurance   Lufttransportversicherung, Luftfahrtversicherung

Aviation insurance is a combination of well-known types of insurance adapted to the conditions of air transport. The main types of aviation insurance available are:
1. Hull insurance, covering accidental loss of, or damage to, the insured's aircraft.
2. Liability insurance, under which the insurer agrees to indemnify the insured (i.e., the aircraft owner) for all sums which the latter becomes legally liable to pay in respect of accidental death or bodily injury suffered by persons on the ground, or in respect of accidental damage to property on the ground, provided such death, injury, or damage is caused directly by the aircraft or by objects falling from it. In addition, liability insurance protects the insured aircraft owner against his legal liability for accidental death or bodily injury to passengers, and for accidental loss of, or damage to, property carried in the aeroplane, such as baggage and cargo. (It should be mentioned that under the contract of carriage by air the air carrier is automatically liable for loss of, or damage to, cargo and baggage if it occurs during the carriage by air. The carrier is not liable if he proves that he and his agents have taken all necessary measures to avoid the

damage or that it was impossible for him or them to take such measures. In Austria, the maximum limits of the air carrier's liability are: AS410,- per kilogram; or the value declared by the consignor when the package was handed over to the carrier and for which he has paid any supplementary charge.)

3. Personal accident insurance, which provides for the payment of fixed amounts to injured aircrew or passengers, irrespective of the question of legal liability for an accident. Passengers may purchase two types of flight accident policy. The first is the well-known trip policy, available at airports (frequently obtainable from slot-machines) and travel agencies, which insures the purchaser for a specific trip or a specified number of hours. The second is a policy which is bought on an annual basis by persons who are regular airline passengers and which covers scheduled flights anywhere in the world.

4. Air cargo insurance: firms sending goods by air may effect insurance either for each individual consignment in the form of trip transit policies, or for recurring air shipments in the form of floating policies or open covers. It is customary for all these policies to be written on an all-risks basis. Under air cargo insurance, the insurer will have subrogation rights against the air carrier for any loss of, or damage to, the goods for which the latter is liable under the contract of carriage by air.

B

balance of payments

Zahlungsbilanz

The balance of payments is a systematic record of all the economic transactions of the residents of a particular country with the rest of the world, i.e., with all non-residents, in a given period, usually one year. This means that the balance of payments, in spite of its name, is a flow concept.

The balance of payments is generally divided into three accounts: first, the current account, which includes the balance of trade (i.e., exports and imports of goods), the invisible account (i.e., exports and imports of services, plus investment income), and unilateral transfers; second, the capital account (i.e., exports and imports of capital, mainly in the form of direct and portfolio investments); and finally, an account dealing with official transactions in gold, foreign exchange, and related items. If a country's foreign exchange receipts (arising from visible and invisible exports, unilateral transfers received from non-residents, and capital imports) fall short of its payments (arising from visible and invisible imports, unilateral transfers made to non-residents, and capital exports), in other words, if the current account and the capital account together show an unfavourable balance, then the country in question is said to have a 'balance-of-payments deficit', which has to be financed in some way: for instance, the country may run down its official gold and foreign currency reserves, and/or increase its foreign borrowing, and/or draw on credit facilities provided by international financial institutions, such as the International Monetary Fund (IFM, set up in 1945), whose main purpose is to lend foreign currencies to countries which need these to finance their balance-of-payments deficits.

A country should try to keep its balance of payments in equilibrium and ensure that, in the long run, its exports of goods and services equal its imports in value, and that, in the short run, it has the necessary foreign currencies to settle any balance-of-payments deficit. For a time such deficits can be met by the debtor country from its reserves of foreign currency and gold, but these reserves are exhaustible, and the only long-term solution is to ensure that more money flows in than out, thus increasing the country's foreign currency reserves. Therefore, a country which runs a persistent deficit on its balance of payments must make every effort to increase its exports and curb its imports of goods and services. This may be achieved, for example, by government-supported export promotion (e.g., export credit guarantees), by imposing import controls (e.g., import quotas, tariffs), by a devaluation of the domestic currency (which makes exports cheaper for foreign buyers and imports more expensive for home buyers), etc.. In addition, a country may also try to improve its capital account by reducing outgoing and increasing incoming investment. This may be achieved, for instance, by imposing controls on outflows of capital, or by increasing domestic interest rates, thus attracting the inflow of foreign capital.

It would be a wrong policy, however, to single out one item and hope that by eliminating this item the deficit can be reduced by an equivalent amount. Two examples illustrate this point. It is often contended that controls on direct

31

investments made abroad can reduce a deficit. It should not be forgotten, however, that usually a large amount of exports in the form of capital equipment, raw materials, and semi-finished goods is associated with the outflow of investment capital, and that, in addition, capital investments in a given year result in investment income in the form of dividends and profits several years later, thus having a positive impact on the current account. Moreover, a country may decide to curb its imports by imposing import controls, which, however, may cause foreign countries to take retaliatory measures. Consequently, government policy should be aimed at eliminating a deficit by implementing appropriate general economic measures, and not by controlling individual balance-of-payments items by administrative means.

balance of trade

Handelsbilanz,
Bilanz des Warenverkehrs

The balance of trade, also termed the 'visible account' ot 'trade account', is part of the balance of payments and records a country's exports and imports of goods (known as 'visible exports' and 'visible imports') during a certain period ot time, usually one year.

If a country's imports of goods exceed its exports, the country is said to have a '(visible) trade deficit', which means that the balance of trade is unfavourable (adverse) / is in deficit / shows a deficit / is in the red / . It is advisable to add 'visible' because in British English the term 'trade deficit' may be used for 'current account deficit'. The opposite of a (visible) trade deficit would be a '(visible) trade surplus', i.e., the balance of trade is favourable / is in surplus / shows a surplus / is in the black /. In the unlikely event that exports equal imports, the trade account would be in balance, or in equilibrium.

balance sheet

Bilanz

The balance sheet, in the U.S.A. also known as the 'statement of financial position' or 'statement of financial condition', is one of the financial statements, or final accounts, drawn up at the end of an accounting period. The most common is the annual balance sheet, although quarterly, or even monthly, statements of (financial) condition are not unknown.

The main purpose of a balance sheet is to provide a 'snapshot' of the assets, liabilities, and (equity) capital of a business unit at the accounting date, or balance sheet date. In contrast to West German and Austrian balance sheets, British and American balance sheets do not normally show the profit or loss for the period under review. This is quite logical since profit or loss figures are flow concepts, i.e., they relate to a period of time, and therefore belong properly to the income statement, or profit and loss account. The balance sheet, on the other hand, represents a stock concept, showing the position at a particular point of time, viz., the accounting date.

Balance sheet data is frequently arranged in account form (although other formats, especially the report form, are quite common), with assets on one side and liabilities and capital on the other side of the T-account. This arrangement reflects the basic balance sheet equation (assets = liabilities + owners' equity), with liabilities and owners' equity representing the source of funds and assets the application of funds. In British balance sheets, the assets appear traditionally on the right-hand, i.e., on the credit, side of the balance sheet, whereas American and Austrian balance sheets show them on the left-hand (or debit) side.

The various types of assets (fixed assets, current assets, investments) and liabilities (short-term liabilities, long-term liabilities), and the equity capital are dealt with under their appropriate headings elsewhere in the book. It should be noted that in the balance sheets of British and American companies, the proprietary interest, i.e., both capital and retained earnings, or reserves, appears under such headings as 'shareholders' equity' or 'stockholders' equity'.

balance sheet ratios   Bilanzkennzahlen

Balance sheet ratios, as the name implies, express relationships between balance sheet items. They are mainly used to analyse the financial position of a business firm at a given time. The following is a summary of the most common balance sheet ratios:

1.   'Current ratio', computed by dividing current assets by current liabilities. (see: current ratio)
2.   'Acid-test ratio', computed by dividing quick (current) assets by current liabilities. (see: acid-test ratio)
3.1. 'Current liabilities to capital (or owners' equity) ratio', computed by dividing current liabilities by owners' equity.
3.2. 'Total liabilities to capital (or owners' equity) ratio', also called 'debt-equity ratio', computed by dividing total liabilities by owners' equity.

    These last two ratios measure the degree of protection from loss afforded to the firm's creditors by the owners' investment; the higher the ratios, the less protection creditors have. If, for example, the ratio of current liabilities to capital is 0.98 : 1, this indicates that current creditors (i.e., lenders of short-term funds) and owners are providing funds of about the same amount to the business. A 'debt-equity ratio' of, for example, 1.30 : 1 indicates that the firm's current and long-term creditors are providing 30 per cent more funds than are the owners. (see: capital structure)

4.   'Owners' equity to total assets ratio', computed by dividing owners' equity by total assets. It shows the percentage of total assets which has been financed by the owners in the form of capital stock and earnings retained in the business. This ratio is of special interest to long-term creditors because it is a measure of financial strength and reflects the long-term liquidity of a firm. Generally speaking, the higher the ratio, the stronger the long-run financial position of the firm. The difference between this ratio and 100 per cent is represented by the 'ratio of total liabilities to total assets', i.e., the percentage of total assets financed by creditors.
5.   The 'ratio of fixed assets to net worth', also known as the 'fixed assets to equity ratio', computed by dividing the firm's net fixed assets (i.e., gross fixed assets less accumulated depreciation) by net worth. This ratio shows the proportion of fixed assets financed by the owners of the firm. If the ratio is larger than 1, this means that the fixed assets exceed the owners' equity and that creditors' funds have been used to finance part of the fixed assets. Especially from a creditor's point of view, it is desirable that all fixed assets should be financed by owners' funds; consequently a 'fixed assets to equity ratio' of 1 : 1 indicates that the firm in question is totally dependent on creditors' funds to finance its current assets. A ratio of less than 1 indicates that the funds provided by the firm's owners have been used to finance all the risky fixed assets and part of the current assets.

bank charges

Kontoführungs- und
Manipulationsgebühren

In the U.K. and the U.S., bank customers usually have to pay an account charge for the conducting of a current account and for related banking transactions, unless they keep a certain minimum balance in their accounts throughout the full charging period. The periodical 'account charge' is based on the number of transactions effected, and is usually collected at the end of each charging period. By contrast, 'service charges' for individual transactions, such as stopping a cheque, providing additional copies of a bank statement, or overdrawing an account without previous agreement, may have to be paid either when they arise or at the end of each charging period.

The introduction of new, and the increase of existing, bank charges in the past few years have provoked many consumer protests, as free banking services had long been used as a marketing tool to spread the banking habit. Due to the decline in interest rates and free balances (i.e., non-interest-bearing current account balances), banks have, however, become more cost-conscious with regard to running personal accounts. In particular, the introduction of NOW accounts, i.e., of interest-bearing checking accounts, in the U.S.A. has been an incentive for banks to move towards charging customers the true cost of the checking account services they receive.

bank deposits

(Bank-) Einlagen

In everyday commercial usage, the term 'bank deposit' refers to an amount credited to a customer's deposit account. Such credits may be the result of cash, cheques, drafts, or similar instruments placed with the bank, or of credit transfers to the customer's account.

On the basis of withdrawal, deposits may be classified as 'demand deposits' and 'time deposits'. Demand deposits may be withdrawn by the depositor (e.g., by cheque) or transferred by him to someone else's account at any time, without prior notice to the bank. They are held by depositors who need a liquid balance for their financial transactions, and usually bear no, or only very little, interest.

Time deposits are covered by a contract stipulating that the depositor may not make any withdrawal prior to maturity (fixed deposits) or prior to the expiry of the period of notice (notice deposits). In the U.S., for example, both periods are 30 days or more.

Other types of time deposits are savings deposits, held in what is referred to as 'passbook savings accounts', and deposits covered by time certificates of deposit.

Time deposits cannot be withdrawn by cheque, nor can they be transferred to other accounts, although deposits held in U.S. NOW accounts do in some respects represent an exception to this rule.

bank draft

Bankenscheck;
Institutsscheck

Technically, a bank draft, or banker's draft, is a negotiable instrument drawn by a bank either on itself (including a branch or the head office) or on another bank at home or abroad. Strictly speaking, this definition is only valid for Great Britain, since in the United States, the first variety, i.e., the instrument drawn by a bank on itself, is referred to as a 'cashier's check', a term not used in the United Kingdom.

Bank drafts provide a very safe method of payment where ordinary cheques would not be acceptable. This is particularly true of payments to parties residing abroad. If a bank customer wishes to make a payment to, let us say, his foreign supplier, he may purchase, for a small fee, a bank draft drawn by his bank on a correspondent bank in the payee's country. He, or the bank itself, will then forward the draft to the payee, and, at the same time, the bank will send to the foreign bank a special letter of advice containing all details of the draft. This letter serves as a protection against fraud, since the draft is not paid until the communication has been received by the payee's bank.

Bank drafts denominated in a foreign currency and payable abroad are a specific form of foreign exchange.

banking services   Bankdienstleistungen

Many present-day banks are practically "financial department stores", i.e., full-service banks, engaging in many kinds of banking and related services, such as: -
1. receiving demand deposits, paying customers' cheques drawn against them, and providing various other mechanisms for the domestic and international transmission of funds, including electronic funds transfer facilities;
2. receiving time and savings deposits and paying interest on them;
3. discounting promissory notes and bills of exchange;
4. extending credit to business firms, with or without security;
5. granting personal loans and credit card facilities to individuals, mainly to finance private consumption;
6. issuing letters of credit and accepting bills of exchange drawn under them;
7. handling documentary collections;
8. issuing bank drafts, cashier's checks, and money orders, and certifying cheques;
9. providing safe deposit vault facilities and custodianship for customers' securities and other valuables;
10. acting in a fiduciary capacity and providing various trust services for private and business clients;
11. underwriting and dealing in securities, subject to the country's legal provisions;
12. providing factoring and leasing services;
13. dealing in foreign exchange and issuing travellers' cheques; and, increasingly,
14. providing related financial, legal, insurance, management, and consulting services.

bank lending   Kreditgeschäft der Banken,
Aktivgeschäft der Banken

Lending by banks, which is an important source of business finance, can be classified in a number of ways: e.g., according to maturity (i.e., according to the time allowed for repayment), according to the purpose for which the funds are used, and according to the security provided by the borrowers. On the basis of maturity, it is customary to distinguish between 'short-term', 'medium-term', and 'long-term' finance.

Short-term finance, which has a duration of up to one year (although some British authors would say, up to three years), includes overdrafts (mainly British) and their American near-equivalents (viz., credit lines and revolving credits), discounts (i.e., bills of exchange discounted by banks), acceptance credits (where a bill of exchange is accepted by one bank but discounted by another), and, finally, ordinary short-term loans. In Britain, the expression 'advance' is sometimes used to describe the principal forms of short-term bank finance.

Medium-term finance usually comes in the form of ordinary loans (referred to as 'term loans' in the United States) which have a duration of between one and five years (between three and ten years, according to some British sources). It is, however, possible to extend revolving credits beyond the usual one-year period, and many overdrafts are, in effect, a form of medium-term finance.

Until very recently, British and American banks were not prepared to grant long-term loans, i.e., loans with maturities of over five (some would say, 10) years. Although the situation has changed in the past few years, British and American firms normally obtain their long-term creditors' funds from other sources, e.g., from insurance companies, pension funds, or by issuing debentures (U.S.: corporate bonds).

Loans and other forms of bank lending may be either unsecured (unsecured loans) or secured (secured loans). Security can be either in the form of some valuable property or charge upon valuable property (as in the case of receivable loans, inventory loans, and mortgage loans), or in the form of a guarantee.

bank reference   "Bankreferenz"

By bank reference (also 'banker's reference') we mean the name of the customer's bank from which the supplier can get information about the customer's creditworthiness. (For example, a customer may supply the following bank reference: "For information concerning our credit standing we refer you to Barclays Bank, 25 - 27 The Arcade, Southampton.")

It should be noted that banks give information only to other banks. Therefore, a supplier seeking information from his customer's bank can obtain this information only through his own bank.

bankruptcy   Konkurs

If persons or businesses become insolvent, i.e., unable to meet their obligations as they mature, either they themselves or their creditors may file a petition in bankruptcy with a competent court of jurisdiction. If the person or business is adjudged bankrupt, his/its property will be administered under the court's order for the benefit of the creditors. This may mean that the bankrupt's property, also referred to as the 'bankrupt's estate', is liquidated to satisfy the claims of the creditors on a pro-rata basis. But it may also mean that the debtor's business is allowed to continue free of interference from creditors, while it reorganises its management and reschedules payments of its obligations. This is the case in the United States when a bankruptcy petition is filed under Chapter 11 of the Bankruptcy Reform Act of 1978, which permits firms to seek protection from their creditors.

In other countries, including Great Britain and Austria, schemes of arrangement, or composition, between the debtor and his creditors, usually involving payment of the obligations in part, are possible. This enables the debtor to avoid bankruptcy.

Bankruptcy is a highly complicated matter, and it is obviously impossible to deal with all its aspects and variants within the scope of this short article. In conclusion, it should, however, be mentioned that in the United Kingdom, the terms 'bankruptcy' and 'bankrupt' are applied only to persons and unincorporated businesses, while companies unable to pay their debts are 'wound up, or liquidated, compulsorily'.

bank statement   Kontoauszug

A bank statement is a typed or computer-printed loose-leaf summary of all transactions involving a customer's account within a certain period of time. The following details of payments made or received are shown: the date of payment, the amount paid or received, and the method of payment used (e.g., cheque, individual credit transfer, standing order).

Under customary banking practice, statements are supplied to customers regularly (e.g., once a month) or, for instance, whenever a payment has been made to the account. Where ATMs are used, customers may have their statements printed out at any time.

bank transfer   Banküberweisung (ins Ausland)

A bank transfer, or banker's transfer, is an international funds transfer, i.e., a transfer of funds from a bank account in one country to a bank account in another country. Acting upon the debtor's request, a local bank instructs the payee's bank abroad to credit the payee's account with the amount transferred, typically in the payee's own currency.

As delays may occur when the instructions are sent by mail or air mail (M.T. - mail transfer), it has become customary for banks to communicate by telegram or telex (T.T. - telegraphic transfer; telex transfer).

In Europe and North America, an international interbank telecommunications system, known as S.W.I.F.T. (Society for Worldwide Interbank Financial Telecommunications), has been established to transmit messages relating to international payments speedily and efficiently between member banks (SWIFT transfer).

barge   Lastkahn,
Frachtkahn

A barge is a slow-moving, flat-bottomed boat for carrying goods, especially large quantities of bulk goods (e.g., coal, sand), on rivers and canals.

barter   Tausch(handel), Tauschgeschäfte;
                                                Gegengeschäfte; Eigenkompensation

Barter is the exchange of goods and/or services for other goods and/or services without the use of money. Barter is characteristic of primitive societies, but it can also be found in modern societies, for instance, when there is a war and the monetary system of a country breaks down, or where a country is short of foreign exchange for the purchase of essential imports. In the latter case, the arrangements involved are usually more complicated than the simple, direct exchange of goods or services between two parties, and are called 'countertrade'.

batch processing   Stapelverarbeitung

In batch processing, data is collected in "batches" and processed periodically. So there is some delay between the occurrence of original events (e.g., withdrawing cash from a cash dispenser or keying in a text for word processing) and the eventual processing of the data generated by these events. The data collected off-line for batch processing may be transferred to the processing unit either manually (e.g., in the form of tapes) or over data transmission lines. Batch processing is contrasted with 'real-time processing'.

bear   Baissier

A bear is a speculator who expects that the price of a security or other investment medium (e.g., property, currency, commodity) will fall. He therefore sells the security, etc., short in the hope that he will be able to buy it more cheaply at a future time. This means that the bear is a short seller and takes what insiders refer to as 'short positions'.

A market situation dominated by bears (or short positions) is called a 'bear market', which is characterised by falling prices and, generally, by a bearish (i.e., pessimistic) sentiment.

bearer bill   Inhaberwechsel

A bearer bill is a bill of exchange drawn payable to bearer. This means that it can be transferred without indorsement by mere delivery and must be paid by the drawee to whoever presents it for payment at maturity.

Usually, a bill of exchange is a bearer bill if the bill itself so states (e.g., "30 days after sight pay to bearer 500 pounds"). But any order bill can be transformed into a bearer bill by the indorser putting only his signature to the bill, i.e., indorsing it in blank.

Bearer bills are very rare in practice, and original bearer bills (i.e., those drawn payable to bearer) are not known in Austria.

bearer cheque   Inhaberscheck

A bearer cheque is a cheque made payable to bearer (e.g., "Pay to the bearer of this cheque £250"). It needs no indorsement and is paid to anyone who presents it at the bank, and, therefore, affords less security than an order cheque. The person presenting the cheque may have found or stolen the cheque and, though he has of course no legal right to it and is committing a criminal offence in trying to cash it, he may be able to get it paid. As a safeguard against this, the cheque may be "crossed", which means that it can be paid only into an account, making it possible for the lost or stolen cheque to be traced back to the person having found or stolen it.

If the drawer of a bearer cheque wishes to withdraw money from his account, the only thing he has to do is cash it at the drawee bank. In this case, the drawer and the bearer are the same person. In addition, he may also cash it at a bank other than the drawee bank by showing his cheque card.

The cheques used in Austria are bearer cheques. Order cheques are only customary in dealings with foreign countries and in interbank transactions.

bill of exchange   Wechsel

Under British and American law, the bill of exchange (abbreviated B/E), also called the 'draft', is defined as "an unconditional order in writing, addressed by one person to another, signed by the person giving it, requiring the person to whom it is addressed to pay on demand or at a fixed or determinable future time a sum certain in money to, or to the order of, a specified person, or to bearer". In simple terms, a B/E is an order given by one person (the drawer) to another (the drawee) to pay a specified sum of money to a particular person (a named payee or the bearer). "Person" includes not only individuals, but also organisations.

All points laid down in the legal definition of the B/E are essential and require some comments:
1. "Unconditional order" means that the order must not be dependent on some event which may or may not happen, e.g., it must be independent of the underlying contract of sale. An example of the usual wording used would be: "90 days after sight pay to me or my order 500 pounds". A conditional order, rendering the B/E void, would be for instance: "Pay Mr. Brown if the goods are up to sample".
2. "Writing" includes printing and typing, and a B/E can be written on any available material except metal. In contrast to Great Britain and the United States; Austrian law requires the word "WECHSEL" to be included in the wording of the B/E.
3. "Addressed by one person to another, signed by the person giving it": the person giving the order is the 'drawer', who must sign the B/E, and the person to whom the order is addressed is the 'drawee'.
4. "On demand or at a fixed or determinable future time": a bill of exchange payable on demand is referred to as a 'sight bill', one payable at a fixed or determinable future time is called a 'time bill'.
5. "A sum certain in money" means that a B/E cannot order payment in, for instance, gold coins or kind. If the sum payable is stated in both words and figures and the two do not agree, the sum denoted by the words is the sum payable.

6. "To, or to the order of, a specified person, or to bearer": a bill payable to a named person or his order is known as an 'order bill', and the person to whom payment has to be made is the 'payee'. A bill payable to bearer is referred to as a 'bearer bill'.

There are three original parties to a bill of exchange: the drawer, the drawee, and the payee (or the bearer). In commercial practice, the drawer and the payee are usually the same person, which means that the drawer orders the drawee to pay a specified sum of money to him or his order. Bills payable to one's own order are very common in connection with contracts of sale. The seller ships goods and draws a bill of exchange for the purchase price on the buyer, instructing the latter to pay the amount to him or his order (e.g., "On May 31, 1985, pay to me or my order 200 pounds"). The seller is the drawer and also the payee, and the buyer is the drawee, i.e., the person to whom the bill is addressed.

A bill of exchange, however, is of no practical value unless the drawee accepts it by writing the word 'Accepted' and his name across the face of the bill to show that he is willing to pay the bill when it matures, i.e., when the time for payment stated in the bill has arrived or elapsed. By accepting the bill the drawee undertakes to honour (pay) the bill when it is presented by the holder for payment at maturity.

A holder of the bill (this is a person in possession of a bill which is payable to him, i.e., the payee, the indorsee to whom the bill has been transferred, or any person in possession of a bearer bill) can use it in any of the following ways: firstly, he can keep it until maturity and then present it for payment; secondly, he may pass it on in payment of a debt, i.e., he may transfer it to someone to whom he owes money; or thirdly, if he is in immediate need of funds, he may discount it with a bank, which is referred to as 'discounting' a bill.

Attention should be paid to the fact that the bill of exchange is a negotiable instrument, which means that it can be transferred by indorsement and delivery of the bill (order bill), or by mere delivery of the bill (bearer bill).

In international trade, bills of exchange play an important role in connection with documentary credits and documentary collections.

bill of lading   Konnossement

The bill of lading (abbreviated B/L) is a document which is issued when goods are entrusted to a shipping company for carriage by sea. It is completed by the shipper (e.g., consignor, consignee) or his agent and then signed by the master of the ship or by some other person authorised by the shipping company.

A B/L usually contains the following points: the name of the shipper; the name of the consignee (or order); the name of the carrying vessel; the port of shipment; the port of discharge; a description of the goods, including the number and kind of packages, any shipping marks, gross weight, measurements, etc.; full details of the freight, including when and where it is to be paid; the terms of the contract of carriage; the date the goods were received for shipment and/or loaded on the vessel; the signature of the ship's master or his agent and the date.

Bills of lading may be either 'order bills' or 'non-negotiable bills'. An order bill of lading (also known as a 'negotiable bill of lading') is made out to, or to the order of, a particular person and can be transferred by indorsement and delivery of the bill, which means that, at least in this respect, it is a negotiable instrument. In practice, an order bill of lading is made out either to the shipper's order (in which case 'order bill' has to be translated by 'Orderkonnossement'), or to the consignee or his order (in this case, 'order bill' is to be translated by 'Namenskonnossement'). In the first case, the consignee is not specified in the B/L, which enables the shipper to name the consignee by indorsing the bill to him when the goods are already in transit. In the second case, the shipper has to insert the name of the consignee when completing the bill.

A non-negotiable bill of lading (in U.S. practice referred to as a 'straight bill of lading') is issued to a named consignee, but not to his order, and is therefore not transferable by indorsement.

From the legal point of view, a bill of lading is: -

1. A formal receipt by the shipowner, acknowledging that goods of the stated quantity and condition have been shipped to a stated destination in a certain ship ('shipped B/L'), or that they have been delivered into the custody of the shipowner for the purpose of shipment ('received B/L'). When the shipowner affirms that the goods shipped or received for shipment are in apparent good order and condition, he issues a 'clean bill of lading', otherwise a 'claused B/L'. For example, where payment is arranged under a documentary letter of credit, the B/L to be presented to the paying bank has to be a clean, shipped order B/L.
2. A memorandum of the contract of carriage between the shipowner and the shipper, repeating in detail the terms of the contract, which was in fact concluded prior to the signing of the bill.
3. A document of title to the goods, giving the holder of the bill (either the consignee, or any other person to whom the bill may have been transferred) the right to claim delivery of the goods from the shipping company when they arrive at the port of destination.

The function of the B/L as a document of title – which is the main characteristic of the B/L – requires further explanation. In law, possession of the B/L is equivalent to possession of the goods, and transfer of the B/L has the same effect as delivery of the goods themselves. The B/L is, therefore, a symbol of the goods represented by the bill, and transfer of the B/L is deemed to operate as a symbolic transfer of the possession of the goods, but not necessarily as a transfer of the property in them. Transfer of the B/L passes such rights in the goods as the parties intend to pass, e.g., the ownership only if the parties intend to pass the ownership on delivery of the bill. On arrival of the goods at the port of destination, the shipowner or his agent (e.g., the master of the ship) is entitled to deliver the goods only against presentation of the B/L, and only the holder of the B/L is entitled to claim delivery of the goods from the shipowner. If the shipowner (or his agent) delivers the goods to a person who cannot produce the B/L, he does so at his own risk if that person is not in fact entitled to the goods. In such a case, the shipowner is liable to the holder of the bill for breach of contract and would have to pay him the value of the goods.

Logically, the function of the B/L as a document of title is distinct from its quality as a "negotiable" instrument. According to Schmitthoff, even a non-negotiable B/L operates as a document of title, because the consignee named therein can claim delivery of the goods from the shipowner only if he is able to produce the B/L.

The practical value of the B/L, which is based on the fact that it is both a document of title and a negotiable instrument, is to enable the person entitled to the goods represented by the bill to dispose of the goods while they are in transit. This, however, does not apply to a non-negotiable B/L, which enables the shipper to pass the ownership and/or possession of the goods to the consignee by delivering the bill to him, but does not permit the latter to dispose of the goods in transit by transferring the bill (by indorsement and delivery).

Finally, it should be mentioned that the bill of lading is issued in a set, usually consisting of three originals (copies), anyone of which may be presented to obtain delivery of the goods from the shipping company. The various originals of the set should be sent to the consignee by alternative mails to ensure that at least one will arrive (the shipper usually sends two originals by different air mails and one by the ship carrying the goods). It is of great importance that at least one original should be in the consignee's hands before, or at the time of, the arrival of the goods, because the shipowner is not entitled to hand over the goods without production of the B/L. If one original of the B/L has been surrendered in exchange for the goods, all other originals become void. It should be noted that in the case of a transfer of the B/L, all originals must be delivered to the indorsee. In addition to the originals, not-negotiable copies of the B/L may be prepared in any desired number, e.g., for internal statistical purposes.

binary system   Dualsystem

In contrast to the decimal system, which is based on the number ten, the binary system is based on the number two. This means that a digit in the binary system represents a power of two. Just as in the decimal system, it is the postion of the digit in a combination of digits that determines which power is involved. In a binary number, the right-most digit represents 2^0 (two to the power of zero, which equals one), the next digit represents 2^1 (which equals two), the next 2^2 (which equals four), and so on. The number 101 in binary notation would, therefore, correspond to 1 multiplied by 2^0 (one), plus 0 multiplied by 2^1 (zero), plus 1 multiplied by 2^2 (four). In decimal notation, this would obviously equal five (one plus four equals five).

From the above it is clear that the binary system needs only two digit values, namely, 1 and 0. This is what makes it so suitable for computer operations, because every piece of logic in computer systems may be reduced to a network of switches, each of which is either "on" or "off". The "on"-state could be represented by 1, and the "off"-state by 0.

biodegradable substance   biologisch abbaubare Substanz

Biodegradable substances can be broken down by bacteria or sunlight into basic elements and compounds. For example, biodegradable plastic, unlike ordinary plastic, disintegrates after some time if thrown away, and is therefore less of a burden on the environment.

bit   Bit

Bit is the abbreviation of binary digit and refers to one of the two digits (0 and 1) used in binary notation. The term also denotes the actual representation of a binary digit in different forms, such as a magnetised spot on a magnetic tape or on a magnetic disk.

blue chips   erstklassige Aktien,
                                                  Spitzenwerte

Blue chips are the shares of highly reputable companies and, consequently, have the highest status as investments. The term is derived from poker (and similar games), where the blue chips are usually the ones with the highest value.

board of directors   Führungsgremium einer britischen/
                                                  amerikanischen Kapitalgesellschaft,
                                                  (erweiterter) Aufsichtsrat,
                                                  Verwaltungsrat

The board of directors, also simply called the 'board', is a group of persons elected by the shareholders of the company at the annual general meeting (AGM). Any person - including a body corporate, referred to as a 'corporate director' - may act as director; he is not required to be a member of the company unless a share qualification is stipulated in the articles of association. The office of director is vacated in the event of his retirement, resignation, removal (which is possible at any time by an ordinary resolution of the members at a general meeting), disqualification, or death. A director has no inherent right to be paid for his services. The articles will, however, normally give a right to remuneration to cover his incidental expenses.

In the U.K., the board of a public limited company must consist of at least two directors, whereas private limited companies need have one director only. The American Model Business Corporation Act specifies that there shall be at least three directors, but a number of states permit a corporation to have only one director.

The powers of the board are laid down in the articles of association (U.S.: bylaws) and are vested in the directors collectively as a board; they can act only when properly convened as a board. In most companies, the directors elect a permanent chairman, who takes the chair at board meetings and normally also presides over meetings of members. He is the company's leading representative in its dealings with the outside world.

The board of directors is responsible for both management and supervision. It sets the general company policy and supervises the day-to-day management, which it delegates to paid managers. Surprisingly, American and British company law requires, or at least permits, also members of the board to be appointed as paid managers (see below: executive director). This is in sharp contrast to the Austrian and West German two-tier board system, under which no member of the 'supervisory board' (Aufsichtsrat einer AG) may become a member of the 'board of management' (Vorstand einer AG). It should be noted that the terms 'supervisory board' and 'board of management' are not original English terms, but are only used to describe bodies which cannot be found in British and American companies.

As a rule, British and American companies have both executive and non-executive directors.

The 'executive director' (also referred to as the 'full-time director' or 'inside director') is a member of the board who, in addition to his board duties, carries out executive (i.e., management) functions in the company. He normally enters into a service agreement defining his powers and duties, and is remunerated separately for his services as a manager.

The number of executive directors varies with the size of the company, small companies frequently having only one. The chief executive director is referred to as the 'managing director' in British companies and as the 'president' in American corporations, but an increasing number of both British and American companies prefer to call their "top man" 'chief executive (officer)'. It should be noted that there are many companies that combine the roles of managing director/president and chairman of the board in a single person. While the managing director, or president, is a kind of "general manager" with overall responsibilities for the operations of the company, the other executive directors are responsible for such specific areas as finance (finance director), marketing (marketing director), purchasing (purchasing director). The term 'director' indicates that they are members of the board, in contrast to other top-level managers/top-level executives, such as the purchasing manager and the marketing manager, who are not on the board.

The 'non-executive director' (also known as the 'part-time director' or 'outside director') is a board member who helps to plan, decide, and supervise the execution of, the policy of the company, but has no executive responsibilities himself. To avoid conflicts of interest, he should have no contractual relationship with the company. Because of his larger independence and his general experience and knowledge (many of them have a full-time occupation in banking and finance), the non-executive director contributes to the long-term strategic function of direction and helps to safeguard the interests of the company where these may conflict with the personal interests of individual directors (e.g., board appointments and remuneration). The appointment of non-executive directors, therefore, serves a similar purpose as the supervisory board under the Austrian system.

bonded warehouse   Zollager

A bonded warehouse is a warehouse, either privately or government owned, where goods which are subject to import duty may be stored without the importer being required to pay the duty. Goods so stored are termed 'bonded goods'. Bonded warehouses are under customs supervision, and goods are not admitted and may not be removed without the permission of the customs officers on duty. Duty levied on bonded goods does not become payable until the goods are removed from the warehouse for domestic consumption. On the other hand, if the goods are withdrawn to be re-exported, no duty has to be paid at all. Bonded goods may be withdrawn in small quantities as needed, and they may also be sold while in storage, in which case payment of duty becomes the responsibility of the buyer. Goods in a bonded warehouse, like those in other warehouses, may be sorted, blended, packed, bottled, labelled, inspected by potential buyers, etc., all under customs supervision.

The bonded warehouse system is widely used for such merchandise as wines, spirits, and tobacco, which have to be stored to mature.

As regards the customs procedure for dutiable goods not required immediately, the importer has to prepare an entry for warehousing. This document is sent to the warehouse after having been inspected by the customs authorities. On arrival of the goods at the warehouse, where they are examined by a customs officer, a warehouse warrant is issued to the importer. From that point the warehouse keeper becomes responsible for their safe keeping until they are officially released for home consumption or for re-exportation.

brand   (Produkt-)Marke

The American Marketing Association defines a brand as "a name, term, symbol, or design, or a combination of them, which is intended to identify the goods or services of one seller or a group of sellers and to differentiate them from those of competitors". In most cases, producers or distributors register a brand, or label (as it is often referred to), in order to prevent competitors from using it. A brand, or that part of a brand, which is protected by law is called a 'trade mark'. A trade mark is created by registration and gives the seller the exclusive right to use the brand.

branding   Markenpolitik

Branding, i.e., the use of brands, is an element of a firm's product strategy. Its main purpose is to help prospects and customers to identify the product or products of a particular seller and to differentiate them from those of his competitors. This is extremely important in today's marketing environment, characterised by keen competition, self-service retailing, and heavy promotional activities.

Putting a distinctive sign, word, or symbol on a product or package does not in itself constitute a brand policy. It creates an opportunity, not more; an opportunity that must be exploited by skilful advertising, pricing, standardisation, and by emphasising quality and reliability, to create a positive brand image and brand loyalty among the consumers. Ultimately, a particular brand must become a kind of unwritten guarantee for the product features a customer is looking for.

What are some of the main decisions a firm has to make in connection with branding? A manufacturer may decide to sell his product under his own brand (manufacturer's brand) or he may allow his distributors or dealers to put their own labels on the product (dealers' brands, distributors' brands, own labels, private brands). A firm may decide to use only one brand for all its products (family or blanket brand) or a separate one for each line or product it sells. This last decision will be influenced by various considerations. For instance, a company marketing baby food and dog food will be well advised to use a different brand for each line. Finally, a firm may choose to drop branded goods altogether, concentrating on what is called 'generic products', a strategy that has proved quite successful for a number of discount stores and supermarket chains.

breach of contract (of sale)   (Kauf-)Vertragsbruch

Breach of contract means the unexcused non-performance of a contract. It occurs when one party to the contract
1. fails to perform, wholly or in part, or
2. makes performance impossible, for himself or for the other party, or
3. gives notice beforehand that he will not perform the contract when the time for performance arrives.

A breach of a contract for sale of goods occurs, for example, if the seller fails to deliver the goods; if he delivers wrong quantities or defective goods; if the goods delivered are not in accordance with their description in the contract; if the goods delivered are not up to sample; etc.. Likewise, if the buyer does not accept the goods which have been delivered in conformity with the contract, or if he fails to pay for the goods, this also constitutes a breach of a contract for sale of goods.

If one party breaks the contract, the other party has certain legal rights, some of which are mentioned below:
1. If the buyer has failed to pay for the goods delivered, the seller may sue for payment of the price.
2. In the case of non-delivery of the goods by the seller, or non-acceptance of the goods by the buyer, the other party may sue for damages.
3. If the seller has delivered less or more than ordered, the buyer may reject the lot, or may accept the lesser quantity or the agreed quantity only and pay a proportionate price.
4. If the goods are not in accordance with the description or sample, etc., the buyer can reject the goods or, if he chooses, accept them and sue for damages.

break-even analysis

Gewinnschwellenanalyse,
Break-even Analyse

Generally speaking, break-even analysis is concerned with determining the break-even point in a business firm. The break-even point can be defined as the volume of sales where total revenues and total costs, or total expenses, are equal, or, to put it in a slightly different way, it is the sales volume which produces neither a profit nor a loss. If the actual sales volume exceeds the break-even sales volume, the firm concerned will make a profit; in the case of a sales volume being lower than the break-even sales volume, the firm will suffer a loss.

The break-even point can be determined by means of a graph or it may be computed mathematically. In either case, it is necessary to divide the costs, including all production, selling, general, and administrative costs, into two groups: -
1. 'Fixed costs', or 'fixed expenses', which do not vary with changes in the level of activity. Fixed costs are incurred, and remain unchanged, regardless of the volume of production. Typical examples are: depreciation on plant and equipment, fire insurance, property tax, and certain other overhead costs.
2. 'Variable costs', or 'variable expenses', which change in direct proportion to changes in the volume of production. Direct materials (e.g., raw materials entering the production process) and direct labour are directly related to the volume of production, and are, therefore, typical examples of variable costs.

The assumption, however, that all costs are either of a fixed or variable nature is an over-simplification. For example, the expenses incurred for electricity, fuel, and certain administrative functions contain elements of both fixed and variable costs. Such expenses are, therefore, classified as 'semi-variable costs'. In a break-even analysis, semi-variable costs have to be separated into their fixed and variable components, the components of each item usually being estimated.

The break-even point can be computed in two different ways:
1. Equation method.
   Since the break-even point is defined as the volume of sales where total

revenues and total costs are equal, it can easily be calculated from the following equation: sales = variable costs + fixed costs. The following example is intended to help understand the foregoing: unit sales price: $10; unit variable costs: $4; fixed costs per year: $150,000. The break-even point in terms of units sold is 25,000 units ($10X = $4X + $150,000, X being the number of units to be sold to break even). This corresponds to a break-even sales volume of $250,000 (i.e., $10 x 25,000).

2. Contribution margin method.

This method is based on the unit contribution margin, which is the difference between unit sales price and unit variable costs. In the above example, the unit contribution margin is $6. This means that every unit sold "contributes" $6 to the recovery of fixed costs (hence the term 'unit contribution margin'). The break-even point in units can be calculated by dividing the unit contribution margin into fixed costs (150,000 : 6 = 25,000 units).

Break-even analysis is a vital management tool. It may be used, for instance, to develop profit estimates for a firm at various levels of sales and production, or to establish or review a firm's pricing policies. If a price increase is being considered, break-even analysis will help estimate the maximum reduction in sales volume that the firm can tolerate without reducing profits. On the other hand, if the firm considers cutting its prices, it will help determine what changes in sales volume would be necessary to offset a given reduction in price.

Although break-even analysis seems simple and effective, this effectiveness is limited in several ways. The major limitations of break-even analysis are (i) the complexities due to changes in a firm's product mix from month to month, season to season, and year to year; (ii) the fact that fixed costs are not always constant and variable costs do not always increase in a straight line with output, especially when a firm's operations approach full capacity; and (iii) the fairly common practice of varying selling prices by offering cash and/or quantity discounts.

broker   Makler,
                                                    Handelsmäkler

A broker is an agent whose main duty is to bring buyers and sellers together. He represents either the buyer or the seller in negotiating purchases or sales, usually in return for a brokerage (mainly in the form of a broker's commission, calculated as a percentage of the amount of business done). A broker does not physically handle the goods, and his authority as to prices and terms is usually limited by his principal.

A broker is very similar to a commercial agent in that he acts in the name and for the account of his principal and does not take title to the goods, but he differs from the agent in one important respect, viz., he does not work on a continuing basis with his principal; in other words, there is no permanent contractual relationship between the principal and his broker.

budget   Budget,
                                                    Haushaltsplan

In economics, the term 'budget' normally refers to the estimate of government revenue and expenditure for the next fiscal year. Depending on the relationship between these two elements, the budget will show either a deficit (expenditure exceeding revenue), a surplus (revenue exceeding expenditure), or it will be balanced (revenue equalling expenditure). Since revenue is raised mainly by imposing taxes, a surplus means that government is taking more money out of the economy than it is putting back. In the case of a deficit, the reverse is true, i.e., on balance, government is pumping money into the economic system.

From the point of view of financial management, surpluses present no problem, but deficits have to be financed by borrowing money either domestically or abroad. Up to a point, this is not difficult since governments frequently enjoy excellent credit ratings, and banks are only too willing to lend to them (even to not so creditworthy ldcs). But a stage may be reached where the payment of principal and interest pre-empts a large portion of revenue, severely restricts the government's room for manoeuvre, and forces it to cut back on, maybe essential, expenditure ("fiscal crisis").

Quite apart from these problems of financial management, although not completely separable from them, the budget represents an important instrument of fiscal policy, which can be used to regulate the level of economic activity. A deficit (more precisely, a reduction in surplus or an increase in deficit) has, ceteris paribus, a stimulatory effect (reflationary policy), while a reduction in deficit or an increase in surplus will normally put a brake on economic activity (deflationary policy).

Budgets are, however, not only used by governments. Also business firms have found them useful management instruments in planning and controlling the allocation of resources. Firms may draw up a variety of budgets (e.g., for capital expenditure, sales, cash, etc.) at the beginning of a business period and compare actual and budgeted performance at the end of the period.

budgeting

(kurzfristige) Planungsrechnung, Budgetierung

The planning process for the inflow and outflow of funds, described in some detail under the heading of "financial management", is referred to as 'budgeting'. A budget is a financial plan covering the expected receipts and expenditure over a relatively short period of time (typically a year). Usually, there is a master budget, which states the movement of funds in global terms, and a number of subsidiary (or supplementary) budgets, each dealing with a particular category of receipts and expenditure. Supplementary budgets include the sales budget, the capital expenditure budget, the personnel budget, the cash budget, etc..

Budgets can be regarded either as forecasts or as targets. In the latter case, they can be used for control purposes, i.e., actual results are compared with the targets set by financial management, and corrective action can be taken where necessary.

buffer stock

Pufferlager, Marktausgleichslager

The prices of primary commodities (e.g., copper, zinc, tin, cotton, sugar, cacao) on which many less developed countries depend for their export revenues are subject to violent fluctuations on world markets. This has a disruptive effect on their economies since, among other things, it tends to discourage long-term planning. This is especially true of capital expenditure, a critical area for ldcs.

One way of remedying this situation is to set up buffer stocks for individual commodities by international agreement. Buffer stocks try to stabilise export prices by intervening in the open market, buying the commodity in question when its price falls below a predetermined minimum level, and selling it when the price exceeds a predetermined maximum.

Factors relevant to the success or failure of commodity buffer stocks include: the durability of the commodity concerned, the amount of funds at the disposal of the buffer stock manager, realistic intervention levels, the extent of speculation in the commodity, the cost of carrying the necessary stock (e.g.,rent, interest on capital tied up, insurance). The relative failure of existing buffer stocks to stabilise commodity prices (e.g., the failure of the buffer stock operated by the International Tin Council) seems to be attributable basically to a lack of funds.

Buffer stocks belong to the field of international commodity agreements, or commodity pacts, which also include international supply and purchase commitments and export quotas.

building society   Bausparkasse

British building societies are specialised financial institutions organised as co-operatives. They are similar to Austrian 'Bausparkassen' and U.S. 'savings and loan associations' (S&Ls). Their principal purpose is to finance the purchase or building of owner-occupied dwellings (including houses and free-hold flats) by their members, finance being provided mainly in the form of long-term home loans, secured by mortgages on the properties involved.

As building societies are non-profit organisations, they keep the rate of interest charged on mortgage loans to the minimum necessary to cover expenses and to make appropriate transfers to reserves.

To gather the funds which they lend out to borrowing members, most building societies offer savings schemes under which the depositor agrees to save a fixed amount regularly, over a number of years. Nowadays, the majority of depositors are not saving to buy or build a private dwelling, but are using these savings schemes as an attractive form of investment. The interest paid on building society deposits is subject to preferential tax treatment, which enables building societies to attract - relatively cheap - private sector funds for the politically important financing of private housing.

The main differences between Austrian and British building societies are: firstly, in Austria a member must have saved a specified amount with his building society before he can get a loan; and secondly, in addition to enjoying certain tax privileges, the interest paid on Austrian building society deposits is supplemented with a government bonus.

bulk goods   Massengüter,
                             Schüttgüter

Bulk goods (also known as 'bulk commodities' or, in sea transport, as 'bulk cargo') are loose substances, such as coal, sand, stones, iron-ore, grain, etc., which are normally transported in large quantities without packing. It follows from the nature of bulk goods that they are carried in tramp ships, as waggon-loads (U.S.: carload, abbreviated CL), or as lorry-loads (U.S.: truckload).

bull   Haussier

A bull is a speculator who hopes that security prices or the prices of other property (e.g., currencies, commodities) will rise. He therefore buys, or contracts to buy, the securities in question with the intention of selling them when the prices have actually moved in his favour, the difference between the lower buying prices and the higher selling prices (less commissions) being his profit (capital gain). Bulls take what is called in stock exchange jargon 'long positions', i.e., they hold more securities - or obligations to purchase securities - than they have at the moment engaged to sell.

A situation on the stock exchange dominated by bulls (or long positions) is referred to as a 'bull market', which is characterised by rising prices and, generally, by a bullish (i.e., optimistic) mood.

business administration   Betriebswirtschaftslehre

Business administration is the American term for the applied social science dealing with business organisations and the activities and problems involved in running them. Other terms used for this discipline are 'business studies' (especially at British universities) or simply 'management'. The most important academic degree in this field is the MBA (Master of Business Administration), offered by 'Business Schools', which have university status (e.g., Harvard, Wharton, London, Manchester, INSEAD).

Since business administration is an applied science, its purpose is not only to gain theoretical insights into its subject-matter, but mainly to assist managers in solving the problems connected with their task. Business administration is an interdisciplinary science and draws heavily on other social sciences, such as economics, psychology, politology, and sociology. In common with these disciplines, business administration has found the systems approach particularly useful. Regarding business organisations as complex socio-technical systems deliberately created for the purpose of achieving specific objectives (e.g., output and profit) and interacting with a complex environment has not only yielded important theoretical insights, but has also proved useful in solving practical management problems.

In addition to analysing the basic nature and objectives of business organisations, business administration has been traditionally concerned with the following aspects:
1. the decisions involved in setting up a business organisation (e.g., choice of legal form, location, basic organisational structure, and organisational procedures);
2. the general process of management (e.g., goal-setting, planning, implementation, and control, as well as management styles and techniques);
3. the functional units or subsystems of business organisations (e.g., procurement, storage, production, marketing, finance, personnel, information, research and development, and the management activities related to them). It should be noted that this functional approach does not imply a commitment to

a functional organisation. Functional aspects and problems have to be taken into consideration also if other types of organisation (e.g., divisional organisation) are adopted.

business communication — betriebliche Kommunikation

Business communication is the exchange of messages in a business context. Like any other form of communication, it involves senders and receivers of information, media to convey the messages, and, finally, the messages themselves.

A typical business unit may send messages to, and receive messages from, customers, suppliers, banks, insurance companies, advertising agencies, shareholders, trade unions, environmental organisations, and, alas, the revenue authorities. But business communication has a role to play also inside the business units. Messages have to be exchanged between the various offices, sections, or departments of a business, such as Accounts, Goods-Inwards, Goods-Outwards, General Office, Mail Room, Warehouse, etc..

Businesses use a wide variety of media for internal and external communications. Messages may be transmitted by letter, by postcard, by telegram, or by telephone. Alternatively, one of the more modern media, such as electronic mail or telecopying, can be used.

The number of different types of messages is legion. A useful distinction is the one between external messages (such as inquiries, offers, orders, complaints) and internal messages, frequently referred to as '(internal) memos'.

business organisation[1] - general — Unternehmen - allgemein

Business organisations, also referred to as 'firms', 'concerns' (not to be confused with the German term 'Konzern'), 'enterprises', and, occasionally still, as 'undertakings', are economic units providing a legal, financial, and organisational framework for productive activities in the widest sense of the word (i.e., for the production and/or distribution of goods and/or services). From the point of view of economic history, business organisations are the result of the continuing process of specialisation, which has become the hallmark of modern civilisation. It is often overlooked that, originally, production and consumption took place within the same economic unit (e.g., in a farm household).

Business organisations should not be confused with business establishments, which are the concrete physical facilities required to carry out production and distribution. Examples of establishments are plants, factories, mills, offices, shops, etc..

Business units may be organised in different legal forms, each of which has different financial and organisational implications. A firm may operate as a sole trader, as a partnership, or as a company, with a separate legal personality distinct from its members. Which of these forms is chosen will depend, among other things, on the size of the organisation, on its capital requirements, and on tax considerations.

The above-mentioned forms of business organisation are sometimes classified as 'traditional' to contrast them with 'alternative' forms, such as the various types of co-operative society and the commune.

51

business organisation[2]
- objectives

Unternehmen - Ziele

From the point of view of organisational theory, business organisations are social, or rather socio-technical, systems deliberately created for the purpose of achieving particular objectives.

The two basic objectives are: firstly, to produce an output (goods and/or services) by combining and transforming resources (physical, financial, human, and information resources) purchased, hired, or otherwise acquired from the organisation's environment; secondly, to sell this output to non-members at prices that more than cover costs (at least in the long run), generating income for the providers of capital, who bear the risk, i.e., basically for their members (the profit objective).

All this distinguishes business organisations, firstly, from other types of social groups which are not deliberately set up to achieve a particular purpose, e.g., from families and groups of friends, which exist for their own sake (i.e., basically to satisfy emotional needs of their members); and, secondly, from voluntary-sector non-profit organisations, i.e., organisations that do have a specific purpose and that do produce an output, which they, however, make available to non-members free of charge, or at least at cost.

The two basic objectives of business organisations (output and profits) have already been mentioned. But they can be refined upon and supplemented with subsidiary (or instrumental) objectives. The production of an output (goods and/or services) is only meaningful if it is capable of satisfying the needs of consumers. Thus, the satisfaction of human needs might be regarded as an important − some would say, the most important - goal of a business organisation, a goal it shares with the above-mentioned non-profit organisations. The profit goal may be formulated either as a particular level of profit, as a specific growth rate for the profit, or as a rate of return on capital invested. Subsidiary objectives, which sometimes may become primary goals, are survival, maintaining the capital base of the organisation, sales, efficiency (closely linked with the profit objective), but also employee welfare and prestige, which are less easy to pin down.

The specific goals of a specific business organisation are the result of a balancing act between the demands from the various social groups involved in the organisation: first of all, from its owners, but also from suppliers, customers, employees, trade unions, the government, etc..

buyer credit

Käuferkredit,
Bestellerkredit

A buyer credit involves the extension of a loan by a commercial bank or other financial institution direct to a buyer. The buyer then uses the proceeds of the loan to pay the seller. Repayment of the credit is made by the buyer to the commercial bank. Buyer credits are generally used in long-term transactions, with repayment terms of five years or more. The debt of the buyer is evidenced by a loan agreement with the bank and, in many cases, secured by a promissory note or a similar instrument.

buyers' market   Käufermarkt

A buyers' market is characterised by an excess of supply over demand. This means that buyers have some market power which allows them to hold down prices, while sellers experience difficulty in selling all their output at planned prices. Buyers' markets are characteristic of slumps and depressions but also of affluent societies, where basic wants and needs have largely been satisfied and demand may have to be artificially stimulated by promotional measures.

buying rate   Geldkurs

The buying rate (also called the 'bid rate' or 'bid') is the rate of exchange, either spot or forward, at which a bank/foreign exchange dealer agrees to buy a foreign currency. If a customer wants to sell a certain amount of foreign currency to a bank, he can do so only at the bank's buying rate.

byte   Byte

A byte is a set of adjacent binary digits (bits) operated on as a unit. In many computer systems, a byte is a grouping of eight data bits (plus one control bit), which can represent either one alphabetic character or two decimal digits. Bytes are used to measure the size of computer memories. For example, a 64K RAM is a random access memory containing 64 kilobytes = 65,536 bytes.

A byte may be subdivided into two nibbles (of four bits each). A word, another basic unit of data in a computer memory, may consist of two bytes (16 bits), three bytes (24 bits), four bytes (32 bits), etc., the exact number of bits (word length or word size) depending on the system used.

C

cancellation of order   Auftragsstornierung

A buyer is legally entitled to cancel his order:
1. at any time before it has been accepted by the seller;
2. if the goods delivered are of the wrong type or quality (e.g., if they are not up to sample);
3. if the goods are not delivered by the time stipulated in the contract of sale;
4. if more, or less, than the quantitiy ordered is delivered; and
5. in the case of major defects in the goods that cannot be repaired.

In many cases, however, the seller will permit the buyer to cancel his order even if the latter is not legally entitled to do so, e.g., when an important customer of the buyer goes bankrupt, and the goods are no longer required.

capacity   Kapazität

In business, capacity is the ability to produce, or, to give an operational definition, the maximum output of a machine or plant per unit of time. In other words, capacity indicates how much a machine, etc., can produce in a given period of time. Capacity, therefore, is a flow concept.

capacity utilisation   Kapazitätsauslastung,
                                         Kapazitätsausnutzungsgrad

Capacity utilisation, or operating rate, indicates to what extent the capacity of a machine or plant (or even of the economy as a whole) is used. An operational definition of this concept would be: actual output (per unit of time) expressed as a percentage of capacity. A factory, for example, could be working at 30% of capacity, which means it is producing only 30% of its potential maximum output. If its capacity is fully utilised, the factory is said to be working at full capacity, or to capacity. Capacity utilisation is a very important ratio, since it determines, among other things, the fixed cost per unit of output.

capital account   Kapital(verkehrs)bilanz

The capital account, or balance of payments on capital account, is part of the balance of payments. It is used to record a country's exports and imports of capital, i.e., all long-term and short-term capital flows between the residents of the reporting country and all non-residents, during a certain period of time, usually one year.

Long-term capital transactions may be in the form of direct investments, which give the investor control over foreign operations (e.g., establishment of foreign subsidiaries or branch offices, purchase of a controlling interest in a foreign company, etc.), in the form of portfolio investments, which do not involve controlling interests in foreign enterprises, but are made only for the purpose of earning investment income (e.g., purchases of long-term securities, such as shares and bonds, issued by foreign-controlled firms; long-term bank loans; etc.), and in the form of purchases/sales of real estate.

Short-term capital transactions include changes in bank deposits, purchases/ sales of short-term securities, and similar transactions, either for speculative purposes ("hot money") or commercial purposes. It should be remembered, however, that income on foreign investments - whether interest, dividends, or repatriated profits - is recorded in the invisible account.

It should be clearly understood that all capital outflows - arising from new investments in foreign countries and from the liquidation of foreign investments in the reporting country, e.g., sale of securities, repayment of loans, etc. - have a negative impact on the overall balance of payments, just as have visible and invisible imports and unilateral transfers made to foreign countries, whereas the opposite is true of capital inflow.

Although the causal relationship between the current account and the capital account is rather complex and cannot be fully explored here, one may say that a capital-exporting country must generate large trade surpluses in order to offset the deficit on its capital account. In part, these surpluses are a direct result of capital exports, because foreign investment projects are usually associated with exports of capital equipment, raw materials, etc..

capital gain

Spekulationsgewinn,
(realisierter) Wertzuwachs,
(realisierte) Wertsteigerung,
(realisierter) Kursgewinn

Capital gains are the profits arising from the disposal (e.g., sale) of capital assets, such as houses or other property, shares, and bonds. Capital gains, therefore, occur when such assets are sold at prices exceeding their cost prices (e.g., purchase prices). If the selling price is lower, there is obviously a capital loss.

The term is applied only to gains arising from isolated, non-recurring transactions, i.e., from transactions other than in the ordinary course of business. It is, for instance, not used to describe the profits of a stockjobber, who buys and sells securities on a regular basis as part of his normal business activity.

Strictly speaking, inflation should be allowed for in calculating capital gains for tax purposes. Otherwise, part or all of a particular gain may be fictitious, and any gain below the rate of inflation is a loss in real terms.

capital gains tax

Steuer auf Spekulationsgewinne,
Wertzuwachssteuer,
Kursgewinnsteuer

Strictly speaking, only the United Kingdom has a capital gains tax, i.e., a special tax on capital gains, as defined in the preceding entry. In the United States and in Austria, the taxation of capital gains is simply a special feature of their respective income tax systems.

Under the U.K. tax regime, adopted in 1965, all net capital gains (i.e., capital gains less capital losses) are liable to capital gains tax at a rate of 30 per cent, although there are a number of exceptions and exemptions. Firstly, capital gains accruing to companies are subject to corporation tax and not to capital gains tax; secondly, in the case of private individuals, the first £5,000 in any one year and the gains from disposing of one's principal private residence or of chattels worth less than £3,000 are exempt from capital gains tax. Another interesting aspect of the U.K. system is that the effect of inflation is taken into account when capital gains for tax purposes are computed.

In the United States, where there is no capital gains tax, all (net) capital gains are subject to personal or corporate income tax, but substantial relief is afforded to long-term capital gains, i.e., gains accruing on the sale or exchange of capital assets held for more than one year. For instance, in 1981, long-term private capital gains (i.e., capital gains made by private individuals) attracted a maximum tax rate of 28% (later reduced to 20%), which must be compared with a maximum rate of 70% (later reduced to 50%) on all other forms of personal income, including short-term capital gains.

In Austria, long-term private capital gains are treated even more favourably, being completely exempt from tax, although the time limits prescribed by the Austrian tax law are not uniform: one year for personal property and five years for real property. Short-term capital gains are treated as ordinary income. There is partial relief for certain types of capital gains realised by business firms.

The taxation of capital gains is a sensitive and controversial issue. Critics of the Austrian, British, and American systems argue that, since capital gains represent unearned income, they should be taxed at the rates applicable to other forms of income, if not at higher rates. Taxation of capital gains at lower rates (or complete exemption) represents a loophole, because it is quite easy for individuals with large incomes to select investments on which the return is in the form of capital gains rather than in the form of dividends or other income, subject to income tax at progressive rates. Those supporting the more favourable treatment of capital gains point out that, since appreciation on capital items is often accumulated over several years, the employment of a progressive tax rate at the time when the gain is realised may result in overtaxation. It is also argued that high taxation of capital gains distorts the stock market and investment decisions by discouraging sales when prices are rising.

capital investment analysis   Investitionsrechnung

Capital investment analysis, sometimes referred to as 'investment appraisal' or 'capital (project) evaluation', involves estimating the future benefits of capital projects to the business organisation concerned and comparing these benefits with their costs.

There are various techniques that can be used to test the viability of a planned capital project (e.g., the building of a new plant or the installation of a new machine). They range from the fairly simple payback method to the much more sophisticated discounted cash flow (or DCF) techniques.

Under the payback method, two or more capital projects are compared in terms of the number of years needed to recover the original investment. The payback period is easy to calculate: all that needs to be done is to add up the projected annual net cash flows attributable to the project until the year is reached when the cumulative cash flow equals the original investment. The project with the shortest payback period will be selected. 'Cash flow' in the context of investment analysis refers to the actual inflows and outflows of cash associated with a particular investment project. The 'net cash flow' is, therefore, the difference between these two flows.

The main drawback of the payback method is that it takes no account of the time value of money. This is why the discounted cash flow methods have been developed, which are all ultimately based on discounting the projected cash flows generated by a project over its life. The two best-known DCF methods are the 'net present value method' (NPV method) and the 'internal rate of return method' (IRR method). Under a common variant of the former method, the projected annual net cash flows are discounted to their present value, with the required rate of return being used as the discount rate. If the present value of these net cash flows equals or exceeds the original investment, the project is accepted. Obviously, it is also possible to compare different projects using the difference between the present value and the original investment as a yardstick.

Under the IRR method, the internal rate of return is calculated, which is the discount rate that equates the present value of the expected net cash flows with the original investment. The internal rate of return is then compared with the required rate of return. For a project to be viable, the IRR must exceed the required rate of return. If two or more projects are compared, the one with the highest IRR should be chosen.

capital structure   Kapitalstruktur

The capital structure of a firm is the composition of its capital, mainly with regard to the relative shares of creditors' funds (debt) and owners' funds (equity). The relationship between these two elements can be expressed in the form of ratios, referred to as 'capital ratios' or 'debt ratios'.

Financial analysts use a large number of different ratios, depending on what aspect or what effect of the capital structure they want to highlight. Thus, for example, the numerator of a specific ratio may be either total debt, long-term debt, or sometimes even total debt plus preference share capital, which is similar to debt in that it requires a fixed payment every year. The denominator, on the other hand, may be either total capitalisation or shareholders' funds, or net assets employed. Another wrinkle is that off-balance sheet liabilities (e.g., liabilities arising from lease contracts) may be included in, or excluded from, the total debt figure. Some of the capital ratios most commonly used are: 'total debt to shareholders' funds', 'long-term debt to total capitalisation', and 'total debt plus preference share capital to ordinary shareholders' funds'. The first is often referred to as the 'debt-equity ratio', and the last as the 'gearing ratio'.

The capital structure of a company, as reflected in its capital ratios, plays an important role in determining whether the basic goals of an enterprise - profit, survival, growth - can be achieved. A low debt-equity ratio, for instance, may mean that the firm is foregoing profits. This is the case if the return on total capital employed is higher than the cost of creditors' funds. On the other hand, a high debt-equity ratio may lead to insolvency and bankruptcy if the income generated by the firm is no longer sufficient to meet payments of principal and interest.

capital transfer tax

kombinierte Schenkungs- und Nachlaßsteuer

The capital transfer tax, introduced in G.B. by the Finance Act 1975, applies broadly to all transfers of personal wealth, in the form of both lifetime gifts and transfers on death. The essential feature of the tax is that gifts during lifetime and property passing at death are treated cumulatively. The rates of tax applicable are progressively higher on successive slices of the cumulative total of chargeable transfers, with a lower scale of rates for lifetime transfers than for transfers on death. There are, however, a number of important tax exemptions, such as transfers between husband and wife in life and on death, and - at the time of writing - the first £55,000, on both lifetime transfers and transfers on death.

Property is valued for capital transfer tax purposes at the price it would fetch if it were sold in the open market at the time of the transfer. At the death of the property owner, all liabilities are taken into account in arriving at his net total estate, and all lifetime gifts are included in the taxable estate, which forms the base for computing the capital transfer tax. After deduction of the tax, the remaining part of the estate is divided among the heirs.

Critics of the capital transfer tax claim that its effects, particularly on the survival of the small- and medium-sized businesses, could well be disastrous. Transfer of a family business, for instance, may involve tax payments that cannot be covered out of profits already subjected to income tax.

Finally, it should be noted that the capital transfer tax replaced the former estate duty - a tax on the capital value of property passed on the property owner's death. This means that under the estate duty scheme, lifetime gifts were not taxed at all, this loophole enabling the owner of property to avoid estate duty by passing his property to relatives before death. In one respect, however, the capital transfer tax and the estate duty are broadly similar: both taxes are levied on the benefactor's estate before it is divided among the heirs/donees. This is in contrast to the inheritance tax, i.e., a tax payable by individuals on the value of property which they receive at the death of a benefactor, and where the rates charged may vary according to the degree of consanguinity. From this definition it is clear that the Austrian 'Erbschaftssteuer' is an inheritance tax and not an estate duty.

card index system

Kartei(system)

The card index system is a method of storing information on cards of equal size and shape. The cards are usually arranged alphabetically in drawers or trays. They can be marked with metal tabs, or riders, in various colours to facilitate reference.

cargo insurance

Güterversicherung, Warentransportversicherung

The term 'cargo insurance' means insurance on the goods being transported by a carrier, irrespective of the mode of transport. It may be classified according to the mode of transport into '(ocean) marine cargo insurance', '(goods in) transit insurance', and 'air cargo insurance'.

carriage[1]

Transport,
Beförderung

In its general economic sense, the term 'carriage' refers to the act of carrying goods (e.g., carriage of goods by air, by sea, by rail, or by road) and is, therefore, used as a synonym for 'conveyance' and 'transport'.

carriage[2]

Fracht,
Frachtgebühr,
Transportgebühr

Carriage may also be taken to mean the charge payable to the carrier for transporting the goods. There is a tendency to use 'carriage' in this sense mainly in connection with rail and road transport, whereas the term 'freight' is preferably used in air and sea transport (air freight, sea freight).

carriage of goods by air[1] - economic aspects

Luftfrachtverkehr - wirtschaftliche Aspekte

Air transport, while being one of the youngest forms of transport, is already making a major contribution to the exploitation of the world's resources. The carriage of goods by air has expanded rapidly over the past years as a competitor to other forms of transport, which is mainly due to the following factors: new ranges of aircraft introduced exclusively for freight carrying (e.g., the high-capacity freight version of the Boeing 747); the computerised cargo reception and handling areas at the major airports in many parts of the world (e.g., in 1971, the cargo terminal at Heathrow Airport in London was linked with a cargo electronic data processing system to make Heathrow the world's first airport to control incoming and outgoing cargo by computer); the proliferation of scheduled cargo flights and air cargo charter flights; the provision of more cargo space on board the new passenger air liners (some of the larger passenger aircraft on the major routes are capable of carrying five tons of freight); and the move towards more integrated unit load systems of air freight, including palletisation and containerisation. The use of containers and pallets has greatly improved the handling of air freight. Air containers are designed to fit the contours of the fuselage to make maximum use of aircraft space. A common and useful design is the "igloo"-shaped container, which fits smoothly into the fuselage and which can easily be pushed into position on roller rails. Many airline operators also use standard cargo containers stacked on standard-size pallets which are rolled into the aircraft.

An important characteristic of airborne trade is that, due to the high freight rates and the limited carrying capacity of the majority of aircraft, air freight is restricted to a limited range of goods whose value is high in relation to their bulk, or which are of perishable nature and call for fast delivery. Textiles, chemicals, valuable machinery, scientific instruments, medical supplies, urgently needed spare parts, fruit and flowers, and even live animals and motor vehicles are among the main items carried.

carriage of goods by air[2]
- advantages and drawbacks

Luftfrachtverkehr - Vor- und Nachteile

The major advantages of sending goods by air are:
1. High speed and quick delivery facilitate payment for individual consignments. This means that the seller's capital is not tied up for such a long period as it otherwise would be, which improves the seller's cash flow. In addition, there is no need for the buyer to hold large stocks in warehouses, which leads to lower storage charges and to the capital tied up in stock being released for more productive uses.
2. Low risk of damage and pilferage, resulting in competitive insurance premium rates.
3. Simplified documentation: air freight transit from any point in the world's air network to any other, by any combination of routes, is possible under one air waybill which has been standardised by the International Air Transport Association (I.A.T.A.) and which is interchangeable between all I.A.T.A.-member airlines. The I.A.T.A.-air waybill is, therefore, acceptable on any I.A.T.A.-airline, permitting flexibility of through-routing with no transshipment documentation problems at en route airports.
4. Less packing and, consequently, lower packing costs than incurred in surface transport.

The outstanding disadvantages of air transport are the following:
1. High air freight rates: because of very high operating expenses and initial cost of aircraft, air transport is still relatively expensive and is therefore not suitable for bulk goods.
2. Limited carrying capacity of many air freighters.
3. Despite modern handling facilities, there is still very often a substantial delay between arrival of goods at their airport of destination and delivery to the consignee, which reduces the advantage of speed in flying.
4. Air freight relies mainly on the road for feeder/distributor services, which increases overall transit costs.

carriage of goods by air[3]
- legal aspects

Luftfrachtverkehr
- juristische Aspekte

The international carriage of goods by air is governed by the Warsaw Convention of 1929 as amended by the Hague Protocol of 1955, and by the Conditions of Contract for the carriage of cargo, drafted by the International Air Transport Association (I.A.T.A.).

The document to be used for consignments by air is the air waybill, which is prima facie evidence of the conclusion of the contract of carriage and a receipt for the goods deliverd to the air carrier (see: consignment note). The member airlines of I.A.T.A. issue a common form of air waybill.

Under the Warsaw Convention, the air carrier is automatically liable for any loss of, or damage to, cargo during carriage by air and for damage due to delay, but he can escape liability if he proves that he and his agents or servants have taken all necessary measures to avoid the loss or damage, or that it was impossible for him or them to take such measures. In other words, the air carrier is only liable for negligence. In addition, he is also not liable if the loss or damage is the consignor's or the consignee's fault. The air carrier's liability is limited to U.S.$20 per kilogram, unless the shipper has declared a higher value and paid the appropriate higher freight rate, in which case that higher value will be the sum payable. However, this limitation will not apply if the carrier is guilty of misconduct, or if he fails to issue a proper air waybill for the goods.

International air freight rates are controlled by I.A.T.A., which has approximately 100 member airlines. Domestic rates, however, are controlled by the member airlines themselves. The major aspect of the I.A.T.A.-system is that no competition is permitted on air freight rates; competition exists only through quality of service, frequency of flights, etc..

carriage of goods by rail[1] - economic aspects
Eisenbahnfrachtverkehr - wirtschaftliche Aspekte

In spite of heavy competition from road, rail transport is still an extremely important method of carrying goods. To meet the competition, its efficiency is constantly being improved, and it has become a very modern and high-capacity form of transport.

Rail freight may be carried either by goods trains (U.S.: freight trains) or by passenger trains. Goods trains, consisting of various types of waggons (e.g., open waggons, covered waggons, flat waggons, container waggons, etc.), may be used for conveying bulk goods (e.g., coal, timber, grain) as well as part-load goods (e.g., parcels), whereas passenger trains carry only part-load goods.

The main characteristics of rail transport can best be explained by comparing rail and road.
1. Cost
   Rail is generally cheaper for bulk goods, which, if sent by road, would necessitate using many vehicles. In contrast to rail, capital outlay for road transport is small - because roads are not directly paid for by the road hauliers - and this is reflected in lower charges for many classes of merchandise. In addition, the arrangements often made for return loads enable charges to be reduced still further.
2. Convenience
   The outstanding feature of road transport is its flexibility. Having no fixed tracks, it can provide a direct collection and delivery service (door-to-door service). Routes can easily be varied according to the flow of traffic, and loading and unloading are confined to single operations. By contrast, rail carriage is tied to a fixed track, and to stations and terminals, which are frequently some distance from the points of loading and discharge. This requires the railways to rely on some other form of transport (mainly road) to perform collection and delivery and is, therefore, the outstanding drawback of rail carriage: the transshipments cause delay, involve double handling, call for more careful packing, increase the risk of theft and damage, and send up costs. To overcome this problem, many large firms have their own private sidings (U.S.: sidetracks), which enable the railways to collect the goods at the consignor's premises and to deliver them direct to the consignee's factory yard. In addition, the railways are increasingly trying to alleviate this problem by the use of containers, which can easily be transferred between road and rail without the need to unload and reload.
3. Speed
   For long distances, rail transport is faster than road, but for shorter distances,

the advantage is with road transport, mainly because small lorry-loads can be handled easily and quickly. Railway policy has been to speed rail services by reducing the number of marshalling yards and developing through traffic in train loads between main centres (for example, in the United Kingdom by the introduction of the freightliner system).

4. Safety

The increasing use of containers in rail transport reduces the amount of handling and the risk of damage to goods sent by rail.

The basic principle of the freightliner system, which is an important form of combined transport in the U.K. and which also offers services to Ireland and Continental Europe, is that goods are carried in train loads on the main trunk routes between the major industrial centres and are collected and delivered by road feeder services. Freightliner trains consist of specially-built flat waggons designed to carry high-capacity, standard-size containers. The waggons, which remain permanently coupled, are operated as a unit (unit train) and are hauled at high speed on time-tabled shuttle services between terminals specially equipped with gantry cranes to transfer the containers from road vehicles to waggons, or vice versa. The freightliner system is also integrated with deep-sea and short-sea trade container services, enabling rapid transfer of containers between rail, road, and ship. The major advantages of the freightliner system are: door-to-door service, with the rail and ship conveying the goods on the main trunk routes and road vehicles collecting and delivering the goods; speed; economy of handling; and low risk of damage and pilferage.

The railways also operate a rapidly expanding system of company trains, so called because they carry exclusively the products of individual large companies in complete train loads. The commodities so carried include raw materials, petroleum products, chemicals, and motor vehicles.

Finally, one should not forget to mention the train-ferry services, operating efficiently, for example, between the U.K. and the Continent. The train-ferry system permits through transport between the U.K. and the Continent with no intermediate handling at the ports, as the specially-built train-ferry waggons are merely shunted on or off the train-ferry vessel.

carriage of goods by rail[2] - legal aspects

Eisenbahnfrachtverkehr
- juristische Aspekte

The document used when goods are sent by rail is the rail consignment note, which is prima facie evidence of the conclusion of the contract of carriage and a receipt for the goods delivered to the rail carrier (see: consignment note).

The international carriage of goods by rail is regulated by the Convention for the International Carriage of Goods by Rail (CIM, which is the abbreviation for Convention Internationale concernant le transport des Marchandises par chemins de fer). Under CIM conditions, the rail carrier (also known as 'carrier by rail') is automatically liable for any loss of, or damage to, the goods while they are in his custody, unless the loss or damage is due either to inherent vice, to the consignor's or the consignee's own fault, or to circumstances which are beyond the railway's control (e.g., arson, sabotage, etc.). The carrier's liability for loss or damage is limited to a maximum of 50 gold francs per kilogram (approximately 370 Austrian schillings at time of writing).

carriage of goods by road

Straßenfrachtverkehr,
Straßengüterverkehr

The carriage of goods by road plays a dominant role in a modern and efficient transport system. This can be seen from the fact that in many countries the roads carry more than half of the total volume of freight.

A shipper who wishes to send goods may operate his own delivery services if the extent of his business warrants it. For example, in the U.K. about half of all goods carried by road are transported in the firms' own vehicles, such as delivery vans, light lorries (U.S.: pickup trucks), and heavy lorries, mainly over comparatively short distances. Over long distances, it will, as a rule, be more economical to employ the services of a road haulier, because he can usually operate with return loads and thus cut costs by keeping his vehicles effectively employed in both directions.

The following is a summary of the main features of road transport:
1. Door-to-door service without intermediate handling.
2. Flexibility in operation.
3. Suitability for small consignments.
4. Simple documentation: the document used when goods are sent by road is the road consignment note, which, like the rail consignment note and the air waybill, is prima facie evidence of the conclusion of the contract of carriage and a receipt for the goods delivered to the carrier (see: consignment note).
5. Combination with rail transport (piggyback service) or with sea transport (roll-on/roll-off).
6. Simplified customs procedure by the use of TIR (Transport International Routier) carnets. Under the TIR procedure (laid down by the TIR Convention, to which most European countries have acceded), the road vehicle or container is sealed by Customs before export, making it possible for the goods to be carried from any approved customs office in the exporting country to any customs office in the country of destination with a minimum of customs examinations and documentation.
7. Need for an extensive network of roads, which is likely to have a negative environmental impact (claim on land).
8. Pollution (noise and fumes) produced by rapidly growing volume of traffic and ever larger lorries (juggernauts).

The international carriage of goods by road is regulated by the Convention for the International Carriage of Goods by Road (CMR, which is the abbreviation for Convention relative au contrat de transport international des Marchandises par Route). It deals principally with the documentation for road transport and with the carrier's liability. The road carrier's liability under CMR conditions is basically the same as that of the rail carrier under CIM conditions, the maximum limit of liability, however, being lower than under CIM conditions.

carriage of goods by sea[1]
- general course of business

Seefrachtverkehr
- Geschäftsabwicklung

An exporter who wants to send his goods abroad by ship may have his own shipping department, which is charged with the execution of export orders in general and with the arrangement of shipping in particular. If, however, export sales are too small to warrant the employment of a shipping manager or specialised shipping clerks, he may employ the services of a forwarding agent or sell only on terms which leave the actual shipping arrangements to be made by the buyer, e.g., ex works, f.a.s., etc..

If an exporter of goods engages, for instance under a c.i.f. contract, to arrange for the carriage of goods to the port of destination, the first thing he has to do is conclude a contract of carriage (by sea) with a shipowner (i.e., an individual shipowner or a shipping company), under which the latter commits himself to carrying the goods in his ship from the port of shipment to the port of destination. The remuneration to be paid to the shipowner is the freight, and the exporter, as a party to the contract of carriage, is referred to as the shipper. Depending on the type of goods to be dispatched, the shipper may charter a complete ship, in which case the terms of the contract of carriage are embodied in a document known as the 'charterparty'. This applies mainly to bulk goods, which are almost entirely transported in tramp ships. In most cases, however, the goods are sent as general cargo, i.e., they are carried in a general cargo vessel together with goods of other shippers, and the terms of the contract of carriage by sea are evidenced by a document referred to as the 'bill of lading', which, in effect, is a receipt by the shipowner acknowledging that goods have been delivered to him for the purpose of carriage and repeating in detail the terms of the contract.

In practice, the shipper usually instructs a forwarding agent to procure space on board a vessel for his cargo. The shipowner, on the other hand, likewise employs an agent, the loading broker, to obtain cargoes for his ship.

The shipowner, through his loading broker, advises the shipper or his agent of the name of the ship that is to carry the consignment, of the loading berth, and of the closing date, i.e., the last date when goods are accepted for loading. The shipper is well-advised to send the goods to the named loading berth in time, for if they arrive after the closing date, the shipowner is entitled to shut them out even if the ship has not sailed yet.

When the goods are delivered to the docks and loaded on board ship, the shipper usually receives a document known as the 'mate's receipt', which is signed by the ship's officer in charge of the loading operations and includes complete details of the goods as well as any comments and qualifications in respect of the condition of the goods received. The records of loading taken during the loading operations are handed to the shipowner's port clerks, who compare them with the bill of lading completed by the shipper and sent to the shipowner's office. If the particulars on the B/L agree with the records of loading, the bill is signed by an authorised person on behalf of the shipowner and handed over to the shipper in exchange for the mate's receipt. It should be noted that, in contrast to the bill of lading, the mate's receipt is not a document of title; its transfer does not pass possession of the goods, and, therefore, it is of lower order than the bill of lading.

The shipper then forwards the B/L to the consignee, or arranges for it to be surrendered to him by a bank, as in the case of payment under a documentary letter of credit or a documentary collection. Since the B/L gives its holder the right to control the goods, it enables the consignee/importer to take delivery of the goods from the carrier when they arrive at the port of destination.

carriage of goods by sea[2]
- economic aspects

Seefrachtverkehr
- wirtschaftliche Aspekte

It is common practice to classify ships into 'liners' and 'tramps'. A liner, or liner vessel, which may be a cargo liner for the carriage of general cargo or a passenger liner, is a ship that operates regularly between two ports or a group of ports. Liners follow fixed routes and run to fixed schedules, that is, they sail on scheduled dates/times, irrespective of whether they are full or not.

Competition among the shipping lines as to freight rates has been largely eliminated by the formation of shipping conferences. A shipping conference is an association of two or more liner companies, usually of various nationalities, which provide international liner services for the carriage of cargo on the same particular route or routes within specified geographic limits at uniform freight rates. This shows that a shipping conference is basically a cartel fixing for its members uniform freight rates for the different classes of cargo. Competition among the conference members is limited to the efficient operation of vessels. The freight rates offered by conference shipping lines are normally lower than those which non-conference shipping lines (referred to as 'outsiders') are able to quote. But it should not be forgotten that regular liner services with their advantages for the shipper (e.g., regular sailings and the assurance of definite delivery dates; stable freight rates) can only be profitably maintained if the liner companies can count on regular freight bookings. This is the reason why shipping conferences grant preferential freight rates to regular customers. A shipper, for example, who enters into a contract with a shipping conference by which he undertakes to ship all his cargo only by conference lines is granted lower freight rates than other shippers. There are more than 300 shipping conferences, each main trade route having its own conference. Shipping companies serving two or more routes may belong to two or more conferences.

In contrast to liners, tramps, or tramp ships, do not run to schedule and are not operated on fixed routes. They are cargo ships which can be chartered by anyone for a particular voyage (voyage charter) or for a certain period of time (time charter) and which are particularly suitable for the carriage of such bulk goods as coal, grain, ores, fertilisers, etc., though some tramps are specially equipped to carry meat and fruit. Tramp rates are not fixed, but determined by competition in the market.

The ship most frequently used in practice is still the general cargo vessel, which is capable of carrying a wide range of cargo. However, in recent years, high-capacity ships purpose-built for certain trades or cargoes have become more popular. The most important of these special-purpose ships are:

1. Oil-tankers: tankers exceeding 200,000 d.w.t. (deadweight tons) are called 'very large crude carriers' (VLCCs) and those with a capacity of more than 350,000 d.w.t. 'ultra large crude carriers' (ULCCs).
2. Container vessels: the major advantage offered by the increasing use of containers in sea carriage is the direct collection and delivery service (door-to-door service). In addition, containerisation has reduced transit times and raised quality of service.
3. LASH vessels (Lighter Aboard the Ship): this new type of vessel carries loaded lighters (barges) from one port to another and takes on other pre-loaded lighters for the return voyage. The advantages offered by this combination of inland water and sea transport include: no intermediate handling during transfer from the ship, thus reducing cost and permitting competitive freight

rates to be quoted; low risk of damage and pilferage; exceptionally quick turn-round.
4. Roll-on/roll-off vessels, carrying loaded road vehicles from one port to another, thus combining road and sea transport.
5. Refrigerated meat and fruit vessels; liquefied natural gas carriers; ore carriers; timber carriers; and others.

carriage of goods by sea[3]
- legal aspects

Seefrachtverkehr
- juristische Aspekte

In the majority of countries, the carriage of goods under bills of lading is governed by the Hague-Visby rules. They are the result of amendments drawn up at Visby, Sweden, to the Hague rules of 1921, and came into effect in 1977. Under these rules, the carrier is bound to exercise due diligence to:
1. Make the ship seaworthy.
2. Properly man, equip, and supply the ship.
3. Make the ship fit and safe for the reception, carriage, and preservation of cargo.
In addition, the carrier must properly and carefully load, handle, stow, and discharge the goods carried. The principle underlying these provisions is that the shipowner is only liable for loss of, or damage to, the goods if he acts negligently.

The rules also specify that the carrier is not liable for any loss or damage resulting, for example, from: perils of the sea; act of god; act of war; strikes or lock-outs; riots and civil commotions; inherent vice of the goods; insufficient packing; etc.. (It should be noted that most of the above exceptions to the carrier's liability can be covered by marine insurance.)

Since the Hague-Visby rules are obviously more in favour of carriers than shippers, new rules were adopted at Hamburg in 1978. Unlike the Hague-Visby rules, the Hamburg rules do not provide a list of the carrier's duties and exclusions of his liability, but state that the carrier is liable for any loss of, or damage to, the goods while they are in his custody, unless he proves that he and his agents or servants have taken all necessary measures to avoid the loss or damage. This shows that the Hamburg rules are similar to those adopted for the carriage of goods by air, road, and rail. It can be seen that, compared with the Hague-Visby rules, the Hamburg rules place the carrier in a very weak position. Therefore, it is unlikely that they will be in widespread use in the near future.

carriage of goods on inland waterways

Binnenschiffahrtsfrachtverkehr

Inland waterways (mainly rivers and canals) help to solve a country's transport problems and, in addition, form an integral part of its drainage and water-supply systems.

When goods are carried on inland waterways, the contract of carriage is evidenced by a document called the 'inland waterway bill of lading', which has the same legal characteristics as the ocean bill of lading. Inland waterway carriers provide transport services by barge and push tug assemblies, trains of barges (consisting of a river tug, a tow rope, and one or more barges), and motorised barges.

Inland water transport, or inland waterways transport, is cheap and economical in the use of manpower and is, therefore, particularly suitable for bulk goods of low value, such as coal, iron-ore, lime, sand, and bricks. From the environmental standpoint, it is virtually noiseless and non-polluting. A major drawback of carriage on inland waterways is that it is slow, especially because of transshipments (e.g., rail/craft/rail) and the number of locks needed to raise craft from one water-level to another.

carrier	Frachtführer, Verfrachter

A carrier is an individual or organisation whose business it is to transport goods. He enters into a contract of carriage with a shipper, by which he undertakes, for a consideration (freight or carriage), to carry the goods specified in the contract from the place named to the agreed place of destination.

On the basis of the various modes of transport, carriers may be classified into 'land carriers', i.e., 'rail carriers' (railway companies) and 'road carriers' (road hauliers, U.S.: trucking firms), 'air carriers' (airline operators), 'sea carriers' (shipping companies), and 'inland waterway carriers'.

cartel	(internationales) Kartell

The term 'cartel' denotes a voluntary association of business enterprises on a contractual basis providing for the adoption of some uniform business policy by its members, especially with regard to production, sales, and prices. Cartels fix prices, restrict output (e.g., by assigning production quotas to their members), carve up (i.e., divide) markets, and may even have their own selling organisations (cartel syndicates). In short, they are combinations "in restraint of trade", i.e., intended to restrict competition.

From this description it is clear that the English term 'cartel' does not cover all types of cartel enumerated in the Austrian Kartellgesetz (e.g., gentlemen's agreements, conscious parallelism, resale price maintenance). Moreover, it should be noted that the term is not defined in British or American law, and that there is a tendency to restrict its use to foreign or international agreements in restraint of trade. Some of the English terms used to describe certain types or aspects of what the Austrian law defines as 'Kartelle' have already been mentioned: 'gentlemen's agreement', 'conscious parallelism', 'resale price maintenance'. Other terms are: 'price ring', 'pool', and, in the United States, 'trust'.

Today, most countries have laws prohibiting, or at least severely restricting, cartels and similar practices in restraint of trade, because they are believed to be against the public interest. It is, however, interesting to note that continental laws tend to be more lenient, especially more lenient than the relevant legislation in the United States (see: antitrust law). Before World War II, Germany in common with other continental countries permitted, and even encouraged, associations and combinations in restraint of trade. The existence of restrictive practices legislation does not mean that there are no more cartels, although they are not always called by that name. OPEC, the Organisation of Petroleum Exporting Countries, is a cartel, and so is the International Tin Council. Cartels can also be found in the E.E.C., especially in the steel industry, which is experiencing great difficulties at the moment.

cash[1]

**Bargeld,
Barmittel**

In everyday contexts, cash refers to banknotes and coins. To pay cash (or in cash), therefore means that, in contrast to other methods of payment (e.g., payment by cheque, by credit transfer, by standing order, etc.), actual banknotes and coins change hands in settlement of some financial obligation. Cash in this form can be obtained from banks (either from bank counters or cash dispensers). Although many people have been predicting the advent of a cash-less society, banknotes and coins have persisted in spite of such formidable rivals as the cheque, the credit card, and the debit card. Obviously, it is still convenient for small purchases, and some experts think that the growth of the shadow economy may have contributed to this situation.

It should be noted, however, that in other contexts, e.g., on a balance sheet, the term 'cash' may include sight deposits held with banks. On many British balance sheets the relevant item reads "Cash in Hand or at Banks".

cash[2]

**prompte Bezahlung,
sofortige Bezahlung**

In a business communications context, cash is frequently applied to prompt payment by whatever means. To pay cash, therefore simply indicates that settlement is effected within a few business days of delivery or performance either by banknotes and coins, by cheque, or by transferring the amount owed from one's bank account.

cash[3]

Bezahlung

In a business communications context (e.g., in a business letter), the term 'cash' may occasionally just denote payment. An example would be: "Our prices are quoted for cash within 30 days".

cash-and-carry wholesaler

**Abholgroßmarkt,
Abholgroßhandlung,
Cash-and-Carry Markt**

Cash-and-carry wholesalers do not perform all the services offered by regular wholesalers. In particular, they do not deliver the goods, but their retail customers have to call for them at their premises; moreover, they do not extend credit but insist on payment at the time of purchase, or at least soon after. For this reason, cash-and-carry wholesalers can quote lower prices than regular wholesalers, which makes them attractive to the small independent retailer. It should be noted, however, that the time spent in calling for the goods, the cost of operating the vehicle involved, and the unavailability of credit will, in many cases, offset the lower prices.

cash discount   Skonto

Where goods or services are sold on credit, it is quite common for the supplier to offer the buyer a cash discount as an incentive for early payment. The cash discount - usually 2% or 3% - can be deducted from the invoice price (i.e., from the list price less quantity discount and trade discount, if any) if payment is effected within a stated period of time (discount period). The terms "2/10, net 30", for example, indicate that a 2 per cent cash discount is given if the invoice is paid within 10 days from/of the date of invoice. Should the buyer, however, not settle the invoice within the discount period of 10 days, he must pay the full amount within 30 days (i.e., between the 11th and 30th day of the credit period).

It is important to note that a cash discount represents the implicit interest on the trade credit involved in a sale on deferred terms. If a buyer takes the cash discount, there is no cost for the use of trade credit during the discount period. However, if a cash discount is offered and it is not taken, there is a definite opportunity cost. In the example mentioned above - 2/10, net 30 -, the buyer has the use of funds for an additional 20 days if he does not take the cash discount but pays on the final day of the credit period. In the case of a £100 invoice, he would have the use of £98 for 20 days. On the basis of a 360-day year, the annual interest cost is 36.7 per cent (2/98 x 360/20). This shows that a trade credit can be a very expensive form of short-term financing where a cash discount is offered, and that, conversely, availing oneself of a cash discount can be a very profitable investment, even if a credit has to be taken out to make the early payment.

cash dispenser   Geldausgabeautomat (z.B. Bankomat)

A cash dispenser, or cash dispensing machine, is a self-service terminal, usually installed in the walls of a banking office, which enables holders of cash cards to draw a limited amount of money per day from their current accounts. A cash dispenser, basically an ATM with only one function, is operated by a cardholder inserting his magnetically encoded plastic card into a slot provided for this purpose, and keying in his PIN code (Personal Identification Number) and the amount required.

As cash dispensers may be accessible up to 24 hours a day, they have proved especially convenient for those at work during normal banking hours, or bank opening hours.

cash flow   Cash flow

The cash flow is a significant indicator of the financial strength of a business firm. The term refers to the amount of cash, or funds, generated by a business during a specific period of time. The most common method of calculating the cash flow is to add to the profit for the period any non-cash expenses (mainly the periodic depreciation charge) and to deduct any non-cash revenues (e.g., accrued interest, i.e., interest earned but not yet received or credited).

The cash flow can be defined in a number of ways, depending on the underlying profit concept used: gross cash flow is based on total profit, i.e., both retained and distributed earnings. Net cash flow, on the other hand, is only retained earnings plus non-cash expenses minus non-cash revenues . If used without any qualifying word, cash flow usually means gross cash flow, i.e., the amount of funds generated by the firm and available for distribution, investment, and repayment of debt.

In the widest sense of the term, 'cash flow' refers to any flow of cash into and out of a firm. A statement of changes in financial position on a cash basis lists not only the cash generated by the reporting firm between two balance sheet dates, but also all other sources of cash (e.g., loans raised from banks or an issue of common stock or bonds) as well as all applications of cash for investment purposes (e.g., expenditure on machinery, vehicles, etc.).

cash with order   Zahlung bei Auftragserteilung

'Cash with order' (abbreviated C.W.O.) is a condition of payment indicating that a supplier is prepared to supply a buyer only if he receives payment for the goods together with the order. This means that he receives payment before he parts with the goods and thus eliminates any credit risk. C.W.O. is, therefore, a variant of 'payment in advance'.

catalogue   Katalog

A catalogue (American spelling: 'catalog') is a list, usually in the form of a book, of goods for sale. In most cases, it also states the prices of the goods.

A well-prepared catalogue should include:
1. an index to the different classes of goods;
2. attractively prepared illustrations, preferably in colour;
3. a written description of the items and an explanation of technical terms used;
4. conditions of sale, delivery, and payment.

central bank   Zentralbank, Notenbank

Every country needs a central institution with a wide range of powers to look after its monetary system; in other words, it needs a central bank. Central banks, such as the Bank of England, the Federal Reserve System of the United States (comprising 12 federal reserve banks), the Deutsche Bundesbank, and the Österreichische Nationalbank, are typically charged with all, or at least most, of the following functions.
1. Central banks are responsible for an adequate supply of legal tender, i.e., of banknotes and coins that have to be accepted in settlement of debts. Usually, the central bank is the sole note-issuing bank in a particular country. The minting of coins is frequently the responsibility of a separate institution under the control of the central bank (e.g., the Royal Mint in Great Britain).
2. Central banks are bankers' banks, i.e., they perform certain tasks for commercial and specialised banks, just as these banks perform services for their own clients. Commercial banks keep accounts with the central bank. These accounts may be used to settle the net positions resulting from the clearing of cheques and credit transfers. Moreover, the commercial banks borrow directly or indirectly from the central bank, especially if funds are not available from other sources, the central bank acting as a lender of last resort.

In addition, central banks are frequently charged with supervising and regulating the banking system of the country in which they operate.
3. A central bank also acts as a banker to its government, typically managing the national debt, handling or superintending the issue of government stocks and Treasury bills, making short-term advances to the government, providing advice on financial matters, etc..
4. More importantly, central banks are concerned with the implementation of monetary policies. They regulate a country's money supply by open-market operations, by calling for special deposits (U.S.: legal reserves), by influencing interest rates, and by operating direct controls on bank lending. But they are also active on the external front, intervening in the foreign exchange markets to control the rates of exchange, and generally managing the external aspects of monetary policy, such as exchange controls, foreign exchange reserves (including Special Drawing Rights), etc..

In performing these tasks, central banks in different countries enjoy different degrees of autonomy from their governments. The Bank of England, for instance, is closely controlled by the Treasury, which since 1946 has had statutory powers to give directions to it. The Federal Reserve System of the United States, on the other hand, is able to steer a much more independent course.

central processing unit   Zentraleinheit

The central processing unit (CPU, also called the 'mainframe') is the nerve centre of any digital computer. It coordinates and controls the activities of all the other units and performs all the arithmetic and logical processes to be applied to the data. In many computers, the CPU includes the central processor (arithmetic-logic unit and control unit) and the primary storage unit. In many texts, however, the terms 'central processing unit' and 'central processor' are used interchangeably.

certificate of deposit   Kassenschein,
Kassenobligation,
Einlagenbescheinigung

Certificates of deposit (CDs) are instruments issued by banks in large denominations in return for sums deposited with them. The most popular variety is the interest-bearing negotiable time CD. In contrast to savings deposits, which are evidenced by passbook entries, deposits represented by time CDs have a definite maturity, which means that the funds are tied up with the bank for a fixed period of time. Nevertheless, a negotiable time CD is a very flexible form of investment, since it not only enables the original depositor to obtain the funds plus interest from the bank at maturity, but it can also be sold for cash at any time before maturity. For this reason, negotiable time CDs have recently become a widely used money market instrument.

certificate of origin   Ursprungszeugnis

The certificate of origin is a special document which is required for customs purposes in connection with shipments to certain foreign countries. It may be submitted by an importer and, as the expression implies, certifies the country of origin of imported goods. "Country of origin" means that the goods either have been wholly produced there or, if imported from other countries, have undergone "substantial transformation", for which various operational definitions are used. The certificate of origin may be issued by the exporter or by a third party, normally a chamber of commerce of the exporting country. It may be either a separate document or combined with other documents, as in the Combined Certificate of Value and Origin (customs invoice).

The certificate of origin required in trade between the E.E.C. and associated countries (e.g., Austria) is called the 'movement certificate'.

In commercial practice, a certificate of origin is, for instance, used where a country grants preferential tariff treatment on imports of goods grown or manufactured in a particular country . In such a case, the goods must be accompanied by a certificate of origin, in which the exporter testifies that the goods in fact originate in the country enjoying preferential treatment. The importer is thus entitled to the benefit of the lower rate of import duty, or even to exemption from duty if the goods are admissible duty free.

certified check   bestätigter Scheck

A certified check is an ordinary check on which the drawee bank certifies that the signature of the drawer is genuine and that he has sufficient funds for the bank to honour it on presentation. The amount certified is set aside by the bank for the express purpose of paying the check, and payment cannot be refused because of insufficient funds.

Certified checks are used extensively in the United States, especially in connection with brokerage, security, and real estate transactions involving large sums of money.

C. & F. (Incoterms 1980)   C. & F.
COST AND FREIGHT   KOSTEN UND FRACHT
...*(named port of destination)*   ... *(benannter Bestimmungshafen)*
International code: CFR

Under this clause, the seller must pay the costs and freight necessary to bring the goods to the named port of destination, but the risk of loss of, or damage to, the goods is transferred from the seller to the buyer when the goods pass the ship's rail at the port of shipment. The seller, however, does not have to procure cargo insurance against the risks of the goods during the carriage, which is the concern of the buyer. In this respect, C.& F. differs from C.I.F., but in all other respects, the seller's and buyer's duties as well as the costs to be borne by each are exactly the same as under a c.i.f. contract.

channel of distribution   Distributionskanal,
                                                Absatzweg

The channel of distribution, also referred to as the 'marketing channel', is the set of marketing intermediaries between the producer and the final user. Channels of distribution can be characterised as having a certain number of stages. A zero-stage channel is one which leads directly from the producer to the final user (e.g., door-to-door selling and direct mail). A one-stage channel would feature one type of marketing intermediary, e.g., retailers that are supplied by the producer direct. A two-stage channel would include two types of middlemen, e.g., wholesalers and retailers, intervening between the producer and the final users.

cheque   Scheck

A cheque (in American English spelt 'check') is a written order to a bank, given and signed by a person having a current account with the bank, to pay a certain sum of money stated on the cheque to, or to the order of, a specified person, or to bearer. 'Person' includes not only individuals but also organisations.

There are three parties to a cheque: the person who makes out the cheque and signs it is the 'drawer'; the person to whom it is made payable is the 'payee' or the 'bearer'; and the bank on which it is drawn is the 'drawee' (also called the 'drawee bank').

The drawer can make out cheques for any sum within the limit of his current account balance (in Austria, current account holders are usually allowed to overdraw their accounts up to a specified limit). The major characteristic of a cheque is that it must be paid "on demand", i.e., when it is presented for payment.

Cheques may be classified into 'order cheques' and 'bearer cheques'. An order cheque is payable to a specified person or to order, and can be transferred by indorsement and delivery. A bearer cheque is payable to bearer, and can, therefore, be transferred by one person to another by delivery, without any formality. In practice, banks provide their customers with printed cheque forms, and the only thing the drawer has to do is fill in the name of the payee (only in the case of order cheques), the sum to be paid, the place and date of issue, and add his signature.

Order cheques and bearer cheques may be cross-classified into 'open cheques' and 'crossed cheques'. An open cheque is payable in cash, but, as a rule, only at the bank or a branch of the bank on which it is drawn. In practice, an open cheque may also be presented for payment at a bank other than the drawee bank, provided the holder of the cheque (payee, indorsee, or bearer) has an account with this bank. In such a case, the bank does not pay the cheque in cash over the counter, but pays it into the holder's account. In contrast to an open cheque, a crossed cheque cannot be cashed over the bank counter, but must be paid into an account. Its purpose is to protect the owner against theft or loss. When a cheque is lost, notice should be given at once to the drawee bank with a request for payment to be stopped.

If there are no funds or insufficient funds on the drawer's account, the drawee bank usually refuses to pay the cheque when presented for payment, in other words, it dishonours the cheque. Colloquially, such a cheque is said to "bounce". The holder of a dishonoured cheque has to send a notice of dishonour to the drawer and the indorsers (if any) and can then take recourse in the same manner as in the case of a bill of exchange.

The cheque is a safe and inexpensive form of remittance, e.g., a buyer of goods sends the seller a cheque in payment of the invoice. Over the past few years, the cheque, in combination with the cheque card, has practically become one of the most common means of payment for goods and services of all kinds.

cheque card

The cheque card, or cheque guarantee card, guarantees that any cheque made out by the holder up to a specified amount will be honoured by the bank issuing the card, regardless of whether there are sufficient funds in the account or not. The amount guaranteed varies from country to country. In Austria, for instance, the upper limit is 2,500 schillings, while the corresponding figure in Great Britain is £50. Thus, the cheque card acts as a safeguard for traders and others accepting cheques from customers. The risk involved in accepting a cheque is, therefore, shifted to the drawee bank, issuing the card.

To ensure that payment is not refused by the bank, the person accepting a cheque has to make sure that the customer's signature, his account number, and the cheque card number on the cheque conform to the corresponding items on the cheque card, and that the cheque card is still valid, i.e., has not yet expired.

Cheque cards may also be used, with or without a cheque, to draw cash at any branch of the drawee bank. Some banks offer cheque cards which double as cash cards (e.g., for the Bankomat cash dispenser service) or as credit cards (e.g., Barclaycard).

C.I.F. (Incoterms 1980)
COST, INSURANCE, AND FREIGHT
...(named port of destination)

C.I.F.
KOSTEN, VERSICHERUNG, FRACHT
...(benannter Bestimmungshafen)

International code: CIF

Under this clause, which is frequently used in international trade, the seller must pay the costs and freight necessary to bring the goods to the named port of destination, and he must, at his own expense, procure marine insurance against the risk of loss of, or damage to, the goods during the carriage. The seller's responsibility for the goods ends when he has delivered them on board ship into the shipowner's custody at the port of shipment.

In particular, the seller must:
1. Supply the goods in conformity with the contract of sale.
2. Contract at his own expense for the carriage of the goods to the agreed port of destination, and pay freight charges and unloading costs to the extent that they are included in the freight charges. In other words, in contrast to an f.o.b. contract, it is the seller's duty to enter into the contract of carriage (by sea) with the shipping conmpany, and he must pay all costs incurred thereby.
3. Obtain, at his own risk and expense, any export licence necessary for the export of the goods.
4. Procure, at his own expense, a marine insurance policy against the risks of carriage. In contrast to C.& F., the seller is responsible for taking out marine insurance, which means that he contracts for the insurance of the goods during the carriage and pays the insurance premium. The insurance has to cover the c.i.f. price (i.e., the net price of the goods after deduction of any discounts, plus freight and cost of insurance) plus 10 per cent buyer's anticipated profit. The insurance provided is usually a warehouse-to-warehouse insurance, covering the risks of carriage not only during the ocean transport, but from the seller's warehouse to the final place of destination. In addition, the seller must provide, at the buyer's expense, war risk insurance if requested to do so by the buyer.

5. Load the goods at his own expense on board the vessel at the port of shipment, and bear all costs in respect of the goods up to the time of their loading (e.g., the cost of transport from the seller's warehouse/factory to the port of shipment; all the handling and shipping charges, such as dock dues, wharfage, porterage, lighterage, etc). In addition, he must pay any taxes, fees, or charges levied because of exportation, as well as the costs of any formalities which he has to fulfil in order to load the goods on board.
6. Bear all risks of the goods until they have effectively passed the ship's rail at the port of shipment.
7. At his own expense, deliver to the buyer a bill of lading for the agreed port of destination, as well as the invoice of the goods shipped and the insurance policy.
8. Provide at his own expense the customary packing of the goods.
9. Pay the costs of any checking operations (such as checking of quality, measuring, weighing, counting).

The buyer must:
1. Accept the documents (e.g., bill of lading, marine insurance policy, and invoice) if they are in conformity with the contract of sale, and pay the price as provided for in the contract. Under a c.i.f. contract, delivery does not mean 'physical' delivery of the goods, but 'symbolic' delivery by means of a bill of lading covering the contract goods. The seller fulfils his contractual obligations as regards delivery by furnishing a bill of lading covering the contract goods to the buyer. This is of great importance because, even if the goods are lost in transit, the seller is still entitled to deliver the proper shipping documents to the buyer and claim the purchase price. As regards the loss incurred, the buyer is entitled to make a claim either against the shipowner by virtue of the bill of lading or against the insurance company by virtue of the marine insurance policy.
2. Receive the goods at the agreed port of destination and bear, with the exception of the freight and marine insurance, all costs of the goods during the ocean transport until their arrival at the port of destination (e.g., stowage of the goods on board ship), as well as unloading costs, including lighterage and wharfage, unless such costs are included in the freight. (Note: if the goods are sold 'C.I.F. landed', unloading costs, including lighterage and wharfage, are borne by the seller).
3. Bear all risks of the goods from the time when they have effectively passed the ship's rail at the port of shipment. This provision is important in cases where the goods are lost in transit owing to causes which do not entitle the buyer to make a claim against the shipowner or insurer. Even in these cases, the buyer has to pay the purchase price on delivery of the duly prepared shipping documents, or, if he has already paid, cannot recover the price.
4. Procure, at his own risk and expense, any import licence which he may require for the importation of the goods, and pay all customs duties and any other duties and taxes payable at the time of, or by reason of, the importation.

circular letter   (Werbe-)Rundschreiben

A circular letter (also referred to as a 'circular'; plural: 'circulars') is a duplicated letter (typed or printed) which is distributed to a large number of individuals or firms (for example, a firm informs other firms about the appointment of a new agent). Since a personal letter is more likely to receive attention than a mimeographed one, circulars are often "personalised", that is, given the appearance of personal letters.

A circular letter often serves the same purpose as a sales letter, and is frequently prepared in series of two, three, or more letters (sales series) in order to achieve the highest possible advertising effect.

claim   Schadenersatzanspruch,
                                                      Versicherungsanspruch

A claim, as used in insurance, is a formal demand made by an insured party on the insurer for payment under an insurance policy.

claused bill of lading   unreines Konnossement

A claused bill of lading (also referred to as a 'dirty B/L' or 'foul B/L') is one which bears a clause indicating any defect in the packing or the goods themselves. In other words, a claused bill is a B/L in which the shipowner or his agent has stated that the goods and/or the packing were damaged or otherwise defective when shipped or received for shipment. "Packing cases stained", "bags torn", "goods shipped not quite dry", "cases damaged and repaired", "case No. 52 broken" are all examples of statements making a bill of lading a claused one.

A claused bill is generally of little use to a shipper of goods, because it may cause difficulties in the collection of payment. For example, documentary credits always call for clean bills of lading, and if a claused bill is presented, the bank will refuse payment. If the carrier has issued a claused bill, the shipper may contact the consignee and make sure that the bill is acceptable as issued. This may be the case where the clause is simply the result of an over-careful shipowner, who does not want to be held responsible by a consignee for possible defects in the goods.

clean bill of lading   reines Konnossement

A clean bill of lading may be defined as one which bears no superimposed clause or notation expressly declaring a defective condition of the goods and/or the packing. In a clean bill of lading, the shipowner affirms that the goods shipped or received for shipment are in "apparent good order and condition". This means, the shipowner only states that the goods are externally in good order. He cannot be expected to judge their quality, because this is for the seller and buyer to agree, neither can he be expected to look inside the packing containers, nor otherwise to check the goods in detail. If, at the port of destination, the goods are found not to be in apparent good order and condition, there is an immediate presumption that the damage occurred while the goods were on the ship and in the shipowner's custody, and the owner of the goods will look to him for compensation.

clean collection

einfaches Inkasso,
nichtdokumentäres Inkasso

Clean collection is a method of payment in international trade under which an exporter presents a clean draft (i.e., a bill of exchange with no shipping documents attached) drawn on the foreign buyer to his bank for collection. The exporter's bank, in turn, forwards the draft to its branch office, correspondent bank, or some other bank in the buyer's country, with instructions to present the draft to the buyer/drawee for payment (in the case of a sight draft) or acceptance (in the case of a time draft)

For example, in the case of "payment against two months' acceptance", the exporter draws a time draft for the purchase price of the goods on the foreign buyer, payable two months after sight/acceptance, which he hands to his bank for collection. The exporter's bank then sends the draft to a bank in the buyer's country (usually a branch office or correspondent bank), instructing it to present the draft to the drawee for acceptance. After acceptance, the foreign bank may either keep the accepted draft until maturity and present it then for payment, or, which is very common in practice, may be asked by the exporter to discount the draft and remit the proceeds to his account.

A clean collection offers the exporter less security than a documentary collection, because, under the latter, the shipping documents, representing the right of control of the goods, are attached to the draft drawn on the foreign buyer and released to him only after payment or acceptance of the draft. Under a clean collection, however, the shipping documents are not attached to the draft, and the buyer will probably have already obtained the documents/goods before the draft is presented to him for payment or acceptance.

clearing bank

britische Geschäftsbank,
Clearing-Bank

The six British clearing banks, including the Big Four (Barclays, Lloyds, Midland, National Westminster), with their network of branches and subsidiaries dominate the British banking scene. They are, in effect, Britain's full-service commercial banks, which provide all the usual banking services, ranging from deposit-taking and cheque-drawing facilities to foreign payments and status information.

The term 'clearing bank' reflects the fact that all clearing banks (but not only they) are members and co-owners of the London Bankers' Clearing House, an organisation through which cheques and credit transfers involving different members are 'cleared'. Clearing in this context is a process by which claims and counter-claims arising from payment transactions carried out by the clearing banks are totalled and offset by a central institution. This means that for each pair of banks involved (e.g., bank A and bank B) only the balance, or net position, (i.e., the difference between the total amount owed by A to B and the total amount owed by B to A) is paid.

C.O.D

gegen Nachnahme

C.O.D., which is the abbreviation of 'cash on delivery' (G.B.) or 'collect on delivery' (U.S.A.), means that payment has to be effected on delivery of the goods. When goods are delivered C.O.D., the post office, the railway, or a forwarding agent is entrusted with the collection of the invoice amount. When the buyer has paid the amount due, the goods are released to him. In this way, the supplier makes sure that he will receive payment for goods supplied to customers who are unknown to him. The only risk that the supplier runs when he uses this kind of arrangement is that the buyer may refuse to accept the goods (risk of non-acceptance).

collection   Inkasso

The term 'collection' is applied to the presentation of invoices, bills of exchange, and similar documents to a debtor for payment, and the payment thereof.

collection agency   Inkassobüro

A collection agency is a commercial establishment specialising in the collection of outstanding accounts. Many credit inquiry agencies double as collection agencies.

combined transport   kombinierter Verkehr

The term 'combined transport', also known as 'integrated transport', 'multimodal transport', or 'intermodal transport', means through transport of intermodal unit loads (i.e., standard-size containers, loaded pallets, and loaded trailers and semi-trailers, which can be carried by more than one mode of transport and which can easily be transshipped between the various modes). In other words, combined transport refers to the carriage of unitised freight, such as loaded containers, pallets, and trailers, by a combination of two or more carriers.

Important forms of combined transport are the freightliner system in the U.K. (see: carriage of goods by rail[1]), the piggyback service, and roll-on/roll-off (Ro-Ro).

commercial agent   Handelsvertreter

A commercial agent is an independent business man who, under a contract of agency, is authorised to procure contracts (of sale) from, or to conclude contracts (of sale) with, third parties on behalf of his principal. In the case of a procurement agency, the commercial agent has only authority to introduce customers to his principal, but he is not entitled to accept orders without his prior consent. In all other cases, he concludes contracts of sale with customers on his principal's account and usually in the principal's name, which means that the principal enters into a direct contractual relationship with the customer. The commercial agent, who is not an employee of the principal and does not take title to the goods, is paid a remuneration in the form of a commission, which is calculated as an agreed percentage of the purchase price of the goods actually sold by him. A commercial agent who acts in a foreign country is referred to as an 'overseas agent'.

commercial bank

Geschäftsbank,
Kommerzbank

'Commercial bank' is the name given to those non-governmental banking institutions whose original purpose was mainly to finance the production and distribution of goods by lending short-term funds, to accept current account deposits, and to offer cheque-drawing facilities. As a consequence of the diversification of commercial banks into many other operations (e.g., consumer and personal lending, credit cards, mortgage banking, international banking and foreign exchange trading, investment management, electronic funds transfer services, etc.), the term 'full-service bank' has been promoted in recent years as more descriptive of the functions performed by commercial banks.

Banks classified as commercial banks are allowed to engage in more varied lending activities and to offer a wider range of financial services than are the other depository institutions.

commercial invoice

Handelsrechnung

A commercial invoice is a document used in foreign trade containing a record of the transaction between a seller (exporter) and a buyer (importer). It is made out by the seller in triplicate or quadruplicate and should contain the following information:
1. the names and addresses of both exporter and importer;
2. the date and number of the invoice;
3. the date and number of the order;
4. a complete description of the goods;
5. the number of packages, and details of shipping marks;
6. the weight and/or quantity of the goods;
7. the unit price, where applicable, and the total invoice price against trade terms (e.g., c.i.f. price);
8. the terms of payment (e.g., documentary credit; D/A; D/P; etc.), including the currency, place and time of payment;
9. the export licence number and/or import licence number, where applicable;
10. the name of the vessel, if known or applicable.

The following points are sometimes required to be shown, usually for the customs authorities in the buyer's country:
11. the seller's signature and a statement by the seller that the invoice is correct and true;
12. the origin of the goods;
13. the ports of loading and discharge;
14. the details of freight and insurance charges specified separately, where applicable.
Since exports are zero-rated, no V.A.T. is shown on a commercial invoice.

The primary purpose of the commercial invoice is to inform the importer of the amount due. In addition, a commercial invoice is often required in the importing country for customs purposes (e.g., as basis for the assessment of import duty) and other official purposes, and must, therefore, conform to the regulations of the importing country. This is mainly true of countries which do not require any customs or consular invoices. Many of these countries, e.g., Middle East countries, require that one or more copies of the commercial invoice be certified by the chamber of commerce of the exporting country, and/or be legalised by the consulate of the importer's country located in the country of the exporter.

commercial traveller

Handlungsreisender, Reisender

A commercial traveller (also called a 'sales representative' or 'sales rep'; in the U.S.A., a 'traveling salesman' or 'field executive') is a person who is employed by a manufacturer or wholesaler. His main duty is to promote the sales of his firm by calling on prospective customers (usually retailers) to obtain orders. A distinction must be made between a traveller who is authorised to conclude contracts of sale on behalf of his firm, and one who has authority to submit offers and accept orders, but only with the firm's prior consent. Normally, the remuneration of the traveller is a fixed salary, enlarged by a commission on the purchase price of the goods sold by him. By contrast, a commercial agent is not an employee of the firm he represents, but an independent business man who works exclusively on a commission basis.

commodity

Ware, (Wirtschafts-)Gut; (international gehandelter) Rohstoff, Welthandelsgut; Massenartikel

The term 'commodity' may refer either to goods (and even to goods and services) in general or to raw materials traded internationally (frequently on commodity markets), such as cotton, rubber, tin, and vegetable oils. Recently, the term has also been applied to mass-produced articles, which are in some respect similar to raw materials (e.g., commodity chips). This similarity is not physical, but economic, and relates mainly to the importance of price competition and the difficulty (if not impossibility) of product differentiation.

commodity exchange

Warenbörse, Rohstoffbörse

Commodity exchanges are highly organised markets for internationally traded raw materials, such as cotton, wool, grain, cocoa, sugar, copper, lead, tin, zinc, and a whole host of minor commodities (copra, spices, etc.). Examples are the London Metal Exchange, the New York Metal Exchange, the New York Sugar Exchange, and the Chicago Board of Trade (which specialises in grain and other agricultural products). Recently, some of the commodity exchanges have branched out into currency trading.

Trading on commodity exchanges is highly standardised. In most cases, business is transacted in the form of "lots" of standard quantities and to an agreed level of quality, the form of contract being laid down by the board, or committee, responsible for running and controlling the exchange concerned. Therefore, for a commodity to be traded on an exchange, it must be capable of being graded, i.e., classified into well-defined levels of quality. Thus, the actual inspection of the commodities or of the samples can be dispensed with. Commodities which are difficult or impossible to grade are commonly sold by auction, with the lots being inspected beforehand by the potential buyers. Raw wool, for instance, is sold by auction, although "tops" (i.e., bundles of combed wool, an intermediary stage in the processing of this commodity) can be bought and sold through commodity exchanges.

The transactions carried out on commodity exchanges are either 'actuals' (also called 'physicals'), involving physical delivery of the commodity in question, or 'futures', where, generally speaking, no such delivery is contemplated.

Actuals, which can be either spot or forward, i.e., for immediate delivery or for delivery at some future time, are less important, since a very large proportion of the world's raw materials are, in fact, sold by direct contract between exporter and importer. Commodity exchanges usually handle physical quantities of the commodities they trade in only to the extent that they are necessary to balance out a marginal and temporary excess of either demand or supply. In spite of this, the exchanges tend to set the market prices for their particular materials all over the world and have, therefore, an importance quite out of proportion to the actual volume of physical trade handled.

Futures, which on most exchanges account for 95 per cent of total volume, are used for speculative or for hedging purposes. The contractual obligations which they represent are not performed by physical delivery, but by engaging in an offsetting transaction, which amounts to either paying or receiving the difference between the agreed futures price and the market price, or new spot price.

commune   Kommune

Communes, especially agricultural (or rural) communes, might be regarded as alternative forms of business organisation, although they are certainly more, viz., social experiments in alternative life-styles. What sets the communes apart from other types of alternative enterprise, such as the worker co-operatives, with which they have much in common, is that the communes, at least the more radical ones, abolish private property and try to break down the barriers between work and private life.

A typical commune, as described in the Commune Directory 1977, is located in a rural area; the members have built their own accommodation or have remodelled an old farmhouse; they go in for organic farming, knitting, weaving, wood-carving, and similar activities; they might rear sheep; and they generally try to be as self-sufficient as possible.

Communes are a deliberate step back to a less differentiated (critics will say, more primitive) form of existence. They are a - minority - answer to the frustrations of modern civilisation, especially to the alienation and loss of involvement arising from the excessive specialisation characteristic of modern life.

company[1] - general aspects   Kapitalgesellschaft - allgemeine
Aspekte

The company (in the U.S. 'corporation') is the most prominent form of business organisation in many fields of the economy. This is borne out by the fact that the majority of large-, medium-, and even small-size businesses in the U.K. and the U.S.A. are run as companies/corporations.

A company, in particular a public or a private limited company, is normally formed with a view to making a profit for its members by engaging in manufacture and/or trade. The capital of the company is divided into shares. It is raised by each member taking a certain number of shares, which are paid for in cash or occasionally given in exchange for some other consideration. The members, called 'shareholders' (U.K., U.S.) or 'stockholders' (U.S.), share in the profits of the company in accordance with the size of their holding. Profits are usually distributed in the form of a cash dividend, which is expressed as a percentage of the nominal value of a share. The company is a legal entity, which means that it has corporate personality and a legal existence separate from that of its individual members. As such, it is the owner of all the business assets, and liable for all its debts and obligations. The liability of the shareholders is limited to the nominal value of the shares held by them. Should the company fail, there will be no call on an individual shareholder to meet the company's debts provided that he has fully paid up his shares. In other words, a shareholder is personally liable only for the amount, if any, remaining unpaid on the shares held by him.

company[2] - types of company   Kapitalgesellschaft - Arten

In the U.K., companies may be incorporated
1. by registration under the Companies Acts (registered companies);
2. by royal charter (chartered companies); or
3. by statute, that is, by the passing of a special Act of Parliament (statutory companies and public corporations).

The most important and most common method of incorporation is by registration. On the basis of the liability of their members, registered companies may be classified into 'unlimited companies', 'companies limited by guarantee', and 'companies limited by shares'. Unlimited companies - very rarely formed - are enterprises whose members have unlimited liability, i.e., they are fully liable for all debts and obligations of their companies. The members of a company limited by guarantee undertake to be liable for their company's debts up to a stated limit. Companies limited by guarantee are not very numerous. This form of organisation is suitable for non-profit-making bodies. In a company limited by shares, the members' liability is limited to the nominal value of the shares held by them. Since this is the form of organisation adopted by most commercial profit-making businesses, companies limited by shares account for the large majority of registered companies. (It is worth mentioning that the old-fashioned term 'joint-stock company' is still used, namely, as a synonym for 'registered company', although not in the relevant laws.) There are two types of company limited by shares, viz., the 'public limited company' and the 'private limited company'.

The public limited company (the approximate equivalent of the 'Aktiengesellschaft' in Austria and West Germany) is a company the memorandum of which states that the company is to be a public (limited) company. Its name must end with 'public limited company' or 'plc', and its authorised and issued capital must not be less than £50,000, of which at least 25 per cent (plus the whole of any premium) must be paid up at the time of incorporation. Although it is called a 'public (limited) company', it need not necessarily sell its shares to the general public, but may also sell them privately (private placing, mainly in the case of fairly small companies). Shares of public limited companies, which are freely transferable, may be sold in a number of ways, for instance, by direct invitation to the public or by an offer for sale (see: primary market). Moreover, many large companies apply for stock exchange quotations to facilitate dealings in the shares they have issued. Both public and private limited companies must have a minimum of two members.

The private limited company (the approximate equivalent of the 'Gesellschaft mit beschränkter Haftung' in Austria and West Germany) is defined as any company limited by shares which is not a public limited company. The company's name must be followed by the word 'Limited' or its abbreviation 'Ltd.'. The major characteristic of the private limited company is that it must not offer its shares or debentures to the general public. The majority of private limited companies are small family businesses run as companies to secure the benefits of continuity and limited liability.

In the U.S.A., the corporation statutes traditionally have never distinguished between the large 'publicly held corporation' (also known as the 'open corporation') and the small 'close corporation' with one or several shareholders. In recent years, a number of states have adopted close corporation statutes, which define a close corporation as one which has no more than a specified number of shareholders and which restricts the transfer of shares in a manner permitted by the statutes. Such a company may dispense entirely with the board of directors by including a provision to this effect in the articles of incorporation. The open corporation is the approximate equivalent of the British public limited company and the Austrian 'AG', and the close corporation is the equivalent of the British private limited company and the Austrian 'GmbH'.

To avoid misunderstandings, it should be noted that, in this book, the term 'company' is taken to mean a company limited by shares or an American corporation respectively.

company[3] - legal aspects, management and control

Kapitalgesellschaft - juristische Aspekte, Geschäftsführung, Verfügungsgewalt

The main characteristics of a company are its legal personality and the separation of ownership and control/management.

In contrast to the sole trader and the partnership, the company is a legal entity (also referred to as an 'artificial person', 'body corporate', or 'legal person'), having a legal existence independent of that of its members. This means that it has its own life (i.e., neither the death of a member nor the transfer of shares affects the existence of the enterprise), and that it can enter into contracts in its own right, hold property, buy and sell, sue and be sued in its own name, just like an ordinary natural person. But it differs from an ordinary person in that it can act only through its properly constituted agents. Its members as such cannot be held individually responsible for the acts of the company, though its directors and officers may, in certain circumstances, be held personally liable for the failure to comply with the provisions of the Companies Acts. As a legal entity, the company is the owner of the business assets, and liable for all its debts and obligations. The liability of the shareholders is limited to the nominal value of the shares held by them. At the time of incorporation, each shareholder must pay up at least 25 per cent of the nominal value of his shares, plus the whole of any premium. If the company fails, a shareholder is personally liable only for the amount, if any, remaining unpaid on the shares held by him. Once set up, the company continues in existence until it is brought to an end in some prescribed legal manner. The formal method of ending a company's existence, as envisaged in the Companies Acts, is by winding up, or liquidation. Winding up means that the company's assets are disposed of, creditors are paid, and the remaining amount of money, if any, is distributed to the shareholders. The winding up of a company follows a decision of the shareholders at a general meeting (voluntary liquidation, e.g., if the company wants to alter its powers and objects in an important way, to amalgamate with another company, or to give up business altogether), or it may be ordered by the courts (compulsory liquidation, e.g., if the company is unable to pay its debts, or if it fails to fulfil its statutory obligations).

Control of the company is ultimately in the hands of the owners (i.e., the shareholders), whose investment is at risk. The owners exercise their ultimate control by voting at meetings, the general rule being that voting power is proportional to the number of shares held. The principal meeting of shareholders is the annual general meeting (AGM), at which, among other things, the accounts are presented to the members. The owners, however, do not have any power to participate in the management of the company. Management, supervision, and day-to-day control over the company are vested in the board of directors, elected by, and responsible to, the shareholders. It must be realised, of course, that the election of directors is effectively in the hands of the members with the largest holdings. The board of directors sets the general policy (it would obviously be impossible for the shareholders to lay down the general policy of a complex, modern business) and supervises the day-to-day management, which it delegates to paid managers. Although, therefore, in a superficial sense it would be correct to say that a company is ultimately controlled by the shareholders, the real distribution of power is frequently quite different, especially in large companies. It is true that the directors are elected by the shareholders. But the vast majority of shareholders are either unable to attend company meetings or are not sufficiently interested in doing so. Provided the periodic dividend is satisfactory, they are usually content to leave the control of the company to the directors.

Owing to the privilege of limited liability and the divorce of ownership from control, a company is in a position to affect the affairs of both shareholders and creditors in many ways. There has, therefore, been a steady trend in the relevant company legislation towards increased publicity and disclosure, which means that the companies are required to make available to the public a certain minimum amount of information. A wide disclosure of the relevant facts prevents prospective shareholders from making investments on the basis of inadequate information, and enables those who supply goods or lend money to assess the creditworthiness of the company concerned. The principal publicity/disclosure requirements may be summarised as follows:

1. Each year, the company must send a copy of the directors' annual report, a copy of the audited balance sheet (which must show, among other things, the names of all its subsidiaries, and details of the classes of shares held in them), and a copy of the profit and loss account to the Registrar of Companies. All these documents are available for public inspection on payment of a nominal fee.

2. The company must also keep certain statutory books, such as a register of members (containing their names and particulars of shares held) and minute books, as well as proper books of account showing, among other matters, receipts and payments of cash, and details of assets and liabilities.

company[4] - advantages and disadvantages

Kapitalgesellschaft - Vor- und Nachteile

The major advantages of a company may be summarised as follows:
1. A company has a continuous existence, independent of its members or directors.
2. The shares in a company are freely transferable and can, therefore, easily be sold without affecting the company's capital or existence.
3. The members' liability is limited to the nominal value of the shares held by them. This limitation of involved risk encourages individual and institutional investors (such as life assurance companies and pension funds) to invest their money not only in the gilt-edged market but also in business enterprises. This makes it possible for a company to raise the huge amounts of capital necessary for large-scale operations, which, in turn, may result in considerable economies of scale.

The advantages listed above may be offset by the following disadvantages:
1. The publicity/disclosure requirements make it difficult for a company to conceal its business affairs. The company's books must be available for inspection by its members and the public.
2. Especially in a large company, the directors and managers have direct control over the company's affairs without being effectively accountable to the real owners (divorce of ownership from control).
3. There is room for conflicts between the shareholders, who are interested in the short-term profitability of the business, the board of directors and the management, concerned with long-term growth and efficiency, and the workers, interested in higher wages and better working conditions.
4. Lack of personal contact with customers and employees.
5. Slow and inflexible decision making.

company[5] - legislation

Kapitalgesellschaft - Gesellschaftsrecht

It is not surprising that entities created by law (either directly or indirectly) should be subject to detailed legal regulations throughout their existence. The main purpose of the relevant laws is to protect shareholders, creditors, and the general public from possible abuses of the legal entity device.

The relevant piece of legislation in the United Kingdom is the Companies Act 1948, as amended by the Companies Acts 1967, 1976, 1980, and 1981. The situation in the United States is slightly more complicated, because company legislation is a prerogative of the individual states, each of which has its own corporation statute to regulate the formation, operation, and winding up of companies. This is not a very satisfactory state of affairs, since corporation statutes may differ considerably from state to state. For instance, in the state of Delaware, legal requirements are much less stringent than in the other states. It is for this reason that the federal government has drawn up a Model Business Corporation Act and has recommended the individual states to adopt it. About half of them have acted upon this recommendation, thus taking an important step towards a complete harmonisation of American company legislation.

complaint

Mängelrüge,
Reklamation

A complaint is an expression of discontent which may be made by a buyer to the seller if the goods delivered are defective, or if the seller has delivered wrong quantities or wrong goods, etc.. 'Wrong goods' are goods which are not in accordance with the quality or description in the contract, or which are not up to sample, or which are unsuitable for a particular purpose for which, with the knowledge of the seller, they have been ordered, etc..

A complaint must be communicated to the seller, usually in the form of a letter of complaint, which should indicate clearly what is wrong. If the seller is not exactly informed of the nature of the defect and all the other relevant details, he cannot take any measures (e.g., repair the goods, send a replacement, grant a price reduction) to settle the complaint. The letter of complaint should also contain such details as order number, date of order, and so on, to enable the seller to identify the consignment in question.

computer

Computer,
Rechenanlage,
Elektronenrechner

A computer is an electronic data processing device, i.e., a machine which accepts data in a prescribed form (input), processes it (i.e., carries out logic and/or arithmetic operations on it), and supplies the results (output) as information, or as signals to control automatically other machines or processes. The computer does this on the basis of a computer program without human intervention at great speed.

Computers may be classified according to size (microcomputers, minicomputers, mainframe computers), according to the basic method of operation (digital, analogue, and hybrid computers), or according to use (home computers, personal computers, etc.).

computer applications in business

betriebliche Computeranwendungen

The computer can be used to solve, or at least to assist in solving, many business problems. Computer applications in business range from simple record-keeping chores to complex management information systems. The business user can either write his own application program (or rather have it written) or buy one of the many application packages offered by computer manufacturers or special software houses.

Typical business applications are: order processing, stock control, invoicing and sales analysis, accounts receivable and pay-roll accounting, general accounting, word processing, point-of-sales systems, computer-aided design (CAD), process control (numerical control, computer-aided manufacturing/CAM).

computer graphics — Computergraphik

Computer graphics is the branch of electronic data processing concerned with the conversion of digital (numerical) information into visual images, and vice versa. Specialised hardware and software (including graphics terminals and plotters) are used to generate lines, curves, charts, etc., from numerical inputs. For example, breakdowns of total sales by product line or by customer can be displayed graphically in the form of pie charts, whereas cost developments can be represented by means of bar charts.

Computer graphics plays an important part in computer-aided design (CAD), which involves also the reverse process, i.e., the transformation of visual images into numerical data.

computer program — Computerprogramm

A computer program (never spelled 'programme') is a set of instructions formulated in a special computer language (e.g., BASIC, FORTRAN, COBOL) which cause the computer to carry out a specific task.

confirmation — Bestätigung

Confirmations are business letters sent out either in connection with incoming or outgoing messages. It is, for instance, common practice to confirm offers made orally or by telephone in order to reassure the offeree and to provide him with some evidence in writing. In all cases where the seller is free to accept or refuse an incoming order (e.g., if the buyer's order is placed in response to an offer without engagement; if the order is a qualified acceptance of the seller's offer, that is, a counter-offer; or if the order was not preceded by an offer), the confirmation constitutes the seller's formal acceptance of the order, resulting in a contract between the buyer and the seller . Both types of confirmation involve a repetition of the essential points and an indication that the confirming person or firm agrees to be bound by them.

While 'confirmations' are used to validate both incoming and outgoing messages, 'acknowledgements' relate only to the former variety. Moreover, the term 'acknowledgement' tends to be restricted to situations where the intention is merely to inform the sender of the receipt of his message. This distinction applies also to the verbs, as can be seen in the following sentence from a business letter: "I acknowledge receipt of your order and confirm it as follows".

confirmed irrevocable (documentary) letter of credit — bestätigtes, unwiderrufliches Dokumentenakkreditiv

An irrevocable L/C is a definite undertaking on the part of the issuing bank to honour a draft on presentation of the shipping documents as specified in the L/C; in other words, the buyer's bank guarantees payment provided all the terms of the credit are complied with by the beneficiary/exporter. Such an undertaking cannot be modified or cancelled without the approval of all parties concerned.

In the case of a confirmed L/C, the advising bank is instructed by the issuing bank to confirm the irrevocable credit before advising/informing the beneficiary of the terms of the credit. Such confirmation constitutes a definite undertaking on the part of the advising bank - which by confirming the credit becomes the confirming bank - to honour a draft drawn on it by the exporter in conformity with the terms of the credit, irrespective of whether or not it can obtain reimbursement from the issuing bank. This shows that the advising/confirming bank's undertaking is independent of, and in addition to, that of the issuing bank.

The confirmed irrevocable L/C gives the seller the greatest protection, because he has the irrevocable commitment of two banks to make payment against documents specified in the L/C. Since the confirming bank is usually located in the beneficiary's country, the act of confirming a credit provides the beneficiary with an undertaking from a local bank, thus eliminating the risk of a default by the issuing bank, the transfer risk, and any other political risks. Consequently, an advising bank being asked to confirm a credit checks on the financial standing of the issuing bank and on the economic and political situation of the issuing bank's country. Credits issued by the world's largest banks are not usually confirmed, as the undertaking of such a bank - even though in another country - is normally sufficient for the beneficiary.

In practice, it is most common for the beneficiary to be instructed to draw his draft on the confirming bank, in which case the confirmed irrevocable L/C sent by the advising/confirming bank to the beneficiary may have the following wording: "We are instructed by (name of the issuing bank) to inform you that they have opened their irrevocable credit in your favour for account of (name of the applicant) for a sum not exceeding (amount of credit), available by your draft on us at sight/at 30 days sight, to be accompanied by: (shipping documents). We hereby confirm the credit and undertake that the draft drawn and presented as specified will be duly honoured by us". (By contrast, in the case of an unconfirmed irrevocable letter of credit, the advising bank would state something like: "This letter is solely an advice of credit opened by (name of the issuing bank) and conveys no engagement by us".)

The procedure for an export transaction on the basis of a confirmed irrevocable L/C available by a time draft includes the following steps:

1. An exporter and an importer sign a contract of sale providing for the shipment of goods under a confirmed letter of credit available by a time draft.
2. The importer asks his bank
   (i) to open an irrevocable L/C for a specified amount in favour of the exporter, and
   (ii) to have the credit confirmed by a bank in the exporter's country.
3. The advising bank receives the L/C from the issuing bank along with the latter's request to confirm it. The advising/confirming bank sends its confirmed L/C to the exporter, stating the conditions of the credit under which it will accept a time draft (usually payable a certain period of time after sight/ acceptance) drawn on it.
4. The exporter prepares the documents and the draft in accordance with the L/C terms and ships the goods.
5. The exporter presents the documents and his draft to the advising/confirming bank, which examines the documents and, if they are in conformity with the L/C terms, accepts the draft. It then sends the documents to the issuing bank and returns the accepted draft to the exporter.
6. The issuing bank delivers the documents to the importer.

7. Since the documents give their holder the right to control the goods, the importer takes possession of them from the carrier.
8. At maturity, the exporter presents the time draft to the advising/confirming bank for payment.
9. The advising/confirming bank pays the exporter and obtains reimbursement from the issuing bank, usually by debiting the account of the issuing bank.
10. The issuing bank obtains reimbursement from the applicant.

It should be noted that the beneficiary, instead of keeping the accepted draft until maturity, may discount it with the advising/confirming bank or with some other bank.

In cases where an exporter receives a L/C which calls for a draft to be drawn on the foreign issuing bank, it is very often stipulated in the credit that it is available for negotiation in his own country. If so, he can, if he wishes, take the credit together with the draft and the documents to the advising bank or some other bank for negotiation, which simply means that the negotiating bank purchases the draft and claims reimbursement direct from the issuing bank.

Finally, the question may arise why exporters sell, for example, on a collection basis, although payment by a confirmed, or even by an unconfirmed, irrevocable L/C is so much safer. For one thing, the foreign buyer may not agree to payment by a L/C, because his line of credit with his bank may be tied up during the validity period of the L/C. For another, a L/C may be too costly for the buyer, because he has to pay a commission to his bank for issuing a L/C. In addition, an advising bank charges a commission for confirming a letter of credit, which is much higher than the one charged for merely advising it. Such a commission has to be borne by the issuing bank, which, of course, passes it on to the buyer/applicant.

consequential loss insurance   Betriebsunterbrechungsversicherung

Consequential loss insurance (U.S.: 'business interruption insurance') is a type of insurance that protects the insured from any loss resulting from the interruption of his business caused by fire, earthquake, explosion, or any other event insured against.

A consequential loss policy may cover
1. loss of profit of a business;
2. standing charges, e.g., rent, taxes, salaries, directors' fees, interest on loans and debentures, etc., which all remain payable during the period of business interruption;
3. increased operating costs, e.g., the additional expenditure incurred in keeping the business going while the property is being replaced or repaired; and
4. the increased cost of restarting the business caused by a rise in the price of materials or the cost of labour after the event insured against has occurred.

consignee[1]   (Waren-)Empfänger

In general, a consignee (whether a private individual, a firm, a government agency, etc.) is the recipient of a consignment of goods.

consignee[2]   (Verkaufs-)Kommissionär

In a restricted sense, a consignee (frequently a retailer) is a party to the consignment contract, by which he undertakes to sell goods (or securities) in his own name, but for the account of his principal, the consignor (usually a manufacturer or wholesaler).

Title to the goods sent on consignment remains with the consignor until the consignee has sold them to a third party; in other words, in the case of a consignment transaction, the consignor retains title to the goods not sold by the consignee, and, consequently, he can recover them if the consignee becomes insolvent. Legal title thus passes directly from the consignor to the third party (buyer) when the sale is completed. Another important characteristic of consignment transactions is that the consignee, who is not a buyer of the consigned goods, has to pay the purchase price of the goods to the consignor only after he has completed a sale to a customer. The consignee is paid a remuneration in the form of a commission, which is usually calculated as an agreed percentage of the purchase price of the goods actually sold by him.

The relationship between the consignor and the consignee is governed by the consignment contract. It should contain all important provisions, such as the percentage of commission to be paid to the consignee; the terms of sale agreed upon by the parties; reimbursement for necessary expenses incurred by the consignee (e.g., storage, freight, insurance); cost of maintenance of the consigned goods; periodic reports to be rendered by the consignee to the consignor; etc.. The periodic report is referred to as the 'account sales'. It should specify the goods received on consignment, those sold, relevant expenses, the amount owing to the consignor, and the amount remitted.

Consignment arrangements are frequently used for new products, particularly where the demand is uncertain. Additionally, if the risks of obsolescence and price change are great, retailers may hesitate to purchase such goods; yet, they may be willing to display and sell them on a consignment basis.

consignment[1]   Warensendung,
                                    Posten

In general, the term 'consignment' is applied to a set of articles sent by a supplier to a buyer at one time. In this sense, consignment is used as a synonym for 'shipment'.

consignment[2]   Kommission(sgeschäft)

In a more restricted sense, the term 'consignment' refers to a transaction under which one person (the consignor) sends goods to another person (the consignee) for sale on commission, title to the goods remaining with the consignor until the consignee has sold them to a third party. Goods sent under these conditions are said to be sent 'on consignment'.

consignment note   Frachtbrief

The consignment note (U.S.: 'waybill') is a document used when goods are sent by rail (rail consignment note) or by road (road consignment note). In the case of carriage by air, the document used is referred to as the 'air waybill', formerly known as the 'air consignment note'.

Both the consignment note and the air waybill have to be prepared by the consignor on a prescribed form and delivered to the carrier (railway company, road haulier, airline operator) together with the goods. The air waybill, for example, must contain the following particulars: air waybill number; airport of departure; airport of destination; names and addresses of the consignor, the consignee, and the carrier; description of the goods; number of packages, method of packing, and the particular marks or numbers on them; weight, quantity, volume, or dimensions of the goods; total freight amount prepaid; date of the flight; details of any special route to be taken; signature of the consignor or his agent; signature of the issuing carrier or his agent.

From the legal point of view, the completed consignment note or air waybill is prima facie evidence of the conclusion of the contract of carriage, and a receipt for the goods delivered to the carrier. Unlike the bill of lading, however, it is not a document of title and not negotiable. This means that it cannot be used to transfer ownership and/or possession of the goods by indorsement and delivery.

The consignment note is usually issued in triplicate. (By contrast, the air waybill consists of twelve copies, three of which are treated as originals having equal validity. The remaining copies are for use by subsequent air carriers when goods are transshipped en route, and for customs and internal statistical purposes). One original copy of the consignment note or air waybill remains with the carrier, one is given to the consignor, and one accompanies the goods. At the destination, the goods are delivered to the consignee on proof of identity, without further formality.

Under the terms of the contract of carriage, the carrier undertakes to deliver the goods to the consignee named in the consignment note or air waybill, unless he gets instructions to the contrary from the consignor under the latter's "right of disposal in transit". The original copy of the consignment note or air waybill received by the consignor entitles him to instruct the carrier (i) to stop the goods in transit, (ii) to change their place of destination, or (iii) to change their consignee. The consignor's right of disposal ends when the consignment note or air waybill has been handed over to the consignee and the latter has signed it.

consignment stock   Konsignationslager

Consignment stock refers to goods which an exporter has shipped out of the country to his agent, branch, or subsidiary for display or subsequent sale. Title to the goods is retained by the exporter until they have been sold to a third party.

consignor[1]   (Waren-)Absender

In general, the term 'consignor' is applied to a firm sending goods to another firm, a private individual, a government agency, etc. (i.e., to the consignee).

consignor[2]   Kommittent

In the case of a consignment transaction, the consignor is a party to the consignment contract, under the terms of which he sends goods (or securities) on consignment to the consignee. He retains title to the goods until they have been sold by the consignee.

consular invoice   Konsulatsfaktura

A consular invoice is a special invoice which the customs authorities of several countries require importers to present together with the commercial invoice before the goods may be cleared.

The consular invoice, which usually contains the same details as the customs invoice, is prepared by the exporter on a special form, obtainable from the consulate of the importing country located in the country of the exporter. Unlike the customs invoice, however, it must be legalised by the consulate, which means that the consulate certifies that the particulars in the invoice are realistic and correct. For legalising consular invoices consulates charge a consular fee, which is normally a certain percentage of the commercial invoice value of the goods. The consulate of the importing country retains one copy of the invoice, returns one copy to the exporter, and forwards further copies to the customs authorities in the importer's country.

Today, consular invoices are required by many Latin-American countries, particularly by those which charge their import duties 'ad valorem', i.e., on the value of the goods. The purpose of the consular invoice is twofold: first, the selling price (export price) is examined in the light of the current market price in the exporter's country to ensure that dumping is not taking place, and second, it forms the basis for determining the import duty levied by the importing country.

consumer goods   Konsumgüter

Consumer goods are goods capable of satisfying human wants directly, and therefore, in contrast to producer goods, they are desirable in themselves. The number of consumer goods is legion, and, apart from their intrinsic value, the demand for them plays an important role in determining the level of economic activity, e.g., in a consumer-led recovery.

Consumer goods are traditionally classified into a durable and a non-durable variety. 'Durable consumer goods' (also referred to as 'consumer durables'), such as T.V. sets and motor cars, can be used more often than once, they give off a stream of services over a period of time, and are, therefore, used up only gradually. 'Non-durable consumer goods', represented for instance by food, are used up in the act of consumption. Although this is not true of clothing, it is normally classified as 'non-durable'. 'Non-durable' should not be confused with 'perishable', i.e., with goods that spoil easily, or go bad quickly (e.g., fruit, flowers, vegetables). Non-durable consumer goods may have a very long shelf-life. The term simply indicates that they are used up in the act of consumption and are not capable of giving off a stream of services.

consumerism

Consumerism is a social movement which sprang up in the 1960s (although there are antecedents) in protest against the unfair deal many consumers were getting in their relationships with business (but, to some extent, also with other organisations, such as schools, government agencies, etc.). Common targets of the consumer movement were (and still are) unsafe products (remember Ralph Nader's "Unsafe at any Speed"?), deceptive advertising and packaging (Vance Packard's "The Hidden Persuaders"), deceptive credit terms, hard selling, price fixing. Another area of concern are the "external effects", i.e., the mainly negative impact of business activities (production and distribution) on (uninvolved and frequently unsuspecting) third parties. Consumerism, therefore, is not only concerned with consumer protection in the narrow sense of the word, but also with pollution, urban decay, and similar environmental problems.

The main aim of this movement is, of course, not only to voice grievances but to remedy them, either by lobbying for legislative measures or by putting pressure directly on business organisations to prod them into "voluntary" action and self-regulation.

Although there are still many problems to be solved (especially in the area of pollution and chemicals in food), the movement has been quite successful. Witness only the statutory regulation of marketing activities in many countries, e.g., truth in lending, truth in packaging, cooling off, and similar legislation.

container[1]

Behälter

A container, in its widest sense, is anything in which goods are packed, e.g., a box, case, crate, barrel, drum.

container[2]

Container

In a more restricted sense, a container is a large standard-size metal box designed for carrying goods by specially-built road vehicles, aircraft, railway waggons, and ships. According to the International Organization for Standardization (ISO), a freight container should be
1. of a permanent nature, thus permitting its repeated use;
2. specially designed to facilitate the safe carriage of goods by one or more modes of transport without intermediate handling; and
3. fitted with devices which make it easy to handle, especially during transshipment from one means of transport to another.

Containerisation is a form of unitisation, i.e., goods packed in a container are capable of being handled as a unit (unit load). Large containers enable rail, road, sea, and air transport to be combined, thus offering a door-to-door service. The transfer from one means of transport to another can be effected more speedily and cheaply, because only a few large standard-size containers have to be handled instead of a huge number of individual packages of different sizes. There are many types of container, and the range is being constantly extended. For example, they include covered and open containers, refrigerated containers (suitable for such perishable products as meat, dairy products, fruit, and drugs), top loader containers (for large and heavy pieces of machinery), bulk liquid containers (for wine, spirits, oil, etc.), and bulk powder containers (e.g., for fertilisers and cement).

Container transport is normally handled by a combined transport operator (CTO), who is either a forwarding agent or a carrier (e.g., a container shipping line). In the case of a full container load (FCL), the container - either owned by the consignor or provided by the CTO - is usually loaded and sealed at the consignor's premises and collected there by the CTO, who arranges for it to be transported to the agreed destination. In the case of a less than container load (LCL), the consignor usually sends the goods to an inland container base/container depot of a container shipping line or of a forwarding agent. Here, the goods from different consignors destined for the same area/country may be grouped together/consolidated by the CTO into a full load and shipped in one container (mixed container), thus reducing carriage costs for the individual consignors involved.

Finally, it is worth mentioning that the International Chamber of Commerce has drawn up rules for a combined transport document, which the parties are well advised to adopt to avoid the many legal problems involved in container transport. Such a combined transport document is not a document of title, but evidence of the conclusion of the contract of carriage and a receipt for the goods. It is subject to the Uniform Rules for a Combined Transport Document. In addition, other documents used in container transport are the container bill of lading and the house bill of lading. Container bills are issued by container shipping lines to the consignors of FCLs and LCLs (provided the goods from different consignors are consolidated by the shipping line itself) to cover the multi-modal transport of goods in a container from an inland place of dispatch to the final place of arrival. Several types of these bills are in use, but no common form has yet been developed. All container bills are "received for shipment" bills, and not "shipped" bills, and most contain clauses defining the responsibility of the door-to-door carrier. If, however, the consolidation of cargoes shipped by several exporters is carried out by a forwarding agent, he issues, if required by the consignors, house bills of lading (see: house bill of lading). The mixed container itself, as distinguished from the individual cargoes contained therein, is normally shipped under a groupage bill of lading, issued by the carrier to the forwarding agent.

contingent liability   Eventualverbindlichkeit;
                                            (bestimmte Art von) Rückstellung

A contingent liability is one that may materialise as a legal debt dependent upon the future occurrence of certain reasonably probable contingencies. In other words, contingent liabilities are potential liabilities arising from acts, events, or circumstances occurring before the balance sheet date or from conditions existing as of that date, but for which any legal indebtedness is contingent, i.e., dependent, on some future event or circumstance. Typical examples are contingent liabilities arising from pending lawsuits, assigned accounts receivable, and from discounted bills or notes.

There is often some confusion between estimated liabilities and contingent liabilities. An estimated liability is a known liability whose value cannot be ascertained with certainty on the balance sheet date. A contingent liability, on the other hand, will probably not result in a specific obligation, but there is a chance that a specific obligation may arise if an event or events occur. For example, obligations under product guarantees (U.S.: warranties) are considered as definite liabilities, because it is highly probable that some payments will be required even though the total amount must be estimated. A legal suit against a company for damages, however, involves a contingent liability if it appears most likely that the firm will win the case. If it is almost certain that the case will be lost, a liability exists and the main problem is to estimate the probable amount of damages to be awarded.

contract   Vertrag

A contract is a legally binding agreement between two or more persons (natural or artificial persons), which is enforceable at law. The persons entering into a contract are referred to as the 'contracting parties', or 'parties to the contract'.

Most contracts can be made in any form, i.e., orally, in writing, by telephone, telegram, etc., but in special cases the law requires a particular form to be adopted (e.g., in Great Britain, contracts of apprenticeship are void unless they are in writing).

For a contract to be valid, it must contain the following important elements:
1. There must be an offer by one person (the offeror), and unqualified acceptance by the person to whom the offer is made (the offeree).
2. It must be supported by consideration, which may take the form of money, goods, services, etc..
3. The contracting parties must have full capacity to contract, which means they must be legally capable of entering into binding contracts.

contract of agency   Agenturvertrag,
                                                    Vertretungsvertrag

The contract of agency is an agreement between a principal and his (commercial) agent under the terms of which the former authorises the agent to procure contracts (of sale) from, or to conclude contracts (of sale) with, third parties on his behalf.

The contract of agency lays down the rights and duties of the two parties, the scope of authority granted to the agent, and the commission payable on the purchase price of the goods actually sold by him. Usually, the commission is earned when the purchase price is received by the principal. For example, the parties may stipulate in the contract of agency that "commission shall be paid at a rate of .. per cent on all moneys received by the principal as purchase price for goods sold by the agent". On principle, the agent is entitled to commission if the transaction for which commission is claimed is the direct result of his efforts. Consequently, even if the customer with whom he has negotiated eventually orders goods direct from the principal, he is entitled to claim commission. It may also be provided that the agent shall be entitled to commission on all sales emanating from his territory, no matter whether they have been procured by his efforts or not. This arrangement is customary where an agent is appointed sole agent for a given territory.

contract of carriage   Frachtvertrag

The contract of carriage is an agreement between a shipper of goods and a carrier by which the latter undertakes, against payment of a consideration termed 'freight' or 'carriage', to carry specific goods from one place to another. The following main types of contract of carriage may be distinguished:
1. the contract of carriage by rail;
2. the contract of carriage by road;
3. the contract of carriage by air; and
4. the contract of carriage by sea.

In the case of carriage by rail, by road, or by air, the contract of carriage is evidenced by a rail consignment note, road consignment note, or by an air waybill. If the goods are dispatched by sea, the shipper may either charter a complete ship, in which case the terms of the contract of carriage are embodied in a document referred to as the 'charterparty', or he may send the goods as general cargo, i.e., they are carried in a ship together with goods of other shippers. In the latter case, the contract of carriage by sea is evidenced by a document known as the 'bill of lading'. It repeats in detail the terms of the contract, which was in fact concluded prior to the issue of the bill. (Further details are dealt with under the headings of "bill of lading" and "consignment note".)

contract of employment   Dienstvertrag

A contract of employment, or contract of service - not to be confused with a 'contract for services' -, establishes an employer-employee relationship. It can be made in any form, i.e., by deed, in writing, or orally, although under the Contracts of Employment Act 1972, employers must give detailed written information to their employees of the terms of their employment. These terms include the rate or the basis of remuneration; hours of work, holidays and holiday pay, sickness and sick pay, and occupational pensions; length of notice to terminate employment; the employee's rights in respect of trade union matters and activities.

Like any other contract, the contract of employment lays down or implies a number of duties for the parties to the contract, i.e., for the employer and the employee. The main duties of the employer are to pay the agreed or appropriate remuneration, to reimburse the employee for expenditure reasonably and properly incurred, and to indemnify him against liabilities incurred in the proper performance of his duties. The employee's duties include his duty to obey the lawful instructions of his employer; to exercise care and skill in the performance of his tasks; to conduct himself properly (laziness, negligence, and bad time-keeping are examples of misconduct); and, finally, to act in good faith all the time.

The termination of a contract of employment is partly regulated by the Employment Protection Act 1975, which specifies the minimum periods of notice to which a full-time employee is entitled.

contract of insurance   Versicherungsvertrag

A contract of insurance, or insurance contract, is a contractual arrangement between the insurer and the policyholder, by which the former undertakes, in return for the payment of a consideration (the premium), to indemnify the insured/beneficiary for any loss of, or damage to, the subject-matter insured on the occurrence of a stated event (event insured against). In the case of life insurance, the insurer undertakes to pay a fixed sum of money to the beneficiary on the death of the insured or on the expiry of the policy period.

The parties to an insurance contract, therefore, are the insurer and the person effecting the insurance. The latter, who receives the policy and has to pay the premium, is referred to as the 'policyholder'. As a rule, the policyholder is identical with the insured/beneficiary. But he may also take out the insurance for a third party, as is the case, for instance, under a c.i.f. contract, where the seller (policyholder) has the   goods insured for the benefit of the buyer   (insured and beneficiary). In the case of life insurance, there are four parties: the insurer, the policyholder, the insured (i.e., the person whose life is insured), and the beneficiary (i.e., the person entitled to receive payment under a life insurance policy). Frequently, the policyholder is identical either with the insured or with the beneficiary.

The insurer may be an insurance company, a Lloyd's underwriter, the government (e.g., in the case of export credit insurance), or a separate government-sponsored fund (as in the case of social security).

A person seeking insurance is called a 'proposer'. Usually, he has to complete a proposal form and submit it to the insurer (or his agent). As soon as the insurer accepts the proposal, the insurance contract comes into existence. In the case of a Lloyd's insurance, the contract is deemed to be concluded when the "slip", which the broker presents to the insurers, is initialled by the last underwriter and thus the risk is fully covered.

Frequently, the insurer issues a cover note. This is an acknowledgement in writing which proves that a certain insurance contract exists. It is a document to be used until the policy itself has been drawn up and issued to the policyholder.

From the legal point of view, it is important to note that the insurance policy is not the insurance contract. The contract is the invisible agreement between the contracting parties; the policy is only written evidence of the contract. A simple example will illustrate the difference: suppose, a life insurance contract was negotiated with a sum insured of £10,000, but, owing to an undetected typing error, the policy document was issued showing a sum insured of £100,000. The contract would be for £10,000 only, as this represented the intention or agreement between the parties, and in the event of the insured's death (assuming that the intention of the parties could be proved by reference to a proposal form or by other means), the beneficiary would not be able to insist on receiving £100,000.

contract of sale   Kaufvertrag

A contract of sale (also referred to as a 'contract for sale of goods' or 'contract of sale of goods') is a contract whereby a seller (also called a vendor) transfers, or agrees to transfer, the property in goods to a buyer (vendee) for a money consideration, called the price. The word 'property' here means rights of ownership of the goods. A contract of sale is one in which the consideration is payable in money. Consequently, it does not apply to barter transactions, where payment is made in kind.

An (international) contract of sale may include the following provisions:
1. Goods: description and quantity of the goods (technical specifications).
2. Price: unit price and total contract value; contract currency (currency of the seller's country, of the buyer's country, or of a third country, e.g., the U.S. dollar).
3. Trade terms, e.g., INCOTERMS: method of quotation; rights and duties of the contracting parties; costs to be borne by the parties (e.g., packing, documents, export licence); passing of the risks from the seller to the buyer.
4. Passing of property: e.g., retention of title.
5. Packing and marking: type of packing; marking instructions.
6. Terms of payment: time; method; place; discounts.
7. Terms of delivery: time; place; method.
8. Inspection of the goods: to enable the buyer to ascertain whether they are in conformity with the contract.
9. Insurance: party responsible for taking out insurance; party bearing the cost; risks to be covered.
10. Documents.
11. Force majeure.
12. Jurisdiction.
13. Arbitration.
14. Law of contract.

control   „Kontrolle" (und „Lenkung") (Managementfunktion)

Although there is no generally accepted definition of the management function of control, it is probably safe to say that its main purpose is to ensure that business objectives and plans are accomplished as they were originally conceived. This involves measuring actual performance, comparing it with predetermined standards, and taking corrective action if results differ substantially from targets. Control in this sense can be applied to many aspects of a business operation: for example, to inventories (inventory control), to quality (quality control), and, perhaps most importantly, to costs (cost control). Standard costing, for instance, is an accounting method that has been developed primarily for control purposes. Under this method, actual costs are compared with standard costs (a process referred to as 'variance analysis') with a view to correcting the situation if necessary.

From the above explanations it should be clear that 'control' is not only concerned with supervision or checking procedures, although these certainly do play a role. The English concept of 'control' is wider and more dynamic than its German counterpart and includes both "Kontrolle" and "Lenkung".

controller   Controller

The term 'controller' is highly misleading, if not an outright misnomer. Although a controller's functions include some measure of 'control' in the accepted management sense of the word (see: control), this is by no means his only, nor even his main duty. A controller is an executive who is primarily responsible for the accounting (both financial and cost), reporting (external and internal), and planning (or budgeting) functions of a company. In addition, by developing satisfactory standards against which to measure performance and by providing guidance and assistance to other members of management in ensuring conformance of actual results to standards he participates in the control function. Moreover, his responsibilities may include tax management, risk management (insurance), supervision of certain treasury functions, managing relations with internal and external auditors, etc..

controls

Lenkungsmaßnahmen,
Beschränkungsmaßnahmen,
Restriktionen,
Bewirtschaftung

Controls represent the most direct form of government intervention in the economy. The idea is for a government not satisfied with the results produced by the market to select one or several strategic variables and to determine their value by administrative action instead of leaving this to the free interplay of supply and demand. Variables selected for regulation include prices (price control), wages (wage control), rents (rent control), interest rates, and exchange rates.

Controls are frequently only temporary. They are imposed (adopted) when free market results begin to diverge too much from policy goals. They may be tightened if they fail to produce the desired results, and relaxed (loosened) or abolished (lifted) when considered too harsh or unnecessary.

conversion

Konvertierung

Conversion is the actual exchange of the currency of one country for that of another. For example, a remittance of Austrian schillings to the United Kingdom is converted into sterling at the rate of exchange prevailing at the time of the remittance; there is no question as to what exchange rate is applicable.

By contrast, 'translation' is the restatement of amounts denominated in a given currency in terms of another currency by applying an exchange rate. For example, the accounts of a foreign subsidiary or branch are restated in terms of the domestic currency by applying appropriate exchange rates (e.g., the historical exchange rate, i.e., the rate in effect at the time a specific transaction occurred, or the closing exchange rate, i.e., the rate ruling at the balance sheet date).

co-operative society

Genossenschaft

Ideally, a co-operative society, or simply co-operative, is an organisation that exists primarily for the benefit of its members, by whom it is democratically controlled, usually on the principle of "one man - one vote". The members are either the customers of the organisation (as in the case of the consumer co-operative or the credit co-operative), its employees (as in the case of the worker co-operative), or its suppliers (e.g., in the case of the agricultural marketing co-operative). In each case, the co-operative breaks down barriers that exist between traditional business organisations and various groups in society, trying to replace antagonism and exploitation by mutual help, participation, and co-operation.

It must be admitted that the co-operative spirit has to some extent been lost. Especially the consumer co-operatives, which were forced to merge to be able to compete with the large traditional retail institutions, have little to distinguish them from their traditional competitors. Today, the co-operative spirit is kept alive in the small worker co-operative, which is certainly the most radical form of alternative business organisation, with the possible exception of the commune.

The co-operative movement, which is thought to have originated in England with the foundation of the first consumer co-operative by the Rochdale Pioneers in 1844, has spread all over the world, and co-operatives can be found in nearly every country. In some countries (such as Great Britain), the consumer co-operative (also called 'co-op') is the predominant form, while in Italy, Spain, and France the worker co-operative is much more prominent. Credit co-operatives are a characteristic feature of the co-operative scene in Austria, West Germany, and the United States, while agricultural co-operatives play a vital role in many less developed countries, such as Tanzania.

copier	Kopierer, Kopiergerät

Virtually all modern copiers are based on an electrostatic process known as 'xerography' (literally, 'dry drawing'), which involves the exposure to the original of a positively charged selenium-coated plate and the application of a negatively charged powder plus heat to produce the copy. In contrast to spirit duplicating and stencil duplicating, this process does not require the preparation of a master, and the number of copies is practically unlimited.

In addition to basic copying, modern copiers offer one or more of the following features: reduction and enlargement; automatic feeding, sorting, collating, stapling; push-button selection of paper size; counters; and self-diagnosis capability (optical signals indicating where the paper jam is located, or that the unit is running out of toner or has to be serviced). Modern copying machines are able to produce copies at high speed (up to 150 copies per minute).

copy[1]	Kopie, Durchschrift, Duplikat

Copy, in the widest sense of the word, refers to the imitation, transcript, or reproduction of an original work, as of a letter, document, painting, etc., and is therefore synonymous with 'duplicate'.

copy[2]	Exemplar, Ausfertigung

The term 'copy' may also be used for one of several originals of the same text, each original having equal standing. Typical examples are the copies of a book, or the three copies making up a full set of bills of lading.

copy[3]

Werbetext

In advertising, copy (also referred to as 'advertising copy') is taken to mean the text of an advertisment, in contrast to non-textual elements, such as pictures, drawings, layout.

corporation[1]

Körperschaft,
juristische Person

The most important corporation in law is the 'corporation aggregate', usually abbreviated to 'corporation'. A corporation in this sense is a group of persons who have formed themselves into an association having a separate legal existence, or artificial personality, quite distinct from the persons who compose it.

corporation[2]

Kapitalgesellschaft;
Aktiengesellschaft;
Konzern

The American corporation is the equivalent of the British company. In most cases, the term refers to a large publicly held corporation. Since many of these corporations have subsidiaries, 'corporation' may also be used to describe a group of companies.

corporation[3]

wirtschaftliche Unternehmung der öffentlichen Hand

In British commercial usage, the term 'corporation' is applied to a public corporation, i.e., to a business organisation created by an Act of Parliament and owned and controlled by government.

corporation tax

Körperschaftssteuer

Corporation tax, or corporation income tax, as it is called in the United States, is a levy on the profits of corporations, i.e., of organisations with a separate legal personality of their own. These include private and public limited companies in the United Kingdom, close(d) and open corporations in the United States, and GmbHs and AGs in Austria and West Germany. Corporation tax may be either a flat rate tax (as in the United Kingdom) or a progressive tax, as in Austria and the United States.

Under the classical system of company taxation, as, for instance, in Canada and in the United States, the dividends paid out of already taxed corporate profits are taxed again in the hands of the shareholders, i.e., they are added to the shareholders' other income and attract income tax at the appropriate rate.

Since the double taxation of dividends has been, and still is, considered discriminatory and unfair, there have been constant attempts to abolish, or at least to mitigate, it. Austria, for instance, has opted for a split-rate system, under which dividends, although subject to both corporation tax and income tax, attract lower rates of corporation tax than do retained profits.

The United Kingdom and the Federal Republic of Germany, on the other hand, operate an imputation system, which avoids the double taxation of dividends altogether. Under this system, a shareholder has to include the dividend he receives in his income-tax return, but may use the corporation tax paid by the distributing company on this dividend as a tax credit against his own income tax liability. This means that the corporation tax paid by the distributing company satisfies two tax liabilities (viz., the company's and the shareholder's), which gets around the double taxation problem.

Some of these corporation tax systems, which are quite complicated anyway, are made even more complicated by the introduction of withholding taxes on dividends.

correspondent bank   Korrespondenzbank

A correspondent bank is a bank which regularly performs services for another bank, i.e., it acts as its agent in a place where the other bank has no branch office. Most of the large banks have correspondents in foreign countries.

cost accounting   Kostenrechnung

Cost accounting is that branch of accounting which is concerned with identifying, classifying, recording, allocating, and reporting the current, projected, or planned costs of a business organisation. Its main purpose is to enable management to set selling prices (costing products), but also to control, i.e., to bring down and keep down, costs.

Costs may be classified in a number of ways. One classification hinges on the fact that costs may be applied to a particular period (in which case they are appropriately called 'period costs'), to units of output (unit cost), or, as an intermediary step, to cost centres, i.e., to departments, machines, etc..

An extremely important distinction is the one between fixed and variable costs. 'Fixed costs', as the term implies, do not vary with the volume of output but remain constant, at least in the short run. Rent for a factory building is an appropriate example. While fixed costs as a whole are by definition static, fixed costs per unit obviously are sensitive to changes in volume. The higher the number of units produced, the lower the fixed costs per unit will be.

'Variable costs' (which in many cases are identical with 'marginal costs') vary proportionately with output. The cost of raw materials is a case in point. Obviously, there are costs, like lighting, heating, etc., which contain fixed and variable elements. They are called 'semi-variable costs'. A certain minimum of lighting and heating may be required whatever the level of output, but beyond that the cost of lighting may well be determined by how much is produced. Semi-variable costs may be split into a fixed and a variable component.

The distinction between 'direct costs' and 'indirect costs' (which are also referred to as 'overhead costs', 'overheads', or 'burden') is similar to, although not identical with, that between variable and fixed costs. Direct costs can be readily traced and attributed to the units to be costed (i.e., to products and activities), while indirect costs cannot be so traced. If they are to be allocated, they have to be collected and subsequently spread over the various units by allocation on the basis of some index (overhead rate). Direct labour and direct material are examples of the former variety, while administrative overheads and manufacturing overheads are meant to serve as illustrations of the latter type.

Cost accounting methods may be classified on the basis of which costs are allocated to the cost units. First, there is 'full absorption costing', under which, as the name suggests, all costs, i.e., both fixed and variable, are allocated to the product involved. The main disadvantage of full absorption costing is that it leads to unstable product unit costs under conditions of fluctuating volume. Two ways of dealing with this serious accounting problem are 'marginal costing' and 'direct costing'. Under these costing methods, the product is charged only with marginal or direct costs, while fixed costs or indirect costs (both fixed and variable) are charged direct to profit and loss for the period concerned. The term 'direct costing' is often applied to both methods, although strictly speaking it should be reserved only for the second one.

Closely related to direct costing is the concept of the contribution margin, which accountants define as the excess of selling price over direct or marginal costs. Direct costing and the contribution margin are important management tools, which, like other tools in this field, have to be applied with skill and understanding. They are particularly useful in short-run decision-making, e.g., in deciding whether or not to accept an order at a special price.

Another important method of costing is 'standard costing'. Standard costing is based on the concept of standard costs, i.e., on an estimate of what actual costs should be under projected conditions. The basic idea is then to compare actual costs with standard costs and to take remedial action if the 'variance' (i.e., the difference between these two types of cost) is too great. Standard costing is, therefore, ideal for purposes of cost control.

cost of goods sold

Selbstkosten des Umsatzes;
(Handels-)Wareneinsatz - bei Handelsbetrieben;
Herstellungskosten (der verkauften Waren) - bei Produktionsbetrieben

'Cost of goods sold', frequently also referred to as 'cost of sales', is an important accounting concept and plays a major role in the income statement.

In a retail or wholesale business, 'cost of goods sold' is taken to mean the total cost of the goods sold during a given accounting period. It consists of the following elements: the purchase price of the goods bought and then sold, the cost of storage, transportation, and delivery to the seller,as well as other costs pertaining to their procurement and receipt.

In a manufacturing business, 'cost of goods sold' refers to the cost of production, or manufacturing cost, of all semi-finished and finished goods sold during a given accounting period. The principal elements of manufacturing cost are direct material (i.e., raw materials and parts), direct labour, and manufacturing overhead (also called 'factory overhead' or 'indirect manufacturing cost'). Manufacturing overhead includes indirect material and indirect labour, i.e., all costs incurred in production which cannot be classified as direct material or direct labour, or, to put it slightly differently, which are not directly chargeable to the units produced.

counter-cyclical policy — antizyklische Konjunkturpolitik

Counter-cyclical policy is a government policy aimed at eliminating, or at least mitigating, the cyclical fluctuations in the level of economic activity. It is called 'counter-cyclical' because its direction is the exact opposite of the cycle itself.

In a boom, when the economy is overheated, deflation would be the appropriate counter-cyclical policy, while in times of recession, stimulatory policies (reflation) would be called for. The main problems of counter-cyclical policy are timing and calibrating the measures correctly, and avoiding negative side-effects (inflation, unemployment) as far as possible.

counter-offer — Gegenangebot

A counter-offer is a statement by the offeree to the effect that he will not accept an offer submitted by the offeror, but will enter into a contract only on his own terms.

Depending on the circumstances, a counter-offer may be submitted either by the buyer or by the seller. If the buyer is interested in the goods offered, but does not agree to the prices and/or terms proposed by the seller, he may make a counter-offer. When the supplier receives a counter-offer - which is an 'offer' within the meaning of the law of contract -, he must decide whether or not he wants to accept it.

Also a seller who receives an order which he cannot meet for some reason may make a counter-offer or regretfully decline the order. This is possible in all cases where the buyer's order does not result in a contract, e.g., if a firm offer is accepted after the time limit for acceptance has expired; if the order is placed in response to an offer without engagement or on the buyer's own initiative, without a preceding offer. In all these cases, the buyer's order is an offer within the meaning of the law of contract.

If the supplier cannot meet an order for some reason (e.g., the goods ordered are no longer manufactured or carried in stock), he, whenever possible, does not refuse the order outright, but makes a counter-offer, for example by recommending substitutes. Therefore, the buyer needs to be persuaded that the suggested substitutes are at least as good as the goods ordered.

countertrade — Gegengeschäfte

The term 'countertrade' covers all foreign trade transactions resulting from exporters' commitments to take products from the importers or from their respective countries in full or part payment for their exports. Countertrade takes many forms, ranging from simple barter transactions, based on a direct exchange of goods and/or services between the two parties to the export transaction, to much more sophisticated deals, frequently involving three or more parties. Some examples are: 'triangular compensation'; 'counterpurchase', or 'offset', where a buyer agrees to purchase goods, subject to the seller using some or all of the proceeds to buy products from the importing country in exchange; and 'product buy back', usually involving the exchange of manufacturing equipment in return for a share of the goods produced by means of this equipment.

Countertrade is typical of trade with East European and less developed countries, which often suffer from a lack of foreign exchange and/or credit facilities. For these countries, barter or similar practices may be the only chance to obtain essential imports, while Western firms accept countertrade commitments in order to increase their exports.

Since there are no reliable statistics in this field, the actual volume of countertrade is anybody's guess. Vienna, being conveniently close to the Iron Curtain, has become an important centre for countertrade activities, and VOEST Intertrading, a subsidiary of VOEST Alpine AG, is muscling in on the act.

credit[1]	Kredit

The original meaning of the word 'credit' is 'trust', especially trust in a person's or firm's ability and willingness to meet his/its financial obligations which arise from buying goods or services on deferred terms or from taking out a loan. For the former type of transaction often the description 'dealing (i.e., buying/selling) on credit' is used.

credit[2]	Kredit, Darlehen

In banking, credit is taken to mean an amount of money placed at a person's or organisation's disposal, and is, therefore, synonymous with 'loan (of money)'. In this sense, it is used more frequently in the United States than in Great Britain. The Concise Oxford Dictionary, for instance, does not even list this meaning. When used in British banking literature, it normally refers to lending in general rather than to a specific amount lent, as, for instance, in 'to grant credit' (but: 'to grant an overdraft, a loan, a credit facility').

credit[3]	Zahlungsziel

Credit may also refer to the time allowed to a buyer for payment for goods or services, as in 'six months' credit' or 'sold on credit terms'.

credit[4]	Haben(-buchung), Gutschrift

In accounting, credit is applied to an entry, or item entered, on the right-hand side of an account, e.g., an addition to a revenue account or a deduction from an expense account or an asset account. Closely related to this is the meaning 'deduction from an amount otherwise due', as in "a tax credit for investments undertaken" or "a credit for goods returned".

credit agreement	Kreditvertrag

A credit agreement (also called a 'loan agreement') is the written agreement between a borrower and a lender of funds, in which the terms and conditions of the extension of funds are specified. These include the term of credit, the principal amount of credit, the rate of interest, the commitment fee, if any, the repayment of the credit, and any guarantee of payment.

credit card   Kreditkarte

Credit cards are issued by financial institutions, such as special credit card companies (e.g., VISA card, Eurocard, Diners Club card, American Express card). A credit card may be used by its holder to make payments in hotels, restaurants, shops, travel agencies, etc., provided that they are members of the appropriate credit card scheme. (The members are referred to as 'merchants' in the U.S.A. and as 'retailers' in the U.K.). American Express cards, for instance, are accepted only in establishments displaying the American Express card sign. Credit cards are, therefore, a convenient alternative to cash or cheques.

The credit card serves as evidence that a credit card company has granted a line of credit to the holder of the card, who must maintain a special credit card account with the card-issuing institution. This line of credit, usually called the 'credit limit', is the maximum amount that the holder may have outstanding at any one time.

The following is intended to illustrate the use of a credit card. Each credit card bears the signature of its holder and is embossed by the issuing institution with the holder's name and the card number. If the card holder wishes to pay by credit card, the only thing he has to do is present his credit card. The retailer will write out a sales slip, or sales voucher, which the card holder is asked to sign. After comparing the holder's signature on the sales slip with that on the card, the retailer puts the slip and the card through a special imprinter to record the holder's name and the card number, and returns the card together with a copy of the sales slip to the holder. The retailer then sends the voucher to the card issuer, who credits the retailer's account with the amount claimed less a discount, and debits the amount involved to the card-holder's account. At the end of each month, the card-issuing institution sends a fully itemised statement to the card holder. If he pays the whole amount outstanding within a certain period of time of the date of statement (usually up to 30 days), he is not charged any interest on the sum due and, therefore, incurs no extra charges on the purchases made. If the holder decides not to settle the monthly account in full within the period specified by the card issuer, he is charged interest on the amount left owing. A credit card holder should retain copies of all his sales vouchers. He will then have a complete record of all his credit card transactions, which he can check against his monthly statements.

Subject to the amount being available within his credit limit, the holder of a credit card may also use it to draw cash advances up to a specified amount at any one time. The total amount withdrawn plus a small handling charge will be included on the next monthly statement.

credit information   Kreditauskunft,
                                        Kreditinformation,
                                        Bonitätsauskunft

Credit information means any information on the creditworthiness of a buyer or borrower. Such information may be obtained from the following sources: 1. the buyer or borrower himself (e.g., he may be asked to fill in a credit application form or to submit a copy of the balance sheet); 2. firms given by the buyer as trade references; 3. banks given by the buyer as references (bank references); 4. trade associations; and 5. credit inquiry agencies (such agencies may provide credit information either in the form of special reports on individual firms in reply to specific credit inquiries, or in the form of rating books).

credit inquiry

Erkundigung(sschreiben),
Auskunftsgesuch,
Anfrage um Bonitätsauskunft

When a new customer asks for goods to be supplied on credit, e.g., he asks for payment on open account terms, the supplier must first find out whether the customer is creditworthy. He is interested in obtaining information about the buyer's reputation, about the volume of his business, and, more particularly, on whether he pays his invoices promptly (payment record). For this purpose, the supplier may send a credit inquiry (also referred to as 'status inquiry') to one of the following: 1. the customer (he may be asked to furnish information about himself, for example, by filling in a credit application form or by submitting a copy of his latest balance sheet); 2. firms which the customer has given as trade references; 3. banks named by the customer (bank references); 4. trade associations; and 5. credit inquiry agencies.

A letter of inquiry should usually include the following points:
1. A request for general information about the prospective customer's reputation and financial standing.
2. A request for an opinion on whether credit within a stated limit should be granted.
3. The assurance that the information will be treated confidentially.

Letters of inquiry and the replies to credit inquiries, and the envelopes in which they are sent, should be marked 'Confidential', 'Strictly Confidential', or 'Private and Confidential'.

Replies to credit inquiries should, among other points, include the following:
1. A statement of the facts and an honest expression of opinion; and
2. A reminder that the information is confidential and that no responsibility for it can be accepted.

credit inquiry agency

Auskunftei

A credit inquiry agency (in the United States referred to as a 'mercantile agency') is a commercial organisation whose business it is to supply information on the financial standing of business firms. It has a considerable store of information, which it keeps up to date from a variety of sources, including its own local agents. If the information asked for is not immediately available from its records, it will make inquiries.

Many credit inquiry agencies operate on a subscription basis. The subscribers pay a subscription fee; in return, they receive the rating books published by the agency and containing commercial and financial information about business firms, and special reports on any firm about which they inquire. The large credit inquiry agencies have branch offices abroad and can also furnish reports on foreign firms. The most famous agency is DUN & BRADSTREET in the United States, which operates all over the world.

credit note   Gutschriftanzeige

A credit note (in the United States referred to as a 'credit memorandum' or 'credit memo') is a document sent by a seller to a buyer to rectify an overcharge in the original invoice, or to acknowledge, and allow credit for, items returned by the buyer, e.g., faulty goods or empty containers. To distinguish it from invoices and debit notes, the credit note is usually printed or typed in red.

creditor   Gläubiger

According to Jowitt, the great English lawyer, a creditor is "a person to whom a debt is owing by another person", debt, according to Jowitt again, being "a sum of money due from one person to another". Therefore, 'creditor' has a narrower meaning than the German term 'Gläubiger', which is based on a wider concept of 'debt' (compare: debtor).

'Creditor' should not be confused with 'lender', which has a narrower meaning since it refers to persons or organisations actually lending sums of money and does not include 'trade creditors', who supply goods and services on credit. In accounting, the terms 'creditors' and 'trade creditors' refer not only to the persons or organisations to whom money is owed by a debtor, but also to the amounts so owed.

creditors' funds   Fremdmittel,
                                                  Fremdkapital

Creditors' funds, also referred to as 'debt', comprise all funds supplied by a firm's creditors, while the term 'loan capital', or 'borrowed capital', is used to describe only the medium- to long-term variety. Creditors' funds, therefore, come in the form of supplier credit, short-term advances (e.g., from factoring companies), time drafts, and promissory notes, but may also be represented by medium- and long-term bank loans, debentures, and by such off-balance sheet items as liabilities arising from leasing contracts.

In contrast to owners' funds, or equity, creditors' funds have to be repaid at maturity, i.e., at the date agreed for repayment. Large loans are, however, frequently repayable in instalments, which means that there are multiple repayment dates (repayment schedule). The cost of creditors' funds is the interest payable to the creditor, either in advance (discount method) or together with the repayment of principal (collect method), although it is not necessary for the interest to be stated explicitly (e.g., as in the case of supplier credit). In addition, there may be other cost elements, such as bank charges, compensatory balances, etc..

The proportion of creditors' funds or loan capital in the total capitalisation of a business is an important factor in achieving (or failing to achieve) the basic goals of a business - e.g., profit, survival, and growth. (see: capital structure; gearing).

credit rating

Bonitätsbeurteilung,
Bonitätseinstufung

Credit rating (or simply 'rating') is the assessment of a borrower's creditworthiness, i.e., of his ability and willingness to pay his debts when they fall due.

Credit ratings are often provided by specialised rating agencies (e.g., Moody's or Standard and Poor's) on the basis of a formal scale. If a bond, for instance, is given an AAA (triple A) rating, this means that the issuer's creditworthiness is exceptionally high.

credit transfer

Überweisung

A credit transfer system enables a person (or firm) wishing to make a payment to a specified payee to instruct a bank or similar institution to credit the payee's account or to arrange for it to be credited if it is with another bank. The funds for this transfer are provided by the remitting person either paying in cash over the bank counter or authorising the remitting bank to debit his account, e.g., handing over a cheque drawn against an account balance with the remitting bank. The main emphasis is, however, on crediting the payee's account. This distinguishes credit transfers from payments by cheque. Since a cheque is basically an instruction to a bank to debit an account, payments by cheque may, by analogy, be classified as a 'debit transfer system'.

Technically, credit transfers can be initiated in a number of ways. As a rule, the paying person has to complete a credit transfer form for each payment, different forms being used by different institutions and for different types of transactions. Where, for instance, the amount is paid in over the bank counter, British clearing banks provide an in-payment form. Under fully paper-based credit transfer systems, these forms are forwarded by the remitting bank to the payee's bank via the credit-clearing system, and the payee's bank credits the payee's account with the amount in question. Credit transfer instructions may, however, also be entered into a data processing system and forwarded either by means of computer tape or over data transmission links. ATMs, EFTPOS systems, and similar facilities involving electronic funds transfers enable customers to initiate transfers without having to worry about filling in forms.

As already mentioned, credit transfer facilities are offered by a variety of institutions. In Great Britain, for instance, they are provided by the ordinary banks and by the National Giro Bank together with the Post Office. The British banks call their payment services (comprising payments by cheque, credit transfers, standing orders, and direct debiting) 'bank giro', while the payment services offered by the National Giro Bank are appropriately called 'national giro'.

The term 'giro' is a tribute to the continental credit transfer systems, which are much older than the British systems, introduced in the late sixties. The term 'giro', which is related to the Italian "girare" (circulate), reflects the fact that the paper-based instructions circulate through the banking system. In the United States, credit transfer systems were introduced even later, American banks skipping the paper-based stage altogether and going straight to electronic funds transfer systems.

Generally speaking, credit transfers are still much less important in the English-speaking countries than in continental Europe. The reason for this is that in the United States and in Great Britain, cheques still dominate the field.

creditworthiness

Kreditwürdigkeit, Bonität

Creditworthiness, also referred to as 'credit standing', means a person's / company's / country's ability and intention to pay the debts in due course, i.e., when they become payable. It is, therefore, a measure of financial strength and influences the amount of credit which suppliers/creditors are prepared to grant.

crossed cheque

gekreuzter Scheck, Verrechnungsscheck

A crossed cheque is a cheque, either an order cheque or a bearer cheque, which cannot be cashed over the bank counter, but must be paid into an account. The bank to which the cheque is presented for payment will collect the amount from the bank on which it is drawn and credit its customer's account. If the holder of a crossed cheque wants cash, he must pay the cheque into his account and then draw his own cheque for the cash.

The purpose of crossing is to protect the owner against theft or loss, since the thief or finder may not have a banking account, and if he has one and uses it, he can easily be traced.

The crossing may be classified into 'general crossing' and 'special crossing'. A general crossing consists of two transverse parallel lines across the face of the cheque, with or without the words "and company" or any abbreviation of them, e.g., "&Co.". A cheque so crossed may be paid into an account at any bank, and the drawee bank will pay it to any bank presenting it for payment. A special crossing consists of the name of a bank written across the face of the cheque, with or without the transverse parallel lines required for a general crossing. A cheque crossed specially must be paid into an account at the bank stated in the crossing, and the drawee bank will pay it only to that bank.

A cheque is a negotiable instrument, and a person who receives a cheque that has been lost or stolen is entitled to keep it, provided he acts in good faith and receives the cheque for value. But if the words "not negotiable" are added to a crossing, the effect is to alter completely the legal position of the person receiving a lost or stolen cheque: he must return it to the true owner. In this context, "not negotiable" does not mean, as it is sometimes taken to mean, that the cheque cannot be transferred. A cheque bearing these words as part of the crossing is just as freely transferable as one without them. Therefore, the phrase "not negotiable" forming part of a crossing does not mean "not transferable". It means quite simply that the title of a transferee to a cheque cannot be better than that of his transferor, even though he receives it in good faith and for value. A 'not negotiable cheque' should, therefore, not be confused with a 'non-negotiable cheque'. The latter is made out to a particular person and includes the phrase "not to his order". Consequently, it is not a negotiable instrument and not transferable at all. It should also be noted that the words "not negotiable" on a cheque do not have the same meaning as the words "not negotiable" on a bill of exchange.

Whereas a cheque crossed "not negotiable" remains transferable, a bill of exchange marked "not negotiable" ceases to be transferable altogether.

The rules and regulations for crossed cheques do not apply in Austria. Crossed cheques made out abroad are treated in Austria as 'Verrechnungsschecks'. Consequently, the German term 'Verrechnungsscheck' may be translated by 'crossed cheque'.

cumulative quantity discount

Umsatzrabatt,
Umsatzbonus,
Umsatzbonifikation

A cumulative quantity discount is based on the total volume purchased over a certain period of time. This discount is an advantage to a seller because it ties customers more closely to him. It is especially used for perishable products and durable consumer goods. This type of quantity discount may be granted in either of the two following ways:

Example 1: 1 per cent discount on annual purchases of over £10,000.
Example 2: quantity discount schedule:

annual purchases in £	discount in %
10,001 - 20,000	1
20,001 - 30,000	2
30,001 - 40,000	3
40,001 - 50,000	4
over 50,000	5

It should be clear from the nature of the cumulative quantity discount that it is paid after the event , e.g., at the end of the business year. This is why certain types of cumulative quantity discount are referred to as 'rebates' (e.g., loyalty rebate). Another possible arrangement is to permit customers to deduct the discount on current orders, the percentage being determined by last year's volume of purchases.

currency[1]

Währung

The term 'currency', in its general economic sense, is applied to the money of a particular country, such as the U.S. dollar, the Canadian dollar, the French franc, the Swiss franc, the Belgian franc, the Dutch guilder, the German mark, the Austrian schilling, the British pound, the Italian lira, the Japanese yen, the Mexican peso, the Spanish peseta, the Australian dollar, the New Zealand dollar, the Hong Kong dollar, etc..

According to their convertibility, currencies can be grouped into three general categories: 'convertible currencies', 'semi-convertible currencies', and 'non-convertible currencies'. Convertible currencies are those which can be freely bought and sold in the foreign exchange markets, at the rates of exchange prevailing at the time of purchase or sale. Semi-convertible currencies can be bought and sold only through the local central bank, at predetermined rates of exchange. A large number of third-world currencies fall into this category. Transactions are limited to commercial deals. Non-convertible currencies are those whose circulation is restricted by the local monetary authorities. The rates of exchange are artificially pegged, usually at a level much higher than the rates prevailing on the black market, or parallel market, which inevitably develops. Most Eastern European countries have non-convertible currencies.

In practice, there are three main convertible currency areas: the U.S. area, which comprises essentially the U.S. and Canadian dollars; the European area, with the currencies of Western Europe; and the Asian area, with the Japanese yen and the Hong Kong, Malaysian, and Singapore dollars. The governments of these countries allow unregulated purchases and sales, and the amounts of money exchanged in the foreign exchange markets are very large.

The world's major currency is the U.S. dollar, followed by the pound sterling, the D-mark, and the Japanese yen. The importance of the U.S. dollar stems from a number of factors, some domestic and some international: the United States has the world's largest capital market, and there are more dollars in the world than all other major currencies put together. Invoicing for raw materials and commodities, especially oil, gas, and wheat, is in U.S. dollars. It is also interesting to note that the dollar is by far the largest component of the foreign currency reserves held by the world's major central banks (reserve currency).

currency[2]

Bargeldumlauf,
Münzen und Banknoten,
Papiergeld

In American English, the term 'currency' is taken to mean the tangible, circulating portion of a nation's money supply, composed of banknotes and coins. The term sometimes refers to paper money only.

current account[1]

Leistungsbilanz

The current account, also referred to as the 'balance of payments on current account', of a particular country is a record of all its exports and imports of goods and services along with unilateral transfers. In other words, the current account consists of the balance of trade (i.e., exports and imports of goods), the invisible account (i.e., exports and imports of services), and unilateral transfers.

If a country's imports of goods and services together with its unilateral transfers to non-residents exceed its visible and invisible exports plus the unilateral transfers received, the country is said to have a 'current account deficit'. The opposite would be a 'current account surplus'.

If a country's balance of trade is in the red, this does not necessarily imply a current account deficit, because the deficit on visible trade may be more than offset by an invisibles surplus, the result being an overall current account surplus.

current account[2]

Kontokorrentkonto,
Girokonto,
Scheckkonto

A current account, or 'cheque account' (U.S.: 'checking account'), is a bank demand deposit account from which withdrawals can be made by writing out cheques. A person wishing to open a current account is often required to provide references, and is asked to state whether the account is of a business or a private nature. A specimen signature is kept at the customer's local branch.

The holder of a current account is provided with a personalised cheque book - i.e., a booklet of blank cheque forms bearing the client's name and account number -, and is usually issued a cheque card. Moreover, the account holder is entitled to a number of bank services, including, among others, credit transfers, standing orders, direct debiting, overdrafts, and cash cards. He is usually charged for the cost of handling the account.

As current account deposits earn no, or only very little, interest, many customers arrange for amounts in excess of current needs to be transferred to deposit accounts on which interest is paid.

It should be noted that British current account holders are offered a much wider range of services than are holders of American checking accounts.

current assets

Umlaufvermögen

According to the American Institute of Certified Public Accountants (AICPA), and also to British and Austrian accounting rules, current assets are defined as cash and other resources which can be expected to be realised in cash or sold or consumed within a one-year period.

Current assets are usually listed on the balance sheet according to their liquidity. The major items are:
1. Cash: cash as shown in the current asset section represents the total amount of money immediately available to be used without restriction for general business purposes. It includes 'cash on hand', or 'cash in hand', such as coins, banknotes, negotiable cheques, and bank drafts, and 'cash at bank', i.e., demand deposits.
2. Short-term (or temporary) investments (see: investment[3]).
3. Notes receivable.
4. Accounts receivable.
5. Inventories.
6. Deferred expenses, or prepaid expenses: these are expenses that have been paid before the balance sheet date, but are incurred in the following accounting period. Typical examples are: prepaid rent, prepaid interest, and prepaid insurance premiums.
7. Accrued revenues, or accrued income: these are revenues, such as accrued interest income, earned before the balance sheet date, but collected/received during the following accounting period.

In the United States, in Great Britain, and in Austria, there are a variety of accounting rules applying to the valuation of current assets. In Austria, for instance, all current assets have to be valued at each balance sheet date at the lower of cost or market. 'Cost' means 'historical cost' (i.e., cost of acquisition or production cost), and 'market' refers either to the 'current replacement cost' (i.e., the current cost of replacing an existing asset, either by purchase or by reproduction, with an equivalent asset) or to the 'net realisable value' (i.e., the amount of cash expected to be derived from the sale of an asset, net of costs required to be incurred as a result of the sale).

current liabilities   kurzfristige Verbindlichkeiten

In accounting, current liabilities, or short-term liabilities, may be described as debts which are usually payable (due) within one year of the balance sheet date. The term 'current liabilities' is used principally to designate obligations whose liquidation is expected to require the use of current assets or the creation of other current liabilities. The 12-month time period in the definition of current liabilities is the most significant factor in the segregation of current and long-term liabilities.

The extent to which current liabilities are detailed in the balance sheet, and the sub-captions used for classifying them, depend largely on the type of business firm and the purpose for which the balance sheet is to be used. The principal types of current liabilities are:
1. Trade accounts payable (see: accounts payable).
2. Short-term notes payable to trade creditors (see: notes payable).
3. Notes payable to banks.
4. Loans from other financial institutions.
5. Dividends payable (i.e., cash dividends declared but not yet paid, including unclaimed dividend cheques from prior declarations). Stock dividends are not reported as liabilities, because they represent retained earnings and are, therefore, properly shown as an element of shareholders' equity.
6. Advance payments from customers: this item refers to payments received in advance from customers for goods and/or services. The advances are originally recorded as liabilities, and are transferred from the liability account to the revenue account when the goods or services are delivered.
7. Accrued expenses, or accrued liabilities: these are expenses, such as accrued interest on bonds payable, that have been incurred before the balance sheet date, but are payable in the following accounting period.
8. Deferred revenues, also known as 'deferred income', 'prepaid revenues', 'prepaid income', and 'deferred credits': these are revenues received before the balance sheet date, but earned only during the following accounting period. Rent and interest received in advance are common examples.
9. Estimated liabilites: an estimated liability is a known liability whose value cannot be ascertained with certainty on the balance sheet date. In such a case, the amount must be estimated as accurately as possible on the basis of all information available. A typical example is the liability for product guarantees, the amount of which depends on the number of items expected to need repair or replacement during the guarantee period. The amount estimated is usually based on past experience and may approximate one half of 1% of annual sales.

Normally, each of the current liabilities listed above should be separately accounted for and separately reported on the balance sheet.

current ratio   Liquidität 3. Grades

The current ratio, also referred to as the 'working capital ratio', is computed by dividing current assets by current liabilities. For example, if the ratio is 2:1, the firm in question has twice as many current assets as current liabilities, and, therefore, it should have no difficulty in paying its short-term liabilities. The higher the current ratio, the better the creditors' position, because of the greater probability that the short-term debts will be paid when they fall due. Thus, the current ratio indicates the degree of safety with which short-term credit may be extended to a business firm by current creditors.

It follows from the foregoing that the current ratio is an important liquidity ratio, i.e., it is a useful measure of a firm's ability to meet its short-term financial obligations. A current ratio of 2:1, or, to put it in a slightly different way, a current ratio of 200%, is considered to be adequate. However, it should be kept in mind that the current ratio is influenced by many factors, so that this traditional absolute standard cannot be regarded as appropriate for all business firms. The peculiarities of the industry in which a firm operates and other factors, such as methods of operations and seasonal influences, should also be taken into account in evaluating the current ratio.

Finally, it should be noted that the current ratio also has some weaknesses. One major criticism is that the inclusion of inventories in current assets impairs the ratio's usefulness as a measure of a firm's liquidity. It is argued that inventories are usually the least liquid of the current assets because they are not readily convertible into cash. This criticism has led to the use of the acid-test ratio.

customs duty   Zoll(-gebühr)

A customs duty, in its general economic sense, is a tax levied by the government on goods crossing the customs border. As the practice of levying customs duties on exports is very rare, the term 'customs duty' is frequently used as a synonym for 'import duty'.

An import duty, or import tariff, is a tax levied on a wide range of dutiable goods which becomes payable when the goods cross the customs border, in other words, when they enter the customs territory. The customs territory comprises either the territory of one country or – in the case of a customs union – the territories of two or more countries. The customs duties levied on imports are included in the customs tariff, which consists of two parts: a list of commodities, classified under various tariff headings, and the tariff rates applicable to these commodities. As a very broad generalisation, it would be true to say that foodstuffs and raw materials for manufacture are duty free, and that manufactured and semi-manufactured goods are dutiable.

Import duties may be broadly classified into 'protective tariffs' and 'revenue tariffs'. Protective tariffs, as the name suggests, are intended to protect domestic industries/producers from foreign competition. Revenue tariffs are levied merely for the purpose of raising revenue for the government. Occasionally, a country levies a tariff or increases its tariffs on goods imported from a particular country as a retaliatory measure if its exports encounter tariff discrimination in that country. Such a tariff is known a 'retaliatory tariff'. 'Preferential tariffs', on the other hand, are used to grant favours to particular countries. The E.E.C. and the United

States, for instance, admit certain goods from ldcs and similar countries at reduced tariff rates to help improve their export performance (aid through trade).

With regard to the method of assessment, there are basically three types of import duty: 'ad valorem duties', which are assessed on the basis of the value of the goods, 'specific duties', based on some measure of quantity, such as weight, length, or number of units, and 'compound duties', which are a combination of the two (e.g., £100 per unit of the imported goods, plus 2 per cent of value).

Import duties are in fact a form of indirect tax, because, though they are in the first place paid by the importer, they are ultimately borne by the final consumer in the form of higher prices.

Import duties, like any other form of protectionism, or trade barrier, are a double-edged instrument of trade policy: on the one hand, they tend to reduce imports, which may help domestic industries and the balance of payments; on the other hand, they prevent a country from reaping the full benefits of the international division of labour, increase the cost of living, reduce international competitiveness, and invite other countries to retaliate by increasing their import duties.

customs invoice   Zollfaktura

A customs invoice is a special invoice for customs purposes which importers in many countries have to present to the customs authorities when filing a customs entry, and which serves as the basis for the assessment of import duty.

The customs invoice has to be prepared by the exporter on a prescribed official form, issued by the customs authorities of the importing country. On this invoice, the exporter must show, in addition to the usual invoice details and the export price, the domestic value of the goods in the exporting country, as well as the country of origin. (If the domestic price in the exporting country is higher than the export price, the import duty is assessed on the basis of the domestic price, which is an anti-dumping measure.) Moreover, the exporter declares that the price shown on the customs invoice is the actual price charged to the customer, that there are no secret discounts, and that there is no second invoice with a different price. This helps to prevent illegal capital transfers.

Customs invoices are required by the Commonwealth countries and a few other countries (but not by the United Kingdom). In the Commonwealth countries, the official designation of the customs invoice is 'Combined Certificate of Value and Origin'.

customs procedure   Zollverfahren

All goods which are imported into a country must be cleared through Customs, which enables the customs authority to examine the goods and calculate the amount of import duty to be paid by the importer.

When goods are imported, the importer, or the agent acting for him, has to file a customs entry. This is a written declaration on an official form, obtainable from the customs authorities, describing the goods in accordance with the Customs Tariff and in sufficient detail to enable them to be clearly identified. In addition, the importer must present all documents required for customs clearance, such as the commercial invoice, customs invoice, etc.. The goods are checked by a customs officer against the entry, and, if it is found to be in order, duty has to be paid at the applicable rate, unless the goods are duty-free. The customs authority then returns a stamped and signed copy of the entry to the importer, enabling him to get the goods released from customs custody.

Special customs procedures have been adopted for goods which are imported only for a limited period of time and then re-exported, and for dutiable goods which are not required for immediate use. In the latter case, payment of the import duty may be deferred by storing the uncleared goods in a bonded warehouse under customs supervision. These special procedures are dealt with in greater detail under the headings of "temporary importation of goods" and "bonded warehouse" elsewhere in the book.

customs union   Zollunion

A customs union is an association of two or more countries which abolish all, or major groups of, internal tariffs (i.e., imports into a member country from any other member country are exempt from duty) and adopt a common external tariff (i.e., a tariff levied on imports from non-member countries). The best example of a customs union is the European Economic Community (E.E.C.).

By contrast, in a free trade area, such as the European Free Trade Association (E.F.T.A.), of which Austrias is a member country, internal tariffs are removed, but each member country retains its own external tariff.

D

damages   Schadenersatz

Damages are a remedy for breach of contract. They are money compensation for a loss suffered. The purpose of granting damages is to put the injured party, as far as money can do it, into the position in which he would have been if the loss had not been suffered, i.e., if the contract had not been broken.

Sometimes, the parties themselves, when entering into a contract, fix the amount of damages payable in the event of a breach of contract. Such an amount is called 'liquidated damages', and is a genuine pre-estimate of the loss which a breach of the contract is likely to cause.

data processing   Datenverarbeitung

The term 'data processing' denotes the operations performed on data, usually by automatic equipment, for the purpose of deriving information. In the wider sense, data processing involves numerical, alphabetic, symbolic, and voice data, and is, therefore, synonymous with 'information processing'. In a narrower sense, the term is restricted to numerical data, while the manipulation of alphabetic characters would be called 'word processing', that of symbols 'image processing', and that of voice data appropriately 'voice processing'.

data transmission   Datenübertragung

Data transmission is the automatic transfer of computer-type information from one computer to another or between a central computer and some remote peripheral device (e.g., an airline reservation terminal or a cash dispenser).

Data can be transmitted over telephone and telex lines, via private circuits, or by radio link, with the help of specialised hardware (modems) and software (communication protocols). Modems are required since, in many cases, the data to be transferred is in digital form, while it can be transmitted only in analogue form. An exception are the digital circuits, which are slowly gaining ground at the time of writing, and where modulation is only necessary if analogue signals (e.g., voice) are to be sent. Data is transferred over these communication facilities either in a continuous stream or in the form of packets (packet switching), which use the transmission capacity more efficiently.

dealer   Händler

The word 'dealer' generally refers to a firm which makes a business of buying and selling goods, usually without altering their condition (e.g., car dealer). A dealer differs from a commercial agent or a broker in that he acts in his own name and on his own account, taking title to the goods. Since a dealer usually sells to ultimate consumers, the term is, for all practical purposes, synonymous with 'retailer'.

debit card

„Debit"-Karte,
„Kreditkarte" mit sofortiger Belastung
des Kundenkontos,
Lastschriftkarte zur Abbuchung von
Rechnungsbeträgen

Like the credit card, the debit card is used to pay for goods and/or services by the cardholder signing a sales slip. In contrast to the credit card system, however, any amount spent is immediately deducted from the cardholder's account when the issuer bank receives the sales slip. As under the debit card system the customer's account must always show a sufficient credit balance, the use of free credit, a hallmark of the credit card system, is thus eliminated. Debit cards, which are issued by financial institutions only, therefore merely provide immediate access to a customer's personal account. Apart from its use in shops and restaurants, a debit card may also enable its holder to draw cash from cash dispensers and to pay for purchases through an EFTPOS terminal.

Often, bank 'credit cards' also serve as 'debit cards' and perform the functions outlined above.

debit note

Lastschriftanzeige

A debit note (in the United States known as a 'debit memorandum' or 'debit memo') is a document which serves the same purpose as an invoice. It is sent by the seller to the buyer to rectify an undercharge in the original invoice, e.g., it is used when an error or omission in an invoice has to be corrected.

debtor

Schuldner

Jowitt, in his famous Dictionary of English Law, defines debtor as "a person who owes a debt". Debt, in turn, is defined as "a sum of money due from one person to another". This means that, at least in British law, the terms 'debtor' and 'debt' have a narrower meaning than their apparent German equivalents 'Schuldner' and 'Schuld', which do not restrict what is owed to money, but include goods and services. In fact, any kind of 'performance (Leistung), i.e., any act or refraining from doing an act, may be the subject-matter of a debt (Schuldverhältnis). Under an Austrian contract of sale, for instance, both the buyer (who owes the purchase price) and the seller (who owes delivery) are regarded as 'debtors'.

Apart from these legal complications, it should be noted that the English term 'debtor' has a wider meaning than the term 'borrower'. 'Debtor' also includes 'trade debtors', who are not classified as borrowers since they have not borrowed money, but have merely obtained goods or services on credit.

In accounting, the terms 'debtors' and 'trade debtors' refer not only to the persons or organisations owing money to a creditor, but also to the amounts so owed.

debt securities

(börsengängige) schuldrechtliche
Wertpapiere

A debt security represents a loan made by the holder of the security to the issuer. Debt securities, therefore, have to be redeemed, that is, the principal has to be repaid by the issuer at maturity, although there are certain exceptions (irredeemable bonds). Strictly speaking, the amount to be repaid (the redemption price) need not be the same as the issue price, and both may vary from the nominal value of the security. The reason for this is that the difference between issue price and redemption price is an element of the return to be obtained from the debt security and can be used to modify, and, in rare cases, even to replace, other elements (e.g., the interest rate). Most debt securities, however, are interest-bearing securities. The interest rate can be fixed (fixed-interest or fixed-interest-bearing securities) or variable (variable-interest securities). Zero-coupon bonds, or deep discount bonds, are non-interest bearing, and the return to the investor is only in the form of the difference between the higher redemption price and the lower issue price.

Debt securities are issued by governments, in which case they are referred to as 'government bonds' (mainly U.S.), 'government stocks' (U.K.), 'gilt-edged securities' (U.K.), or, if issued by local governments, as 'local authority stocks' (U.K.), 'corporation stocks' (U.K.), 'municipal bonds' (U.S.). But also companies may issue debt securities, which are then called 'debentures' in the U.K. and 'corporate bonds' in the United States. In the United States, debentures are unsecured corporate bonds, i.e., bonds that are not secured by a charge on a specific asset or group of assets of the issuing corporation.

Debentures/corporate bonds may carry an option for their holders to convert them into ordinary shares (U.S.: common stock) at a predetermined price and within a specified period of time. In this case, they are referred to as 'convertible debentures' (U.S.: 'convertible bonds'). Debenture holders, or bondholders, will decide to exercise this option if the dividends and/or the share prices of the company in question develop satisfactorily.

There is a tendency for short-term and medium-term debt securities to be referred to as 'notes' (e.g., Treasury notes, capital notes, floating rate notes, i.e., variable-interest notes).

deductible   Selbstbehalt,
                                                 Abzugsfranchise

The term 'deductible', which is used in the U.S.A., has the same meaning as the British expression 'excess'. It is a specified amount or a certain percentage of the sum insured up to which the insured must bear any loss of, or damage to, the subject-matter insured for his own account. When the deductible is exceeded, only the amount in excess of the deductible is recoverable under the policy.

Such a deductible may be compulsorily applied by the insurer, or the insured may voluntarily agree to it, in which case a certain reduction in premium is allowed.

default   Nichterfüllung einer (vertraglichen oder
                                                 gesetzlichen) Verpflichtung

In its most general sense, default denotes failure to fulfil any contractual or legal duty, in particular, failure to pay one's debts when they fall due. For instance, in connection with export credit guarantees, protracted default means the importer's failure to pay the contract price within six months of the due date.

defective goods

mangelhafte Waren

Defective goods may be described as goods which have one or more major or minor defects. A major defect is one which prevents the buyer from using the goods in the ordinary or stipulated way. All other defects are deemed to be minor.

If the seller has delivered goods showing a major defect that cannot be repaired, the buyer may reject the goods, thus rescinding the contract. If, however, the goods show minor defects that are irreparable, the buyer has the right to claim a reduction in price (allowance), but he is not entitled to reject the goods. In the case of repairable defects, irrespective of whether they are major or minor, the buyer is given the right to choose between a reduction in price or having the goods repaired.

deflation[1]

restriktive Wirtschaftspolitik;
Deflation

Today, the term 'deflation' is usually used to describe an economic policy intended to reduce the level of overall (or aggregate) demand. The main purpose is to calm down an overheated economy and to slow down the rise in prices. Some economists would call such a policy 'disinflation' and would reserve 'deflation' for a policy that aims at an absolute fall in the general price level. The reason for this distinction is that deflation originally denoted a fall in prices.

Deflation may be brought about by monetary policies, e.g., by increasing interest rates and contracting the money supply, and/or fiscal policies, e.g., by increasing taxes and/or reducing government expenditure.

Deflationary measures frequently have nasty side-effects, the most important being an increase in the rate of unemployment and a fall in incomes. To avoid this, some economists recommend an incomes policy (either voluntary or mandatory) to get inflation under control.

deflation[2]

Inflationsbereinigung

The term 'deflation' refers also to the correction of an economic quantity (e.g., income) for a rise in price to indicate its real (as distinct from its nominal) value.

delay in delivery

Lieferverzug

Delay in delivery means that the supplier does not deliver the goods within the time stipulated in the contract of sale, which results in a breach of contract.

If the delay in delivery is not the supplier's fault, the buyer may allow him an additional period of time and may rescind the contract in the case of non-delivery. Should the supplier be responsible for the delay, the buyer may, even if the supplier performs the contract within the additional time allowed, sue him for damages in respect of late delivery. If the supplier fails to deliver the goods, he may be sued by the buyer for damages in respect of non-delivery.

delay in payment   Zahlungsverzug

Delay in payment means that the buyer fails to pay for goods and/or services within the time stipulated in the contract.

If a buyer fails to pay his debts in time , the seller usually sends him a reminder, which, if it does not produce any results, may be followed by more severely worded collection letters. Should the customer fail to respond to these letters, the seller may take steps to collect the amount due, either by entrusting a collection agency or a bank with the collection or by bringing legal action against the debtor.

Collection through banks is effected, in most cases, by means of a sight draft. The seller/creditor draws a sight draft on the debtor and hands it to his bank with instructions to pass it on to the buyer's/debtor's bank, which will present it for payment. Legal action is the last resort in the collection of outstanding accounts. In such a case, the seller's lawyer may try once more to induce the debtor to pay, but if this very last attempt to bring about an amicable settlement also fails, he will institute legal proceedings.

del credere agent   Handelsvertreter mit Übernahme des
                                        Delkredere

A del credere agent is a commercial agent who undertakes to indemnify the principal for any loss which the latter may sustain owing to the non-payment of the purchase price by a customer introduced by the agent. The agent, however, is not liable if the non-payment is due to the principal's failure to perform the contract. Usually, agents who accept the del credere for customers are paid an additional commission, called a 'del credere commission'.

DELIVERED AT FRONTIER (Incoterms 1980)   GELIEFERT GRENZE
... *(named place of delivery at frontier)*   *...(benannter Lieferort an der Grenze)*

International code: DAF

'Delivered at frontier' means that the seller's obligations are fulfilled when the goods have arrived at the frontier of the country named in the contract of sale. Thus, the seller must bear all costs and risks of the goods until they have been delivered at the frontier. To avoid misunderstandings, the parties contracting on the basis of this trade term are recommended to specify the word 'frontier' by indicating the two countries separated by that frontier, and also the named place of delivery, e.g., "delivered at German-Austrian frontier (Walserberg)". It should also be noted that this term is only suitable in cases where the transport is interrupted at the frontier. Otherwise, in the case of loss of, or damage to, the goods, it may be difficult, or even impossible, to determine where the loss or damage occurred.

In particular, the seller's primary duties are (i) to contract for the carriage of the goods to the named place of delivery at the frontier, pay the freight, and bear all other costs of transport to that place; (ii) to place the contract goods cleared for export at the disposal of the buyer at the named place of delivery at the frontier on the date or within the period stipulated in the contract of sale, and bear all the risks up to that time; (iii) to bear the unloading costs if it is necessary or customary for the goods to be unloaded on their arrival at the named place of delivery.

The buyer's primary duties are (i) to take delivery of the goods as soon as the seller has duly put them at his disposal at the named place of delivery at the frontier, and bear all risks of the goods from that time on; (ii) to obtain any import licence, pay any import duties, and pay for on-carriage.

DELIVERED DUTY PAID (Incoterms 1980)
... *(named place of destination in the country of importation)*

International code: DDP

GELIEFERT VERZOLLT
... *(benannter Bestimmungsort im Einfuhrland)*

Whereas the term 'ex works' represents the seller's minimum obligation, the term 'delivered duty paid', when followed by words naming the buyer's premises, denotes the other extreme - the seller's maximum obligation. Under this clause, the seller has to bear all costs and risks of the goods until they have been placed at the buyer's disposal at the named place of destination in the country of importation. The term 'delivered duty paid' may be used irrespective of the mode of transport.

The seller's primary duties are (i) to contract for the carriage of the goods to the named place of destination and pay the freight; (ii) to place the goods at the disposal of the buyer at the named place of destination and bear all the risks of the goods up to that time; (iii) to obtain any import licence and pay any import duties, including the cost of customs clearance.

The buyer's primary duty is to take delivery of the goods as soon as the seller has duly put them at his disposal at the named place of destination.

delivery (of goods)   Lieferung (von Waren)

Delivery of goods means the voluntary transfer of possession from one person (the seller) to another (the buyer). The goods are normally regarded as having been delivered to the buyer when he, or his agent (e.g., the carrier), has been enabled to exercise control over them (actual or physical delivery). In cases where the seller has obtained a bill of lading, as under a c.i.f. contract, the goods are deemed to have been delivered when the bill of lading has been delivered to the buyer (symbolic delivery).

The time, place, and mode of delivery are stipulated in the contract of sale. In export sales, however, standardised trade terms (e.g., the INCOTERMS) are normally used to specify mode and place.

delivery period   Lieferfrist

Delivery period is the time interval between placing the order and the moment when the goods come under the control of the buyer or his agent (e.g., the carrier).

demand

In economic theory, demand means the amount of a commodity or service that economic units are willing to buy, or actually buy, at a given price. In economic theory, therefore, demand is always effective demand, i.e., demand supported by purchasing power, and not merely the desire for a particular commodity or service.

Obviously, demand is not only influenced by price, but also by many other factors, such as the incomes of the demanders and the prices of substitutes. In economic analysis, these other factors are frequently assumed to be constant (the 'ceteris paribus' or 'all other things being equal' condition). This allows one to relate a range of prices to the quantities demanded in what is called the demand function (with price as the independent and demand as the dependent variable) and to graph this relationship in the demand curve.

demand curve

Nachfragekurve

The demand curve is the graphical representation of the demand function, i.e., of the relationship between price and demand. It tells us how many units of a particular commodity or service would be bought at various prices, assuming that all other factors (such as the incomes of the demanders and the prices of substitutes) remain unchanged. The demand curve normally slopes downwards from left to right, which means that more is bought at low prices than at higher prices. A famous exception to the rule of a downward-sloping demand curve is the "Giffen paradox". If the condition that all other factors remain unchanged (the 'ceteris paribus condition') is relaxed and the incomes of the demanders, for instance, are allowed to change, then the whole demand curve will shift its position.

department store

Kaufhaus,
Warenhaus

Department stores are large retail establishments offering a wide range of goods, with the main emphasis on such shopping items as furniture, women's clothing, curtains, flooring, bedding, etc.. Other lines carried are leather goods, cameras, radio and television sets, home computers, toys, and games. Increasingly, department store customers are also being offered services, including travel and sports, insurance and investment, cleaning, and car-hire services.

The name 'department store' obviously derives from the fact that the goods offered, as well as many activities related to them (e.g., buying and selling), are segregated into separate departments, each under its own manager, or "buyer". Advertising, delivery, staff training, and other general activities are, however, carried out centrally for all departments.

The main selling point of department stores is their ability to supply all, or at least as many as possible, of a customer's retail needs under one roof. Slogans like "one-stop shopping" or "We supply everything from a needle to a crocodile" (the latter being used by Harrods in London) testify to this fact. The convenience of one-stop shopping may help to offset certain disadvantages, such as the rather impersonal atmosphere and the limited range of goods (especially if compared with stockists) in the individual departments.

Department stores may be independent, i.e., single-unit firms, or may belong to a large chain, as is the case with Sears and Roebuck and J.C. Penney stores in the United States.

depletion

Substanzverringerung;
Substanzwertabschreibung,
Absetzung für Substanzverringerung

Depletion, like depreciation, has two different meanings. In its general economic sense, it is applied to the exhaustion of natural resources, such as iron ore, oil and natural gas, gold, silver, coal, timber, gravel, etc.. Assets subject to depletion are referred to as 'depletable assets', 'wasting assets', or 'exhaustible assets'. They may be described as irreplaceable and commercially exploitable stores of natural raw materials.

In the accounting sense, depletion is an accounting process which spreads the cost of a wasting asset (less any residual value) over its estimated useful life, expressed in terms of the estimated number of units that are economically available. In other words, depletion is the periodic allocation of the cost of natural resources to expense, periodic expense being charged against periodic income. The total depletion charge for each period is computed by multiplying the unit depletion rate (i.e., the cost of the asset divided by the estimated number of units in the asset) by the actual number of units extracted during the period. To illustrate, assume that the total cost of a mine with an estimated potential production of 2 million tons is $160,000 (no residual value). The depletion rate per unit is $0.08 (160,000 : 2,000,000). If 10,000 tons are mined during a given year, the depletion charge for the year is $800 (0.08 x 10,000).

depreciation[1]

Wertminderung

Depreciation refers to a loss in the value of assets, e.g., of buildings, plant, machinery, stocks, or in the value, both internal and external, of a currency (especially under a system of floating exchange rates.)

depreciation[2]

Abschreibung,
ordentliche Abschreibung vom
Anlagevermögen

The term 'depreciation' may also be used in a more specific sense. According to the American Institute of Certified Public Accountants (AICPA), depreciation is an accounting process which aims to distribute, or spread, the cost of tangible fixed assets, less residual value (if any), over their useful lives in a systematic and rational manner. It represents a process of cost allocation, as opposed to asset valuation. This definition requires some further comments.

The value of a firm's tangible capital assets is reduced mainly because they are used and worn out in the production of goods and services, although a number of factors other than use may also be responsible for the loss of value (viz., deterioration and decay, obsolescence, time, the firm's maintenance and repair policy). In compliance with the matching principle, this loss of value, however caused, is periodically (usually annually) charged against current income as an expense of operations (operating expense). This expense, referred to as the 'depreciation expense', is one which the business firm hopes to recover by pricing and selling its products, just as it expects to recover the current cash expenditure connected with production, such as labour and materials. Since tangible fixed assets are not completely used up within one year, their costs are spread over their estimated useful lives and allocated through depreciation expense to each unit produced. (In accounting jargon, the assets are said to be "written off" during their useful lives). This shows quite clearly that the annual depreciation expense (also known as the 'annual depreciation charge' or 'annual write-off') is intended to recover as cash the total cost of the depreciable assets (i.e., assets subject to depreciation) over their useful lives. The period during which tangible fixed assets are converted into cash varies with the nature of the assets involved. The costs of buildings are generally recoverable within 25 to 30 years, while the costs of vehicles may be recovered within 3 to 5 years.

It follows from the above explanations that depreciation expense is a non-cash expense (i.e., it does not represent a cash outlay). Therefore, like any other expense, it reduces a firm's pre-tax profit, but, in contrast to cash expenses (e.g., interest expense), does not reduce a firm's cash flow.

The factors to be considered in calculating the annual depreciation expense are: the actual cost of the depreciable asset, its estimated residual value, and its estimated useful life.

If a tangible fixed asset is acquired (i.e., purchased) by a firm, cost is taken to mean 'acquisition cost' and includes all expenditure incurred in acquiring the asset and placing it in usable condition. Thus, acquisition cost includes the purchase price plus such incidental expenditure as freight and installation costs. By contrast, if a machine or other tangible asset is constructed by a business firm for its own use, cost is taken to mean 'production cost'.

The usual basis of depreciation is cost less any estimated residual value. The residual value, or salvage value, of a tangible asset is the estimated amount which may be recovered at the time the asset is finally retired from service. The asset may be scrapped, sold, or traded in. A common synonym for residual value is 'scrap value', which may be misleading because the asset may not be scrapped. In practice, the residual value, unless material in amount, is usually ignored, and the depreciation charges are based on cost.

The useful life, also known as the 'service life' or 'economic life', is the period of usefulness of an asset to its owner. It is mainly influenced by the following factors: wear and tear (i.e., loss of value sustained as a result of ordinary use), deterioration and decay, passage of time, inadequacy, obsolescence, and the firm's repair and maintenance policy. Because of inadequacy and obsolescence, the service life of an asset may be much shorter than its physical life. Depending on the nature of the asset, service life may be measured in terms of years, units of output, or hours of operating time.

Some typical examples of depreciable assets are: buildings, furniture and fixtures, machinery, equipment, motor vehicles, etc.. It is worth mentioning that land is not subject to depreciation.

Finally, 'depreciation' should not be confused with 'depletion' and 'amortisation'. All three are accounting processes, the purpose of each being to allocate systematically the cost of fixed assets to expense. The difference is that depreciation relates to tangible fixed assets, depletion to natural resources, or wasting assets, such as mines, quarries, and oil wells, whereas amortisation is usually used to describe the periodic allocation of the cost of certain types of intangible fixed assets, such as patents and copyrights.

depreciation[3] (for tax purposes)   Abschreibung (im steuerlichen Sinn)

The amounts provided for depreciation in the financial accounts of a business organisation are usually not equal to the amounts allowed by the revenue authorities for tax purposes. These amounts are referred to as 'capital allowances' (including 'first-year allowances' and 'annual writing-down allowances') in the United Kingdom and as '(accelerated) depreciation allowances' in the United States. To arrive at the profit assessable for income tax or corporation tax, it is necessary to add back the depreciation recorded in the financial accounts and then to deduct the amounts permitted for tax purposes.

As a rule, the revenue authorities allow firms to write down their tangible fixed assets much faster than would be warranted on the basis of their actual useful lives. In the United States, for instance, the Economic Recovery Act of 1981 permits most machines to be written off in five years, with the highest depreciation allowance (32%) coming in the second year. In Great Britain, the Finance Act 1972 increased the first-year allowance for machinery to 100%, which means that it can be written off in the first year. (It should be noted that this generous depreciation policy has since been reversed, and that the British government has started phasing out first-year allowances.)

The effect of all this is to reduce dramatically profits for tax purposes, the corporation tax or income tax charge, and, consequently, the cost of capital, which makes capital allowances a powerful investment incentive. Strictly speaking, however, accelerated depreciation for tax purposes, in the U.S. also referred to as 'accelerated cost recovery', does not reduce, but only defers, corporation tax. Whenever a firm reduces its level of capital expenditure, the taxman will catch up with it.

depreciation methods   Abschreibungsmethoden

Methods of depreciation are concerned with computing the amount of depreciation expense that should be recorded each period. A number of methods have been developed, each of which provides a somewhat different pattern of depreciation charges over the useful life of the tangible asset.

The most popular depreciation methods are the 'straight-line method' and the 'reducing-charge methods' (also known as the 'decreasing-charge methods'). The straight-line method of depreciation allows the cost of the asset to be spread evenly over its useful life; in other words, this method results in an equal depreciation charge in each period of the asset's useful life. The depreciation charge per period (usually per year) is calculated by dividing the asset's depreciable cost (i.e., cost minus residual value) by its useful life. For example, if a machine with a ten-year life costs $100,000, the depreciation charge in each of the ten years is $10,000. The straight-line method is widely used in practice, mainly because of its simplicity. One weakness of this method is that it relates depreciation expense to the passage of time rather than to the degree of use.

The reducing-charge methods are designed to allocate the depreciable cost in such a manner that periodic depreciation charges are higher in the early years and lower in the later years of the asset's life. These methods are based on the assumption that new assets are more efficient than old ones. Several different methods may be employed to achieve the objective of assigning a decreasing depreciation charge to each period the asset is in use.

The principal reducing-charge methods currently being used are the 'declining-balance method', or 'diminishing-balance method', and the 'sum-of-the-years'-digits method'. Both are methods of accelerated depreciation, i.e., they allow a firm to recover a greater proportion of the cost of the asset in the early years of the asset's life than is possible with the straight-line method.

Under the declining-balance method, the annual depreciation charge is computed by multiplying the book value of the asset (i.e., cost less accumulated depreciation) by a fixed percentage (which is to be calculated from a formula). Since the book value declines each year (hence the term 'declining-balance method'), this method results in decreasing annual depreciation charges. For example, if the acquisition cost of a machine is $10,000, its useful life 3 years, and its estimated residual value $1,250, the annual depreciation rate would be 50%. Consequently, the depreciation expense in the first year would be $5,000 (i.e., 10,000 x 50%), in the second year $2,500 (i.e., 5,000 x 50%), and in the third year $1,250 (i.e., 2,500 x 50%).

Under the sum-of-the-years'-digits method, the periodic depreciation charge declines each year by the same amount. Each year, the depreciable cost of the asset is multiplied by a rate of depreciation which decreases from year to year. The rate to be applied in a particular year is expressed as a fraction, the denominator of which is equal to the sum of the years' digits for the asset's useful life, and the numerator of which is the asset's remaining life, including the current period. In other words, the numerators of the various fractions are the years' digits in inverse order. The following example shows the annual depreciation charges for a machine with a cost of $150,000 and an estimated service life of 5 years. The sum of the years' digits is 15 (i.e., $1 + 2 + 3 + 4 + 5$); therefore, the depreciation charge in the first year is $50,000 (i.e., 150,000 x $\frac{5}{15}$), in the second year $40,000 (i.e., 150,000 x $\frac{4}{15}$), in the third year $30,000, in the fourth year $20,000, and in the fifth year $10,000.

As has been shown above, both the straight-line method and the reducing-charge methods allocate an asset's depreciable cost on the basis of time. In practice, however, there are also methods which allocate cost on the basis of use, viz., the 'productive-output method', or 'units-of-output method', and the 'service-hours method'. These methods require the service life of an asset to be estimated in terms of the number of units of output or of the number of hours it is used. The primary justification for the use of these methods is that they distribute the cost of the asset in proportion to its use. The reason why they are only rarely used is that it is much more difficult to estimate the life of an asset in terms of use than in terms of years.

Finally, a few remarks on the recording of depreciation are in order. The most widely used procedure is to debit the annual depreciation charge to a depreciation account, entitled Depreciation Expense, which is an operating expense account, and to credit a valuation account entitled Accumulated Depreciation, Allowance for Depreciation, or Provision for Depreciation. In accounting terminology, the double entry for each year's depreciation charge is: "debit Depreciation Expense, and credit Accumulated Depreciation". On the balance sheet date, the Depreciation Expense account is closed to the profit and loss account, and the Accumulated Depreciation account, like the related asset account, is carried to the balance sheet. The major advantage of this method of recording depreciation is that it permits both the cost of the asset and the accumulated depreciation to date to be shown on the balance sheet. It may be of interest to mention that the annual depreciation charge may also be credited direct to the related asset account, which is called 'writing down' the asset. This method is usually not desirable, mainly because the cost of the asset will be lost sight of.

The tax implications of depreciation, another important aspect of this complex subject, are dealt with under the heading of "depreciation[3] (for tax purposes)".

desk-top computer   Tischcomputer

Desk-top computers are portable microcomputers designed for single-user applications. The term is, therefore, virtually synonymous with 'personal computer'.

devaluation (of a currency)   Abwertung (einer Währung)

The term 'devaluation' is used where a country with a fixed rate of exchange officially reduces the value of its home currency in terms of other currencies.

By contrast, under a system of floating rates, a decline in the exchange rate is referred to as a 'depreciation'. But since in practice the prevailing system is "dirty floating" (i.e., a compromise between "clean floating" and fixed rates), the distinction between 'devaluation' and 'depreciation' has become blurred.

In practice, devaluation is typical of countries with "soft" currencies, i.e., weak currencies, which are the result of serious balance-of-payments difficulties.

Devaluation means that a smaller amount of foreign currency is needed to buy the home currency, and a larger amount of home currency to buy the same amount of foreign currency. Consequently, the major effect of a devaluation is that, on the one hand, it makes exports of goods and services cheaper for foreign buyers and encourages the inflow of foreign investment capital, whereas, on the other hand, it makes visible and invisible imports dearer for domestic buyers and discourages the outflow of capital.

From the foregoing it can be seen that devaluing the domestic currency is an appropriate method of reducing a country's balance-of-payments deficit, provided other countries do not follow suit (competitive devaluation). In addition, it should not be forgotten that, due to the increase in import prices, a devaluation tends to produce strong inflationary pressures. Since labour and, in many cases, imported materials and components are required to produce goods for exports, this may offset some or all benefits which theoretically may be obtained from a devaluation. A further complication is that a devaluation will be counter-productive, i.e., lead to a higher deficit, in cases where the demand for exports has a low price elasticity.

While it is true that a devaluation may provide relief in a crisis, it may well give rise to a fear of further devaluations and lead to a loss of confidence. A devaluation may immediately spark off a round of speculation on a possible further devaluation. Any consideration of devaluing a currency is usually kept secret and denied publicly to prevent unbearable speculative pressure against the currency. Public suspicion of a possible devaluation inevitably invites speculative activity by holders of the currency and by bears, the former trying to avoid losses by selling the devaluation-prone currency, the latter, on the other hand, trying to make a profit by selling the currency short/forward.

development aid   Entwicklungshilfe

Development aid represents a transfer of real resources from one country or international organisation (the donor) to a less developed country (the donee). Its main aim is to promote and encourage economic development in the donee country to narrow and, eventually, to eliminate the gap between developing and industrialised countries. It should therefore be distinguished from emergency aid, which tries to solve or alleviate basically short-term problems, such as crop failures, droughts, earthquakes, floods, etc.. For a transfer to be classified as development aid , it is immaterial whether it represents a sacrifice for the donor country or not.

Although development aid certainly represents a moral obligation for the richer countries, it is by no means certain that the transfer of resources involved is in all cases really beneficial to the donee countries. The radical view is that the developing countries should be left alone ("follow a policy of dissociation" in the jargon of development economics). However that may be, it is certainly necessary to study carefully the real needs of the donee countries and to devise methods that would minimise the negative side-effects of aid-giving. One lesson that seems to have emerged from aid-giving is that, in many cases, huge, capital-intensive projects are unsuitable for less developed countries, and that the main emphasis should be on small-scale schemes incorporating what is called "appropriate technology" geared to the real needs of the recipients of development aid.

Development aid can be classified in many ways: we can distinguish between official (i.e., government) aid and private aid; between capital aid (designed to increase the donee's net capital imports), aid through trade (designed to improve the donee country's export performance, e.g., by tariff concessions), and technical aid (transfer of technology mainly through training of local staff and the provision of qualified personnel). Another distinction is the one between project aid and programme aid, i.e., between aid tied to a particular project and aid that can be spent at the discretion of the donee country. Unilateral aid is aid granted by one specific country, while in the case of multilateral aid, the donor is an international organisation funded by several countries.

digital   digital

Digital refers to the representation of data by means of a finite set of discrete symbols (e.g., the numbers 0 - 9) instead of by a continuously variable physical entity (e.g., the flow of electric current). Digital computers are based on the system of binary notation, where the set of symbols is restricted to two, viz., 0 and 1. The process of converting continuous (analogue) signals or data into digital form is referred to as 'digitalisation'.

direct debiting

Lastschriftverfahren,
Lastschrift-Einzugsverkehr,
Abbuchungsverfahren

Direct debiting is a method of payment which - in contrast to standing orders - is ideal for the payment of varying amounts at irregular intervals. It differs from the standing order in being more flexible, and in that it is the payee, and not the payer, who gives instructions to the bank for payment.

Direct debiting, which is used for settling suppliers' invoices and for paying such accounts as telephone and electricity bills, works as follows: by previous arrangement between the parties the debtor signs a general authority giving his creditor permission to claim the amounts due to him from the former's bank. A supplier of goods and/or services, for example, sends the buyer an invoice in the ordinary way and, usually after an interval of a few days, submits through his own bank a direct debit form for the amount due to him to the buyer's bank. The bank then debits the buyer's account with the amount due, transferring it to the supplier's account with his bank.

direct exporting

direkter Export

By direct exporting is meant a method of exporting under which a manufacturer sells his goods direct to foreign customers, and not to an export merchant in his country (indirect exporting). To achieve a steady volume of direct exports, many manufacturers establish their own permanent sales organisation abroad, whose duty it is to create and maintain a demand for the goods in question.

The exporter who wishes to put his export trade on a permanent basis has to examine various possibilities, some of which are mentioned below:
1. The exporter may grant the exclusive distributorship to an importer abroad (exclusive importer); or
2. he may entrust his representation to an independent agent abroad or to a commercial traveller; or
3. he may establish his own branch offices and employ his own sales organisation abroad; or
4. he may act through a subsidiary company there, etc..

direct quotation

Preisnotierung

The term 'direct quotation' refers to a method of quoting rates of exchange. An exchange rate quoted on a direct basis (in the U.K. called a 'pence rate') indicates the number of units of home currency per unit or 100 units of a foreign currency. In other words, it states the amount of home currency that can be obtained, or has to be paid, for one unit or 100 units of a foreign currency.

In the case of a direct quotation/pence rate, a bank/foreign exchange dealer works on the principle of "buy low and sell high". This means that a bank, when buying a foreign currency from a customer, gives as few units of the home currency as possible for each unit of foreign currency bought, and, when selling, wants to get as many units of the home currency as possible for each unit of foreign currency sold. Let us assume that on a particular day the U.S. dollar is quoted in Vienna at AS18.25/18.50. This means that the bank buys dollars at 18.25 Austrian schillings and sells dollars at 18.50 schillings. This example shows that the first price quoted is the bank's buying rate, and the second price the bank's selling rate, which is obviously higher than the buying rate, because any bank, in order to make a profit, must sell a foreign currency at a higher price than it pays for it. In banking practice, all direct quotations/pence rates have, without any exception, the buying rate on the left and the selling rate on the right. This applies to both spot rates and forward rates.

direct tax   direkte Steuer

Taxes are traditionally classified as 'direct' and 'indirect'. Direct taxes affect the economic fortune of the economic unit (person or firm) on which they are levied by reducing its income and/or wealth. In contrast to indirect taxes, direct taxes are not shifted to other economic units in the form of higher prices or wages, but are borne by the original taxpayer; or, to put it in a slightly different way, the point where the tax is paid and the point where the tax is borne (the incidence of the tax) coincide.

Direct taxes in G.B. are: taxes on income (income tax and corporation tax) and taxes on capital (capital gains tax and capital transfer tax). They are paid to the Inland Revenue authorities, either by the person/firm taxed or by the person's employer under the P.A.Y.E. system.

Empirical research has shown that the distinction between direct taxes and indirect taxes is less clear-cut than the traditional classification suggests. Income taxes may be, and are, passed on to customers or employers in higher prices or wages, although less openly and formally than indirect taxes. If, for instance, income tax and/or corporation tax is increased, business firms will try to maintain their after-tax rate of return by putting up their prices, unless the market prevents them from doing so.

discount[1]   Preisnachlaß (Skonto, Rabatt)

Discount may be defined as a reduction on the list price or invoice price. The most important types of discount are: 'cash discount', 'quantity discount', 'trade discount', 'seasonal discount'.

discount[2]   Deport

In the foreign exchange market, the term 'discount' refers to the difference between the higher spot rate and the lower forward rate. Consequently, the foreign currency concerned can be bought more cheaply in the forward market (i.e., for delivery at a specified future time) than in the spot market (i.e., for immediate delivery). (see: forward rate)

discount[3]   Disagio

In connection with securities, discount refers to the amount by which a share or bond stands below its nominal (or par) value. As in the case of premium[3], a discount may be calculated also with reference to some other value, e.g., the 'asset value' of a share. If a share stands at a discount to its asset value, this means that the share's current price is lower than the value of the assets attributable to that share. The asset value of a share is simply calculated by dividing the number of shares of a company into the total value of its assets.

discount[4]   Wechseldiskont

When used in connection with bills of exchange, the term 'discount' is applied to the interest deducted by a bank from the face value of the bill when discounting it. (see: discounting (of a bill of exchange))

discount house[1]   Diskontladen,
                                  Diskonter

Discount houses, also referred to as 'discount stores' or 'cut-price stores', are retail institutions that sell consumer goods at a discount from nationally advertised list prices. In contrast to other retailers which may occasionally discount prices, they do so openly and consistently, offsetting their lower margins by high volume and by operating in austere warehouse-type premises in low-rent locations and offering only a minimum of service (e.g., no credit and delivery, no after-sales service).

Discount houses typically specialise in consumer durables, such as electrical appliances and furniture, although they can also be found in food retailing. Recently, many of the traditional discount houses have added clothing to their range of goods, and some of them have moved up-market, although their main appeal is still to the budget-minded, price conscious low-income earner.

discount house[2]   Diskontbank,
                                  Spezialbank für das Wechselgeschäft

In Great Britain, a discount house is a banking institution whose business is mainly confined to the discounting of trade and bankers' acceptances, especially those arising from export and import transactions, and of Treasury bills. A trade acceptance is a bill of exchange accepted by a firm buying goods and/or services on credit. In recent years, the discount houses have expanded their activities to dealings in negotiable certificates of deposit and foreign exchange.

discounting (of a bill of exchange)   (Wechsel-)Diskontierung

The holder of an accepted bill of exchange (or of a promissory note) may wait until it matures and then present it for payment. Should he require the money before the bill matures, he may discount the bill with his bank. Most textbooks define 'discounting a bill' as "selling a bill to a bank". Banking practice, however, makes a clear distinction between 'discounting' a bill and 'selling' a bill (i.e., 'purchasing' a bill, from the point of view of the bank). If the bill includes an interest clause (e.g., "Three months after date pay Mr. Brown or order £1,000 with interest at 10% per annum"), the bank will 'purchase' it, pay the holder the face value plus interest accrued until the day of purchase, and collect both the face value and the interest when it presents the bill to the acceptor for payment. By contrast, if the bill does not contain an interest clause, which means that the interest is included in the face value, the bank will 'discount' the bill, pay the holder the face value minus interest accruing from the day of purchase to the date of maturity, and collect the face value on presentation.

The interest deducted from the face value of the bill is known as the 'discount', which is calculated at an agreed percentage per annum for the remaining life of the bill. The rate of discount varies and is influenced by the current market rate of interest, the remaining life of the bill, the credit standing of the various parties to the bill, and possibly by other factors.

If the holder of a bill discounts it with a bank, he must transfer it to the bank by indorsement and delivery if it is payable to order, or by delivery only if it is payable to bearer. By discounting the bill the bank becomes the holder and may either rediscount it with the central bank or keep it until maturity and present it for payment.

dishonoured bill   notleidender Wechsel

A bill is deemed to be dishonoured if it is not accepted by the drawee when presented to him for acceptance (dishonour by non-acceptance), or if it is not paid by the drawee/acceptor when presented to him for payment (dishonour by non-payment). If a bill is dishonoured, either by non-payment or non-acceptance, the holder has an immediate right of recourse against the drawer and any indorsers, which means that he can demand payment from them, provided they have received notice of dishonour by the holder. It should be noted that an indorser can exclude his liability by adding the words "without recourse" to his signature when indorsing the bill.

In the case of inland bills, notice of dishonour can be in any form, oral or written. As regards foreign bills, however, formal notice of dishonour in the form of a protest is required. (A foreign bill is a bill either drawn by a person resident abroad, or drawn by a person resident in the domestic country on a person resident abroad and payable abroad.) Whereas foreign bills must be formally protested upon dishonour by non-acceptance or non-payment, no protest is required for inland bills. In this respect, British and American law differs from Austrian law, which requires inland bills also to be protested. 'Protesting' a bill means that the bill is re-presented for acceptance or payment by a notary public, who notes on the bill the reason for dishonour. The notary public then issues a formal certificate of dishonour, called the '(deed of) protest', setting out the circumstances of dishonour. A protest, therefore, is a formal declaration by a notary public to the effect that on a certain day the bill was presented for acceptance or payment and that acceptance or payment was refused ('protest for non-acceptance', and 'protest for non-payment'). A copy of the protest and a copy of the bill are then sent by the holder to the drawer or indorser(s) he intends to make liable. (In Austria, the protest is written on the reverse side of the bill). The party paying the bill may, in turn, have recourse to any prior party, and so on.

disposable (personal) income — verfügbares (persönliches) Einkommen

Disposable income is the money available to individuals or households for spending and saving after personal taxes, employee's national insurance contributions, and similar payments have been deducted.

In the national income accounts, disposable income is roughly calculated by taking net national product at factor prices (national income in the narrower sense), deducting corporate profits and employer's national insurance contributions, adding government transfers and dividends (which gives personal income), and, finally, deducting personal taxes in the widest sense of the term.

distributed data processing — dezentralisierte Datenverarbeitung

Distributed data processing refers to the decentralisation of the data processing function in an organisation. Smaller computers are placed in functional units (such as offices, sections, or departments) and connected to a central computer.

distributing agent — Vertreter mit Auslieferungslager

An agent either passes orders on to his principal, who then dispatches the goods to the customers direct, or he carries stocks of specific products, spare parts, etc., and is authorised to supply customers direct from his stock. This latter type is called a 'distributing agent' or 'agent carrying stock'. Title to the goods in stock remains with the principal until they have been sold to a customer. Consequently, the principal can recover the goods in stock if the distributing agent becomes insolvent.

distribution — Distribution

Distribution, in the widest sense of the word, is the economic activity concerned with getting the goods from the manufacturer to the final consumer, i.e., it provides a link between production and consumption. It includes buying and selling (i.e., the transfer of ownership) and other activities of marketing intermediaries in the channel of distribution, physical distribution (transportation and storage), but also such auxiliary functions as banking, finance, insurance, and promotional activities that speed up and generally facilitate the distribution process.

In contrast to production, distribution creates utility and adds value, not by changing the form of the products, but by making them available to the ultimate consumer where and when required. Distribution creates time and place utilities and is, therefore, productive in the wider sense of the word.

distribution of income — Einkommensverteilung

Distribution of income refers to the way in which the aggregate income or product of a community - either a national economy or the world as a whole - is divided among its members. Since the subject is related to questions of poverty, equity, and redistribution, it would seem intuitively to be one of the fundamental problems of economic science and practice. But some schools of economic thought either neglect the subject or play down its importance.

From a technical point of view, income distribution can be divided into various types, depending on the way in which the members of the community concerned are grouped. Functional distribution is based on the division into recipients of wages and salaries, recipients of property income (interest, rent, capital gains, etc.), and recipients of profits. Occupational distribution shows how income is shared by the various occupations or industries, while in the case of racial or sexual distribution it is race or sex that forms the basis.

A comprehensive treatment of the subject would involve, among other things, measuring existing income distributions, trying to explain the present situation, and suggesting ways of changing it according to some operational definition of equity, or fairness.

diversification

Diversifizierung,
Diversifikation

According to Kotler, the doyen of marketing scholars, diversification is the product policy that offers "new products for new markets". A firm may decide to expand its product mix by adding a new product line or new lines, which will presumably be sold to different target groups. The idea is to create new sources of income which are independent of the existing sources and would, therefore, help to spread the risk inherent in any particular product line. This aspect of diversification can be epitomised by "Don't put all your eggs in one basket".

The term 'diversification' can also be applied to the policy of placing one's investments in a wide range of investment media, e.g., shares of different companies, bonds, property, and so on.

dividend[1]

Dividende

The dividend is that portion of a company's profit which is distributed to the shareholders owning shares ranking for dividend. Dividends, which may be paid out annually or twice a year (i.e., as an interim dividend and as a final dividend), are expressed either as a percentage of the face value of the shares on which they are paid, or as a fixed sum per share. Although dividends are usually paid out in cash (cash dividend), it is not impossible to have a distribution, either wholly or partly, in the form of shares (stock dividend).

The dividend policy of a company is the responsibility of the company's directors. The shareholders have, at best, only an indirect say. There are, however, constraints, the main one, of course, being the amount of profits, or earnings, generated by the company in question. If there is no or only little profit, a company will normally pass its dividend, i.e., it will not declare a dividend in that year, although it is always possible to fall back upon reserves, if any. If profits are sufficient, it is up to the directors to decide what portion should go to the shareholders and what portion should be retained in the business (ploughback, or self-financing).

The relationship between total earnings and paid-out earnings can be expressed either in the form of the payout ratio, indicating the percentage of total earnings that is distributed, or in the form of the dividend cover, which is calculated by dividing the dividend into the retained earnings. From the above it should be clear that a high payout ratio involves a low dividend cover.

The actual payout ratio, decided upon by the directors, will be the result of conflicting motives: on the one hand, a high payout ratio is likely to keep shareholders happy and increase the demand for the company's shares, which raises their price and facilitates future issues; on the other hand, the directors will want to set aside funds for further development, especially if external finance is expensive and/or difficult to obtain. There is, however, a body of opinion that favours a 100 per cent payout ratio, i.e., the elimination of self-financing. A well-run company, it is argued, will have no difficulty in raising external funds (including those from its own shareholders), while a badly run company should, in any case, not be allowed to use funds belonging to the shareholders.

dividend[2]   Rückvergütung

The consumer co-operative societies pay a dividend - colloquially referred to as a 'divi' - to their members. This dividend is not a return on capital invested, but comes in the nature of a rebate calculated at a specified percentage (two to three per cent) on the total amount of purchases by a member during a year.

docker   Hafenarbeiter

A docker is a worker who is employed in loading and unloading ships in the docks (port area).

docks   Hafenanlagen

The term 'docks' is often used in a generic sense to describe the range of port basins together with the surrounding port facilities, such as piers, wharves, repairing appliances, offices, etc.. If a ship enters or leaves port, the shipowner has to pay charges for the use of the docks. These charges, which are usually based on the net register tonnage, are referred to as 'dock dues' or 'dockage'.

documentary collection   Dokumenteninkasso

Documentary collection is a method of payment used in international trade under which the shipping documents relating to a particular shipment of goods are released to the importer on payment or acceptance of a documentary draft drawn on him by the exporter. Under this method, an exporter who handles a shipment on a draft basis presents the draft together with the shipping documents (e.g., bill of lading, commercial invoice, insurance policy, etc.) to a bank in his country for collection (the exporter's bank is referred to as the 'remitting bank'). In addition, the exporter must give his bank - on a printed instruction form - complete and precise instructions as to the handling of the collection. The remitting bank, in turn, forwards the documents and the draft together with the completed instruction form to its branch, correspondent bank, or some other bank in the buyer's country (collecting bank), advising it whether the documents are to be surrendered on payment or acceptance of the draft, whether the importer is to be allowed to inspect the goods before payment or acceptance, how the collection proceeds are to be remitted (e.g., by air mail, cable, or SWIFT), what is to be done if the draft is dishonoured, etc..

In the case of a sight draft, the collecting bank is instructed to deliver 'documents against payment' (abbreviated D/P). This means that the buyer does not receive the documents, which will enable him to take delivery of the goods from the carrier, unless he has honoured/paid the draft. After payment, the collecting bank remits the collection proceeds to the remitting bank for the credit of the exporter's account.

In the case of a time draft (usually payable a specified period of time after sight), the collecting bank is instructed to deliver 'documents against acceptance' (abbreviated D/A). Under D/A terms, the collecting bank is authorised to release the shipping documents to the buyer only after he has accepted the draft. After payment at maturity, the collecting bank remits the amount to the exporter's account with the remitting bank. In practice, however, the exporter usually does not want to wait until the draft matures and, therefore, asks the collecting bank to discount the accepted draft.

A documentary collection offers the exporter more security than a clean collection or payment on open account terms, because the documents - giving the buyer the right to obtain the goods from the carrier or dispose of the goods while they are still in transit - are not released to the buyer without payment or acceptance of the draft. In other words, by instructing the collecting bank to deliver 'documents against payment' or 'documents against acceptance' the exporter keeps control of the goods through the collecting bank until the buyer has paid or has incurred the obligation to pay at a specified future time. Although a documentary collection offers the exporter a high degree of security, he may suffer losses resulting from the buyer's failure to take up the documents/goods (risk of non-acceptance). Such failure, which is, of course, a breach of contract, may be due, for example, to the buyer's inability or unwillingness to pay, a decline in the market price of the goods, or an increase in tariff rates. If, in such a case, the exporter is not able to find another buyer, the goods have to be returned to him or, if this should be impossible because of their perishability or the high costs involved, they have to be sold by public auction. Occasionally an importer, after failing to take up the documents, avails himself of the services of a "dummy" to buy the goods cheaply at the auction.

documentary draft · Dokumententratte

A documentary draft is a bill of exchange accompanied by shipping documents, such as the bill of lading, the commercial invoice, the certificate of origin, the marine insurance policy, etc.. A bill with no shipping documents attached is referred to as a 'clean draft'.

Documentary drafts are used in connection with documentary collections (D/P and D/A) and documentary credits. The main purpose of using a documentary draft under collection arrangements is to ensure that the buyer will not be given the documents (and, therefore, the right of disposal of the goods) without having first paid or accepted the attached bill of exchange in accordance with the arrangement between the parties. Under a documentary letter of credit, the advising bank or the issuing bank will pay or accept the exporter's draft only on presentation of the shipping documents called for by the letter of credit and attached to the draft.

documentary letter of credit   Dokumentenakkreditiv

A documentary letter of credit (L/C), also known as a 'documentary credit', is an arrangement for payment in international trade under which a bank, acting at the request and in accordance with the instructions of a customer (the foreign buyer), undertakes to pay, either directly or through another bank, a certain sum of money to a third party (the exporter) against presentation of specified shipping documents. Most documentary credits are subject to the 'Uniform Customs and Practice for Documentary Credits', issued by the International Chamber of Commerce.

Where payment under a documentary credit is arranged, the procedure in simple outline is as follows:
1. The exporter and the foreign buyer enter into a contract of sale calling for settlement by documentary credit.
2. The foreign buyer (the 'applicant', or 'principal') instructs his bank (the 'issuing bank', or 'opening bank') to issue/open a documentary credit in favour of the seller (the 'beneficiary') on the terms specified by the buyer in his instructions to the issuing bank.
3. The issuing bank sends the L/C to a bank in the exporter's country (the 'advising bank'), instructing it to advise/notify the beneficiary of the terms against which payment will be made, in particular of the documents required under the L/C.
4. The exporter ships the goods and surrenders the required documents to the advising bank.
5. In the majority of cases, the advising bank pays, or undertakes to pay, the purchase price.
6. The advising bank forwards the documents to the issuing bank, which releases them to the importer to enable him to take delivery of the goods from the carrier.
(For further details on the steps involved see: "confirmed irrevocable documentary letter of credit").

It should be clearly understood that, apart from payment in advance, the most favourable method of payment for the exporter is payment by documentary letter of credit. The main characteristic is that, in documentary credit operations, all parties concerned deal in shipping documents and not in goods. Thus, a documentary L/C is completely separated from the underlying contract of sale, on which the credit requirements are based. Broadly speaking, the exporter's major advantage is that - provided he complies with all the terms of the credit - payment is guaranteed by a bank, which must look to the buyer for reimbursement. The only thing the exporter has to do is present the shipping documents as provided for in the L/C. Consequently, the exporter is independent of the buyer's ability and willingness to pay. The documentary letter of credit practically eliminates both the risk of non-acceptance and the risk of non-payment and is, therefore, safer than documentary collections.

There are four parties to the usual procedure:
1. The buyer: he is referred to as the 'applicant for the credit', because it is he who takes the first step by applying to his bank to open a L/C in the exporter's

favour. It is also the buyer who lays down the terms. If he fails to have a L/C opened as stipulated, the seller is entitled to claim damages for breach of that stipulation.

2. The issuing bank: the buyer's bank must strictly comply with the buyer's instructions and has no authority to do otherwise. The issuing bank can either inform the seller directly that a L/C has been opened in his favour or, as is common in practice, ask a bank in the seller's country to do so. The L/C issued by the buyer's bank may be 'revocable' or 'irrevocable'. A 'revocable credit' may be amended or cancelled at any time without prior notice to the beneficiary and, therefore, offers only little protection to the exporter. By contrast, an 'irrevocable credit' cannot be amended or cancelled by the issuing bank without the beneficiary's consent and, thus, constitutes a definite undertaking on the part of the issuing bank to make payment against presentation of the shipping documents.

3. The advising bank: this is the bank that acts on behalf of, and in accordance with the instructions received from, the issuing bank. As it is the issuing bank that chooses the advising bank, it normally uses its own branch office or correspondent bank in the exporter's country, unless the applicant specifically requests the L/C to be advised through the exporter's bank. If the advising bank receives an irrevocable L/C from the issuing bank, it may act in one of two ways: firstly, it may be instructed merely to advise, i.e., notify, the beneficiary that an irrevocable L/C has been opened in his favour, in which case the L/C is referred to as an 'unconfirmed irrevocable L/C'. Secondly, it may be requested to confirm the credit before notifying the beneficiary, such confirmation constituting a definite undertaking on the part of the advising bank to pay according to the terms of the credit. In other words, when confirming an irrevocable credit, the advising/confirming bank, in addition to the issuing bank, undertakes to make payment against the shipping documents specified in the L/C. In contrast to irrevocable credits, revocable credits are always unconfirmed.

4. The seller: he is also known as the 'beneficiary' of the letter of credit because he is entitled to payment under the L/C provided he complies with the terms of it.

From what has been mentioned above it should be clear that there are three different types of L/C used in practice: 'confirmed irrevocable credits', 'unconfirmed irrevocable credits', and 'unconfirmed revocable credits'. Credits of the kind considered above may or may not call for bills of exchange to be drawn by the exporter, though in Great Britain and in the United States the drawing of bills is common practice. If the L/C is unconfirmed, the bill would normally be drawn on the foreign issuing bank, and if it is confirmed, then the bill would be drawn on the confirming bank. The bank on which the draft is drawn and which, therefore, has to pay according to the terms of the credit is called the 'drawee bank' or 'paying bank'.

For the buyer's bank to be able to issue a L/C in favour of the exporter, the buyer has to complete an Application to Open a Documentary Credit, which contains the full terms and conditions under which the beneficiary will receive payment. The instructions given to the issuing bank will cover:

1. whether the credit is to be issued as revocable or irrevocable, and whether the advising bank is to be requested to add its confirmation;
2. the name and address of the beneficiary;
3. the name of the bank on which the draft (sight draft or time draft) is to be drawn;

4. details of the shipping documents required in evidence of the transaction (e.g., clean on-board bill of lading issued to order, blank indorsed; rail or road consignment note; air waybill; insurance policy or insurance certificate; commercial invoice; customs invoice; consular invoice; certificate of origin; packing list; etc.;
5. a description of the goods, including details of the quantity and the unit price;
6. the place of shipment and the place of destination;
7. the total credit amount and the currency of the credit;
8. the expiry date, i.e., the date by which the beneficiary must present the shipping documents.

When the advising bank receives the letter of credit from the issuing bank, it usually rewrites the L/C on its own stationery and forwards the rewritten version to the beneficiary. A L/C which has been rewritten may run something like, "We are instructed by (name of the issuing bank) to advise you that they have issued/ opened their irrevocable credit in your favour for account of (name of the applicant)....".

For the exporter to get payment from the paying bank (advising/confirming bank or issuing bank), he must comply with the terms laid down in the credit. If, for example, the documents presented by the exporter to the paying bank are not strictly in conformity with the terms of the credit (e.g., the B/L is not "clean"; the B/L is not marked "on board"; the invoice value exceeds the amount available under the credit; the insurance policy or certificate does not stipulate coverage of risks as required by the credit; etc.), the bank is entitled to reject them, in which case the exporter should immediately contact the foreign buyer and ask him to instruct the bank to accept the documents as presented. If the documents presented appear to be in conformity with the terms of the credit, the paying bank has to accept them and honour the draft drawn on it by the exporter, even if he has shipped wrong or inferior goods and has falsified or cleverly forged the documents.

document of title

Traditionspapier, Dispositionspapier

A document of title (also called a 'document of title to goods') is a document which serves as proof of the possession of goods, authorising the possessor of the document to receive the goods represented by such a document. In commercial practice, the most important documents of title are the bill of lading and the warehouse warrant.

As can be seen from the above definition, a document of title is a symbol of goods; consequently, possession of the document is equivalent to possession of the goods, and transfer of the document has the same effect as delivery of the goods themselves.

The two main characteristics of a document of title are: first, transfer of the document acts as a symbolic transfer only of the possession of the goods, but not necessarily as a transfer of the property in them. Transfer of the document passes such rights in the goods as the parties intend to pass. The following example is meant to illustrate this: if a consignor ships goods to a foreign consignee on consignment, it is evident that the consignor, by delivering the bill of lading to the consignee, intends to pass only the right to claim delivery of the goods from the shipowner, but not the property in them. This shows quite clearly that, in this

141

context, the term 'title to the goods' means simply 'rights in the goods', without specifying what rights are actually meant.

Second, only the holder of the document may claim delivery of the goods - in the case of a B/L, from the shipowner (or his agent), and in the case of a warehouse warrant, from the warehouse keeper, who, in turn, are entitled to deliver the goods only on presentation of the document.

In commercial practice, documents of title also play an important role as security for overdrafts, bank loans, etc.. For example, a bank may advance money on the security of the goods in storage, in which case the borrower/depositor has to hand over the warehouse warrant as security to the bank, which can rely on the warehouse keeper not to part with the goods without the depositor presenting the document.

documents against acceptance   Dokumente gegen Akzept

'Documents against acceptance' (D/A) is a form of documentary collection under which the shipping documents relating to a shipment of goods are released to the importer on acceptance of a documentary time draft drawn on him by the exporter.

'Documents against acceptance' offers the exporter less security than 'documents against payment' or 'cash against documents', as he has control over the goods only until the buyer has accepted the draft, and not until payment has been made.

documents against payment   Dokumente gegen Zahlung

'Documents against payment' (D/P) is a form of documentary collection under which the shipping documents relating to a shipment of goods are released to the foreign buyer on payment of a documentary sight draft drawn on him by the exporter. D/P is a typical transaction on concurrent terms, i.e., the foreign importer receives the documents (bill of lading, etc.) and, therewith, the right of control of the goods only against payment of the draft.

The procedure for an export transaction on the basis of a sight draft for collection includes the following steps:
1. An exporter and an importer sign a contract of sale providing for the shipment of goods payable by a sight draft for collection.
2. The exporter draws a sight draft for the purchase price of the goods on the importer, completes the instruction form obtained from his bank, prepares the documents, and ships the goods.
3. The exporter presents the shipping documents (e.g., bill of lading, commercial invoice, insurance policy or insurance certificate, certificate of origin, etc.), the draft, and the completed instruction form to his bank (remitting bank).
4. The remitting bank forwards the documents, the draft, and the exporter's instructions to its branch office or some other bank in the buyer's country (collecting bank).
5. The collecting bank notifies the importer
    (i) that the documents covering the contract goods have arrived,
    (ii) that the shipment is covered by a sight draft, and
    (iii) that, in accordance with the exporter's instructions, the documents will be delivered to the importer on payment of the draft.

6. The importer visits the collecting bank to settle the transaction. According to the exporter's instructions, the collecting bank
    (i) collects the face value of the bill, bank charges, and charges for the remittance of the collected funds to the remitting bank, and
    (ii) releases the documents to the importer.
7. Since the documents give their holder the right to control the goods, the importer takes delivery of the goods from the carrier.
8. The collecting bank remits the collected funds to the remitting bank, which, in turn, will credit them to the exporter's account.

In practice, the contracting parties may also agree that payment has to be made on 'cash against documents' terms. 'Cash against documents' (abbreviated C.A.D.) is very similar to 'documents against payment'; it differs from the latter only in that it does not involve the drawing of a sight draft. In other words, under C.A.D. terms, the collecting bank is instructed to release the shipping documents to the importer on payment of the invoice price of the goods, and not on payment of a sight draft.

double taxation   Doppelbesteuerung

In general, double taxation means that the same tax object/tax base (i.e., the objective basis on which a tax is imposed, such as a person's income or a company's profit) is taxed twice in the same period. Double taxation may occur because the same base is assessed twice by the same tax jurisdiction, or because it is assessed by two competing tax jurisdictions.

An example of the first kind of double taxation, common in many countries (e.g., in the United States), is the taxation of company profits. A company is liable to corporation tax on its profits, and, when they are distributed to the shareholders in the form of dividends, the same profits are subject to personal income tax in the hands of the shareholders. Double taxation of the second kind often occurs through the imposition of taxes on the same base by different levels of government, as is the case with federal and state taxation in the United States. Another example of the second kind is international double taxation, where the same tax base is assessed in two different countries. International double taxation may result particularly from a double residence (that is, individuals and companies have a residence also in a foreign country, in which case they will, as a rule, be subject to tax on world-wide income in both countries) or from income arising in a foreign country. International double taxation may be mitigated or avoided by double taxation agreements between countries.

down payment   Anzahlung

The term 'down payment', or 'deposit', is especially used in connection with instalment sales, where it refers to a certain percentage of the purchase price of goods which has to be paid on delivery, the balance being payable in periodic instalments until the full amount has been paid off.

In international trade, the term 'down payment' is applied to that portion of the contract price which the buyer is required to pay to the exporter on or before the delivery of goods or the performance of services, e.g., 5% of the contract price when the contract is signed, and 10% on delivery of the goods. The remainder may be subject to a variety of credit terms.

143

drawee (of a bill of exchange) (Wechsel-)Bezogener

The drawee of a bill is the person on whom the bill of exchange is drawn. He is the person instructed by the drawer to pay a specified sum to, or to the order of, the payee, or to bearer.

In the case of a sight bill, the drawee is primarily liable to pay the bill when it is presented for payment, without any prior presentation for acceptance. In the case of a time bill, however, he is under no liability on the bill unless he accepts it, thus becoming the acceptor and assuming primary liability on the bill.

drawee (of a cheque) (Scheck-)Bezogener, das bezogene Kreditinstitut

The drawee of a cheque is the bank which is instructed by the drawer to pay a certain sum of money to, or to the order of, the payee, or to bearer. In contrast to the drawee of a bill of exchange, the drawee of a cheque is always a bank.

drawer (of a bill of exchange) (Wechsel-)Aussteller

The drawer of a bill is the person who makes out the bill of exchange. He draws the B/E on the drawee, instructing the latter to pay a specified sum of money to, or to the order of, a named person (payee), or to bearer. In the case of a bill to one's own order, the drawer is also the payee. The act of making out a bill is known as the 'drawing of a bill'.

Like the indorser(s), the drawer is secondarily liable on the bill. Consequently, if the bill is dishonoured, the drawer and all indorsers become liable for its payment.

drawer (of a cheque) (Scheck-)Aussteller

The drawer of a cheque is the person who makes out the cheque. He draws the cheque on the drawee bank - with which he must have a current account -, instructing the latter to pay the sum stated to, or to the order of, a named person (payee), or to bearer. The drawer is permitted to make out cheques up to the amount standing to the credit of his current account, or up to the overdraft limit, if any.

dumping Dumping

Dumping refers to the practice of selling a product in a foreign country at a price lower than that charged for the same product in the home market in order to gain a competitive advantage over other suppliers. To make the prices comparable, export packing, freight, insurance, etc., have either to be added to the domestic price or deducted from the export price. The General Agreement on Tariffs and Trade (G.A.T.T.), which almost all the world's major trading nations have signed, prohibits this practice and provides for a defence against it through higher tariffs. Charges of dumping, however, are difficult to prove. This is especially true when the exporter's government subsidises exports, which enables the exporter to cut his export price. Whereas an individual firm dumps its product abroad mostly for competitive reasons, a government will encourage this practice for political or balance-of-payments reasons.

The most common measure to counteract dumping in the importing country is the imposition of a countervailing duty. This is an import tax levied on a commodity sold at a dumping price, irrespective of whether the exporter has been paid a subsidy or not. The main purpose of a countervailing duty is to place the imported goods on an equal footing with other imports and with domestic products. In the case of subsidised exports, for instance, the countervailing duty usually equals the amount of the subsidy. For example, such a duty is provided for in the U.S. tariff legislation, but its imposition requires elaborate proceedings to prove that dumping does in fact exist.

duplicating   (mechanische) Vervielfältigung

Copies, which are frequently required in large numbers in the modern office, can be produced by various methods. Duplicating is one of them. In contrast to (photo)copying, where copies are produced straight from the original, duplicating requires a master copy or stencil as an intermediary step. In the case of spirit duplicating, the master is prepared on a sheet of glossy paper backed by a carbon paper with the coated side up to face the master. The master copy can then be used on the duplicator to run off 200 to 300 copies. In the case of stencil duplicating, the material to be copied is typed on a waxed sheet (cutting the stencil) after the typewriter ribbon has been disengaged. The stencil is inserted in the duplicator, and ink is forced through the incisions of the stencil to form the required image.

E

ecology   Ökologie

First coined by the German zoologist Ernst Haeckel in 1866 as a technical term to denote that division of biology which deals with the relations between organisms and their environment, the word 'ecology' has, from the 1960s onwards, spread rapidly into common usage. It now has a wider meaning and includes all sorts of scientific, educational, and even political activities, aimed at protecting the environment from pollution which might unsettle the delicate ecological balance of a region or of the earth as a whole, thus threatening the survival of mankind itself.

"Ecological thinking" in this wider sense means thinking in terms of: conservation of nature rather than ruthless exploitation; organic farming rather than energy-intensive agribusiness, based on toxic pesticides and heavy machinery; truly durable consumer goods rather than built-in obsolescence; decentralisation rather than concentration of production and decision-making; conservation and efficient use of energy rather than continuing waste; environmentally benign, renewable flow energies (solar, wind, water) rather than exotic energy technologies, such as coal liquefaction, nuclear fission and fusion, or solar satellites; certain changes in life-style; man's position as an integral part of nature rather than its dominator.

As the translation of these concepts into reality may sporadically bring about some economic hardship (e.g., redundancies in heavily polluting industries), a fundamental contradiction between ecology and economy has been erroneously construed by some traditional ideologists. Etymologically, however, both words derive from the same root, viz., Greek oikos = house, and both mean "the science of the management of the house". And if it is the task of the economy to secure material well-being, long-term implications must no longer be ignored. If certain economic activities prove to be counter-productive in the long run (e.g., because they damage our biosphere), then the economy is failing to fulfil its avowed task. Economy and ecology could thus be regarded as two facets of one and the same conception, viz., the promotion of the material well-being of humankind, and ecology could be defined as the long-term aspect of economy.

economic indicator   Konjunkturindikator

Economic indicators (U.S.: 'business indicators') are statistical series sensitive to changes in the level of economic activity. They may be classified into three types on the basis of their relationship to the timing of general economic fluctuations as measured by the gross national product.

The most interesting variety are the 'leading indicators', such as new orders for capital goods, which "lead" turns in the trade cycle, i.e., they rise or fall in advance of marked changes in economic activity. Leading indicators play an important role in forecasting and are used to predict changes in the economic situation. 'Coincident indicators' change at the same time as the level of economic activity (e.g., industrial production), while 'lagging indicators' are supposed to move up or down after general economic activity has altered its course. In many countries, unemployment is a lagging indicator, because firms tend to hang on to their workers until the situation gets really bad and tend to hire new workers only when the recovery is in full swing. From the last example it should be clear that the relationships between movements in the gross national product and in the economic indicators are empirical, may differ from country to country, and may change with time.

economic policy   Wirtschaftspolitik

Economic policy comprises all measures planned or taken by a government to regulate the economic affairs and, ultimately, the economic welfare of a nation or other administrative unit. Economic policy may take the form of direct intervention in the economy (e.g., price controls, subsidies, taxation) or of indirect intervention by changes in the legal, or even constitutional, framework of economic activity (e.g., antitrust law, company law, laws regulating public finance). Direct intervention usually aims at achieving some short-term goal (e.g., price stability), while indirect intervention generally implies a somewhat longer-term perspective (e.g., economic growth, redistribution of incomes, etc.).

The proper conduct of economic policy requires in principle the following steps: determining the goals, analysing the present situation, selecting suitable instruments to achieve these goals, arranging for the instruments to be applied, and, finally, checking the results and taking corrective action if necessary.

The traditional goals of economic policy are: price stability, full employment, economic growth, an ever increasing volume and variety of goods and services, balance-of-payments equilibrium, redistribution of income. In the present circumstances, most people would, however, regard this list as woefully inadequate, and would supplement it by adding protection of the environment, a careful use of resources, and, perhaps rather vaguely, although not less pertinent, an improvement in the "quality of life".

One problem about these goals, which are basically determined outside the economic sphere by a political process, is that many of them are not compatible with each other and are, therefore, subject to trade-offs. The classic example is the trade-off between price stability and full employment. In many circumstances, a low rate of inflation can be achieved only by deflating demand and, therefore, at the expense of full employment. But there are many others: for example, if we take the protection of the environment really seriously, we shall have to sacrifice some economic growth - at least some of the traditional, purely quantitative expansion, which has so far dominated the list of policy goals.

Economic policy may be classified in various ways. One widely accepted classification is based on the key variable in the economic system that a particular form of economic policy tries to control. In the case of 'fiscal policy', this key variable is aggregate demand, which can be influenced by changes in the volume and pattern of government revenue and government expenditure. 'Monetary policy', on the other hand, tries to control the money supply or the level of interest rates, while in the case of 'incomes policy' the key variable is represented by the various forms of income generated by an economic system. 'Exchange rate policy' tries to control the exchange rate, 'industrial policy' the pattern of industry, and 'regional policy' the spatial distribution of economic activity.

147

All of the foregoing is based on the assumption that the economic system is amenable to outside intervention and can actually be guided in the direction laid down by the policy makers. There are some economists who would question this assumption and maintain that the economy develops according to its own laws and should, therefore, not be tinkered with. Although the number of people subscribing to this radical view may be small, many seem to have become alive to the limitations of economic policy-making, at least to the extent that they do no longer believe in "fine tuning", i.e., in the possibility of achieving the economic policy goals with any degree of precision.

economics[1]   Volkswirtschaftslehre

Economics, like any other science, tries to make sense of the field of objects it investigates, i.e., it tries to understand what makes the economy, or some part of it, tick. This task involves identifying, describing, quantifying, and correlating such economic phenomena as production, saving, investment, consumption, prices, employment, unemployment, to mention only some of the more important elements, with a view to developing a coherent picture, or model, of the economic system. For this purpose, it is necessary to set up hypotheses and test them against the facts, which in economics basically means observation and collecting statistics, since it is not possible to conduct controlled experiments.

The analysis can be carried out at different levels of aggregation. Macro-economic theory deals with such broad aggregates as gnp, the general price level, national saving, etc., while micro-economics is geared to small economic units, such as firms, households, and individual industries or markets.

The relationships between the various elements, or variables, of the economic system, i.e., the functions, can either be described verbally, or the economist may use graphs and charts or mathematical symbols. Each of these notations, which can be used either singly or in combination, has its advantages and disadvantages. Modern economic theories are often couched in mathematical terms, a development which a number of important economists consider as having gone too far.

Quite apart from the notation chosen, different schools of economic thought emphasise different elements of the economic system and correlate them in different ways, giving different answers to the questions involved. The neoclassical school (e.g., Paul Samuelson) does not include the distribution of income among the factors determining the level of national income, whereas the Cambridge school (e.g., Joan Robinson) considers it to be extremely important. Monetarists and Keynesians have different views on the role of interest rates and the money supply, and supply-siders do not see eye to eye with Keynesians on the question of investment and consumer demand. Political economists, as the name suggests, stress the interdependence of the political and economic systems and, consequently, the role of trade unions, of employers' organisations, or of power in general, while neoclassical scholars tend to play this institutional aspect down.

This diversity of opinion is, no doubt, partly due to the sheer complexity of the subject-matter, but partly also to the fact that economics is a social science. This means that the economist is part of the social system he describes and tries to understand, and that complete objectivity is impossible. Class interest, ideological background, and similar factors of necessity play a greater role than in the natural sciences.

As has already been mentioned, economics tries to gain insights into the functioning of the economic system. But, obviously, there is also a more practical side to it: economic theory may be applied to concrete economic problems and used as a basis for economic policy-making.

economics[2]

(volks-)wirtschaftliche Aspekte, Rentabilitätsfaktoren

Just as acoustics refers to the science of sounds as well as to the acoustic conditions of a particular room or facility, the term 'economics' may be used to describe the social science defined in the preceding entry as well as the more concrete economic aspects of some activity, or operation. The expression 'economics of advertising' denotes the economic aspects of this promotional activity, in contrast to psychological, moral, or artistic aspects, which may be equally important in a different context. The 'economics of the cash discount' are the considerations governing the granting of discounts for early payment. In the sentence "The economics of coal mining have changed", the term refers to the factors determining the feasibility and profitability of this particular industry. From the last example it can be seen that 'economics' in the more concrete sense of the word takes the plural, while 'economics' as a social science takes the singular (e.g., "economics is a social science").

economic systems

Wirtschaftssysteme

Economic systems can be classified by the method they employ to solve the basic economic problem of satisfying human wants through the allocation of scarce resources. 'Free market economies' rely on the market forces of supply and demand and the price mechanism, 'centrally planned economies' use central planning agencies to do the job, while 'mixed economies' contain elements of both. Obviously, this is an over-simplification. There are many elements of central planning even in the most laissez-faire economies, while, on the other hand, it is impossible to centrally plan all of the millions of transactions that make up an economic system. All economies fall somewhere between the two extremes, some closer to the one, some closer to the other, and are really mixed economies.

From a purely economic point of view, each basic type has its merits and demerits: free market economies are better at meeting the varied demands of the consumer, but less efficient in the provision of public goods (medical care, national defence, etc.). Centrally planned economies may have certain advantages in the heavy industries, the armament industry, and in public goods, but have quite obvious weaknesses in catering for the daily needs of the private consumer. Surprisingly, centrally planned economies have been rather less efficient than free market economies in dealing with environmental problems, although the latters' record in this field is nothing to write home about either. The worst sins against the environment seem to be perpetrated in the eastern bloc countries (atomic power stations, air pollution, leading to acid rain). Apparently, in spite of all the differences, the two systems share certain basic assumptions, one of which seems to be a growth ideology.

But economic systems are not simply economic affairs, they also involve political choices, which may outweigh the more obvious economic considerations. Free market economies are based on private property and on democratic political systems, while centrally planned economies tend to go with authoritarian regimes.

economies of scale   Kostendegression

Economies of scale are the benefits, in the form of lower unit costs, derived from an increase in the scale of some economic activity, like production or selling. A doubling or trebling of output, for instance, will, in many cases, not require a doubling or trebling of inputs, since the increase in the level of output is likely to permit specialisation (of both workers and machines) and will, therefore, result in higher productivity. Mass production techniques, as used in the motor industry, would be a case in point. Another example is an increase in capacity utilisation, where unit costs come down because fixed costs can be spread over a larger number of units produced.

External economies of scale may be derived from the bulk buying of raw materials and components, or may take the form of lower financing charges for raising larger amounts of loan capital.

Of course, there is a point beyond which economies of scale will disappear, or even turn negative (diseconomies of scale). Business units may become inflexible and unwieldy if they exceed a certain size. Capital-intensive, high-volume production methods using what is called "dedicated" (i.e., highly specific) equipment cannot easily be adapted to changes in market demand and product characteristics, which may imply underutilisation or even obsolescence. Moreover, large-scale production may give rise to monopolies and overcentralisation and may, therefore, involve higher social costs, such as high prices and proneness to crises, which may offset the original benefits.

Economies of scale should not be confused with 'increasing returns to scale', which is a much narrower concept and denotes only the benefits derived from a proportionate increase in all inputs.

economy[1]   (Volks-)Wirtschaft

The economy is a subsystem of the socio-political system and comprises economic institutions (manufacturing firms, banks, railways, retail shops, etc.) and economic activities (production, buying and selling, lending and borrowing, and so on).

The term 'economy' normally refers to the economic system of a particular country, although there is evidently also a world economy, and, at a lower level of aggregation, there are regional economies, and smaller economic units, such as business firms. The latter, which are referred to as 'Betriebswirtschaften' in German, are, however, not normally classified as 'economies' in British and American usage.

Historically, the economy as a distinct subsystem is of fairly recent origin. In the Middle Ages, for instance, economic matters were much more closely linked with social life as a whole and subject to customs and the like (e.g., in the guild system). The emancipation of the economic systems is one of the important characteristics of modern times.

The main task of the economy is the satisfaction of human wants through the efficient and equitable allocation of scarce resources. This, however, does not mean that all the participants actually pursue this goal. In fact, the motivation of those participating in the economic process, most conspicuously that of business men, is far from being so altruistic and is dominated by self-interest (i.e., the profit motive). Adam Smith was obviously not right in assuming that these - often conflicting - interests are guided by an invisible hand to produce the best possible overall result. Private self-interest and public interest may, and do, clash in many areas, and the market may fail to prevent injustice and a waste of resources ("market failure", e.g., poverty, pollution, unemployment).

In view of the complex nature of modern economic systems, it is not surprising that they should not always function properly: there are (short-term) cyclical problems, (long-term) growth problems, structural problems, to mention only the most obvious ones.

economy[2]

Einsparung,
Sparmaßnahme,
Wirtschaftlichkeit

The term 'economy' may also refer to an act or instance of saving, or, to put it in a slightly different way, to the careful use of resources. A firm, for instance, may practice economy (or make economies) by eliminating waste and cutting costs to the absolute minimum wherever possible. It may economise on raw materials, on factory supplies, such as fuel and lubricants, and on labour; or it may make economical use of office space or reduce lighting expenses and other overheads.

Economies of scale are the savings (in the form of lower unit costs) attributable to large-scale operations.

ecosphere

Ökosphäre,
Biosphäre

The ecosphere, or biosphere, is the zone of our planet in which all living things exist and interact. As there is life in and on the ground, in the water, and in the air, the ecosphere can be said to comprise parts of the lithosphere (the solid portion of the earth, i.e., soil and rocks, from Gk. lithos = stone), of the hydrosphere (the water bodies of the earth), and of the atmosphere.

If the earth were the size of an apple, the ecosphere would be no thicker than the skin. It extends from a thin layer of usable atmosphere (about 7 miles high) to a few miles into the earth's interior and is thus a relatively thin film enclosing the planet, an intricate film of life which contains all the water, minerals, oxygen, carbon, phosphorus, and other chemical building blocks necessary for life. These chemicals must be recycled again and again for life to continue, because essentially no new matter enters or leaves the earth.

The intact survival of the ecosphere has in the last few decades been increasingly threatened by technological developments which are poisoning it with the waste products of the chemical and nuclear industries, of agribusiness, and of various combustion processes in the domestic, industrial, automotive, and electricity-generating fields.

elasticity   Elastizität

Elasticity is a concept used in economic theory to describe and to measure the responsiveness of one economic variable (the dependent variable) to changes in a second economic variable (the independent variable). The price elasticity of demand, for instance, measures the change in the demand for a commodity caused by a change in its price. But there are many other types of elasticity: e.g., the income elasticity of demand, the price elasticity of supply, the supply elasticity of price, the elasticity of substitution.

Generally speaking, the dependent variable may be 'perfectly elastic', i.e., an infinitesimal change in the independent variable will lead to an infinitely large change in the dependent variable; it may be 'relatively elastic', i.e., a change in the independent variable will cause a more than proportionate change in the dependent variable; it may have 'unitary elasticity', where a change in the independent variable leads to an exactly proportionate change in the dependent variable; furthermore, the dependent variable may be 'relatively inelastic' (i.e., rigid), showing a less than proportionate change; finally, it may be 'perfectly inelastic', i.e., it shows no response to changes in the independent variable, however large.

Elasticities are calculated by dividing the percentage change of the independent variable into the percentage change of the dependent variable (ignoring signs). If, for instance, a 1 per cent decrease in price results in a 2 per cent increase in the quantity demanded, the price elasticity of demand is said to have a value of two.

electronic banking   elektronische Zahlungsverkehrs- und
                                   Informationsleistungen

Electronic banking can be defined as the use of computers and telecommunications technology in the performance of banking services with a view to eliminating paper-based records and allowing the customer direct access to bank payment and information systems. Since from the marketing point of view the last aspect is particularly important, electronic banking is often dubbed 'self-service banking'.

The main elements of electronic banking are electronic funds transfers; the provision of automated teller machines and home banking facilities to retail customers; and corporate cash management services, offered to wholesale customers.

Every user of self-service banking facilities receives a plastic card and a personal code (PIN - personal identification number), which he needs to operate a terminal.

electronic funds transfer   elektronischer Zahlungsverkehr

The term 'electronic funds transfer' (EFT) covers any transfer of funds initiated through a customer- or teller-operated electronic terminal (ATM, POS terminal, etc.), through a telephone or similar instrument, or through a computer. The messages originated by these devices either instruct/authorise a financial institution to debit or credit an account or cause these entries to be made automatically. EFT, therefore, is a fast and paper-less type of payment service, which has to be distinguished from transfers originated by cheque, bank draft, credit transfer form, or similar paper instruments.

The most obvious benefits offered by EFT systems are an increase in speed and a tremendous reduction in paperwork.

electronic mail   elektronische Post

Electronic mail involves the transmission of text from a word processor or similar device to another. The messages can be transmitted either over public (Teletex) or private networks (intra-office or intra-company).

Electronic mail is much faster (up to fifty times) and more efficient than Telex. Electronic mail systems can produce soft or hard copies and may feature electronic mail boxes, which will store incoming messages until they are called up.

employment office   Arbeitsamt

An employment office is a facility run by a government agency (e.g., Employment Service Agency in the U.K., Department of Labor in the U.S.A.) where people seeking employment (job-seekers) are given information about existing vacancies. The term has completely ousted the older 'labour exchange' and is itself being replaced in the U.K. by the more fashionable 'jobcentre'.

energy conservation   Energiesparen

Energy conservation is the generic term applied to any measures directed at reducing our enormous energy consumption, preferably without considerable sacrifices in our standard of living. Energy conservation is made possible by means of technological innovations which increase energy efficiency by eliminating some of the waste that is the hallmark of our present energy systems. Thus, the energy efficiency of the typical motor car is still pathetically low, as is the efficiency of thermal power-stations: fossil fuel plants lose as much as 60 per cent of their energy input as waste heat, and the Dürnrohr plant has been called a giant immersion heater to warm up the river Danube, with more energy lost than the Hainburg plant could ever generate; nuclear power-plants, moreover, lose 70 per cent. Technical improvements can be made by means of fluidised bed combustion, co-generation, and district heating, measures which together could reduce waste heat dramatically from 70 per cent to less than 10 per cent.

In households, most of the heat energy that is lost escapes through insufficiently insulated walls, especially in the case of buildings constructed in Vienna and other cities in the 1950s and 1960s. Here, the solution lies in the retrofitting of old houses with better insulation or in introducing double glazing in areas where single-pane windows have traditionally been predominant, as in many parts of Britain and the U.S..

Energy conservation can also be achieved by changes in life-style, such as by reducing the use of the private car in favour of public transport, by cycling or walking wherever feasible, and by wearing sweaters rather than insisting on overheated rooms in the winter. Also, it is rather mysterious why architects still incorporate unhealthy and energy-devouring air-conditioning systems in their buildings in moderate climate zones (a case in point is the Vienna Wirtschaftsuniversität), when the wisdom of air-condition-based architecture is beginning to be doubted even in tropical regions.

An increasing number of energy experts maintain that conservation measures could bring down overall energy consumption considerably without much "belt-tightening". Conservation is the prerequisite for a soft energy future.

energy crisis   Energiekrise

When the OPEC countries drastically raised oil prices in 1973, this came as a shock to industrialised countries. For the first time, the wisdom of complete reliance on oil was questioned, and the term 'energy crisis' became a household word. Some temporary conservation measures were introduced (in Austria, for example, car owners had to forgo the use of their vehicles for one day per week), but on the whole it appears that the lesson of 1973 still has not been fully understood.

Basically, there are two interpretations of the energy crisis. The first is that in order to make up for the doubtful oil base, energy independence must be sought by relying on other sources, e.g., lots of nuclear power-stations. We need ever more energy because there is a direct correlation between gnp and energy input in any given country, i.e., each per cent of economic growth necessitates a one per cent increase in energy consumption.

This philosophy is based on a future projection of past trends that were valid into the mid-seventies. From the end of the seventies onwards, however, a "de-coupling" of primary energy input and gnp has taken place to an extent that has come as a complete surprise even to optimists. In Austria, for example, overall energy consumption has decreased each year since 1978, the year of the Zwentendorf referendum. Some modest economic growth, on the other hand, has been upheld. At the time of writing (1984), yearly overall energy consumption in Austria is short of 1976 official government forecasts by the equivalent of approximately 8 times Zwentendorf's capacity. Electricity consumption, however, has not been stabilised yet, and there is still a yearly increase, though much smaller than projected. Electricity consumption is now short of 1976 government projections by 1.5 Zwentendorf equivalents.

Similar developments have taken place in many other countries and have supported the second interpretation of the energy crisis, viz., that we should employ all our ingenuity to find ways to manage with much less energy. Energy conservation should be possible by means of technological innovations which increase energy efficiency, and by changes in life-style.

An increasing number of energy experts maintain that if mankind were to decide in favour of a soft energy future, there would be no energy crisis. Conservation measures could bring down energy consumption considerably, and the remaining energy needs could eventually be covered by the environmentally benign, renewable soft energies, such as solar, wind, and water-power. This would mean that energy generation from "violent" processes, such as nuclear fusion, nuclear fission, and the combustion of fossil fuels, could be given up.

environment   Umwelt

The environment is the region, surroundings, or part of nature in which any organism exists. The word is now often used synonymously with 'nature', as in environmental protection.

equity capital   Eigenkapital

The term 'equity capital', or simply 'equity', refers to the owner's (or owners') funds in a business organisation, i.e., to the funds provided by the owner(s) as well as to those internally generated. These funds do not, of course, all exist in liquid form - they may have long been invested in various assets -, but simply represent the proprietary interest(s) in the business organisation.

A firm's equity is recorded in its balance sheet under such headings as "net worth", "shareholders' funds", "stockholders' funds", "shareholders' equity", "stockholders' equity", depending, to some extent, on the type of business organisation involved. In a public limited company, for instance, the shareholders' equity comprises the company's (paid-up) capital, represented by ordinary shares (or by ordinary shares and preference shares), and both capital and revenue reserves. In an American corporation, the corresponding items would be '(paid-up) capital stock' (common stock, and preferred stock if any) and 'retained earnings', occasionally still referred to as 'earned surplus'. Since sole proprietorships and partnerships are not required to separate capital and reserves in this way, the proprietary interests in them are shown under one heading, entitled "proprietor's equity", "partners' equity", or "net worth".

Occasionally, the terms 'equity' and 'equity capital' are used in a narrower sense, in which case they are synonymous either with 'share capital' (U.S.: capital stock) or with 'ordinary share capital' (U.S.: common stock). 'Equities', the plural of equity, refers to 'ordinary shares'.

The relationship between equity capital and loan capital or creditors' funds is a key financial ratio and of critical importance to the financial health of a firm. (see: capital structure)

equity securities   mitgliedschaftliche Papiere,
                                                   Aktien

The term is used rather vaguely to describe either ordinary shares (U.S.: common stock) or both ordinary shares and preference shares (U.S.: preferred stock).

In contrast to debt securities, which represent "creditorship", shares are colloquially said to represent "ownership". From the strictly legal point of view, however, this is not true. A shareholder, by owning shares, does not own the assets of his company, for these are the property of the corporate entity. The ownership of a share entitles the shareholder only to vote at the annual general meeting (AGM) or at extraordinary general meetings (voting right), and to share proportionately in the net profits (dividend) as well as in the distribution of assets on winding up (liquidation dividend). Equities, consequently, represent risk capital: shareholders may lose their investment if the company fails, and the dividend to which they are entitled is contingent upon the profits made. In good years, it might be higher than the interest paid on debt securities, and in bad years, it may be passed, i.e., shareholders may receive nothing.

estimate   Kostenvoranschlag

An estimate is a statement, sent by a contractor to a prospective customer, of the approximate cost at which certain work will be done (e.g., an estimate for the installation of central heating). The estimate, usually based on the specifications sent in by the customer, gives a detailed description of the work to be done and the materials to be used.

Usually, a contractor includes a cost escalation clause in his estimate, which protects him from unforeseen cost increases (e.g., "We want to stress that the price quoted is based on present costs of materials and labour. Should these costs rise we would have to add the increased costs to our price").

eurocheque   Euroscheck

The interbank eurocheque scheme is operated in nearly all European and a few non-European countries (e.g., Israel, Egypt, Tunisia, Morocco). Under this scheme, cheque cards and forms bearing the eurocheque symbol may be used by their holders to draw cash in local currency at member banks abroad. In addition, in some countries, holders of eurocheque cards can make payments by cheque in the appropriate local currency to hotels, shops, etc.. It should be noted that all eurocheque transactions are subject to specified limits per cheque.

Euro-markets   Euro-Märkte

Euro-markets are markets for financial claims, such as bank deposits or bonds, denominated in one of the Euro-currencies. Euro-currencies represent deposits held outside the country which issued the currency. Euro-dollars, for instance, are dollars acquired by a person, a firm, or a bank not resident in the U.S.A. and held outside the U.S.A..

exchange control   Devisenbewirtschaftung

Exchange control, or foreign exchange control, is a system whereby the state controls/regulates some or all purchases and sales of foreign exchange effected by its citizens. The main purpose of exchange control is to ration limited supplies of foreign exchange and to manipulate exchange rates.

In fact, all countries have developed some sort of exchange control system, which, however, differs from country to country. It is true that, in some countries, these controls have been relaxed in recent years. For example, Great Britain abolished all her controls on capital exports in the early 80s, although applications for foreign currency by importers of goods and services and by persons travelling abroad must still be approved.

The agency responsible for exchange control is the central bank. It is assisted in its work by the commercial banks, requiring their customers to complete the necessary exchange control forms, which are then submitted by the banks to the central bank. The commercial banks are allowed much discretion in that they may approve applications themselves up to certain limits, and submit the forms after approval.

exchange rate	Wechselkurs (Devisenkurs, Valutenkurs)

The exchange rate, or rate of exchange, is the price, or value, of a country's currency expressed in terms of another country's currency (e.g., U.S.$1 = AS18; read: "one U.S. dollar equals 18 Austrian schillings", or "there are 18 Austrian schillings to the U.S. dollar").

Generally speaking, an exchange rate may either be fixed by the monetary authority (i.e., the central bank) of the country concerned (fixed, pegged, or official rate of exchange) or may be determined by the free interplay of supply and demand in the foreign exchange markets, without any government intervention (floating, flexible, or fluctuating rate of exchange).

In banking practice, there are different rates for different types of foreign exchange, e.g., a rate for foreign coins, a rate for foreign banknotes, a rate for telegraphic or cable transfers (T.T. rate or C.T. rate), a rate for cheques (cheque rate), etc.. Whereas the English term 'exchange rate' is an inclusive term for all the various rates mentioned above, the German terminology is much more differentiated. The expression 'Wechselkurs' is a collective term for both 'Valutenkurs', which is the rate for foreign banknotes and coins, and 'Devisenkurs', i.e., the rate for sight deposits denominated in a foreign currency.

Banks/foreign exchange dealers always quote two rates (e.g., in Austria, U.S.$1 = AS18.25/18.45): one at which they are prepared to buy a foreign currency, known as the 'buying rate', 'bid rate', or simply 'bid', and one at which they are prepared to sell a foreign currency, the 'selling rate', 'offered rate', or 'offer'. The 'middle rate' is the arithmetic mean of these two rates. It is obvious that the selling rate is higher than the buying rate, because any bank, if it is to make a profit, must sell a foreign currency at a higher price than it pays for it. The difference between the buying and the selling rate, i.e., the bank's margin, is referred to in banking jargon as the 'spread'.

The normal rate of exchange quoted in the market is the 'spot rate', i.e., the rate quoted for immediate delivery of (and immediate payment for) the currency concerned. By contrast, the 'forward rate' is the price of a foreign currency which is bought or sold for delivery and payment at some future time. If the forward rate is above the spot rate, the difference is known as the 'premium', in the opposite case as the 'discount'.

In general, foreign exchange quotations may be either on a direct or on an indirect basis. A 'direct quotation' (in the U.K. called a 'pence rate') gives the number of units of the home currency per unit or 100 units of a foreign currency. In other words, it is the home currency price of a unit or 100 units of a foreign currency (e.g., in Austria, U.S.$1 = AS18.25/18.45). By contrast, an 'indirect quotation' (in the U.K. called a 'currency rate') is the price of one unit of home currency in terms of a foreign currency (e.g., in the U.K., £1 = U.S.$1.68/1.70). Today, in most countries, foreign exchange quotations are made on a direct basis. In the United Kingdom and in the United States, however, all quotations (in the United States except for the pound sterling) are made on an indirect basis.

To simplify matters, all definitions in this book which relate to foreign exchange and exchange rates imply the direct quotation/pence rate. The major aspects associated with the indirect quotation/currency rate are dealt with in detail under the heading of "indirect quotation" elsewhere in the book.

exchange risk[1] - general   Wechselkursrisiko - allgemein

Generally speaking, (foreign) exchange risk may be defined as the possibility of loss or gain arising to an economic unit from movements in exchange rates, irrespective of whether these movements are due to the free interplay of supply and demand or caused by central bank intervention. Experts distinguish between three main types of (foreign) exchange risk: 'transaction risk', 'translation risk', and 'economic risk'.

The transaction risk occurs whenever individuals or organisations are due to receive, or due to make, payment in a foreign currency at a future time. It refers to exchange gains or losses that may arise from the settlement of transactions denominated in a foreign currency. A typical example of a transaction involving the transaction risk is the sale or purchase on credit of goods and/or services invoiced in a foreign currency, such sales or purchases resulting in foreign currency receivables or payables.

Suppose that an Austrian exporter sells goods to a U.S. importer, the invoice price of $10,000 being payable in three months. Assuming that the exchange rate ruling on the date of invoice is U.S.$1 = AS18.00, the Austrian exporter expects to exchange the $10,000 for AS180,000 when payment is received. But what happens if the exchange rate goes up or down in the period between the date of invoice and the date of settlement? If, for example, the dollar has declined to 17.00 schillings by the date of payment, the exporter will get only AS170,000 when converting the invoice amount, i.e., he will make an exchange loss of 10,000 schillings. If, on the other hand, the exchange rate moves in his favour, he will make a corresponding exchange gain.

The opposite is true of an importer of goods and/or services invoiced in a foreign currency. If the value of the foreign currency in terms of the home currency goes down between the date of invoice and the date of payment, the importer will make an exchange gain, and vice versa, because he will need a smaller/higher amount of the home currency to buy the foreign currency amount required for the payment of the invoice price.

It is obvious that all economic units which will have to make payment in a foreign currency are more or less in the same position as an importer. For example, a firm that takes out a foreign currency loan will normally have to (re)pay principal and interest in the foreign currency. On the other hand, those who are due to receive payment in a foreign currency at some future time (e.g., an investor who buys foreign bonds and is to receive repayment of the capital at maturity) are in a position similar to that of an exporter.

The translation risk plays an important role where a multinational group has to prepare a consolidated balance sheet. For this purpose, the foreign subsidiaries' balance sheets, which have to be drawn up in the local currency concerned, must be consolidated with the parent company's balance sheet. Therefore, all assets and liabilities expressed in a foreign currency must be restated in terms of, i.e., translated into, the parent company's currency. The main problem involved is that there are two possible exchange rates that can be used to translate assets and liabilities: the exchange rate prevailing at the time the asset or liability came into existence (the historical rate), or the exchange rate ruling on the balance sheet date (the closing rate). For example, one specific translation method requires all foreign currency-denominated assets and liabilities to be translated at the closing rate. If this closing rate is higher or lower than the closing rate of the preceding period, in other words, if the rate of exchange has risen or fallen in the period between two balance sheet dates, a translation gain or loss will result.

The economic risk is defined as the possibility of a change in the net present value of a firm's expected cash flows due to unexpected fluctuations in foreign exchange rates. This change can be positive or negative, depending on the effect of the exchange rate fluctuations on sales volume, prices, and costs.

In addition, it may be of interest to point out the difference between '(foreign) exchange risk' and '(foreign) exchange exposure'. Whereas the (foreign) exchange risk is the possibility of loss or gain arising from exchange rate fluctuations, the (foreign) exchange exposure denotes the foreign currency amounts which are subject to the (foreign) exchange risk. Thus, one may speak of a U.S.$-exposure, a £-exposure, etc.. On the basis of the three types of (foreign) exchange risk, (foreign) exchange exposure may be classified into a 'transaction exposure', a 'translation exposure', and an 'economic exposure'.

exchange risk[2] - protection from transaction risk (covering)   Wechselkursrisiko - Kurssicherung

The following is a brief outline of the most important methods of neutralising, minimising, or avoiding the transaction risk. The first group comprises preventive and risk-minimising measures, such as invoicing in domestic currency and currency escalator clauses in contracts.

A firm selling goods and/or services abroad may invoice in domestic or in foreign currency. If the invoice price is denominated in the exporter's currency, the foreign buyer has to bear the exchange risk, i.e., he will make any gain or loss resulting from exchange rate fluctuations. This shows that the exporter, by invoicing in his domestic currency, shifts the exchange risk to the importer. If, on the other hand, the importer is in a stronger bargaining position, he may insist on the goods and/or services being invoiced in his currency, which leaves the exporter to bear the exchange risk.

Frequently, the contracting parties agree on a currency escalator clause being included in the contract. The idea is to fix the rate of exchange of the contract currency vis-a-vis the home currency. For example, an Austrian exporter may insist on the following clause being included in the contract: "The invoice price of $...... has been calculated using today's exchange rate U.S.$1 = AS......, and should this rate drop by more than 2% by the date of settlement, we reserve the right to adjust our price accordingly".

The second group comprises more or less all "classic" methods of eliminating the transaction risk, such as forward cover, taking out a foreign currency loan (used by an exporter), buying and depositing foreign currency (used by an importer), discounting foreign currency receivables, and exchange risk guarantees.

Forward cover means that an exporter/importer protects himself against the exchange risk by selling/buying in the forward market the amount of foreign currency which he will receive/have to pay at a future time. Further details are dealt with under the heading of "forward cover".

Another possibility for an exporter who has an account receivable denominated in a foreign currency which he expects to weaken is to take out a loan in the foreign currency concerned for the tenor of the outstanding receivable and to convert the loan proceeds into his home currency at the spot rate. At maturity, the exporter will repay the loan with the foreign currency amount obtained on collection of the invoice price. By immediately selling the loan proceeds spot for his home currency the exporter protects himself against any loss arising from fluctuations in the exchange rate between the date of invoice and the date of payment. But by the same token he cannot make an exchange gain either, because he cannot have it both ways.

By contrast, an importer who has an account payable denominated in a strong foreign currency may buy spot the foreign currency amount required to settle the invoice and place it on deposit with a domestic or foreign bank until the date of payment. The importer may also prepay the invoice amount and ask for a cash discount.

If an exporter has a claim against a foreign importer which is evidenced by a bill of exchange or promissory note denominated in a foreign currency, he may discount the bill or note with a bank, thus passing the exchange risk on to the bank.

Since commercial insurers do not provide insurance cover against the exchange risk, the governments of the major industrial countries have introduced for their exporters exchange risk guarantees, which are a form of export credit guarantee. These guarantees, however, are issued only for long-term transactions, where forward cover or other measures are not available.

Finally, it should be noted that none of the methods mentioned above can be considered as the best and most effective one. The decision as to which of these methods should be used in a particular case is influenced by many factors, the most important perhaps being availability and cost involved.

excise tax   Verbrauchssteuer

Excise taxes, or excise duties, are narrow-based sales taxes, i.e., they are imposed on a limited range of commodities. In this respect they differ from V.A.T., which covers a very broad range of goods and services. An excise tax is usually levied on the manufacturers of particular commodities, but it can be shifted to the consumers by including the amount of tax in the selling price (indirect tax). In the U.S.A., for example, the tax is frequently paid by the purchase of tax stamps, which must be affixed to the commodity before it enters the distribution channel.

It is a fundamental principle of indirect taxation that a commodity which is subject to duty if imported should be similarly taxed, i.e., bear an excise duty, if produced at home, otherwise the home producer would be given an unfair advantage over his competitor abroad. Great Britain, under the Treaty of Accession to the European Community, has gone one step further and has converted its customs revenue duties into internal taxes chargeable alike on imported and home-produced goods and known as 'excise duties'.

Commodities subject to excise duty usually are widely consumed and have a relatively inelastic demand. In Great Britain, for instance, there are excise duties on tobacco, alcohol (e.g., spirits, beer, wine), hydrocarbon oils, matches and mechanical lighters, betting and gaming, etc.. Excise duties may be either 'ad valorem', amounting to a fixed percentage of the selling price of the commodity, or 'specific', amounting to a fixed sum per measure of quantity. In G.B., the cigarette duty, for example, is based partly on a charge per 1,000 cigarettes and partly on a percentage of the retail price. Duty on other tobacco products is based on the weight of the finished product.

Although excise taxes are considered regressive, placing a larger burden on the poor than on the rich, they offer the advantages of stable revenues and low cost of collection.

exclusive dealer   Vertragshändler

An exclusive dealer is a retailer who has been granted the exclusive dealership by a supplier (e.g., a manufacturer). Under this contractual arrangement, the supplier sells only to that retailer in a given market, and he requires the dealer not to carry competing lines. Like the exclusive distributor, the exclusive dealer acts for his own account, taking title to the goods.

Exclusive dealerships are frequently found in the marketing of new cars (e.g., Ford dealer) and consumer specialty products, such as expensive men's suits.

exclusive distributorship   Generalvertretung

An exclusive distributorship (also called a 'sole distributorship') is a contractual arrangement between a supplier (e.g., a manufacturer) and a wholesaler - frequently referred to as the '(exclusive) distributor' or '(sole) distributor'. The supplier undertakes to sell only to that wholesaler in a given market, or territory, while the distributor is frequently prohibited from handling directly competitive products. In contrast to a sole agent, the exclusive distributor deals for his own account, taking title to the goods.

A foreign merchant who is granted an exclusive distributorship by a manufacturer is called an 'exclusive importer'. He differs from an import merchant in that the latter has no exclusive sales rights.

It should be noted that, in American English, the term 'distributor' is synonymous with 'wholesaler' and does not imply any exclusive rights. Distributors with exclusive rights are always referred to as 'exclusive distributors'. In British English, however, the term 'distributor' always implies exclusive rights (even if used without any qualifying adjective) and, in addition, may also be applied to a retailer.

executive Führungskraft,
Spitzenmanager,
leitender Angestellter

Strictly speaking, executives are top-level managers. In this sense, the term includes not only managing directors, presidents, and all executive directors, but also the top-level managers directly reporting to them, e.g., marketing managers (U.S.: vice-presidents in charge of marketing), purchasing managers, etc.. Particularly in American usage, however, the term is also (euphemistically) applied to managers or even clerks at the lower end of the corporate hierarchy, presumably to enhance their self-esteem and motivation without having to raise their remuneration. There are 'field executives', who are elsewhere simply called 'salesmen' or 'sales representatives', and 'account executives', i.e., employees of banks or advertising agencies responsible for a particular client or group of clients.

The term can also be used as an adjective - this was actually its original use - in such compound words as 'executive suite', 'executive jet', and, yes, 'executive wash-room', to denote things related or belonging to top-level managers.

expense Aufwand

In accounting, expense may be defined as the use and consumption, expressed in terms of money, of goods and services by a business enterprise in the process of generating revenues. According to U.S. accounting practice, expenses are classified into 'operating expenses', 'non-operating expenses', and 'extraordinary expenses'.

Operating expenses, or operating costs, are expenses incurred by a firm in carrying out its ordinary operations. A frequently used classification of operating expenses is a "functional" one. The three most widely recognised items are (i) cost of goods sold; (ii) selling expenses (i.e., expenses directly related to the sale and delivery of goods or services, such as salesmen's salaries, commissions, travel expenses, advertising expenses, collection costs); and (iii) general and administrative expenses (i.e., expenses incurred in the general direction of an enterprise as a whole; items included vary with the nature of the business, but usually comprise salaries of executives and general-office employees, rent, and other general-office expenses.).

Non-operating expenses, often called 'other expenses', are expenses which cannot properly be classified as operating expenses. They are incurred by a firm in conducting other than its ordinary activities, i.e., they are not directly related to the firm's major revenue-earning operations, although they may be regular and typical. They tend to recur, and therefore are not extraordinary. Typical examples are: interest expense, losses from foreign exchange fluctuations, and losses from the sale of securities.

Extraordinary expenses differ from non-operating expenses by their unusual nature and infrequency of occurrence. According to the AICPA, there are only very few types of expense that would normally be classified as extraordinary, such as expenses due to major casualties (e.g., an earthquake).

Finally, it is worth mentioning - without going into detail - that the English terms 'cost', 'expense', and 'expenditure' are not as clearly defined and separated from each other as the German terms 'Kosten', 'Aufwand', and 'Ausgaben', which makes it difficult to compare them and solve terminological problems.

export credit guarantee

Exportkreditgarantie,
Exportrisikogarantie

Export credit guarantees, which, from the legal point of view, contain elements of both guarantee[2] and guarantee[3], are government-insurance facilities covering risks peculiar to export transactions but not normally covered by commercial insurance. They are given for the purpose of encouraging trade with other countries, and are applicable to both visible and invisible exports.

These guarantees are available to exporters granting supplier credits to foreign buyers, and to banks granting buyer credits to foreign buyers or refinancing loans to exporters.

The risks covered by export credit guarantees are referred to as 'commercial risks' and 'political risks'. Commercial risks include:
1. the risk of insolvency of the buyer (risk of insolvency);
2. the risk of the failure of the buyer to pay the amount due within six months after due date (risk of protracted default);
3. the risk of the failure of the buyer to accept the goods (risk of non-acceptance).

Political risks include:
1. the risk of cancellation or non-renewal of export or import licences;
2. war risks;
3. the risk of expropriation or confiscation of the buyer's firm;
4. the transfer risk; etc..

In the United Kingdom, the administration of the scheme of export credit guarantees is in the hands of the Export Credits Guarantee Department (ECGD), which is a separate government department. In the U.S.A., these insurance facilities are offered by the Export-Import Bank of the United States in Washington, D.C. (usually just called the Eximbank), which is a financially self-sustaining, independent government agency. In Austria, the official export credit agency is the Österreichische Kontrollbank AG, a private bank which has been entrusted by the government with issuing export credit guarantees as the agent of the Austrian Ministry of Finance.

export credit insurance

Exportkreditversicherung

The granting of credit in international trade (supplier credits and buyer credits) involves special risks which are not present in domestic transactions. These risks are broadly defined as 'commercial' and 'political'. Because of the importance of exports to the national economy, the governments of all the major industrialised countries provide export credit insurance in the form of export credit guarantees to their export community.

The purpose of export credit insurance is to give exporters and their financing institutions the assurance that the major part of a credit granted by an exporter (supplier credit) or his bank (buyer credit) to a foreign buyer will be paid, even

163

though the buyer has defaulted. In other words, export credit insurance is intended to minimise, or even eliminate, the special commercial and political risks which are peculiar to export transactions.

export distributor

Generalexporteur

An export distributor is an independent merchant who enters into a contractual arrangement with a manufacturer in his country under the terms of which he is granted the exclusive right of distributing the manufacturer's goods abroad, either generally or in a specified market. In doing so, he deals for his own account, taking title to the goods. An export distributor differs from an export merchant in that the latter has no exclusive sales rights.

Two types of export distribution agreement are in use: under the first type, the distributor agrees to place annual orders of a fixed amount with the manufacturer, and under the second type, he merely agrees to place orders if and when he himself receives orders from his customers abroad. In both cases, the export distributor places the orders in his own name and is personally liable for payment of the price.

exporter

Exporteur

The term 'exporter' is applied to a seller who sends goods out of his country. It covers both export merchants and manufacturers selling direct to foreign customers.

export licence

Exportlizenz

An export licence (American spelling: 'export license') is a document which is obtained from the government giving permission to export specific goods to a particular country. For example, export licences may be needed for military or strategic goods, scarce and essential raw materials, works of art and antiques, various forms of livestock, etc.. The actual list of goods requiring export licences changes from time to time.

export merchant

Exporthändler,
Ausfuhrhändler

An export merchant is an independent firm buying goods from manufacturers and exporting them in its own name and on (for) its own account. This is referred to as 'indirect exporting', as opposed to 'direct exporting', where manufacturers sell direct to foreign customers. Generally, merchants specialise either in markets (e.g., the Caribbean islands) or in types of goods (e.g., medical and surgical supplies). Frequently, they have their own branch and/or sales offices abroad. Export merchants operate in two main ways:
1. they buy goods from manufacturers against the requirements of foreign buyers; or
2. they buy goods on their own initiative and promote their sales abroad.

The manufacturer's main advantages in dealing with export merchants are threefold: first, he can sell the goods to the merchant ex works and receive prompt payment, with the export merchant having to bear the credit risk. Second, the merchant usually arranges all shipping and packing details, and third, bears all risks involved in international trade (e.g., political risks).

EX QUAY (Incoterms 1980)   AB KAI

International code: EXQ

'Ex quay' means that the seller undertakes to deliver the goods to the buyer on the quay (wharf) at the port of destination named in the contract of sale. The seller has to bear the full cost and risk involved in bringing the goods there.

The points where costs and risks pass from the seller to the buyer coincide under both 'ex ship' and 'ex quay' terms, but, under the latter, they have been moved one step further - from the ship on to the quay. The seller not only has to contract for the carriage of the goods, pay the freight, and - if he so desires - take out cargo insurance, but also has to bear the additional risks and costs of unloading.

There are two 'ex quay' contracts in use, namely, 'ex quay (duty paid)' ('ab Kai - verzollt') and 'ex quay (duties on buyer's account)' ('ab Kai - Zoll zu Lasten des Käufers'). In contrast to 'ex ship', under 'ex quay (duty paid)' terms, it is the seller who has to clear the goods for import, which means that he has to provide any import licence at his own risk and expense, and has to pay any import duties, taxes, fees, or charges (including the costs of customs clearance) necessary for importation. Under the clause 'ex quay (duties on buyer's account)', the liability to clear the goods for import is to be met by the buyer instead of by the seller.

EX SHIP (Incoterms 1980)   AB SCHIFF
...(named port of destination)   *...(benannter Bestimmungshafen)*

International code: EXS

'Ex ship' means that the seller must place the goods at the buyer's disposal on board the vessel at the usual unloading point at the named port of destination, and must bear all costs and risks of the goods up to that time.

The difference between an 'ex ship' contract and a c.i.f. contract is twofold. First, under an 'ex ship' contract, delivery of the shipping documents is not equivalent to delivery of the goods, which means that this type of contract requires actual delivery of the goods to the buyer at the named port of destination. The buyer is not bound to pay the purchase price before the goods are actually delivered to him at the stipulated port. Consequently, if the goods are lost in transit, the buyer is not obliged to pay the purchase price on delivery of the shipping documents, and can, in certain circumstances, claim recovery of the price he paid in advance. Second, in contrast to c.i.f. terms, the goods are at the seller's risk during the voyage. Consequently, the seller is under no obligation to the buyer to insure the goods. In cases where the seller actually insures them and they are lost or damaged in transit, the buyer cannot claim the insurance money from the insurance company, because the seller, when effecting the insurance, does not act on behalf of the buyer.

'Ex ship' is similar to C.& F. and 'freight or carriage paid to ...' in that the seller has to bear the costs of carriage, but it differs from these two clauses in that the seller also has to assume the risk of loss of, or damage to, the goods during the carriage.

externalities

externe Effekte,
externe Kosten und Erträge

Externalities, or external effects, are social costs or benefits which are caused by the activities of an industry and are not reflected in the price at which the product is sold: they are costs not borne by those who cause them, and benefits not paid for by the recipients.

For example, two externalities in the generation and supply of electricity for domestic heating are:
1. the costs to the community of SO_2 emissions from fossil fuel power-stations, of radiation from nuclear systems, and of deterioration of river water quality, destruction of wetland forests, etc., owing to hydro-electric schemes;
2. the benefits to the community of replacing dirty domestic fuels with electricity, which is clean at the point of use and thus reduces air pollution there.

It has been suggested that externalities should be "internalised" by working them into the cost structure of a product.

EX WORKS (Incoterms 1980)
...(ex factory, ex mill, ex plantation, ex warehouse, etc.)

AB WERK
...(ab Fabrik, ab Mühle, ab Pflanzung, ab Lagerhaus, usw.)

International code: EXW

'Ex works' means that the seller's only responsibility is to make the goods available at his premises (i.e., works or factory). In particular, he is not responsible for loading the goods on the vehicle provided by the buyer, unless otherwise agreed. The buyer bears the full cost and risk involved in bringing the goods from there to the desired destination. This term thus represents the minimum obligation for the seller.

In particular, the seller must:
1. Supply the goods in conformity with the contract of sale.
2. Place the goods at the disposal of the buyer at the time stipulated, at the point of delivery named. The 'ex works' clause may either contain the address of the premises from which the goods are to be collected or refer only to the town where the seller's works, factory, or warehouse is situated (e.g., 'ex works Liverpool'). If the seller's business is carried on at various premises in the same town, the seller is bound to inform the buyer in time of the local address at which the goods are ready for collection.
3. Bear the cost of checking operations (such as checking of quality, measuring, weighing, counting).
4. Bear all costs and risks of the goods until they have been placed at the disposal of the buyer.

The buyer must:
1. Take delivery of the goods as soon as they are placed at his disposal at the place and at the time stipulated, and pay the price as provided for in the contract.
2. Bear all costs and risks of the goods from the time when they have been placed at his disposal, e.g., the cost of loading the goods on the vehicle; the cost of transport to the place of destination; the cost of cargo insurance; all risks of loss of, or damage to, the goods in transit.
3. Provide any export licence at his own risk and expense, and bear any customs duties and taxes that may be levied by reason of exportation.

F

facsimile transmission

Fernkopieren,
Faksimileübertragung

While transmission by telex or electronic mail is restricted to the set of characters incorporated in the printing or receiving devices used, facsimile transmission (remote copying, telecopying) enables you to send (to "fax", in modern office jargon) exact copies of drawings, documents, and letters (including printed letterheads and logos, and even in Japanese script if necessary). The speed of facsimile machines (remote copiers, telecopiers, telefax transceivers) is comparable to that of electronic mail equipment.

factoring

Factoring

Factoring is a commercial service designed to assist firms selling goods and/or services on credit. Under a typical factoring agreement, a specialised financial institution, the factor, purchases all or a specific group of a firm's accounts receivable without recourse to the firm for credit losses (thus assuming the del credere risk), advances an agreed percentage of the value of the accounts receivable to its client, collects the receivables when they fall due, and frequently performs additional services (e.g., the factor may take over the sales ledger and perform all the necessary accounting operations.) Factoring, in contrast to forfaiting, involves a continuing arrangement, based on a master agreement, and cannot be used for isolated transactions.

Under the type of arrangement described above, where the factor assumes the collection function, the firm will notify its customers on the invoices sent to them that the account has been sold (assigned) to the factor and that payment has to be made to it (notification factoring). Under non-notification factoring, the customer is not aware that the account has been sold. He will, therefore, pay the amount of invoice to the seller, who has to pass it on to the factor.

Factoring, like any other commercial service, does not come free: a factor will make a separate charge for each type of service rendered, e.g., for collection and accounting, for assuming the del credere risk, for making advances on the receivables bought. Factoring, therefore, is quite expensive, but may be well worthwhile for firms whose expansion might otherwise be held up by a lack of working capital.

factors of production

Produktionsfaktoren

Factors of production are the scarce resources used in the process of production. They are traditionally classified into three broad categories: 'land', 'labour', and 'capital'.

Land includes everything that is provided by nature and commands a price (thus, gravitation, although an essential ingredient of production, is not considered to be a factor of production). Labour means people with different physical and mental skills and powers. Capital is taken in its physical rather than its financial sense, i.e., it includes machines, tools, and buildings, rather than money.

These three broad categories are quite useful in surveys of a country's resources. Their usefulness in more specific applications, e.g., in the theory of production, is more doubtful. Here, other groupings have been found more helpful (e.g., specific and non-specific factors). The factors of production have also been criticised for their role in the theory of distribution.

F.A.S. (Incoterms 1980)
FREE ALONGSIDE SHIP
...*(named port of shipment)*
International code: FAS

F.A.S.
FREI LÄNGSSEITE SCHIFF
...*(benannter Verschiffungshafen)*

Under f.a.s. terms, the seller must deliver the goods alongside the vessel named by the buyer, at the named port of shipment, at the date or within the period stipulated. The actual loading of the goods on board ship is the buyer's responsibility. Usually, the seller must place the goods alongside the vessel at the quay; in cases where the ship cannot enter the port, the seller has to provide, and pay for, lighters, which will take the consignment alongside the ship. All costs and risks of the goods pass from the seller to the buyer at the time when they have been effectively delivered alongside the vessel.

In many respects, the seller's and the buyer's duties as well as the costs to be borne by each are exactly the same as under an f.o.b. contract. The main difference is that, unlike F.O.B., it is the buyer who must load the goods on board ship at his own risk and expense. It is also the buyer's responsibility to clear the goods for export, which means that he has to obtain any export licence at his own risk and expense, and pay any taxes, fees, or charges levied because of exportation.

file[1]

(Akten-)Ordner

A file is a cover, or folder, in which letters or other papers are kept together in proper order for reference. Files come in many different shapes and sizes, the most common perhaps being the arch file, in which the letters or papers, with suitable holes punched into them, are secured by means of an arch unit and a compressor.

file[2]

Akt

The term 'file' may also refer to a set of papers or documents concerned with a particular matter, and usually kept together in a special folder, or cover. As an example, there will be a separate file for each project under development in a particular firm, and probably one for the records of each employee.

file[3]

Datei,
Datenbestand

In data processing, the term 'file' is generally used to describe a collection of data, of any form, that is stored beyond the time of execution of a single job. A file may contain program instructions or other data, which may be numerical, textual, or graphical.

In commercial data processing, a file is a set of similar or related records that are treated in the same way. For example, in a sales ledger application, a file might consist of a set of customer name and address records.

filing

Ablage,
Schriftgutablage

Filing is a very important office activity. It involves the storing of papers, documents, reports, business letters, and other items of information according to some predetermined arrangement, so that any item, when required, can be located quickly and conveniently. The emphasis is on the finding (information retrieval), not on the storing, aspect.

Information can be filed alphabetically, by subject-matter, geographically, or by other criteria. Filing systems range from simple box files and filing cabinets to microfilm (or microfiche) and optical disk systems. Computer storage devices, such as flexible and hard disks, magnetic tapes, etc., can also be used for filing purposes.

Filing in a business organisation can be either centralised, i.e., there is only one filing department, which serves the whole organisation, or departmental, where each department has its own filing section.

filing cabinet

Aktenschrank

A filing cabinet is a cupboard with shelves used for storing letters, documents, reports, and other items of information. These papers are kept together in files, which are placed laterally along the shelves of the cabinet, and the contents of each file are clearly indicated on an index strip attached to the spine of the file.

financial management

Kapitalwirtschaft,
betriebliche Finanzwirtschaft

Financial management is concerned with planning, implementing, and controlling the flow of funds into, and out of, a business organisation. In other words, it deals with the raising and allocation of the funds required by the organisation to achieve its objectives. Originally, the emphasis was on the sourcing of funds. In older books on financial management, frequently entitled "business finance", the use of funds was dealt with only perfunctorily. The modern tendency is to regard the two aspects as equally important and to devote considerable space to such topics as the management of working capital, capital project planning, and mergers and acquisitions.

The financial manager is, therefore, first concerned with raising the funds required. A wide variety of sources are available. Each has certain characteristics as to availability, cost, maturity, encumbrance of assets, and other terms imposed by the providers of funds.

Funds may be raised internally (internal finance). The ultimate source of all internal finance is the revenue generated by selling products or capital assets. Sales revenue is partly used up in the current period in the form of cash expenditure on materials, labour services, profit distributions, etc., while what is left over - referred to as the 'cash flow' (equivalent to retained earnings and depreciation) - can be used for investment purposes or to repay borrowed funds. Funds can, however, also be obtained from outside sources (external finance), e.g., from partners or shareholders, or from creditors (creditors' funds). The funds provided by shareholders, partners, or proprietors are called 'owners' funds' or 'equity capital'.

The financial manager must determine the best mix of financing for his firm, always taking into account its ultimate objectives. This involves the question of an appropriate capital structure, especially of the proper relationship between debt and equity and its implications for the return on the firm's equity (see: gearing). But also the problem of maturity, e.g., whether to raise short-term or long-term funds, has to be dealt with.

As has already been mentioned, the modern financial manager is also responsible for the use, or outflow, of funds. Outflows are caused by current expenditure on materials, merchandise, outside services, and labour services. This current expenditure results in inventories and, eventually, in cash sales or credit sales (in the latter case, also in accounts receivable). Furthermore, tax payments, interest payments, payments of profits to shareholders, and similar items have to be taken into account.

Since short-term inflows and outflows cannot be co-ordinated perfectly, a business organisation will need a pool of cash and, maybe, short-term credit facilities to even out discrepancies. This raises the problem of liquidity, i.e., the problem of whether the firm will be able to meet its short-term financial obligations when they fall due.

Outflows of funds are also caused by investment, and the financial manager is, therefore, also concerned with allocating funds to expenditure whose benefits will be realised only in the future. This task involves, among other things, capital investment analysis to test the viability of capital projects in terms of cash flow and return on investment. Finally, mergers and acquisitions (of other businesses), which represent only a special type of investment, have to be considered from the point of view of the allocation of funds.

Managing these inflows and outflows is a complicated task and, like most other management activities, requires careful planning. The planning process in this field is often referred to as 'budgeting'.

financial ratios[1] - general

Kennzahlen der Finanzbuchhaltung - allgemein

Generally speaking, a ratio is the quantitative relationship between two numbers based on how many times one is contained in the other. Ratios can be expressed in a number of ways. For example, the ratio of 6 to 4 (6 : 4) may also be written as

3/2 (i.e., as a simple fraction), 1.5 (i.e., as a decimal fraction), or 150% (i.e., as a percentage). Ratios are, therefore, basically calculated by dividing the second number into the first one, or, to put it differently, by dividing the first number by the second one.

Financial ratios are quantitative relationships between balance sheet items (balance sheet ratios), income statement items (income statement ratios), or between balance sheet and income statement items (interstatement ratios). Financial ratios are computed to obtain information about various characteristics and conditions of firms. For example, the ratio of current assets to current liabilities provides some insights into a firm's ability to meet its short-term debt.

Financial ratios are among the best known and most widely used tools of financial statement analysis. The reasons for their popularity as a means of assessing the performance and financial conditions of business firms are: firstly, they are easy to compute, and secondly, they are much more informative in intertemporal and interfirm comparisons than absolute figures (in other words, they facilitate comparisons with previous periods, other business organisations, or with an industry average). In addition, they provide a convenient means of disclosing information that cannot readily be detected by examining the components of the ratio. It should be noted, however, that the use of ratios in financial statement analysis is not a mechanical process. While it is easy to compute a ratio and compare it with one or another "standard ratio", it is far more complex to interpret its meaning and to relate it to the objectives of the analysis.

It can be seen from the foregoing that ratio analysis involves not only the selection but also the interpretation of the relationships between various balance sheet and income statement items at a given time. An additional aspect of ratio analysis is the selection of proper bench-marks, or standards, for the purpose of comparison. Ratios standing alone are generally meaningless. They must always be compared with standards that are meaningful for the firm being analysed.

The three most common types of standard used in ratio analysis are 'absolute', 'historical', and 'industry' standards. Absolute (or independent) standards are those generally considered as desirable, regardless of the business firm, the industry, the time, the stage of the trade cycle, or the objectives of the analysis. The classic examples are the 2 : 1 standard for the current ratio and the 1 : 1 standard for the acid-test ratio.

The firm's own past performance produces a continuous set of historical standards, which provide a high degree of comparability. On the assumption that the past is indicative of the present and the future, those standards can help the analyst determine whether a firm's position is improving or deteriorating.

Industry standards are widely used in ratio analysis. Many trade associations prepare detailed balance sheet and income statement ratios by size of firm and by geographic location. The problem in using industry standards is that no two business firms are exactly the same.

financial ratios[2] - types

Kennzahlen der Finanzbuchhaltung - Arten

In general, the ratios which can be computed from the various items in financial statements fall into the following categories: 'liquidity ratios', 'long-term solvency ratios', 'turnover ratios', and 'profitability ratios'.

Liquidity ratios are indicators of a firm's ability to meet its short-term obligations when they fall due. Two examples of liquidity ratios are the 'current ratio' and the 'acid-test ratio'.

Long-term solvency ratios are measures of a firm's ability to meet its long-term financial obligations. Some examples are the 'owners' equity to total assets ratio' and the 'total liabilities to owners' equity ratio', frequently referred to as the 'debt-equity ratio'.

Turnover ratios, such as 'accounts receivable turnover' and 'inventory turnover', or 'stock turnover', are measures of asset management efficiency.

Profitability ratios are indicators of a firm's effectiveness in achieving profits in relation to sales volume and investments. Some examples of profitability ratios are the 'profit margin ratios', especially the 'net income to net sales ratio', and the various 'return on investment ratios'.

Some of the most commonly used financial ratios are listed under the headings of "balance sheet ratios", "income statement ratios", and "interstatement ratios".

financial statements

Periodenabschluß,
Jahresabschluß,
Finanzausweise,
Abschluß der Finanzbuchhaltung

Financial statements are financial accounting records drawn up at the end of an accounting period - e.g., annually, quarterly, monthly, or even more frequently - to summarise and present in concise form information contained in the ledgers, journals, working papers, etc., relating to the accounting period under review. In the United Kingdom, financial statements are often referred to as 'final accounts' or, where appropriate, as 'annual accounts'.

Financial statements include the balance sheet, the income statement - referred to as the 'profit and loss account' in the United Kingdom -, the statement of changes in financial position, or funds-flow statement (e.g., cash-flow statement), or any supporting statement or other presentation of financial data derived from accounting records (e.g., ledgers and journals).

In a group of companies, the parent company and its subsidiaries are separate accounting entities and have, therefore, to prepare separate financial statements. In many countries, the parent company is additionally required to consolidate (i.e., combine) each period the financial statements of all group companies into one overall set of financial statements, which are referred to as 'consolidated financial statements' (hence the terms 'consolidated balance sheet' and 'consolidated income statement'). In this case, the parent and its subsidiaries are treated as if they were a single economic unit. Consequently, the preparation of a consolidated financial statement involves eliminating such items as intra-group receivables and payables and intra-group investments.

firm offer

festes (fixes, bindendes) Angebot

Every offer is firm unless it contains a clause to the contrary. 'Firm' means that the offer is binding on the seller. If he makes a firm offer, he undertakes to supply the goods in question at the prices and on the terms stated, provided the offer is accepted within reasonable time, or within the time limit for acceptance fixed by the seller (e.g., "This offer is firm for three days only"; "We cannot leave our offer open for more than 48 hours"; "We offer you firm until Friday next"; "This offer is firm subject to acceptance by 10th June").

A firm offer can be withdrawn at any time before the buyer has mailed his acceptance (order). This holds even if a time limit for acceptance has been stipulated. Once the acceptance has been mailed, the seller can revoke his offer only with the buyer's consent. By contrast, in Austria, the offeror cannot change or revoke his offer after it has been received by the offeree, unless, of course, the latter agrees. This applies also to offers with a fixed time limit for acceptance.

From the legal point of view, it is important to note that only a 'firm offer' is an 'offer' within the meaning of the law of contract, whereas an 'offer without engagement' is merely an 'invitation to treat'. This means that an order placed by the buyer against the seller's firm offer results in a contract of sale, provided that the order is placed on time and constitutes an unqualified acceptance of the offer.

fiscal policy

Fiskalpolitik,
Budgetpolitik

Fiscal policy is the government policy concerned with raising revenue through taxation and other means and deciding on the level and pattern of expenditure with a view to controlling aggregate demand. Tax cuts to stimulate economic activity, increases in taxation to skim off excess purchasing power, and budget cuts to slow down inflation are typical examples of fiscal measures taken by governments. Fiscal policy is normally the responsibility of the Minister of Finance (Chancellor of the Exchequer in the U.K., Secretary of the Treasury in the U.S.A.).

fixed assets

materielles und immaterielles
Anlagevermögen

Fixed assets are assets of a relatively permanent nature which are used in the regular operations of a business and are not intended for sale, or, to put it differently, they are assets that will not be completely used up or converted into cash in the ordinary course of business within one year. (see: depreciation[2])

For accounting purposes, fixed assets, also referred to as 'operational assets', may be classified as follows:
1. Tangible fixed assets: these operational assets may variously be described by the terms 'property, plant, and equipment', 'plant assets', or 'capital assets'. Tangible fixed assets have five major characteristics: they are actively used in operations; are not held as an investment or for sale; are relatively long-lived; have physical substance; and provide measurable future benefits to the business. They may be further categorised into:
    (i) Assets subject to depreciation (depreciable assets), such as buildings, machinery, furniture and fixtures, etc..
    (ii) Assets subject to depletion (depletable assets, also known as wasting assets or exhaustible assets), such as mines, oil and natural gas wells, quarries, timber tracts, etc.. These natural resources are called 'wasting assets' because physical elements are actually removed and cannot be

replaced. (It should be noted that 'depletion' differs from 'depreciation' in that the former implies removal of a natural resource, i.e., physical shrinkage, while the latter implies a reduction in the value of an asset due to use, obsolescence, or inadequacy.)

(iii) Assets not subject to depreciation or depletion (non-depreciable assets or non-wasting assets), such as land for plant site, farms, etc..

2. Intangible fixed assets, such as patents, copyrights, trade marks, goodwill, etc.. An intangible fixed asset is an asset which has no physical substance; its value is, for instance, represented by certain rights which it confers on its owner. Further details are dealt with under the heading of "intangible fixed assets".

The accounting for tangible fixed assets is based on the cost principle and the matching principle. Tangible fixed assets, either acquired by the firm or constructed by it for its own use, have to be recorded in the accounts at cost (i.e., acquisition cost or production cost). Acquisition cost includes the purchase price and all incidental costs incurred in placing the asset into usable condition, such as freight and installation costs. This means that both the purchase price and the incidental costs have to be capitalised, i.e., debited to the asset account. Subsequent to acquisition or construction, tangible fixed assets are carried in the accounts and reported at (i) cost (e.g., land), or (ii) in the case of a limited useful life, at cost less accumulated depreciation or depletion (reflecting continuing application of the matching principle).

From the terminological point of view, it is worth mentioning that the term 'fixed assets' is the equivalent of 'materielles und immaterielles Anlagevermögen', and not, as is often wrongly assumed, of 'Anlagevermögen'. This is because 'Anlagevermögen' consists of 'materielles Anlagevermögen', 'immaterielles Anlagevermögen', and 'Finanzanlagevermögen', whereas fixed assets include only tangible and intangible fixed assets, but not permanent investments.

fixed exchange rate

fester Wechselkurs,
fixer Wechselkurs

A 'fixed' (or 'pegged'/'official') exchange rate may be generally defined as one which, in contrast to a floating rate, is not determined by the free interplay of supply and demand in the foreign exchange markets, but is officially fixed by the monetary authority (i.e., by the central bank) in agreement with the International Monetary Fund. The value so fixed is referred to as the 'parity'.

On a technical level, the rate is fixed by intervention in the foreign exchange markets (open-market operations) and by foreign exchange controls. Under a system of fixed exchange rates, governments have to intervene in the foreign exchange markets to protect the pegged rates of exchange against fluctuations arising from the ups and downs in foreign trade, unpredictable capital movements, or speculative foreign exchange dealings. Consequently, central banks must enter the market and buy or sell the foreign currencies in question with a view to preventing the official rates from falling or rising. In addition, countries may impose controls on some transactions, such as on imports of goods and/or services or on capital movements.

The major advantage of fixed rates is that they promote growth in international trade, because exporters and importers can disregard the exchange risk and calculate fairly accurately the sum they will receive, or will have to pay, in their own currency. On the other hand, a system of fixed rates of exchange requires countries to hold reserves of gold and foreign currencies to be able to intervene in the markets and to finance deficits in the balance of payments.

Nowadays, most exchange rates are no longer fixed. Fixed rates played a major role in the period between the end of World War II and the early 1970s. The basis of a new international monetary system was laid down in 1944 at an international conference held in Bretton Woods, New Hampshire, United States. This conference also led to the creation of the International Monetary Fund (I.M.F.) and of the International Bank for Reconstruction and Development (the World Bank), which were intended to assist in implementing the new system.

Under the Bretton Woods agreement, each I.M.F. member country agreed to fix the foreign exchange value of its currency in terms of the U.S. dollar (some countries in terms of sterling). Each country undertook to intervene in the foreign exchange market to prevent the exchange rate from moving more than 1 per cent above or below the parity. The progressive collapse of the Bretton Woods fixed exchange rate system began with the devaluation of the pound sterling in 1967. Meeting at the Smithonian Institution in Washington, D.C. in 1971, the finance ministers of the I.M.F. member countries agreed to a new pattern of fixed exchange rates. The dollar was formally devalued, while most other currencies were upvalued. The Smithonian agreement allowed a wider range of fluctuations (2.25 per cent on either side of the dollar parity). However, the system failed again. For various reasons, the United States was forced to devalue the dollar again, and by March 1973, the Smithonian agreement - together with the system of fixed exchange rates - was a thing of the past, and most major currencies were floating independently.

floating policy   Abschreibepolizze

The floating policy (also called the 'declaration policy') is a type of cargo policy in (ocean) marine insurance and aviation insurance taken out for recurring shipments. It lays down the general conditions of insurance, e.g., the conditions of cover (insurance of goods in transit by sea may be on an all-risks, f.p.a., or w.a. basis, whereas air cargo insurance is usually on an all-risks basis), the premium rates applicable, but not the particulars of the individual consignments intended to be covered. The policy has no time limit and is issued for a lump sum sufficient to cover recurring shipments, the details of which are declared at a later date. Declarations are made by the insured to the insurer as shipments go forward, and the amount insured is reduced by the value of each declaration. The policy remains in force until the amount insured is exhausted, unless it is cancelled by either party. The floating policy might cover, say, shipments in the aggregate amount of £50,000; when the insured dispatches and declares a consignment of £3,000, the available cover is reduced to £47,000, and when the amount insured is exhausted, the policy is written off. The insured should take out a new floating policy before the sum insured has been fully declared, so that there is continuous cover for further shipments.

Under a floating policy, the insured is required to declare all shipments as they go forward. He cannot elect to insure any shipment elsewhere, nor send it uninsured. Another important characteristic of the floating policy is that the insured must pay in advance a lump sum premium on the full sum insured. When the sum insured has been exhausted, the actual premium is calculated at the agreed rates on the various shipments declared, and a return or additional premium paid if the total due differs from the amount originally paid.

This type of cargo policy is gradually falling into disuse, its function in practice being replaced by the open cover procedure.

floating rate of exchange — flexibler Wechselkurs

A 'floating' (or 'flexible'/'fluctuating') rate of exchange is determined by the free interplay of supply and demand in the foreign exchange markets. In other words, the market price of one currency in terms of another is allowed to move up and down according to the supply of, and the demand for, the currency concerned. Supply and demand are mainly determined by the following factors: exports and imports of goods and services, unilateral transfers, exports and imports of capital, i.e., all long-term and short-term capital flows (e.g., in the form of direct and portfolio investments, including speculative flows).

If, in a free market, demand exceeds supply at a given price, then the price of a particular commodity is bid up until demand equals supply. The opposite would be true of an excess of supply over demand. The same applies to a free foreign exchange market. Since the price of a currency is allowed to adjust continuously so as to equate demand and supply, an overall balance-of-payments deficit or surplus cannot occur.

From the foregoing it can be seen that the principal advantage of floating exchange rates is that they act as automatic regulators of the balance of payments, restoring equilibrium whenever it is disturbed. Consequently, there is no need for central banks to keep foreign currency reserves to finance balance-of-payments deficits, inherent in a fixed exchange rate system. The main disadvantage is that freely floating exchange rates create uncertainty and may discourage trade. The exchange risk to be borne by the exporter or the importer may, however, be covered in the forward exchange market.

If a country's exchange rates are left to be determined by competitive market forces without any government/central bank intervention, this is referred to in economic jargon as 'clean floating'. The main characteristic of the present world-wide monetary system is that, although most exchange rates are no longer fixed, they are not allowed to float freely either. The prevailing system is 'dirty floating', i.e., a compromise between clean floating and fixed exchange rates. This means that most governments/central banks intervene in the foreign exchange market. They influence supply and demand by selling and buying the foreign currencies concerned (open-market operations) to keep their exchange rates at a certain level or to smooth fluctuations, without being tied to any official rate.

An example of a system of jointly floating currencies is the 'European Monetary System' (EMS), which came into being in March 1979. Under this scheme, the currencies of the E.E.C. member countries are not allowed to exceed a defined margin of fluctuation vis-a-vis the other members' currencies. The margin of fluctuation is defined both on a bilateral and a multilateral basis. First, each currency in the EMS is free to float 2.25 per cent above and below the parity fixed in terms of each of the other currencies. In addition, each currency has a central parity, defined in terms of the ECU (European Currency Unit), and is allowed a margin of fluctuation above and below this parity. The ECU - which exists only on the books of the EMS member countries, and not as a circulating currency - represents a weighted basket of all the member currencies, the weight assigned to each national currency being based on the distribution of trade between the members of the Community and on the relative size of the country's gnp. The ECU was originally worth $1.40, but its value varies over time as the member currencies float jointly in terms of the U.S. dollar and other non-member currencies.

flow concept

Stromgröße,
Periodengröße

A flow concept represents an economic variable whose quantity or value is measured over a period of time. Many of the better-known economic variables belong to this group: e.g, sales (quantity sold or revenue received per unit of time), capacity (maximum output per unit of time). The list of flow concepts also includes the gnp, since it denotes the total amount of goods and services produced by a nation's economy during a year or any other span of time. Other examples would be the revenues and expenses as shown in a profit and loss account, or exports and imports of goods, services, or capital, which are recorded in the balance of payments.

F.O.B.[1] (Incoterms 1980)
FREE ON BOARD
... *(named port of shipment)*

International code: FOB

F.O.B.
FREI AN BORD
... *(benannter Verschiffungshafen)*

Under f.o.b. terms, the seller undertakes to place the goods on board a ship at the port of shipment named in the contract of sale. The risk of loss of, or damage to, the goods is transferred from the seller to the buyer when the goods pass the ship's rail.

In particular, the seller must:
1. Supply the goods in conformity with the contract of sale.
2. Deliver the goods on board the vessel named by the buyer, at the named port of shipment, on the date or within the period stipulated, and notify the buyer, without delay, that the goods have been delivered on board.
3. Obtain, at his own risk and expense, any export licence necessary for the export of the goods.
4. Bear all costs and risks of the goods until they have effectively passed the ship's rail at the named port of shipment. These costs include: the cost of transport from the seller's warehouse/factory to the port of shipment; all the handling and shipping charges (e.g., dock dues, wharfage, porterage, lighterage, and similar charges); the costs of any formalities which he has to fulfil in order to load the goods on board; and, in contrast to F.A.S., the loading charges (unless these are included in the freight which has to be paid by the buyer) and any taxes, fees, or charges levied because of exportation. The passing of the risks from the seller to the buyer can best be explained by an example: if the goods are lifted by a crane and are then dropped on the quay or into the water, the seller is responsible for the damage. If, however, the goods

are dropped on the deck after having crossed the rail, it is the buyer who has to bear the loss.

5. Provide at his own expense the customary packing of the goods.
6. Pay the costs of any checking operations (such as checking of quality, measuring, weighing, counting).

The buyer must:

1. At his own expense, charter a vessel or reserve the necessary space on board a vessel and inform the seller of the name of the vessel, and of the loading berth of, and delivery dates to, the vessel. In other words, the buyer must contract with a sea carrier for the carriage of the goods to the port of destination, pay the freight, and inform the seller of the arrangements that have been made.
2. Bear all costs and risks of the goods from the time when they have effectively passed the ship's rail at the named port of shipment, and pay the price as provided for in the contract. The costs to be borne by the buyer include: the port rates falling due when the ship carrying the goods leaves port; the stowage of the goods on board ship; the loading costs to the extent that they are included in the freight; cargo insurance; import duties; and all the landing and delivery charges (e.g., unloading charges; wharfage, porterage, lighterage, etc., at the port of destination; transport charges from the port of destination to the buyer's address).

F.O.B.[2] (Revised American Foreign Trade Definitions 1941) F.O.B.

In U.S. American practice, F.O.B. has become a general delivery term which may be used irrespective of the mode of transport. The Revised American Foreign Trade Definitions contain 6 different f.o.b. clauses, but only two of them are mentioned in the following:

1. F.O.B. VESSEL   F.O.B. SCHIFF
...(named port of shipment)   *...(benannter Versandhafen)*

Under this term, the seller must bear all costs and risks of the goods until they have been delivered on board the vessel at the named port of shipment. F.O.B. VESSEL is the exact equivalent of F.O.B. (Incoterms 1980).

2. F.O.B.   FREI
*...(named place of destination   ...(benannter Bestimmungsort
in the country of importation)*   im Einfuhrland)*

If F.O.B. is used in the form of 'F.O.B. place of destination', it denotes free delivery at that place. The seller must place the goods at the buyer's disposal at the named place of destination. He must bear all costs (e.g., transportation, insurance, customs duties, etc.) to the named place, and he is responsible for any loss of, or damage to, the goods until their arrival at the named place. An important example is 'F.O.B. buyer's warehouse' ('Frei Haus'). Under this term, the seller must bear all costs and risks until the goods reach the buyer's address.

The term 'F.O.B. ...(named place of destination in the country of importation)' is the exact equivalent of 'DELIVERED DUTY PAID ...(named place of destination in the country of importation)' (Incoterms 1980).

F.O.B. AIRPORT (Incoterms 1980)
...(named airport of departure)

International code: FOA

F.O.B. FLUGHAFEN
...(benannter Abgangsflughafen)

In relation to air transport, the expression F.O.B. is not to be taken literally. Whereas under the clause 'F.O.B. ...(named port of shipment)' the costs and risks of the goods pass from the seller to the buyer at the time when the goods have been delivered on board ship, the costs and risks under 'F.O.B. airport' are transferred when the goods have been delivered into the custody of the air carrier at the airport, and not when they have been lifted into the aircraft.

In particular, the seller must:
1. Supply the goods in conformity with the contract of sale.
2. Deliver the goods into the custody of the air carrier named by the buyer, or, if no air carrier has been so named, of an air carrier chosen by the seller. Delivery is to be made on the date or within the period agreed for delivery, and at the named airport of departure or at such other place named by the buyer in the contract.
3. Contract at the buyer's expense for the carriage of the goods to the airport of destination named by the buyer, unless the buyer or the seller gives prompt notice to the contrary to the other party. Usually, it is the seller who enters into the contract of carriage (by air) with the air carrier. The air freight, however, must be paid by the buyer. In practice, the seller, when entering into the contract, pays the freight, and the buyer must reimburse him for the amount paid. It should be noted that air freight is not included in the f.o.b. airport price. Therefore, the seller should make out two separate invoices, one for the price of the goods and one for the air freight. By contrast, under the clause 'F.O.B. ...(named port of shipment)', the buyer himself must contract with a sea carrier for the carriage of the goods to the destination.
4. Obtain, at his own risk and expense, any export licence necessary for the export of the goods, and pay any taxes, fees, and charges levied because of exportation.
5. Bear any further costs payable in respect of the goods and all risks of the goods until they have been delivered into the custody of the air carrier (e.g., the cost of transport to the airport of departure).
6. Provide adequate protective packing at his own expense.

The buyer must:
1. Inform the seller of the airport of destination.
2. Bear all costs and risks from the time when the goods have been delivered into the custody of the air carrier (e.g., the cost of transport from the airport of destination to his premises).
3. Pay the price invoiced as provided for in the contract.

folder[1]

Mappe,
Schnellhefter

A folder is a cover - usually a piece of stiff paper or card folded in two - for holding or filing loose papers.

folder[2]
Faltprospekt,
zusammengefaltete Druckschrift

A folder is also a folded sheet of printed paper providing some information (as in a railway timetable folder) or advertising a product or service. Usually, the printed matter does not cross the fold.

follow-up letter
Nachfaßbrief

A follow-up letter is a letter which is sent if the original letter has not produced the desired results. Such letters are often sent by firms to customers who have made an inquiry, but have not yet placed an order or have not even acknowledged the quotation.

force majeure
höhere Gewalt

By force majeure is meant any cause or event which neither party to a contract can anticipate or control, such as wars, strikes, lock-outs, and acts of god (e.g., earthquake, storm, volcanic eruption, flood, etc.).

It is common practice to include in a contract of sale a force majeure clause, under which the seller accepts no liability for any delay in shipment or non-delivery of the goods due to force majeure.

forecasting
Prognoseerstellung

Forecasting involves the prediction of the value of economic variables - such as sales, production, gnp, money supply, inflation - at some future time. Forecasting is intended to eliminate or reduce risk and uncertainty and to permit rational economic planning for firms, governments, and other economic units. Depending on the period of time involved, we may distinguish between short-term, medium-term, and long-term forecasting. Forecasting techniques may range from simple projections of past trends to the use of leading indicators or econometric models incorporating thousands of equations.

Although forecasts are often out, i.e., wrong, they frequently represent the best information available at the time and are indispensable in the sense that most economic decisions have to rely on some kind of forecast, whether formal and explicit or informal and implicit.

foreign exchange
Fremdwährung,
Devisen

The term 'foreign exchange' has a comprehensive meaning and is normally used as a synonym for 'foreign currency' in whatever shape and form.

German terminology is much more differentiated. Whereas the term 'Valuten' is applied to foreign banknotes and coins, the term 'Devisen' refers to sight deposits denominated in a foreign currency and held by residents with non-resident banks. Consequently, foreign currency deposits held by domestic non-banks, e.g., firms, with domestic banks do not count as "Devisen", but as "Fremdwährung".

Transmission of foreign exchange may be by cheque, traveller's cheque, mail transfer (M.T.), telegraphic or cable transfer (T.T. or C.T.), SWIFT transfer, etc..

Foreign exchange is a country's principal means of settling its transactions with other countries. Thus, a country's demand for foreign exchange depends on its imports of goods and services, its unilateral transfers to foreign countries, and its capital exports, while the supply of foreign exchange available to it depends on its exports of goods and services, its unilateral transfers received, and its capital imports. If foreign exchange expenditures exceed foreign exchange receipts, the country has a balance-of-payments deficit, which it may finance from reserves of foreign exchange accumulated in the past.

foreign exchange market   Devisenmarkt

The foreign exchange market is a market in which convertible currencies can be freely bought and sold. In contrast to other types of market, it is not a formal location where buyers and sellers meet, but it is a vast, world-wide network of buyers and sellers of currencies, linked by video screens, telephone, and telex. The exchange of communication is rapid and to the point: quotation of exchange rates on request, and dealing at those rates. Actual currency is rarely seen, it is usually transferred by cable from one account to another.

The foreign exchange market has two main sections: first, the 'spot market' for transactions in spot exchange (i.e., foreign currencies bought or sold for immediate delivery and payment). In practice, spot transactions have to be settled in two working days' time, the delay allowing completion of the necessary paperwork. Second, the 'forward market', in which foreign currencies are bought or sold for delivery and payment at a specified future time (forward exchange).

Participants in the foreign exchange market are commercial banks (a bank acts through foreign exchange dealers/forex dealers/FX-dealers who have been authorised to buy and sell foreign exchange for their bank and its customers), their customers, foreign exchange brokers, and central banks, the latter acting as agents for their governments, e.g., in trying to influence the market by intervention.

Commercial banks are by far the most important institutions participating in the foreign exchange market. They deal with each other on a permanent basis, hence the term 'interbank market', through which most of the foreign exchange dealing is directed. While banks deal actively in foreign exchange for their own account to make profits, they also act as agents on their customers' behalf. The banks' customers range from multinational companies engaged in international trade to individuals who need foreign exchange for some purpose or other (e.g., tourists purchasing small amounts of foreign banknotes).

The function of foreign exchange brokers is to bring together buyers and sellers of foreign currencies. In other words, they act as intermediaries between banks, and between banks and the public. Banks with business to transact would find it too time-consuming to shop around (i.e., to call other banks) for exchange rate quotations, while brokerage firms have the necessary personnel and communication links to contact a maximum number of clients in a minimum of time. When approached by a bank with an order to buy or sell, the broker will contact other banks to find a counterparty. Brokers are paid a commission, termed 'brokerage', which is based on the type and size of the transaction and paid in equal halves by the buyer and the seller. For example, a typical commission in New York involving a 3 million dollar/mark operation is $96.

Business in the market is done almost entirely by telephone, transactions frequently involving millions of dollars, pounds, etc.. The major banks have separate dealing rooms, equipped with facilities (video screens, telephones, teleprinters, direct wires, etc.) for direct communication with brokers, other dealers, important customers, and also with the foreign exchange departments of banks in foreign dealing centres. Most dealers are in permanent contact with the principal financial centres and thus able to quote competitive buying and selling rates for all the major currencies.

The world's major dealing centres are located in three areas: the Far East and Middle East (Tokyo, Hong Kong, Singapore, and Bahrein), Western Europe (Frankfurt, London, Paris, and Zurich), and North America (New York, Chicago, Los Angeles, San Francisco, and Toronto).

Finally, it is worth remarking that the foreign exchange market is a very close approximation to a "perfect market". There are many sellers and buyers of homogeneous/identical "commodities", such as dollars, pounds, francs, etc.. Through their excellent system of communications they are able to watch closely the prices of these currencies. This means that they have perfect knowledge of existing market conditions, so that there tends to be only one price for a currency in terms of another at any one time.

F.O.R./F.O.T. (Incoterms 1980)
FREE ON RAIL/FREE ON TRUCK
...(named departure point)

International code: FOR

F.O.R./F.O.T.
FREI WAGGON
...(benannter Abgangsort)

F.O.R. and F.O.T. are used synonymously, since the word 'truck' also refers to a railway waggon. These terms should only be used when the goods are to be carried by rail.

Under f.o.r./f.o.t. terms, the seller's and the buyer's duties are as follows: in the case of goods constituting a waggon-load, the seller must obtain a waggon and load it at his own expense on the date or within the period stipulated, and deliver it into the custody of the railway. In the case of a load less than a waggon-load, the seller must deliver the goods into the custody of the railway, usually at the dispatching station. He must bear all costs and risks of the goods until the waggon on which they are loaded, or the goods themselves, have been delivered into the custody of the railway (e.g., the cost of transport to the railway station). In addition, the seller must provide at his own expense the customary packing of the goods, and pay the costs of any checking operations (such as checking of quality, measuring, weighing, counting).

The buyer must: take delivery of the goods when they have been delivered into the custody of the railway; pay the price as provided for in the contract; bear all costs and risks of the goods from the time when the waggon on which the goods are loaded, or the goods themselves, have been delivered into the custody of the railway; provide any export licence at his own risk and expense, and bear any customs duties and taxes that may be levied by reason of exportation.

format

Format,
Präsentation(-sweise),
Darstellung(-sweise)

In data processing, the term 'format' refers to the predetermined arrangement of data, e.g., the layout of a printed page, the arrangement of data on a punched card or in a magnetic tape block, or the composition of a printed line.

forward cover

Kurssicherung am Devisenterminmarkt,
Terminsicherung

Generally speaking, 'forward cover' refers to a forward (exchange) transaction intended to protect a buyer or seller of foreign exchange from unexpected fluctuations in the exchange rate.

In the case of a forward transaction, a bank and its customer enter into a forward exchange contract, whereby each party agrees to deliver at a specified future time a specified amount of one currency in exchange for a specified amount of another currency. The main characteristic of a forward transaction is that the rate of exchange is agreed upon at the time the contract is entered into, but delivery and payment are not required until maturity. This makes it possible for individuals and organisations who will have to make, or will receive, payment in a foreign currency at a future time to protect themselves against the risk of fluctuations in the spot rate by buying/selling the amount of foreign currency concerned in the forward market. Forward cover is used by exporters and importers of goods and/or services, banks, investors, etc..

The following examples are meant to assist the reader in understanding the foregoing: suppose that an Austrian exporter sells goods to a U.S. importer, the invoice price of $10,000 being payable in three months. Assuming that the exchange rate ruling on the date of invoice is U.S.$1 = AS18.00/18.50, the Austrian exporter expects to exchange the $10,000 for AS180,000 when payment is received. But if the exchange rate goes down in the period between the date of invoice and the date of settlement, the exporter will get less in domestic currency when converting the invoice amount, i.e., he will make an exchange loss. It is for this reason that the exporter may decide to enter into a forward exchange contract with his bank. Let us assume that on the date of invoice the three-month forward dollar is quoted at a premium of 20/30 groschen against the schilling; thus, the three-month forward rate is AS18.20/18.80. The Austrian exporter, who expects to receive $10,000 in three months, may sell the dollar amount three months forward at 18.20 schillings to the dollar. In three months, he will have to deliver $10,000 to the bank and, in return, will be paid AS182,000. By doing so he protects himself from any movement in the spot rate against him between the date of invoice and the date of payment (but by the same token he cannot make any exchange gain either). But what happens if the U.S. importer fails to pay the invoice price? Since the exporter has to fulfil his obligations under the forward exchange contract, he will have to buy the dollar amount in the spot market, thus bearing the full exchange risk.

Similarly, an importer may protect himself against the transaction risk by buying in the forward market the amount of foreign currency which he will have to pay at a future time. An Austrian importer, for instance, who will have to pay $10,000 in three months to a U.S. exporter in payment of an invoice may buy the dollar amount three months forward at 18.80 schillings to the dollar (the figures used are those of the first example). In three months, he will have to pay AS188,000 to the bank and, in return, will get the $10,000 which he needs to pay the invoice price.

forwarding agent   Spediteur

A forwarding agent, or freight forwarder, acts as intermediary between those having to send or collect goods and those who are to transport them, i.e., between a consignor or consignee and a carrier. Acting on the instructions given by either the consignor or the consignee, the forwarding agent arranges, in his own name but on his client's account, for the carriage (conveyance/transport) of goods to the agreed place of destination. For this purpose, he employs the services of a carrier, with whom he enters into the contract of carriage for his client's account.

The general course of business is that the forwarding agent collects the goods from the consignor, delivers them to the carrier, and - through his branch offices or correspondents - makes arrangements for transshipments, if necessary. At the consignor's request he issues a 'forwarding agent's (certificate of) receipt'. A forwarding agent usually has his own vehicles (lorries, vans, etc.) and transports the goods himself, for example, from the consignor's warehouse to the railway station or airport. In doing so, he acts as a carrier.

Since a forwarding agent handles goods for many different customers, he can obtain lower freight rates by combining several small consignments into larger ones. These grouped consignments (U.S.: consolidated shipments) are addressed to a correspondent or a branch office at the place of destination, who split them up again and deliver the individual consignments to the various consignees. It is therefore often cheaper, and certainly much simpler, for suppliers to employ a forwarding agent than to deal direct with the carrier.

A forwarding agent specialising in international dealings has a network of foreign correspondents or branch offices and is, therefore, able to make arrangements for the carriage of goods to and from all parts of the world. Consequently, the services of a forwarding agent are of great value to those engaged in the export trade, particularly to small firms which do not have their own export organisations and shipping departments. It is customary for the forwarding agent to collect the goods from the exporter, make all arrangements for shipping them, and, after they have been shipped, send an advice of shipment to his branch office or correspondent in the buyer's country. The latter takes delivery of the goods and either forwards them to the buyer or arranges for them to be warehoused if the buyer does not want them immediately.

In addition to forwarding goods, a forwarding agent renders many important services to his customers, either directly or through his foreign contacts. Among other things, he obtains the necessary shipping documents, takes out marine insurance, and handles all customs formalities as well as documentary and clean collections. Many forwarding agents have special facilities for export packing and warehousing, and some also provide container services.

forward rate (of exchange)   (Devisen-)Terminkurs

The term 'forward rate' is taken to mean the price of a foreign currency which is bought or sold for delivery and payment at a fixed future time. It is the rate of exchange at which forward transactions are carried out in the forward market.

In the case of a forward transaction, a bank and its customer enter into a forward exchange contract, whereby each party agrees to deliver at a specified future time a specified amount of one currency in exchange for a specified amount of another currency. The main point is that the rate of exchange is agreed upon at the time the contract is entered into, but delivery and payment are not required until maturity. Forward transactions enable individuals and organisations who will have to make, or will receive, payment in a foreign currency at a future time to protect themselves against the risk of fluctuations in the spot rate by buying/selling the amount of foreign currency concerned in the forward market (forward cover). This strategy is used by exporters and importers of goods and/or services, banks, investors, and so on.

Forward rates are normally quoted by banks/foreign exchange dealers for fixed periods of one, two, three, six, and twelve months, but forward exchange contracts can also be arranged for other periods on special request.

In banking practice, a forward quotation is usually expressed in terms of a premium or discount in relation to the spot rate. If a currency is at a premium against another currency, this means that the forward value of that currency is higher than the spot value, whereas the opposite is true of a currency at a discount. Consequently, if the rate of exchange is quoted on a direct basis (direct quotation), a premium has to be added to the spot rate, i.e., the forward rate is higher than the spot rate, and, consequently, more units of the home currency can be obtained for each unit of the foreign currency than at the spot rate. By contrast, a discount has to be deducted from the spot rate, i.e., the forward rate is lower than the spot rate.

The following example is meant to illustrate the foregoing: let us assume that the U.S. dollar/Austrian schilling spot rate in Vienna is AS17.90/18.05, and that the three-month forward dollar is quoted at a premium of 10/15 groschen against the schilling. In banking jargon, the Austrian schilling is said to be at a dollar premium in the forward market, or, to put it differently, the dollar is said to be at a premium against the schilling, which means that the forward dollar is more expensive than the spot dollar when quoted in schillings. In the example chosen, the three-month dollar premium of 10/15 groschen has to be added to the spot rate, which results in a three-month forward rate of AS18.00/18.20. Thus, banks will buy dollars three months forward at 18.00 Austrian schillings and will sell dollars three months forward at 18.20 schillings. Therefore, when selling a dollar three months forward to a bank, one gets 10 groschen more than when selling a dollar spot. On the other hand, one needs 15 groschen more to buy a three-month forward dollar than to buy a spot dollar.

An Austrian exporter, for example, who expects to receive $1,000 in three months from a U.S. importer in payment of an invoice may sell the dollar amount three months forward at 18.00 schillings to the dollar. In three months, he will have to deliver $1,000 to the bank and, in return, will be paid 18,000 schillings. By doing so he protects himself from any movement in the spot rate against him between the date of invoice and the date of payment (but by the same token he cannot make any exchange gain either).

Assuming that the three-month forward dollar is quoted at a discount of 15/10 groschen against the schilling, the three-month forward rate would be AS17.75/17.95. In this case, the Austrian schilling is said to be at a dollar discount, or the dollar is said to be at a discount against the schilling. This means that the forward dollar is cheaper than the spot dollar when quoted in schillings.

The above example shows, among other things, that a premium or a discount is also quoted as bid and offer, the bid being lower than the offer in the case of a premium and higher in the case of a discount.

Finally, according to the theory of forward exchange, a discount or premium on one currency against another is directly related to the difference in interest rates prevailing in the two countries. The currency of the higher interest-rate country should be at a discount against the currency of the lower interest-rate country, and vice versa.

f.p.a.   f.p.a.

F.p.a. (which is an abbreviation for 'free from particular average') is a type of insurance cover for goods in (ocean) marine insurance.

The f.p.a. clause in an (ocean) marine insurance policy establishes the principle that the insurer is not liable for any particular average loss (i.e., partial loss of, or damage to, the goods not due to a general average act), but the strictness of this rule is mitigated by a number of exceptions. For instance, the insurer is fully liable for partial loss of, or damage to, the goods (i) if the ship is stranded, sunk, or burnt, or (ii) if the loss or damage is attributable to fire, explosion, collision or contact of the vessel with any external object (ice included). An example of a partial loss or damage which is not recoverable at all under an f.p.a. policy is one caused by heavy weather provided the vessel has not been stranded, sunk, or burnt during the voyage.

No question of particular average arises when there is total loss of, or damage to, the goods due to stranding, sinking, fire, explosion, collision, heavy weather, etc.. In all these cases, the insured can always hold the insurer liable. In addition, the insurer also undertakes to pay the insured value of any package which may be totally lost or damaged in loading, transshipment, or discharge. In other words, the insurer undertakes to treat each package as separately insured, and the total loss of an entire package in loading, transshipment, or discharge is treated as a "total loss of part of the goods", and not as a "particular average loss of the whole of the goods". If, for example, the goods are packed in 20 cases, one of which is totally lost in loading, the insurer will pay the total insured value of that one case. If, on the other hand, all 20 cases are partly damaged, the insurer is free.

It should also be mentioned that f.p.a. policies - as is the case with all-risks policies and w.a. policies - give the insured full cover against general average damage/loss and contribution.

franchise   Integralfranchise

The term 'franchise', as used in insurance, may be defined as a specified amount or a certain percentage of the sum insured which must be reached before a claim is payable. Once the amount or percentage is attained, the claim is payable in full.

In other words, claims for less than a specified amount or percentage will not be paid by the insurer; however, claims for more than that amount or percentage will be paid in full.

The franchise - as is the case with the deductible - is fixed by the insurer in the policy and is intended to eliminate trivial claims. In modern practice, the franchise is used, for example, in w.a. policies, but it is no longer used in hull insurance, where it has been replaced with the deductible.

franchising   Franchising

Franchising is a vertical distribution arrangement where one independent contractor (the franchisor) grants another independent contractor further down the distribution channel (the franchisee) certain rights in return for a franchising fee and the latter's commitment to fulfil certain duties. The main right involved is the franchisee's right to manufacture and/or sell a specified product or service for his own account, using the franchisor's trade mark, logo, patent rights, commercial and technical know-how, etc.. The franchisee is required to comply with the standards of the franchisor's business organisation in a manner laid down in the franchise contract.

Franchising can be found in the fast food industry (e.g., McDonald's), in the car rental business (e.g., Hertz), in the hotel industry, and in many other fields.

FREE CARRIER (Incoterms 1980)   FREI FRACHTFÜHRER
...(named point)   ...(benannter Ort)
International code: FRC

This clause has been designed to meet the requirements of modern transport, particularly of combined transport, frequently involving the use of containers.

The seller's primary duty is to deliver the goods at the named point into the custody of the carrier named by the buyer. In most cases, the cargo terminal owned or used by the carrier would be the proper point where all costs payable in respect of the goods and all risks of loss of, or damage to, the goods pass from the seller to the buyer. In other words, once the goods have been delivered at the named point into the charge of the carrier, the buyer has to bear any unforeseen costs and risks in bringing the goods to the destination. He has to pay the sales price, no matter what happens to the goods, provided that the cause of any loss or damage cannot be attributed to the seller. 'Free carrier' implies an export sale, which means that the seller has to obtain any export licence at his own risk and expense, and has to pay any taxes, fees, and charges levied in respect of the goods because of exportation.

The buyer's primary duty is to contract with a carrier for the carriage of the goods from the named point to the destination, pay the freight (usually including the loading costs), and inform the seller of the name of the carrier and of the time for delivering the goods to him. The buyer may select any type of carrier, including a combined transport operator, who conveys the goods to the destination under one contract of carriage, involving different modes of transport.

freight[1]

Fracht,
Frachtgebühr,
Transportgebühr

The term 'freight' is taken to mean the consideration payable to the carrier for transporting the goods as provided for in the contract of carriage. There is a tendency to use 'freight' mainly in connection with the carriage of goods by sea (sea freight) or by air (air freight), whereas the term 'carriage' is preferably used in rail and road transport.

freight[2]

Fracht,
Frachtgut

Freight may also be used as a general term for goods carried from one place to another, irrespective of the mode of transport (e.g., sea freight, air freight, rail freight).

The term 'cargo' (plural: cargoes; U.S.: cargos), however, is generally used to describe goods carried by air ('air cargo', a synonym for 'air freight') or by sea ('sea cargo', synonymous with 'sea freight').

FREIGHT/CARRIAGE AND INSURANCE PAID TO (Incoterms 1980)
...(named point of destination)

FRACHTFREI VERSICHERT
...(benannter Bestimmungsort)

International code: CIP

This term is the same as 'freight or carriage paid to...', but with the addition that the seller has to procure cargo insurance against the risk of loss of, or damage to, the goods during the carriage. The seller must contract with the insurer, pay the insurance premium, and provide the buyer with the insurance policy or other evidence of insurance cover. The insurance has to cover the contract price plus 10 per cent.

Under the term 'freight or carriage and insurance paid to...', the risk of the goods passes from the seller to the buyer when the goods are delivered to the first carrier, which means that the goods are transported at the buyer's risk. Consequently, the buyer has to rely mainly on the terms of the cargo insurance for protection. It is true that in the case of loss of, or damage to, the goods the buyer also has the right to compensation from the carrier, a right which arises from the latter's liability under the contract of carriage. But in view of various exclusions of the carrier's liability and limitations on the amounts recoverable from the carrier, the buyer normally turns to the insurer. The insurer, on payment of the insurance money, is subrogated to the rights of the insured buyer and is thus enabled to claim against the carrier.

FREIGHT/CARRIAGE PAID TO (Incoterms 1980) FRACHTFREI
...(named point of destination) *...(benannter Bestimmungsort)*

International code: DCP

Like C.& F., 'freight or carriage paid to...' means that the seller pays the freight for the carriage of the goods to the named destination. However, the risk of loss of, or damage to, the goods passes from the seller to the buyer when the goods have been delivered into the custody of the first carrier, and not at the ship's rail. Whereas C.& F. is used for goods carried by sea, the term 'freight or carriage paid to...' may be used for all modes of transport, including combined transport, frequently involving the use of containers.

This term, like C.& F., requires the seller to contract for the carriage of the goods to the agreed destination and to pay the freight. The seller's obligations are fulfilled when the goods have been delivered to the first carrier. This means that the risk of loss of, or damage to, the goods is transferred from the seller to the buyer at that moment and that the goods are transported at the buyer's risk. Since this trade term can be used irrespective of the mode of transport, the carrier could be a road haulier, a railway company, an airline operator, a shipping company, or a combined transport operator.

While under C.& F. terms the point of delivery to the sea carrier has been tied to the means of conveyance, viz., to the ship's rail, 'freight or carriage paid to...' only requires the seller to deliver the goods into the custody of the first carrier, normally at the latter's cargo terminal. If several carriers are engaged (e.g., from Vienna to Hamburg by rail, and from Hamburg to New York City by ship), delivery is already fulfilled when the goods have been delivered to the first of these carriers. This is different from C.& F., where the goods are transported to the ship at the seller's risk.

As 'freight or carriage paid to...' implies an export sale, the seller has to obtain any export licence at his own risk and expense and pay any taxes , fees, and charges levied in respect of the goods because of exportation.

The buyer's primary duty is to take delivery of the goods when they have been delivered to the first carrier, bear all risks of the goods from that time, bear, with the exception of the freight, all costs and charges incurred in respect of the goods in transit until their arrival at the point of destination, and bear the costs of unloading, unless such costs and charges are included in the freight. In addition, the buyer has to obtain any import licence and pay all customs duties due on importation of the goods.

fringe benefit (betriebliche) Nebenleistung

Fringe benefits (often simply called 'benefits' or 'employee benefits') are payments, either in cash or in kind, made to an employee in addition to his "normal" wage or salary. Fringe benefits are either statutory (such as holiday with pay), contractual, i.e., incorporated in the contract of employment, or voluntary, which means they can be withdrawn at the employer's discretion. Examples of fringe benefits are: company cars, subsidised canteens, stock options (for managerial personnel), the free use of recreational facilities, creches and day-care centres, discounts on the firm's goods, etc..

fund[1]   Fonds,
                                                     zweckgebundenes (Sonder-)Vermögen

One of the meanings of the term 'fund' is a sum of money or other resources set apart for a specific objective or activity, as in 'sinking fund'. This is a fund created for the purpose of repaying a debt or replacing an asset.

fund[2]   -fonds (z.B. Investmentfonds,
                                                     Währungsfonds)

By extension, the term 'fund' may also be used to describe an organisation administering sums of money or other resources. Investment funds, which pool and invest monies obtained from shareholders or unitholders, and the International Monetary Fund (I.M.F.), administering funds (quotas) received from its member countries, would be cases in point.

funding[1]   Finanzierung,
                                                     Mittelbereitstellung

Funding denotes the provision of funds, i.e., of pecuniary resources, for a particular purpose, and is, therefore, more or less synonymous with 'financing'.

funding[2]   Fundierung,
                                                     Umwandlung kurzfristiger in langfristige
                                                     (sog. fundierte) Schulden

In a more specialised sense, funding refers to the conversion of a floating (i.e., short-term) debt into a long-term debt, as, for instance, when a company issues debentures to repay a large overdraft or when the British government replaces its floating debt with an issue of gilt-edged securities.

funds[1]   Barmittel,
                                                     finanzielle Mittel

In colloquial usage, the term 'funds' is often used as a synonym for cash (i.e., banknotes, coins, and current account balances at banks) and other financial resources that can readily be converted into cash. For instance, a cheque drawn against an account with an insufficient credit balance or a debit balance may be returned, bearing the words 'no funds'. A fund-raising campaign is an organised effort to find the financial resources required for a particular purpose.

funds[2]   Kapital

The expression 'funds' may also be used to describe the capital of a company, as, for instance, in 'shareholders' funds'.

futures contract   standardisierter Terminkontrakt (ohne
                                          effektive Lieferung)

Commodity futures differ from contracts for forward - physical - delivery in that they are for standard quantities and for standard periods of time. Another, and perhaps more important, difference is that the parties to futures contracts have no intention of either making or accepting delivery of the commodity in question. Instead, futures contracts are, generally speaking, performed by engaging in an offsetting transaction. The sale of a futures contract is completed ("closed out") by buying back an identical contract maturing at the same time. A futures purchase is closed out by selling a contract for the same period. This may be done at any time before the original futures contract matures, and results in the operator either paying or receiving the difference between the price of the original and the price of the offsetting futures contract, depending on which is higher.

Commodity futures can be used for purely speculative reasons. It is, however, also possible to hedge price risks with them. This is dealt with under the heading of "hedging" elsewhere in the book.

It should be noted that the terminological distinction between forward contracts and futures contracts is not always observed. The confusion arises mainly because forward contracts are obviously contracts for future delivery and are often referred to as such.

It may also be of interest to add that futures contracts are increasingly being used in connection with currencies (currency futures), money market instruments (interest-rate futures), and with securities dealt in on stock exchanges (stock-index futures). These futures contracts may collectively be referred to as 'financial futures', although the term is sometimes interpreted in a more limited sense.

G

gains from trade

positive Wohlfahrtseffekte des
Außenhandels

Gains from trade are the positive welfare effects to a country from engaging in international trade. It is generally believed that, in most circumstances, countries are better off economically with international trade than they would be without it. These positive effects on welfare flow mainly from the international division of labour, i.e., from each country concentrating on what it can do (relatively speaking) best. The benefits come in the form of lower costs and prices and a wider range of goods and services.

It should not be forgotten, however, that gains from trade do not come free: against them must be set a number of negative effects, the main one being a loss of independence. Moreover, trade in non-essentials (e.g., table water) may involve a waste of energy; and it has been proved by neoclassical economists that, in certain circumstances, international trade may be positively harmful to a country, especially if that country is an ldc.

gearing

Verschuldungskoeffizient;
Fremdkapitalwirkung auf die
Eigenkapitalrentabilität,
Financial Leverage

There are two types of gearing: 'capital gearing' and 'income gearing'.

Capital gearing in its widest sense is synonymous with 'debt ratio', i.e., it relates creditors' funds to owners' funds (see: capital structure). Some financial analysts, however, reserve the term for a special capital ratio, namely, for the 'gearing ratio', calculated by dividing ordinary shareholders' funds into total debt (including preference share capital).

Income gearing, another financial ratio, is intended to provide information about the effects of capital gearing on the earnings available to ordinary shareholders. Income gearing, in the U.S. referred to as 'financial leverage', is calculated by dividing earnings before interest and tax (EBIT) by EBIT minus annual interest expense of borrowed funds and/or the preference dividend on a pre-tax basis. In other words, it relates EBIT to what remains for the ordinary shareholders after fixed-interest payments, including the preference dividend, if any, have been deducted, i.e., to earnings per share.

In conclusion, it should be noted that the term 'gearing' is sometimes used simply to describe the amount of borrowed funds in a firm.

general average

Havarie-grosse,
große Havarie

General average is not strictly an insurance term, but relates to a practice which is very similar to insurance in its intention. General average is an accepted rule of the sea and applies only to maritime transport. During the sea voyage, the main interests at risk are the ship and the cargo. They form a common adventure and are exposed to the same risks. When these risks encounter a common peril, it may become necessary to make an extraordinary sacrifice or to incur an extraordinary expenditure in order to preserve the ship and the cargo. For instance, the ship may encounter heavy weather, and it may be necessary to jettison part of the cargo and/or part of the ship's equipment in order to lighten the ship and save it and the cargo from total loss. General average may be defined as a deliberate partial loss to save all the interests in the adventure from total loss. It is only just and fair that the owners of all the interests saved by a deliberate sacrifice of property should contribute proportionately towards covering this loss.

Under the contract of carriage by sea, the party suffering a general average loss is entitled to a rateable contribution from each of the other parties. If, for example, a cargo owner suffers a general average loss, he is entitled to claim contribution from the shipowner and the other cargo owners, irrespective of whether he has taken out (ocean) marine cargo insurance or not.

Finally, it should be mentioned that the risks which may fall upon the shipowner or a cargo owner under the law of general average are fully covered by his (ocean) marine insurance (hull insurance on the vessel and cargo insurance on the goods). These risks are twofold: first, physical loss of, or damage to, the ship (including its machinery and equipment) or goods, and second, the shipowner's or cargo owner's liability to pay a general average contribution. The insurance cover of physical loss of, or damage to, the ship or goods caused by a general average act enables the shipowner or cargo owner to claim payment of the insurance money from the insurer without becoming involved in the complications of the average adjustment. On payment of the insurance money, the insurer is subrogated to the rights of the insured arising from the contract of carriage by sea and is thus enabled to pursue the shipowner's or cargo owner's claim for contribution.

general cargo

Stückgut

The term 'general cargo' is used in air and sea transport and means cargo consisting of different kinds of goods, i.e., not of any particular kind. It is, therefore, the opposite of bulk cargo. The proper term in land transport would be 'part-load goods' (in U.S. railroad terminology 'less-than-carload freight', abbreviated LCL).

general inquiry

allgemeine Anfrage

In a general inquiry (also referred to as a 'routine inquiry'), the prospective buyer merely asks the supplier to send him general information about the goods in question, such as catalogues, leaflets, a price-list, and, where appropriate, samples.

gilt-edged securities — britische Staatsanleihen

The Radcliff Report 1959 defines "gilt-edged securities (also referred to as 'government bonds' or 'government stocks') as the securities issued by Her Majesty's Government or by the nationalised industries and guaranteed by Her Majesty's Government that are dealt in on the London Stock Exchange; these terms do not include Treasury bills".

It should be noted that the expression 'mündelsichere Wertpapiere', which virtually all dictionaries offer as a translation of 'gilt-edged securities', has a much wider meaning and includes all kinds of securities in which a trustee is allowed to invest his ward's money without making himself liable for any losses. The closest English equivalent of 'mündelsichere Wertpapiere' is 'trustee securities', although these two terms are by no means coextensive either.

Gilt-edged securities, or simply gilts, are used by the British government and the nationalised industries to raise long-term funds. They are also an important instrument of monetary policy (open-market operations).

goods — Güter, Ware(n)

Goods are objects capable of satisfying human wants. They are traditionally divided into 'free goods' and 'economic goods'. The former do not command a price because they are in abundant supply and their marginal utilities are very low. The opposite is true of the latter: they are scarce, their marginal utilities are high, and they can normally be acquired only by giving up something valuable for them. There is no hard and fast borderline between the two categories. What may be a free good in one place (e.g., water in temperate zone mountain areas) may be an economic good in another place (e.g., in a desert country). Generally speaking, there is a tendency for originally free goods to change over to the economic category because of the increasing pressure of demand and uncontrolled economic growth (e.g., water).

Economic goods can be divided into 'consumer goods' and 'producer goods'. Only the former are desirable in themselves, while the demand for the latter is a derived demand based on their usefulness in ultimately producing consumer goods. If the criteria of durability and non-durability are applied to the two categories, we get 'durable consumer goods' (or 'consumer durables', such as radios and T.V. sets) and 'non-durable consumer goods' (e.g., food and clothing); 'durable producer goods' (or 'capital goods', e.g., machines, buildings, etc.) and 'non-durable producer goods' (e.g., factory supplies and fuel).

goods-in-transit insurance — Binnentransportversicherung von Gütern

Goods-in-transit insurance, also called 'transit insurance', is a type of insurance indemnifying the insured for any loss of, or damage to, the goods in transit by land (i.e., by road or by rail) or on inland waterways. Insurance coverage attaches from the time the goods leave the initial point of shipment (warehouse, factory, etc.) until they are delivered at the place of destination.

Transit insurance policies usually enumerate specified perils, and loss of, or damage to, the goods is covered only if resulting from those perils. The risks covered include fire, lightning, earthquake, landslide, theft (particularly hijacking of whole loads), collision, derailment, overturning of the transporting vehicle, etc.. In addition, transit policies may also be available on an all-risks basis. Certain risks, however, are excluded from the all-risks cover, e.g., risks of war, riots, strikes, inherent vice, defective packing, radioactive contamination, etc..

Transit insurance policies may be written either as 'annual transit policies' or as 'trip transit policies'. An annual transit policy covers all shipments of the policyholder effected during the policy period of one year. The premium for an annual transit policy is based on the total value of all the goods covered during the term of the policy, and varies with the mode of transport, the routes used, the distance, and other factors. It is impossible for the policyholder to determine accurately in advance the value of his shipments to be covered. Consequently, it is customary for annual transit policies to be written either on an annual or on a monthly reporting basis. In the first case, the policyholder estimates the value of his shipments to be covered during the policy period and pays an estimated annual premium. On expiry of the policy, he makes a report to the insurance company of the actual values covered by the policy. An adjustment is then made in the premium, and he pays any extra premium due or receives a refund of any overpayment. In the second case, the policyholder has to make monthly reports of shipments, the premium being due when the reports are made. It is customary for premium payments to be sent with the reports.

In contrast to the annual transit policy, the trip transit policy is designed to cover a specified shipment on a particular trip. It is meant for persons or firms who do not have sufficient shipments to justify an annual policy. It is used, for example, to cover shipments of household furniture, heavy machinery, and merchandise or livestock en route to and from exhibitions.

The benefits of transit insurance for the insured are threefold. Firstly, it guarantees immediate payment of damage or loss, even though the carrier may be held liable under the contract of carriage. Secondly, it indemnifies the insured for any loss of, or damage to, the goods in excess of the liability of the carrier. And thirdly, it protects the insured against any damage or loss for which the carrier is not liable, e.g., damage or loss due to acts of god.

gross domestic product — Bruttoinlandsprodukt

In contrast to the gross national product, the gross domestic product, or gdp, is a geographical concept. The gnp (output measure) of a particular country includes all final goods and services produced by the nationals of that country, no matter whether they operate inside or outside the country. By contrast, the gdp comprises the final goods and services produced within the boundaries of that country, no matter whether nationals or foreigners are involved in their production.

For a country with large investments abroad (e.g., the U.S.A.) or with a large number of its nationals working abroad (e.g., Turkey), gnp and gdp will differ significantly. The same is true of countries employing a large number of foreign workers and playing host to subsidiaries of multinationals.

gross national product

Bruttonationalprodukt,
Bruttosozialprodukt

The gross national product (gnp) is the total value - at current or at constant prices - of all final goods and services produced by a nation's economy in a year (or any other standard period of time). 'Gross' means before deduction of depreciation charges; 'final' means that intermediate inputs are excluded (no double counting, or duplication). The gnp at current prices is called the 'nominal gnp', the gnp at constant prices the 'real gnp'. The real gnp may be calculated by applying a gnp deflator to the nominal gnp, the deflator corresponding to the rate of inflation for all final goods and services.

The most important items included in the gnp calculated under the expenditure (or flow-of-product) method are: personal consumption (durable and non-durable consumer goods and services), gross private domestic investment, government expenditure on goods and services, and net exports of goods and services. The gnp can also be calculated by adding up all types of income (such as wages, salaries, rents, profits, etc.) and depreciation (income method), or by adding up the values added by the industries composing the economy (output method).

Although the gnp is a very useful concept, its usefulness as a measure of national welfare and in international comparisons is increasingly being called into doubt by economists. The gnp has been criticised because it fails to include the value added by non-market activities (e.g., the work of housewives) and the value of leisure, while, on the other hand, it does include "regrettables" - i.e., expenditure intended to remedy some evil which might never have come into existence but for activities leading to a higher gnp (e.g., treatment of occupational diseases, anti-pollution expenditure). Furthermore, the gnp fails to account for the unwanted by-products ("bads", or "externalities", in economic jargon) of the economic process, which certainly have to be taken into account when assessing the net benefit of this process to society as a whole. The prime example here is certainly pollution. Another shortcoming is that the gnp does not allow for the wealth-creating effect of consumer durables, which are treated as consumer expenditure (and not as investment). Is this misleading practice really only due to accounting problems, or at least also to a reflection of our "throw-away" society?

To remedy some of these defects, different measures of national welfare have been developed, of which the most important are NNW (net national welfare) and indices based on social indicators (e.g., number of cars and telephones, suicides, child mortality, etc.).

group of companies

Konzern

Companies may operate separately or as a group. In a group, one company controls one or more subsidiary companies, usually by holding more than 50 per cent of each subsidiary's equity capital. A large group may also have sub-subsidiaries, i.e., companies controlled by its subsidiaries. The controlling company, also referred to as the 'holding company' or 'parent (company)', quite often restricts its activities to managing the subsidiaries. In contrast to such a non-operating (or pure) holding company, an operating parent additionally engages in the production and distribution of goods and services.

A subsidiary company may be set up by the parent company, but it is also possible for the parent to acquire more than 50% of the equity capital of an already existing company. The second method, by merger or take-over, is probably more common today.

Subsidiaries in which the parent company holds 100 per cent of the capital are referred to as 'wholly-owned subsidiaries'. In cases where the parent's interest, or stake, is between 20 per cent and 50 per cent, the term 'associated company' is used.

Although a group of companies operates for practical purposes as a single enterprise, the separate legal personality of each company is strictly maintained, so that, for example, at least under British law, a creditor of a subsidiary can make no claim against the holding company. Subsidiary companies must, therefore, be clearly distinguished from mere branches, sales offices, and similar units, which are just separate establishments without legal personality of their own. In one important respect, however, groups are recognised as single enterprises: not only must each group company (or affiliated company in American usage) publish accounts relating to its own activities, but the holding company must also publish consolidated group accounts, relating to the activities of the group as a whole. The expression 'consolidated' indicates that the assets and liabilities as well as the revenues and expenses of all group companies have been summarised, and that intra-group accounts receivable and accounts payable have been netted out.

Groups may be formed by vertical integration, i.e., by combining companies from different stages in the chain of production and distribution, or by horizontal integration, under which method companies from the same stage of production or distribution are combined. In the case of a conglomerate group, or conglomerate, the subsidiaries operate in completely unrelated industries. There is no commercial logic behind this combination, although conglomerate mergers may be perfectly logical from the financial point of view. Multinational companies are groups with subsidiaries in more than one other country and operate from a global (or international) perspective. Multinationals may be of the vertical, horizontal, or conglomerate variety.

Groups, which dominate business life in many countries - not in terms of numbers, but in terms of sales, profits, and market share -, are a very useful type of organisation. They combine the advantages of size (e.g., economies of scale, marketing power) with the flexibility of decentralised management. The overall policy is laid down by the group's headquarters (i.e., by the top management of the parent company), while the individual subsidiaries are given considerable latitude in the management of their affairs - although it is, of course, possible to keep subsidiaries on a longer or a shorter leash.

guarantee[1]

Garantie (im Sinne einer Gewährleistungsgarantie)

In many trades, it is customary for the supplier to give the buyer a written guarantee (the term used in the U.S.A. is 'warranty'). Under the terms of this guarantee, the supplier undertakes to replace or repair, free of charge, any article which may prove defective during the guarantee period (usually one year), provided the defect is due to faulty material or workmanship. In other words, a guarantee is a voluntary undertaking by the supplier (retailer, wholesaler, or manufacturer) to make good by repair, by complete or partial replacement, or otherwise, any defect in the goods becoming apparent within a stipulated period of time, provided the buyer is not responsible for the defect.

guarantee[2]   Garantie (im Sinne eines unabhängigen Garantievertrages)

A guarantee, in a broad sense, is a contract between a person (known as the 'issuer of the guarantee') and another person (called the 'beneficiary of the guarantee') by which the issuer undertakes to be answerable for the payment of a debt or the due performance of some contract or duty by a third party. Under this type of guarantee, the issuer is primarily liable, i.e., he assumes a liability independent of the question whether the third party defaults or not.

A guarantee[2] differs from a guarantee[3] mainly in that it is an independent, and not an accessory, contract. This means that it is independent of the existence of an underlying agreement; even if the latter ceases to exist or is void from the beginning, the guarantee[2] remains binding on the issuer. In other words, even if the underlying contract between the third party and the beneficiary is void, the latter may require the issuer to pay the amount guaranteed. For all payments made under the guarantee the issuer has the right of recourse against the third party.

Important examples of this type of guarantee are 'tender bonds' and 'performance bonds'.

guarantee[3]   Bürgschaft

A guarantee, in a narrower sense, is a contract evidenced in writing between a person (known as the 'guarantor') and a creditor by which the guarantor undertakes to answer for the payment of a debt by another person (referred to as the 'principal debtor'), who himself remains primarily liable for such payment to the creditor. The guarantor is only secondarily liable, which means that he becomes liable to pay only if the principal debtor defaults. If the guarantor pays the debt, he has the right to sue the debtor for all sums paid under the guarantee, plus interest.

In commercial practice, a guarantee is frequently used as collateral security for overdrafts and bank loans.

The most important point is that a guarantee[3] is an accessory contract, not a primary contract, which means that it is always subsidiary to the underlying agreement (frequently a credit agreement) between the principal debtor and the creditor. Consequently, if the underlying agreement is or becomes void for any reason, the guarantor is not bound by his guarantee.

H

hard copy

gedruckte Maschinenausgabe,
ausgedruckte Kopie,
Hardcopy

Hard copy is not "hard" in the ordinary sense of the word since the term refers to any more or less permanent physical record of computer output, such as paper tape, punched cards, computer print-outs. The term is contrasted with 'soft copy'.

hard energy path

harte Energiepolitik

Traditional (i.e., hard path) energy philosophy postulates that energy needs will go on rising forever (or at least for a very long period to come). Since fossil fuels are likely to be depleted soon, the gap will have to be filled by increasingly exotic energy sources, such as power from nuclear fission and fusion.

Interestingly, advocates of the hard path exude an infinite belief in the future solution of as yet entirely unsolved problems, such as nuclear waste disposal or the generation of the unimaginably high temperatures that would be necessary to sustain a nuclear fusion reaction. On the other hand, they are not prepared to believe that the cost of soft energy technologies which are already working satisfactorily (e.g., photovoltaic cells) can be brought down to a competitive level. Needless to say, many hard path enthusiasts are in some way or another professionally involved in hard energy technology marketing.

hard energy technology

harte Energietechnologie

Most of the energy technologies currently used or envisaged can be described as 'hard' because:
1. the violent processes used to generate energy engender waste materials and side-effects which pose an increasing threat to the environment and thus to our life-support systems. Cases in point are the SO_2 and NO_x pollution of the air caused by the combustion of fossil fuels (see: acid rain), and the radioactive waste and emission from nuclear fission.
2. they exploit hard energy sources, which are depletable (non-renewable). Oil, for example, will only last for another few decades, uranium hardly much longer, and coal, a few hundred years.
3. they contribute to the entropy (here: heat pollution) of our planet by releasing, within a few decades, energy that has been stored by nature over thousands of millions of years.
4. they entail further centralisation and concentration of generating and distribution systems, of decision-making and political power, and often require elites of specialists, who may attempt to increase their influence by increasing the dependence of consumers. Cases in point are the electricity utilities in Austria and elsewhere.

Typical hard energy technologies are coal and oil combustion, coal liquefaction and gasification, and nuclear fission and fusion.

Some borderline cases are natural gas technology (because natural gas, although non-renewable, is almost clean in its combustion), hydro-electric schemes (because, while water-power is non-depletable, hydro-electric power-stations can wreak ecological havoc if they are disproportionately large or in other ways unfit for the ecology of the region concerned), and solar satellites (because of the hazards involved in the transmission of large amounts of energy in the form of microwaves).

hardware   Hardware

Hardware, in a data processing context, refers to the physical equipment, comprising the central processing unit and the peripherals (such as input and/or output devices, and storage units). Hardware is contrasted with 'software'.

hedging   Hedging

The term 'hedging' is used either in a very vague and general sense or in a precise, technical sense. In the former case, it refers to any kind of transaction intended to protect an actual or prospective owner from losses due to price changes. Thus, people hedge against inflation by buying property or other assets whose prices are expected to at least match the rate of inflation. Hedging in its more precise and technical sense belongs to the world of commodity trading and commodity exchanges, where it is used to describe the buying or selling of futures contracts to protect an operator from losses due to price changes.

A trader or manufacturer, for example, that requires a certain amount of a commodity, say, in three months, may, instead of buying it forward, engage in a hedging operation. He will first buy an equivalent amount of futures to be settled (closed out) at the time he requires the actual commodity, i.e., in three months. Secondly, he will buy the actual commodity in the spot market when required, i.e., again in three months' time. Any fall or rise in the price of the actual commodity will be offset by the profit or loss on the sale of the futures contracts. A trader wishing to sell at some future time will hedge by selling an equivalent amount of futures.

Hedging, therefore, in contrast to forward trading, requires two different, but matching, transactions: the purchase or sale of futures contracts to be settled when the actual commodity is purchased or sold in the spot market.

In conclusion, it might be worth mentioning that financial futures (interest-rate futures, currency futures, stock-index futures) are being increasingly used for hedging against volatile interest rates, floating exchange rates, and fluctuating share prices.

holding company   Muttergesellschaft,
                                    Holding(gesellschaft)

In a strictly legal sense (e.g., as defined in the British Companies Act 1948), a holding company is any company that controls at least one subsidiary (usually by owning more than 50 per cent of its equity capital). In journalistic and business usage, however, the term usually refers to what is sometimes called a 'pure' (or 'non-operating') holding company, i.e., a parent company having many subsidiaries and confining its activities primarily to their management. Holding companies in this sense, therefore, do not engage in the production and distribution of goods and/or services, but typically perform financial, corporate planning, and other overall management services for their subsidiaries.

home banking

Abwicklung von Bankgeschäften über Heimterminals,
„Homebanking"

Home banking refers to self-service banking on interactive terminals (such as adapted telephones and T.V. sets, videotex terminals, or home computers) installed in customers' private homes.

So far, home banking services have been offered to selected customers in various pilot projects designed to help cut personnel cost and facilitate customer access to basic services, such as transferring funds between accounts; purchasing and selling securities; arranging for payments in foreign currencies; creating and cancelling standing order mandates; ordering cheque books; applying for loans, etc.. Furthermore, the home banking terminal may provide the subscriber with continuously up-dated information on banking hours, service fees, foreign exchange rates, share prices, loan and investment schemes, and account balances.

To get access to his own bank account, the customer uses a system of codes and passwords, which protect his account and prevent interference with ordinary data processing in the bank.

hot money

Fluchtgeld,
heißes Geld

Hot money is a colourful name for short-term capital that moves quickly, and often unexpectedly, from one country to another, either to avoid or escape a fall in the exchange rate and/or in interest rates, or to benefit from a possible rise in the exchange rate and/or from higher interest rates. If speculators expect, for instance, a depreciation of the British pound, they will sell their financial assets denominated in sterling for dollar- or D-mark-assets. Conversely, rumours about a possible revaluation of the D-mark will prompt speculators invested in other currencies to move into D-mark-denominated assets. Changes in interest rate differentials may have a similar effect.

These quick movements of short-term capital present a great problem for monetary management, since they are inclined to destabilise exchange rates and tend to lead to sharper fluctuations than might be warranted by the underlying economic factors, such as trade flows, inflation rates, long-term capital movements, etc..

house bill of lading

Hauskonnossement,
Spediteurkonnossement

House bills of lading are issued by forwarding agents who combine goods from different consignors into large consignments. These grouped consignments are, in turn, shipped under groupage bills of lading, issued by the carrier to the forwarding agent. Such a consolidation of cargoes is particularly common where goods are shipped in mixed containers.

The term 'house bill of lading' is a misnomer (the term 'shipping certificate' is more appropriate), because such a document is not a bill of lading in the legal sense of the word. It is not a document of title, giving the consignee a right to claim the goods from the carrier, but only a receipt for the goods delivered to the forwarding agent. Consequently, a house bill of lading cannot be tendered under a c.i.f. contract as a proper bill of lading, and, if the contract allows such a tender, it cannot be regarded as a proper c.i.f. contract. Moreover, if payment is arranged under a documentary credit, the bank will reject a house bill unless it is specifically authorised in the credit to accept it.

hull insurance

(See- und Luft-)Kaskoversicherung

The term 'hull insurance' means insurance both on the ship, including machinery and equipment, (marine hull insurance) and on the aircraft (aircraft hull insurance) itself. It covers physical damage to, and total loss of, an insured vessel or aeroplane.

I

importer Importeur

The term 'importer' refers to a buyer who brings goods into his country from abroad.

import licence Importlizenz,
Einfuhrlizenz

An import licence (American spelling: 'import license') is a document which is obtained from the government giving permission to import specified goods. Primarily, import licensing aims to protect domestic industries in the short term by restricting competitive imports. Moreover, import licensing is sometimes used as a means of exchange control, for an importer may not be allowed to pay for the goods without obtaining such a licence. Also, goods which are subject to an import quota can only be imported if an import licence has first been issued to the importer.

import merchant Einfuhrhändler,
Importhändler

An import merchant is an independent firm buying goods from foreign suppliers for its own account and reselling them to buyers in its home country. It may hold stocks for distribution when it obtains orders, or it may only buy when it itself has orders for the goods from local buyers - this will usually depend on the type of goods in question. Normally, heavy industrial equipment is not bought for stock, but consumer products are generally stocked for resale.

import quota Einfuhrkontingent,
Importkontingent

The term 'import quota' may be defined as the maximum amount of a certain commodity which the government allows into the country during a specified period of time. Import quotas may be fixed in terms of quantity (e.g., the number of HIFI-sets imported within a year may be limited to 200,000) or in terms of value. They may apply to imports of the commodity in question either from all countries (overall or global quota) or from a specified country (allocated quota, e.g., the number of cars imported from Japan may be limited to 150,000 p.a.). Importers wishing to import goods subject to a quota have to apply for an import licence. Import licences are granted until the quota is exhausted.

Import quotas are often adopted as a protectionist device to shield domestic producers from the effects of foreign competition. In addition, they are also intended to cope with balance-of-payments deficits and to protect domestic employment in particular industries.

incomes policy   Einkommenspolitik

Incomes policy is the branch of economic policy aimed at restraining wages, salaries, profits, dividends, prices, or other forms of income, either together or selectively, mainly with a view to slowing down (cost-push) inflation. Examples of incomes policies include wage and price controls, wage and price freezes, voluntary wage and price guidelines, and agreements between government, business, and labour on wage and price restraint. From the above examples it can be seen that incomes policies may be either voluntary or statutory, i.e., the government may rely either on persuasion and exhortation (jawbone, in American economic jargon) or on mandatory controls.

Incomes policies, although difficult to impose and to implement, are preferable to deflationary (fiscal or monetary) policies as a method of dealing with persistent cost-push inflation, since they tend to avoid the latter's nasty side-effects, such as unemployment.

income statement   Erfolgsrechnung, Gewinn- und Verlustrechnung, V+G-Rechnung

The income statement is one of the financial accounting records drawn up at the end of an accounting period, i.e., usually at the end of a fiscal year, although quarterly or monthly income statements are not unknown. The main purpose of this statement is to summarise all revenues earned and expenses incurred during the accounting period and to determine whether the reporting business unit has produced a profit or a loss. Technically, this is done by transferring the balances of the various revenue and expense accounts from the trial balance to the income statement.

Since an income statement is concerned with what has happened over a period of time, it represents a flow concept. By contrast, the balance sheet, which is geared to a specific point of time, viz., the balance sheet date, is a stock concept.

The information contained in an income statement can be shown in a variety of ways. The most common and informative format, or layout, is the multiple-step report form, where the final result, colloquially referred to as the 'bottom line', is worked out step by step, and interesting intermediary differences are shown.

The starting point of an income statement is 'net sales', i.e., sales less returns. 'Net sales' less 'cost of goods sold' gives the 'gross margin', or 'gross profit'. 'Gross profit' minus 'operating expenses', such as distribution and administrative expenses, gives the 'operating profit' (also known as 'income from primary operations' or 'operating income'). To this are added any 'non-operating revenues' and any 'extraordinary revenues', and from this are deducted any 'non-operating expenses' and any 'extraordinary expenses'. Finally, income tax has to be deducted to arrive at the 'net income', or 'net profit', the amount available for distribution and for allocation to retained earnings accounts.

In the United Kingdom, the information contained in a U.S. income statement was originally presented in two separate accounts, viz., in the trading account ('net sales' minus 'cost of goods sold', giving 'gross profit on trading', or 'trading profit') and in the profit and loss account, which started with the gross profit on trading. It is now usual for the trading and profit and loss accounts to be shown under one combined heading, viz., 'trading & profit & loss account' or simply 'profit and loss account'. To avoid confusion, it should be noted that in British accounting statements and in accounting literature, the term 'trading profit' frequently corresponds to the American 'operating profit', and not to the American gross profit, or gross margin.

income statement ratios   Kennzahlen der V+G-Rechnung

Income statement ratios, as the term suggests, express relationships between income statement items. These ratios are used primarily to analyse the profitability of a firm's operations. Two commonly used ratios are the 'operating ratio' and the 'net profit margin'.

The operating ratio provides a general indication of how efficiently the firm in question has been operated in the period under review. It is computed by dividing total operating expenses by net sales. Total operating expenses include the cost of goods sold as well as general, selling, and administrative expenses. An operating ratio of, say, 90% indicates that 90% of the firm's annual sales were consumed by operating expenses. The difference between the operating ratio (expressed as a percentage) and 100% is the 'ratio of operating income to net sales', or the 'operating profit ratio'. Obviously, the lower the operating ratio, the higher the operating profit ratio, and the more efficient the operations of the firm.

The net profit margin indicates the proportionate size of the profit element in the sales of a firm. It is computed by dividing net income (i.e., net profit after taxes) by net sales. A net profit margin of, say, 2% means that the firm concerned realises 2% of sales in profit, or, to put it in a slightly different way, for every dollar (pound, schilling, etc.) of sales, the firm realises 2 cents (2 pence, 2 groschen, etc.) in profit.

income tax - personal   Einkommenssteuer

Personal income tax is levied on the income received by an individual or household, while the income (profit) of a company or corporation is subject to corporation tax (U.S.: corporation income tax). Personal income taxes are very popular with governments, though perhaps less so with taxpayers, not only because they are relatively easy to administer and, therefore, efficient revenue-raisers, but also because they can be used as an instrument of fiscal policy and of social policy (e.g., to stimulate aggregate demand or to redistribute incomes). The popularity of personal income taxes is also due to the belief that an individual's income is the best single index of his ability to contribute to the support of government. In other words, personal income taxes are regarded as equitable, or fair.

Personal income taxes are collected in two principal ways: in the case of wages and salaries, the usual procedure is for the employer to withhold the tax and pay it over to the revenue authorities. In the United Kingdom, this method of withholding personal income taxes is referred to as the 'Pay-As-You-Earn system' (P.A.Y.E. system). Where the income is derived from self-employment or from the operation of an unincorporated business (e.g., of a sole proprietorship or partnership), the taxpayer is required to file a tax return after the end of the fiscal year. On the basis of this return, the revenue authorities issue a notice of assessment in due time. In addition, the taxpayer may have to make advance payments, which are then set off against the final assessment.

In spite of basic similarities, personal income tax systems differ widely from one country to another. For one thing, personal income may be defined differently. In some countries, personal income taxes are imposed on total income, while in others, income from different sources is taxed under separate rules and often at different rates. The United Kingdom operates a mixed system, under which incomes from different sources (e.g., income from dependent employment; income from the occupation of certain woodlands; profits of trades, businesses, and professions) are reported under separate schedules, but taxed jointly. Capital gains, however, are subject to a separate tax (capital gains tax).

Another respect in which personal income tax systems differ widely from each other is the number and size of tax allowances and similar reliefs intended to take account of a taxpayer's special circumstances and to adjust the tax burden to his ability to pay. The British Information Services booklet on taxation (1975) lists a large number of personal allowances, such as single person allowance, married couple allowance, various child allowances, dependent relative allowance, blind person's allowance, wife's earned income allowance, age allowance, etc.. In addition, income tax relief may be claimed for premiums on a life assurance policy taken out on the life of the taxpayer or his wife. Austria has a system of tax credits (including an earned income tax credit and a sole earner's tax credit) and a variety of personal deductions for special types of expenditure (e.g., life assurance premiums and certain types of investments), which serve a similar purpose.

incorporation (of a company)   Gründung (einer Kapitalgesellschaft)

Before a company, especially a public limited company, is set up/established/ formed/ in the U.K., the company promoters (i.e., persons involved in the formation of the company) must enter into negotiations on the acquisition of land, buildings, and other property, obtain the consent of the proposed directors to act as such, and arrange for the underwriting of the shares.

The formalities necessary for the incorporation of a company are quite simple. Certain prescribed documents have to be prepared, usually by a solicitor on the instructions of the promoters, and filed with the Registrar of Companies. They include: the memorandum of association; the articles of association; a list of the names of the first directors and the secretary; a statement of the amount of capital the company is to be authorised to issue. After payment of the proper fees, the Registrar issues a certificate of incorporation, from the date of which the company exists as a legal person. A private limited company may commence business immediately. A public limited company may not commence business or exercise any of its borrowing powers until it has complied with certain other requirements and received a trading certificate from the Registrar. After commencement of business, every company has to hold a general meeting (called a 'statutory meeting'), where the statutory report and any matters relating to the formation are discussed.

The memorandum of association defines the company's powers and regulates its relations with the outside world. It must contain separate clauses setting out the name of the company, the location of the registered office, the objects of the company (i.e., the activities the company is allowed to engage in), the limitation of liability (either by shares or by guarantee), and the amount of nominal share capital and its division into shares. A company established as a public limited company must also state this fact in the memorandum.

In contrast to the memorandum, the articles of association regulate the internal affairs of the company, such as procedure at meetings, the voting rights of different classes of shareholders (ordinary shareholders, preference shareholders), the powers and duties of directors, etc..

The memorandum and the articles of association constitute a binding contract between the company and its members, and can be altered only by special resolution of the latter. The memorandum and the articles together are the approximate equivalent of the 'Satzung' (AG) or 'Gesellschaftsvertrag' (GmbH), both also referred to as 'Statuten'.

In the United States, where the procedure of incorporation is broadly similar, the relevant documents (in particular, the articles of incorporation and the bylaws) have to be filed with the Secretary of State of the state of incorporation. Since the corporation laws of the states are not uniform, some advantage may be gained by incorporating under the laws of a particular state (e.g., the statutes of Delaware give promoters and management much greater freedom than do some other states).

The articles of incorporation, also known as the 'charter', are the approximate equivalent of the memorandum of association in the U.K., but, by contrast, also contain provisions for the regulation of internal affairs. They specify: the name of the corporation - which must be followed by 'Corporation' (abbr. 'Corp.'), 'Company' (abbr. 'Co.'), or 'Incorporated' (abbr. 'Inc.') - ; the duration and purpose of the corporation; the address of the registered office; the number and classes of stock, and the rights of the different classes of stockholders; the names of the directors and incorporators (i.e., the original subscribers of shares).

The bylaws - the approximate equivalent of the articles of association in a British company - include specifications as to the meetings of shareholders, voting procedures, responsibilities of officers, etc..

INCOTERMS INCOTERMS

The INCOTERMS (abbreviation of 'International Commercial Terms') are a set of international rules for the interpretation of specified trade terms used in export sales. They were first published by the ICC (International Chamber of Commerce) in 1936. Amendments and additions were made in 1953, 1967, 1976, and 1980 in order to provide an up-to-date set of rules broadly in line with current practice in international trade.

The main purpose of these terms is (i) to define the method of delivery of the goods sold; (ii) to indicate the seller's and the buyer's duties; and (iii) to indicate the point(s) up to which the costs and risks of the goods are borne by the seller and from which they are borne by the buyer, i.e., the point(s) where the costs and risks pass from the seller to the buyer. 'Costs of the goods' in this context does not mean the cost price of the goods, but all costs incurred in getting the goods to the place of destination, such as cost of packing, loading and unloading charges, cost of insurance, etc.. Under some of the INCOTERMS, the points where costs and risks are transferred do not coincide. This is the case with C.& F., C.I.F., 'freight or carriage paid to...' and 'freight or carriage and insurance paid to...'. The INCOTERMS do not determine, as is often wrongly assumed, the passing of title to the goods.

In addition, they serve as the basis for price quotations. When a supplier quotes a price, for example on a c.i.f. basis (cost, insurance, freight), this means that his quotation includes all the costs he has to assume under the contract. It is evident that the seller, when quoting f.o.b. (free on board), will ask for a lower price than when quoting c.i.f., because, in the latter case, he would include insurance and freight in the purchase price, while he would not do so in the former case.

In some instances, the INCOTERMS may refer only to the calculation of the purchase price, while the delivery of the goods is governed by other terms. For instance, the seller's price-list or catalogue might quote 'ex works' prices for the advertised goods, and the foreign buyer might order goods accordingly, but the parties might agree that the goods are to be dispatched by mail by the seller, who undertakes to pack, invoice, frank, and insure them. In this context, it should be noted that special provisions in the individual contract between the parties will override anything stipulated in the rules. Parties may adopt INCOTERMS as the general basis for their contract, but may also specify particular variations of, or additions to, them. For instance, a buyer may require a c.i.f. supplier to provide war risk insurance as well as marine insurance. In that case, the purchaser may specify "INCOTERMS C.I.F. plus war risk insurance". The seller will then quote his price on that basis.

Finally, it should be mentioned that the application of the INCOTERMS is completely voluntary. If, however, a contract is concluded on the basis of the INCOTERMS, the seller and the buyer know exactly what their duties are, which helps to avoid misunderstandings and disputes in international trade.

For details of the various INCOTERMS see: "ex works"; F.O.R./F.O.T.; F.A.S.; F.O.B.; C.& F.; C.I.F.; "ex ship"; "ex quay"; "delivered at frontier"; "delivered duty paid"; "F.O.B. airport"; "free carrier"; "freight/carriage paid to..."; "freight/carriage and insurance paid to..." - (INCOTERMS 1980). In all the definitions and explanations, the main emphasis is on when the costs and risks pass from the seller to the buyer, and on the most important types of cost to be borne by each party. The question of who is responsible for procuring the various types of transport documents (e.g., bill of lading) is very complex and goes beyond the scope of these definitions. For these and further details please refer to:
ICC: INCOTERMS, International rules for the interpretation of trade terms, 1980 edition; and
EISEMANN/MELIS: INCOTERMS, Ausgabe 1980; Kommentar 1982, GOF Verlag, Wien.

Although these clauses are primarily designed for export sales, the following may also be used in domestic transactions: 'ex works', F.O.R./F.O.T., 'freight/carriage paid to...'.

The following are some illustrative examples of clauses as they may be found in contracts of sale:

1. Delivery c.i.f., Alexandria. (Lieferung c.i.f., Alexandrien.)
2. Our prices are / are quoted / f.o.b. Hamburg. (Unsere Preise verstehen sich f.o.b. Hamburg.)
3. The price of one case is £8.50, f.o.r. London Bridge. (Der Preis einer Kiste beträgt £8,50, 'frei Waggon', London Bridge.)

index

Index

An index is a single number which represents the average value of a set of related items (e.g., wholesale prices) compared with their average value at some base period. The average value at the base period usually equals 100, and a change from it is expressed as a percentage. If, for instance, the Wholesale Price Index is currently 130, this means that the average value of all wholesale prices has risen 30 per cent on the base period. To make indices more realistic, it is customary to calculate not just the simple average of the set of items involved, but to weight the items, i.e., to multiply each item by a number reflecting its relative importance in the whole set.

Index numbers are very useful statistical devices, because they enable huge amounts of data to be reduced to a form which can be more readily understood. Examples of index numbers include price indices (Retail Price Index, Wholesale Price Index, Dow-Jones Index - which is an unweighted index of 30 stocks listed on the New York Stock Exchange), volume indices (e.g., Index of Industrial Production), and several others.

index linking

Indexbindung,
Indexkoppelung,
automatische Valorisierung

Index linking - also called 'indexation' - is a mechanism for periodic adjustments in the nominal values of contracts in line with movements in a specified price index. Escalator clauses in labour contracts and the indexing of income tax rates and exemptions in Canada provide examples of this practice.

Indexing all contracts in an economy would protect everybody from inflation, although it would leave the country vulnerable to international competition. As a recent example, the I.M.F. (International Monetary Fund) has forced Brazil to de-index wages as a condition for extending loans.

indirect quotation

Mengennotierung

Indirect quotation is a method of quoting rates of exchange. An exchange rate quoted on an indirect basis (in the U.K. called a 'currency rate') indicates the number of units of a foreign currency per unit of the home currency. It states the amount of foreign currency that can be obtained, or has to be paid, for one unit of the home currency.

In the case of an indirect quotation/currency rate, a bank/foreign exchange dealer works on the principle of "buy high and sell low". This means that a bank, when buying a foreign currency from a customer, wants to get as many units of the foreign currency as possible for each unit of home currency paid to the customer, and, when selling, gives as few units of the foreign currency as possible for each unit of home currency received from the customer. Let us assume that the Austrian schilling is quoted in London at AS28.20/28.50. This means that the bank in London sells schillings at 28.20 and buys schillings at 28.50. This example shows that the bank's selling rate is on the left and the bank's buying rate on the right. In contrast to direct quotations/pence rates, all quoted currency rates have the selling rate on the left and the buying rate on the right. This applies to both spot rates and forward rates.

In banking practice, forward rates are quoted in terms of premiums or discounts in relation to the spot rates. If currency rates are used, a premium is deducted from the spot rate (both selling rate and buying rate), i.e., the forward rate is lower than the spot rate. This is because a premium means that the foreign currency for future delivery is dearer than for immediate delivery, and, therefore, fewer units of it can be obtained for each unit of the home currency than at the spot rate. The opposite is true of a discount, which has to be added to the spot rate, i.e., the forward rate is higher than the spot rate.

indirect tax   indirekte Steuer

An indirect tax is described as a tax on goods and services which may be shifted by the original taxpayer (i.e., the person who is required by law to pay the tax over to the revenue authorities) to the ultimate consumer, who actually bears/pays the tax in the form of increased prices. This definition shows that an indirect tax is one which is not levied directly on the person on whom it ultimately falls. The original taxpayer (manufacturer, wholesaler, retailer) is not identical with the person who actually bears the tax (ultimate consumer). In other words, in the case of indirect taxes, the tax incidence (i.e., the final place where the tax burden is borne) is on the ultimate consumer, because he cannot pass the tax on to someone else.

The most important indirect taxes are: value-added tax, customs duties, and excise duties. The main purpose of indirect taxation is to raise revenue (V.A.T., excise duties, revenue tariffs) and, in the case of protective tariffs, to protect domestic industries from foreign competition. Any proposal to increase an indirect tax must take into account the possible effects on demand. If the demand for the item taxed is very elastic, a high tax rate may well lead to a fall rather than a rise in total revenue.

indorsement   Indossament

The term 'indorsement' (also spelt 'endorsement') is mainly used in connection with the transfer of instruments payable to order. In contrast to instruments payable to bearer (e.g., bearer cheque, bearer bill of exchange), which can be transferred by delivery of the instrument only, all instruments payable to order (e.g., order bill of exchange, order cheque, promissory note, order bill of lading, warehouse warrant) are transferred by delivery and indorsement. Transfer in this context means that the rights embodied in the instrument pass from one person (the transferor) to another (the transferee).

An indorsement must be written on the back of the instrument. The person who writes the indorsement is called the 'indorser' (also 'endorser'), and the person to whom the instrument is indorsed is referred to as the 'indorsee' (also 'endorsee').

The most important types of indorsement are 'blank indorsements' and 'special indorsements'. A blank indorsement, or indorsement in blank, consists only of the indorser's signature, which means that the instrument becomes payable to bearer and can be further transferred by mere delivery. Bills of lading and warehouse warrants are invariably indorsed in blank.

A special indorsement consists of the indorser's signature and the name of the indorsee, sometimes followed by the date (e.g., "Pay to John Brown. July 18, 1985 - signed: Henry Smith"; or: "Pay to John Brown or order. July 18, 1985 -

signed: Henry Smith"). Further transfer by the indorsee is possible only by means of another indorsement. In rare cases, a special indorsement is used to transform an instrument payable to bearer into an instrument payable to order.

The indorsement may also be in such a form as to prohibit further transfer of the instrument, in which case it is termed a 'restrictive indorsement' (e.g., "Pay to John Brown only"). This, however, does not affect the rights of the indorsee against the indorser.

industrial licensing   Lizenzvergabe

Patents (but also other types of industrial property, such as industrial designs and trade marks) may be commercially exploited by their holders in various ways. One method is for the patent holder, or patentee, to work the patent himself. A chemical company, for instance, having invented a new process may decide to use it exclusively and shut out all other chemical companies. Secondly, it is possible to assign, i.e., to sell, patents to other business firms, which means that the patent holder parts with all his rights in the patent, usually against payment of a lump sum. Thirdly, industrial property may also be licensed. Under the last-mentioned method, referred to as 'industrial licensing', a patent holder (the 'licensor') permits a person or firm (the 'licensee') to use the patent for a limited period of time, usually against payment of a periodic licence fee, or royalty. For instance, VOEST, which invented the L-D steel-making process, or basic oxygen process, in addition to using the process itself, licensed it to U.S. steel firms.

A typical licensing agreement based on a patent licence will include the following points:
1. identity of licensed patent;
2. scope of licence (e.g., whether it is exclusive or non-exclusive);
3. payment of licence fees, or royalties (basis of calculating fee, e.g., net sales of items produced under licence, accounting requirements to be observed by licensee, rights of inspection for licensor);
4. duration of licence (upper limit is duration of patent);
5. arbitration;
6. law of contract;
7. jurisdiction.

Industrial licensing has grown in importance in recent years, especially on the international front. To some extent, this development reflects the shift from product-based to service-based economies in the industrialised world.

industrial policy   Industriepolitik

Industrial policy is the branch of economic policy by which a government tries to influence the industrial structure, or industrial mix, of a particular country. It is concerned with the question of what kinds of industry are desirable for a particular country and what size they should be.

A government may try to encourage 'sunrise' industries or it may help ease the pain of shrinking 'sunset' (i.e., declining) industries back to a healthy size or of phasing them out. The range of instruments that might be used by a government in this area includes selective investment incentives (investment grants, first-year allowances, investment tax credits), outright subsidies, favourable loans, planning procedures, public investment corporations for active intervention in the industrial field, government procurement policies, protective tariffs, and related measures.

Industrial policy is particularly important in times of structural change. Generally speaking, socialist governments are more likely to give a higher priority to this type of policy than conservative ones.

industrial relations

(institutionalisierte) Arbeitgeber-Arbeitnehmer Beziehungen

This term does not, as might be supposed, refer to the relationships between various industries or between business firms within a given industry, but to the relations between the two sides of industry, viz., labour and management, within the framework provided by government. In British usage, the term is normally restricted to the collective relations between employers and employees, i.e., between employers' associations and trade unions, while the term 'human relations' is used to describe certain aspects of the relations between individual workers and employers. Industrial relations is, therefore, concerned with collective bargaining, national or industrial wage rates, trade union recognition, employee-management co-operation and conflict, incomes policy, and related matters. In the U.K., industrial relations are characterised by frequent industrial conflicts and industrial action (such as strikes), while the Austrian system of industrial relations (called 'Sozialpartnerschaft') puts a premium on negotiations and compromise.

industry[1]

Fertigungsindustrie

In certain contexts, industry denotes the sector of the economy made up of manufacturing establishments and is, therefore, coextensive with 'secondary industry'. It should be noted that, in contrast to the German expression 'Industrie', 'industry' includes also small- and medium-scale establishments.

industry[2]

Wirtschaftszweig, Branche, -wirtschaft

In its wider sense, industry refers to any branch of economic activity and is, therefore, not restricted to manufacturing. Agriculture is an industry, just as is the production of chemicals or of steel (chemical industry, steel industry). But there are also service industries, such as the insurance industry or the tourist industry. Moreover, the private sector of the economy is occasionally referred to as 'private industry'.

inflation

Inflation

Inflation is the persistent rise in the price of goods and services (including factors of production) over an extended period of time, as measured by a price index. Inflation leads to a decline in the purchasing power of a given nominal sum of money. This loss of purchasing power is sometimes described as the depreciation of the internal value of a currency.

213

There is no definitive theory of inflation, although many economists regard an excess of demand over supply (demand-pull inflation), an increase in costs (cost-push inflation), and structural imbalances (demand-shift inflation), either singly or in combination, as causes of the inflationary process.

information management   Informationswirtschaft

Information - e.g., information on costs, customers, competitors, supply markets, or on the economy as a whole - has always had a role to play in the successful operation of businesses. But it is only in recent years - probably in connection with the increasing complexity of business organisations and of economic life in general - that its importance has been fully recognised and has merited specific managerial attention. Increasingly, the generation, flow, storage, retrieval, manipulation, and use of information are no longer being left to chance, but are being subjected to standard management procedures, such as analysis, planning, and control. In this context, the application of systems thinking has proved particularly useful: all information-related activities as well as the people and mechanical or electronic aids involved are viewed as elements of an integrated information system. This means that the elements influence each other and that the information system as a whole interacts with the other subsystems (e.g., marketing, finance) of the organisation.

A business organisation wishing to provide and use information efficiently, with maximum benefits and minimum costs to the organisation and its members, will probably set up a central information management unit. This unit will be headed by a top-level executive (e.g., by a vice-president for information, reporting to the president) and will have overall responsibility for all information-related matters, in particular, for designing, implementing, operating, and controlling an efficient information management system. For this purpose, it will first be necessary to analyse the information needs (mainly who needs what kind of information) and the existing information resources of the organisation (e.g., internal and external records, information processing and communication equipment, but also people inside and outside the organisation). In designing the information management system management will probably have to supplement and/or replace existing resources, eliminate redundant elements, avoid duplication, reduce information overload, and, most importantly, integrate all resources to achieve the desired effect.

Although computers and telecommunication devices (e.g., personal computers linked with the organisation's mainframe in a distributed data processing system) are bound to play an important role in any modern information system, it would be wrong to equate their presence with efficiency. Efficiency can only be achieved if the mix of manual, mechanised, and computer-assisted activities fits the requirements of a particular organisation. There are many highly efficient information systems that use computers only sparingly, if at all.

information processing   Datenverarbeitung (im weiteren Sinne), Informationsverarbeitung

The term 'information processing' is synonymous with 'data processing' in the wider sense of the word.

infrastructure — Infrastruktur

Infrastructure is the foundation underlying a nation's economy and is, therefore, essential to its proper functioning. It includes transportation and communication systems, water supplies, electric power, waste disposal, and other public services. The term is often widened to include the educational and administrative systems of a particular country.

initial order — Erstauftrag

An initial order, or first order, is, as the term implies, the first order placed by a customer with a particular supplier.

inquiry — Anfrage

Many business transactions start with an inquiry (also spelt 'enquiry') relating to goods. This is usually a letter addressed to a supplier by a prospective customer (also called a 'prospect' in business).

In a letter of inquiry, the prospective buyer has to state simply, clearly, and concisely what he wants - general information, sales literature (catalogues, leaflets, etc.), a price-list, a sample, a quotation, an estimate, and so on. As most letters of inquiry are short and simple, many firms have adopted the practice of sending printed inquiry forms, thereby eliminating the need for a letter. It is also possible for the prospective buyer to make the inquiry by telephone, by telegram, or by telex. Businessmen usually send inquiries to several likely suppliers, as they want to find out which of these suppliers offers the best quality, the most favourable prices and terms, etc.. From the legal point of view, it is important to note that an inquiry is without any obligation for the inquirer.

insolvency — Überschuldung; Illiquidität

The term 'insolvency' has two different meanings: 'actual insolvency', in which case a firm's liabilities exceed its assets, and 'technical insolvency', where a firm cannot meet its current debts as they fall due. In the case of technical insolvency, assets may exceed liabilities, but they may not be liquid enough to meet current debts.

instalment — Rate

An instalment is any of a number of part payments, usually of equal amount and due at regular intervals. The term is used especially in connection with the purchase of consumer goods under an instalment plan, but may also be applied to the part payments on a debt, e.g., a term loan, each of which is specified as to amount and date due, interest often being included.

instalment sale

Ratenkauf

Where goods are bought on the instalment plan, the buyer is usually required to pay a certain percentage of the purchase price as down payment, or deposit, while the balance is payable in a number of part payments of equal amount at stipulated intervals. Property in the goods purchased under such an arrangement may pass either on payment of the deposit and delivery of the goods (credit sale) or on payment of the last instalment (conditional sale). Hire purchase transactions, although legally more complicated, are similar to conditional sales in that title to the goods passes on payment of the last instalment. It should be noted that the term 'hire purchase' is often indiscriminately applied to credit sales, conditional sales, and hire purchase transactions proper, and has therefore, in everyday usage, become a synonym for 'instalment sale'.

insurance

Versicherung

Insurance may be defined as a contractual relationship under which one party (the insurer) agrees, against payment of a consideration (the premium), to indemnify another party (the insured) for any loss of, or damage to, the subject-matter insured which the latter may incur due to designated events. In the case of life insurance, also called '(life) assurance', the agreement is for the payment of a stipulated sum of money to a third party (the beneficiary) on the death of the insured or on the expiry of the policy period.

The basic principle of modern insurance is the pooling of risks. A large number of persons bearing essentially the same risks pay regular contributions into a common fund, administered by an insurer, which is used to make payments to those who suffer a misfortune. This is of particular importance to business people, who are thereby enabled to transform the basically unpredictable risks incidental to doing business into definite costs.

The amount of the contribution, i.e., the premium, is assessed according to the probability of losses. The work of evaluating risks and assessing premiums is performed by actuaries, who are experts in mathematics and statistics.

The most important types of commercial insurance are: marine insurance, life insurance, fire insurance, motor insurance (U.S.: automobile insurance). Other kinds of insurance are: theft insurance, fidelity insurance (covering losses resulting from an employee's dishonesty), luggage insurance, personal accident insurance, liability insurance, etc..

insurance agent

Versicherungsvertreter

An insurance agent is an independent business man who introduces insurance business to an insurance company in return for a commission. In contrast to the insurance broker, the insurance agent acts as agent of the insurer.

The majority of insurance agents are not primarily engaged in insurance. They are appointed agents on a part-time basis because, usually from their own profession, they are in a position to introduce clients to their principal, the insurer. Thus, it is very common for bank managers, solicitors, tax advisers, car dealers, travel agents, and the like to hold an agency appointment, often with more than one company.

In Austria, the term 'Versicherungsvertreter' is also used colloquially for employees of insurance offices who sell insurance on a salary-plus-commission basis.

insurance broker   Versicherungsmakler

An insurance broker is an independent business man who acts as an intermediary between the insured and the insurer with a view to effecting an insurance. In this, the broker acts as the agent of the insured and not of the insurer.

Unlike insurance agents, insurance brokers profess to be experts in insurance. They are full-time specialists, have special knowledge of the insurance market, and offer advice and professional help in arranging insurances on behalf of their clients. Anyone may request an insurance broker to act for him, and the broker is required to negotiate the most favourable insurance contract for him with the insurers. It should be noted that the most important difference between the insurance broker and the insurance agent is that the former is free to place the insurance with any insurer, and does not represent any particular companies. Strangely enough, although an insurance broker acts as the agent of the insured, he is not remunerated by his client, but receives a commission (termed 'brokerage') from the insurer, in much the same way as do insurance agents, for introducing an insured to him.

In Great Britain, many insurance brokers are members of Lloyd's (Lloyd's broker). A Lloyd's broker is a specially authorised broker, who will not necessarily deal exclusively with Lloyd's, but also with other insurers.

insurance policy   Versicherungspolizze,
                                       Versicherungsschein

The insurance policy is written evidence of the insurance contract. It is a document setting out the exact terms and conditions of an insurance transaction, e.g., the precise risks covered; exclusions of cover, if any; the period of cover; the amount of premium; etc..

insurance premium   Versicherungsprämie

Insurance premium may be defined as the consideration which the insurer receives from the policyholder for his undertaking to pay the sum insured if the event insured against occurs. The amount of premium is purely a matter of contract, depending on the insurer's estimate of the risk. For example, the premium charged for a cargo policy in (ocean) marine insurance depends on the type of goods insured, the sum insured, the risks covered (f.p.a.; w.a.; all risks; war; strikes; etc.), the claims experience over, say, the past three or five years, etc..

The premium is payable in cash, in advance. Where the insurance is effected through a broker, the broker is solely and personally responsible to the insurer for payment of the premium. In other words, the policyholder pays the premium to the broker, who must pay it to the insurer.

intangible fixed assets   immaterielles Anlagevermögen

In accounting, items of intellectual property, such as patents, trade marks, copyrights, etc., are referred to as 'intangible fixed assets'. These are assets whose value resides in the rights which their possession confers upon the owner. In contrast to tangible fixed assets, intangible fixed assets (also known as 'intangible assets' or simply as 'intangibles') have no physical substance, but represent legal rights, privileges, and competitive advantages that accrue to a business enterprise through ownership. The rights inherent in intangibles may be physically evidenced by contracts, certificates, and other supporting documents, but the intangibles themselves do not possess physical substance. The main characteristics of intangible assets may be summarised as follows: (i) they may be purchased from external sources or developed internally; (ii) their ownership confers some exclusive rights upon the business firm; and (iii) they are relatively long-lived.

The most common items classified as intangible fixed assets are:
1. Patents: a patent is the exclusive right granted by the government to an inventor to manufacture, sell, or use his invention for a certain period of time (in the United States, 17 years). At the end of this period, the patent expires and becomes public property available to all.
2. Copyrights: a copyright is the exclusive right granted by the government to its holder to reproduce, publish, and sell a literary product (e.g., a book) or a work of art. In the U.S., for example, copyrights are granted for a period of 28 years.
3. Trade marks (see: brand).
4. Goodwill: although goodwill is in some respects a special case, it is generally classified as an intangible asset since it involves such intangible elements connected with a business firm as favourable and convenient location, customer satisfaction, efficiency of operation, good reputation, quality of products, favourable prices, satisfactory relations between employees and management, financial standing, good business management, etc.. These elements are collectively referred to as 'internally developed goodwill', and are not properly reflected in the balance sheet. Goodwill is recognised in the accounts only when a business is purchased, in which case it is known as 'purchased goodwill'. The amount paid for, and recorded as, goodwill is that portion of the purchase price which exceeds the market value of all assets acquired less any liabilities assumed.

Finally, it should be noted that the cost of some intangible fixed assets can be written off during their useful lives in much the same way as can the cost of tangible fixed assets (see: depreciation[2]) and of natural resources (see: depletion). The accounting process of allocating systematically the cost of intangible assets to expense is referred to as 'amortisation'.

interest[1]   Zinsen

Interest is the price charged by the lender, or, conversely, paid by the borrower, for the temporary use of funds. Interest is normally expressed as a percentage per annum of the principal, i.e., the amount lent or borrowed, in which case it is called the 'interest rate'. Generally speaking, interest rates are determined by the supply of, and the demand for, credit, by the rate of inflation, by monetary controls, by the creditworthiness of the borrower, and by other related factors.

Different types of banks charge or pay a great variety of interest rates on different types of loans or deposits. In many countries, the rate of interest charged by the central bank when lending to the banking system is not just an interest rate, but an important instrument of monetary policy. This interest rate is called the 'discount rate' in the united States, the 'minimum lending rate' (MLR) in Great Britain, and the 'bank rate' in Canada. In Austria, the term 'Leitzinsen' is used, and there are two different rates for two different types of central bank credit (Lombardkredit, Rediskontkredit).

Banks borrow not only from the central bank and from their customers (by accepting their deposits), but also from other banks. The rates of interest charged on interbank lending are called 'interbank rates', e.g., LIBOR (London Interbank Offered Rate) and the Federal Funds rate in the United States.

The next tier of interest rates applies to the financial transactions between the commercial banks and their customers. The 'prime rate' (an American term) is the lending rate charged to a bank's most creditworthy business clients. It is fixed independently by each bank and is used as a bench-mark for all its interest rates. Its approximate equivalent in Great Britain is the 'base (lending) rate'. To compare the U.S. prime rate with the British base (lending) rate, add 1% to the latter. This is because prime borrowers in Great Britain are charged base (lending) rate plus 1%.

'Deposit rates', as the name suggests, are paid by banks on the various types of short- and long-term deposits entrusted to them by their customers. Interest paid on deposits may either be withdrawn at the end of a year or left in the account. In the latter case, it will also start earning interest (compound interest).

interest[2]   Beteiligung (an einer Unternehmung)

Interest is the proportion of equity capital held by an investor in a company. It may also be referred to as 'holding' or, in colloquial usage, as 'stake'. An investor may hold more than 50 per cent of the capital of a company, in which case he is said to have a 'majority interest'. Holdings of less than 50 per cent are called 'minority interests'. An interest enabling an investor to control the company in question is a 'controlling interest'. It need not be a majority holding, since it is quite possible to control a company with a minority stake if the remainder of the capital is split among a large number of investors.

In colloquial usage, the term 'interest' may also refer to a company in which an investor has a holding, or even to one which is wholly owned by him.

interface   Schnittstelle

In data processing, interface denotes a connection between two systems or two pieces of hardware, i.e., the place where output from one unit is converted to a form acceptable as input to another unit. The channels and associated control circuitry providing the connection between a CPU and its peripheral units (VDU, printer, etc.) would be called an 'interface'.

interstatement ratios

kombinierte Bilanz- und V+G-Kennzahlen

Interstatement ratios are financial ratios expressing quantitative relationships between balance sheet items and income statement items. The most commonly used interstatement ratios are: 'inventory turnover', 'receivables turnover', and 'return on investment'.

The inventory turnover is a ratio measuring the liquidity of inventories. It shows how often average inventories are "turned over", i.e., converted into receivables (in the case of credit sales) or cash (in the case of cash sales), within a given period of time, usually a year. Thus, it is a measure of a firm's efficiency in managing its inventories. The ratio is usually computed by dividing cost of goods sold by average inventory (i.e., beginning inventory plus ending inventory, divided by 2). (see: turnover[1])

The receivables turnover, also referred to as the 'collection ratio', measures the rate at which trade accounts receivable are converted into cash within a given period of time (usually a year), i.e., it is an indicator of the liquidity of accounts receivable. This ratio shows how often average accounts receivable are collected during a year. It is computed by dividing credit sales by average accounts receivable (i.e., year-end accounts receivable plus accounts receivable at the beginning of the year, divided by 2). The higher the turnover, the greater the flow of cash into the firm, and, therefore, the higher the liquidity of the accounts receivable. This shows that the turnover of accounts receivable is a measure of the efficiency of a firm's credit and collection policies throughout the year. Finally, one should not forget to mention the average collection period. It shows the number of days average accounts receivable are outstanding. It is computed by dividing the receivables turnover into 365 (days in a year). Assuming a receivables turnover of 5, the average collection period would be 73 days.

Return on investment (ROI), an important profitability ratio, is not a single ratio but a number of ratios, each of which measures the return on a particular type of investment. ROI is considered as a useful indicator of management's general effectiveness and efficiency. The two most important versions of ROI are 'return on total assets' and 'return on equity'.

'Return on total assets' (i.e., total investment) measures the profitability of the total resources available to a business. It indicates the efficiency with which management used the total resources available to them. It is computed by dividing EBIT (earnings before interest and taxes) by total assets.

'Return on equity' is computed by dividing net income (i.e., net profit after taxes) by owners' equity. It measures a firm's profitability from the point of view of the owners; in other words, it measures the return to the owners on their total investment in the business (i.e., the original investment plus retained earnings).

intrapreneurship

Unternehmertum im Unternehmen

Intrapreneurship is a fairly new management technique. It involves encouraging entrepreneurial behaviour within a large business organisation which may have become too rigid and inflexible for quick innovation. The usual method is to establish separate venture groups with their own development, production, marketing and distribution, and set them a specific task. These venture groups are kept on a long leash and normally report to top management, bypassing the complex corporate hierarchy.

inventory
Lager,
Lagerbestand,
Vorratsvermögen

Put simply, the term 'inventory' (in British English referred to as 'stock') is applied to goods owned by a business at a particular point in time and held for the purpose of future sale or for utilisation in the manufacture of goods for sale. The American Institute of Certified Public Accountants (AICPA) defines 'inventory' in a slightly more complicated way as "the aggregate of those items of tangible personal property which (i) are held for sale in the ordinary course of business, (ii) are in the process of production for such sale, or (iii) are to be currently consumed in the production of goods or services to be available for sale".

In a retail or wholesale business, inventory consists mainly of merchandise inventory, i.e., goods purchased for sale without any further processing. This means that the goods carried in the merchandise inventory are not materially altered, although they may be blended, packed, etc., before being resold.

In a manufacturing business, inventory includes raw materials, semi-finished goods, goods in process (also known as 'work in process' or 'work in progress'), finished goods, and factory supplies (also called 'manufacturing supplies').

The accounting rules applying to the valuation of inventories are quite complicated and cannot be dealt with in detail in this short article. According to the concept of conservatism, inventories, like any other item of current assets, have to be valued at each balance sheet date at the lower of cost or market. The term 'market', as used here, means current replacement value (by purchase or by reproduction, as the case may be). 'Cost', on the other hand, is a less clear-cut concept because it may be determined by a variety of methods, the most commonly used of which are: specific cost identification, the moving average method, the weighted average method, FIFO (first-in, first-out method), and LIFO (last-in, first-out method).

The term 'inventory' should not be confused with the German terms 'Inventur' (inventory-taking, or stock-taking) and 'Inventar' (furniture and fixtures).

inventory management
Lagerwirtschaft

Inventories, or stocks, which can take the form of materials, work in progress, and finished goods (in manufacturing), or of merchandise (in retailing and wholesaling), represent an important element of the physical (or technical) subsystem of business organisations. Inventories have to be maintained as a buffer between purchasing and production and between production and selling. Their main purpose is to secure a steady flow of physical resources through the organisation. Stockless production has been tried and is possible, but this only means that stockholding is shifted back to the supplier.

Inventories are also important from the financial point of view, since a lot of capital is tied up in them at any given moment, quite apart from the other cost elements involved (e.g., storage, insurance). Therefore, it is not surprising that inventory management should be regarded as an essential ingredient of profitable management.

From the organisational point of view, inventory management can be grouped with purchasing or with production. The modern tendency is to integrate it with purchasing and certain other functions in a materials management department.

An essential prerequisite for any management decision on inventories are up-to-date inventory (or stock) records. Stock record information includes: code number of item, description, quantity held in stock (stock level), planned minimum and maximum quantities, reorder level, cost data, stock movement (inputs and outputs, or issues). Stock records should be updated continuously, a task for which computers are particularly well-suited. In spite of this, it is usually necessary to ascertain physically (count, weigh, measure) the stock on hand at least once a year (stock-taking, inventory-taking), mainly to satisfy accounting regulations.

The most important aspect of inventory management is, however, inventory control, or stock control, i.e., the decisions involved in having the right amount of stock at any given time (whatever 'right' may mean in this context). Inventory control is faced with a classical trade-off situation, i.e., there are conflicting goals, so that a compromise has to be found. The basic elements to be allowed for in deciding on a particular level of stocks are availability and cost. On the one hand, it is necessary to have a fairly high level of stocks in order to avoid stockouts and a disruption of production and/or sales with negative effects on customer relations; on the other hand, stocks should be kept at the lowest possible level because of the costs and risks involved (risk of obsolescence, cost of storage, insurance, and capital tied up in inventories). There are a number of management techniques that can be used to work out a satisfactory solution to this problem. Buzz-words in this field are: two-bin method, economic order quantity, and safety stocks.

investment[1]

(Real-)Investition,
Realkapitalbildung

In economics, the term 'investment' usually means real investment, or capital formation, i.e., the flow of expenditure designed to maintain or expand the stock of capital goods, such as factories, office blocks, plant and machinery, etc.. Strictly speaking, changes in inventories (called 'inventory investment') and, from the point of view of national accounting, also net exports of goods and services should be included. Some economists would also include expenditure on education, vocational training, and related activities, because, the argument goes, they represent a form of investment resulting in "human capital".

Investment is an important component of gnp and an essential determinant of national income. It is, however, not only necessary to replace and expand the capital stock of a country; capital expenditure must also be directed at modernising and improving it. Only when a country has the latest and most modern technology, can it hope to hold its own against foreign competitors. It should be noted, however, that this applies only to the industrialised nations; less developed countries may require different, possibly more labour-intensive, forms of investment adjusted to their particular needs. Moreover, even in the

222

industrialised countries, people have begun to realise that capital-intensive technologies may create problems, especially if demand is no longer expanding as fast as it used to.

In view of the importance of capital expenditure, it is not surprising that governments should try (or at least have tried until very recently) to stimulate investment by providing investment incentives, such as first-year allowances, investment tax credits, and investment grants, although this may mean that they are subsidising capital at the expense of labour. The actual volume of investment will, therefore, depend on the availability of funds, the expected return, and the existence and extent of encouragement afforded by government.

investment[2]

Finanzinvestition,
Finanzanlage

The term 'investment' may also be used to describe the acquisition of financial assets (i.e., financial claims), such as bank deposits, shares, bonds, Treasury bills, etc.. This form of investment, which does not (or at least not directly) result in tangible equipment, is undertaken to generate current investment income (e.g., dividends, interest) or capital gains.

The investment industry, which includes such organisations as the stock exchange, brokerage houses, investment companies, and banks, acts as intermediary between the ultimate providers and the ultimate users of capital.

investment[3]

Finanzanlagen;
kurzfristige Finanzanlagen,
Wertpapiere des Umlaufvermögens;
langfristige Finanzanlagen,
Finanzanlagevermögen

In accounting, investments are generally classified for balance sheet purposes into 'short-term investments' and 'long-term investments'. This distinction is entirely one of accounting, and not of law, and arises out of the nature and the purpose of the investment.

Short-term investments, also referred to as 'temporary investments' or 'temporary investments of cash', are reported on the balance sheet under the caption of current assets. To be classified as current assets, short-term investments must be easily convertible into cash, and it must be the intention of the firm's management to convert them into cash within a period of approximately one year. The main purpose of holding investments on a short-term basis is to satisfy a firm's precautionary desires for liquidity; in other words, short-term investments are primarily held as a reserve source of cash.

The most common types of short-term investment are time deposits in banks and marketable securities. These are securities which are readily marketable, i.e., securities regularly traded on a stock exchange (listed securities, or quoted securities) or securities for which there is an active market (e.g., the Unlisted Securities Market in G.B. or the Over-the-Counter Market in the U.S.). Best known examples of marketable securities are government securities, such as Treasury bills and gilt-edged securities, and equity and debt securities issued by companies, i.e., shares and debentures.

In Austria and West Germany, the balance sheet item for short-term investments is 'Wertpapiere des Umlaufvermögens'. It is obvious that this balance sheet title does not include time deposits in banks and is, therefore, only an approximate equivalent of 'temporary investments'. A more appropriate translation would be 'kurzfristige Finanzanlagen'.

The rules applying to the valuation of short-term investments are highly complicated and differ from country to country. In Austria, for example, marketable securities are recorded initially at cost (i.e., the value at the date of acquisition). Subsequent to acquisition, they have to be valued and reported at each balance sheet date either at cost or at market, whichever is the lower (lower-of-cost-or-market principle). Market in this context is taken to mean the current market value at the balance sheet date. The application of the lower-of-cost-or-market is in conformance with the concept of conservatism, according to which unrealised losses have to be recognised, whereas unrealised gains must be ignored.

All investments not classifiable as current assets are usually shown in the balance sheet between current and fixed assets. The most widely used balance sheet caption for non-current investments is 'investments' or 'other investments'. Investments classified under this category are referred to as 'long-term investments' or 'permanent investments'.

Permanent investments may or may not be readily marketable, i.e., readily convertible into cash. However, it must be the intention of the firm's management to hold them on a long-term basis. Long-term investments may be made (i) to obtain control of another company; (ii) to earn investment income; (iii) to establish business relationships with other companies; and (iv) to promote diversification of business activities.

Long-term investments include such marketable securities as shares and debentures (U.S.: corporate bonds) of other companies held on a long-term basis; loans to subsidiaries; funds earmarked for specific purposes, such as the replacement of plant and equipment or the payment of occupational pensions; etc.. All these items are excluded from current assets because there is no intention to have them available for the payment of current liabilities or for the use in connection with regular current operations.

According to Austrian accounting rules, short-term investments, as has already been mentioned, have to be valued on the lower-of-cost-or-market basis ("strenges Niederstwertprinzip"). By contrast, the valuation basis for long-term investments is the "gemilderte Niederstwertprinzip". If the current market value at the balance sheet date is lower than cost, the investment to be valued may be shown in the balance sheet at the lower market value or at cost. If, however, the drop in the market value has been material and it is evident that the decline is not due to a mere temporary condition, the value to be reported must be the lower market value.

investment bank   Effekten- und Investmentbank

U.S. investment banks, which are similar to the British issuing houses, act as intermediaries between both companies and government institutions wishing to raise capital and individual or institutional investors. They are, therefore, mainly engaged in marketing bond and other security issues, syndicating international loans, selling and buying securities on the open market, and in dispensing investment advice. Recently, the range of services has been expanded to include merger and acquisition advice and other expert services.

In the United States, commercial banks are legally prevented from engaging in any but a few very restricted investment banking transactions.

investment funds   Investmentfonds

Investment funds are financial institutions set up for the purpose of pooling the funds of small (or relatively small) investors, investing them (hopefully) profitably in a wide range of securities and/or other investment media for the benefit of the said investors. Investment funds are professionally managed and should theoretically be able to achieve a better return than the private investor or a portfolio representing the market average. For one thing, they have, as a rule, more funds at their disposal than the private investor and can, therefore, buy a wider range of securities or other investment media to spread the risk.

From an organisational point of view, there are two main types of investment fund: the 'investment trust' ('closed-end trust' in the United States) and the 'unit trust' ('mutual fund' in the United States).

Investment trusts are not really trusts but investment companies. They are ordinary public limited companies (or corporations in the United States) which, instead of engaging in production or trade, specialise in investing funds in a wide range of securities and/or properties, the funds being raised by issuing shares and, frequently, debentures (U.S.: corporate bonds). This type of investment fund is prohibited by Austrian law, although Austrians were (unfortunately one must say, given hindsight) allowed to buy shares in the ill-fated and fraudulent Investors' Overseas Services (IOS).

Unit trusts, however, can also be found in Austria (e.g., Combirent, a unit trust investing in fixed-interest securities). In the case of a unit trust, two institutions are involved: (i) the management company, which is responsible for the investment policy of the trust and which decides, within the limits of the trust deed, the composition of the trust's portfolio; (ii) the trustee company/bank, which has custody of the actual securities. In contrast to the investment trust, the funds raised and the securities bought with them are quite separate from the capital and the assets of the company responsible for investment. The funds are raised by selling units, each representing a fraction of the portfolio of the trust. Their value is determined simply by adding up the prices of the securities in the portfolio and dividing by the number of units. Therefore units, in contrast to investment trust shares, can never be under- or over-valued. Another difference from the investment trust is that unit trusts charge management fees, and are normally prepared to redeem, i.e., buy back, units no longer required by their holders. This implies that the capital of a unit trust is much more flexible than that of an investment trust, which can only be changed by special resolution of a general meeting.

investment incentive   Investitionsanreiz,
                                             Investitionsförderungsmaßnahme

Investment incentives are measures taken by a government with a view to encouraging capital expenditure by private firms, the idea being that an increase in capital expenditure will stimulate economic activity and provide jobs. Investment incentives can, however, also be used more selectively as an instrument of industrial or regional policy.

Investment incentives can take various forms. The most common are: first-year allowances (permitting firms to charge higher depreciation expenses than warranted by wear and tear), investment tax credits (percentage of capital expenditure can be deducted from tax liability), and investment grants (straight cash payments by government).

investor   (Kapital-)Anleger,
                                                 Investor

Investors, i.e., the ultimate purchasers of securities, may be classified in various ways. An important distinction is the one between 'private' and 'institutional' investors. The former are (more or less) rich individuals who put their money into shares, bonds, property, etc., while the latter are organisations, such as insurance companies, banks, pension funds, and, last but not least, investment funds. Institutional investors are becoming more and more important because, as a rule, they have more funds at their disposal than the private individual investor. This enables them to pursue a more diversified investment policy. They spread the risk by investing their funds in a wider range of securities. The portfolio of a typical institutional investor will comprise shares, debentures, Treasury bills, etc., and, where permitted by law, property.

Investors may also be classified on the basis of their investment strategy, namely, as bulls, bears, and stags. Other classifications are not fully reflected in investment terminology. There is no special term for investors who are mainly interested in current investment income (dividends, interest), while those mainly interested in capital gains are referred to as 'speculators'.

invisible account   Dienstleistungsbilanz

The invisible account forms part of the balance of payments and is a systematic record of all exports and imports of services (also known as 'invisibles', hence the terms 'invisible exports' and 'invisible imports') of a particular country in a given period, usually one year.

Invisible trade between one country and the rest of the world includes such services as shipping; air, rail, and road transport; banking; insurance; licensing; tourism; etc., resulting in payments in the form of freight, tourist expenditure, insurance premiums, licence fees, commissions, etc.. In addition, the invisible account also includes investment income, i.e., interest, dividends, and profits received from, and paid to, non-residents. This income is regarded as a return for services rendered by capital lent or employed abroad. Examples of investment income counting as exports are interest on loans granted by banks or governments to foreign borrowers; interest on foreign bonds; dividends on shares held in foreign companies; profits repatriated by a foreign branch office; etc..

An excess of invisible exports over invisible imports is known as an 'invisible trade surplus' or 'invisibles surplus', which means that the country's invisible earnings exceed its invisible payments. The opposite would be an 'invisible trade deficit' or 'invisibles deficit'.

226

A (visible) trade deficit (i.e., imports of goods exceed exports) may be more than offset by a surplus on invisibles, thus resulting in an overall current account surplus. At the time of writing, this is true of Austria, where the invisibles surplus is mainly produced by tourism.

invitation to treat

Einladung zur Stellung eines Antrages
(im Sinne des Kaufvertrages)

In contrast to an offer[1], an invitation to treat is merely an invitation to people or firms to make offers. From the legal point of view, it is important to note that the acceptance of an offer results in a contract, whereas the taking up of an invitation to treat does not. The following examples are intended to illustrate this:
1. Offer without engagement: this term is misleading, because an offer without engagement is not an offer within the meaning of the law of contract, but only an invitation to treat.
2. An advertisement of goods for sale at a stated price is not an offer to sell the goods at that price, but it is only an invitation to negotiate for the sale of the goods. The same applies to the display of goods in a shop-window with prices mentioned on them.
3. In the case of an auction, the auctioneer's request for bids is not an offer, but an invitation to the persons present to make their bids (offers) for the goods to be auctioned off.

invoice

Rechnung,
Faktura

An invoice is a document which contains a record of the transaction between a buyer and a seller. It is normally prepared by the seller on a printed invoice form, and its primary purpose is to inform the buyer of the amount he has to pay. A complete invoice contains the following details:
1. name and address of both buyer and seller;
2. date and number of the invoice;
3. date and number of the order against which the goods have been delivered;
4. description of the goods;
5. weight and/or quantity of the goods;
6. unit price(s); extension of each item (i.e., unit price multiplied by quantity); deductions (e.g., trade discounts, quantity discounts) and additional charges (e.g., packing); total invoice amount;
7. terms of payment;
8. mode of transport (if the invoice is used as an advice note);
9. in G.B., Austria, West Germany, but not in the U.S.A., the rate and/or amount of V.A.T..

Invoices vary in size and style, but all contain the same basic information. Sometimes, the invoice is enclosed in the parcel with the goods, and sometimes it is sent separately, e.g., where the goods are baled, crated, or supplied in bulk.

Special types of invoice are the pro forma invoice, and - in foreign trade - the commercial invoice, the customs invoice, and the consular invoice.

L

labour force

Arbeitskräftevolumen,
Arbeitskräftepotential

The labour force includes the employed and the involuntarily unemployed, i.e., those at work and those seeking employment but unable to find some at the prevailing wage rates. The labour force is, therefore, a measure of the labour resources available to a society at existing wage rates. In many countries (Austria is one of them), only the registered unemployed are taken into account, while in the United States and Canada a survey is used to determine the number of people actually looking for work, a number which also includes the school-leavers, who are unable to register as unemployed because they have never held a job. Apart from these statistical considerations, the size of the labour force is determined, among other things, by demographic factors (size of the population, age structure, immigration, emigration) and the level of wages.

labour turnover

Fluktuation,
Fluktuationsziffer

Labour turnover, or, more precisely, the rate of labour turnover, is a measure of the stability or instability of a firm's work-force. This ratio can be calculated in various ways. The most popular method is to express the number of workers leaving the firm during a specified period of time (usually a year) as a percentage of the firm's average work-force for the same period. A high rate of labour turnover means that the work-force is rather unstable, while a low rate obviously means the opposite.

leaflet

(kleiner) Prospekt,
Werbeblatt,
Werbezettel

A leaflet, occasionally referred to as a 'pamphlet', is a single sheet of paper, or a few sheets loosely bound together, usually advertising something or giving information. It is frequently distributed free of charge.

leasing

Leasing

Leasing is a popular form of medium- to long-term financing. Under a lease contract, or lease, a firm or private individual, known as the 'lessee', instead of buying a specific asset or assets, acquires from the lessor the right to use the object/objects involved for an agreed period of time. The lessor, of course, retains ownership of the asset or assets involved, and is rewarded for his services with rentals, usually paid to him by the lessee at regular intervals.

Leases may be classified in a number of ways, e.g., according to the type of asset leased (consumer goods lease, equipment lease, lease of land and/or buildings) or according to the services provided by the lessor (net lease, maintenance lease). The most important classification, however, is the one based on the term of the lease and the repayment of the lessor's investment, viz., the classification into 'finance lease' and 'operating lease'.

Under the first type of arrangement, the lessee acquires the right to use an asset for most of its useful life (the obligatory period, or basic period). In addition, he is normally responsible for maintenance, insurance, and repairs, which means that a 'finance lease' is, as a rule, also a 'net lease'. The rental payments from the lessee are intended to recover the lessor's cost of the object leased and to give him a return on his investment. Such leases, under which the lessor's investment is fully recovered, are also referred to as 'full-payout leases'. They are usually non-cancellable.

The term 'operating lease' is generally used to describe a short-term lease, by which the lessee can acquire the use of an asset for a fraction of its useful life, the lessor frequently providing such services as maintenance, insurance, and repairs. This means that 'operating leases' can frequently be cross-classified as 'maintenance leases'. Since under an operating lease the lessor's investment is not fully recovered, such leases are also referred to as 'non-payout leases'.

Another interesting type of lease is the 'sale and leaseback' arrangement. Under such an arrangement, the owner and user of a specific property sells it to a leasing company, which leases it back to him. The owner obtains a large cash payment for the property sold, but nevertheless can go on using it against periodic rental payments.

It has already been mentioned that leasing represents an alternative to buying assets. The decision on whether to lease or to buy is not as easy and as obvious as it is sometimes made out to be (especially by leasing companies). While obviously a finance lease is usually more advantageous than a cash purchase or a purchase on deferred terms, the situation is less clear-cut if a comparison is made with a purchase financed by a long-term bank loan repayable in instalments. In the case of an operating lease, which can be cancelled quite easily, the main emphasis is less on the financing aspect than on the greater flexibility offered by a lease in comparison with an outright purchase.

less developed country   Entwicklungsland

Less developed (or developing) countries used to be called 'backward' or 'underdeveloped', two terms that today are regarded as impolite and are, therefore, hardly used any more. Less developed countries (ldcs) are characterised by poverty (low per capita income and little, if any, per capita wealth), high child mortality, high birth rates, low life expectancy, malnutrition, widespread illiteracy, and, frequently, by a very uneven income distribution.

The reasons for this state of affairs are controversial. There are, however, many scholars and experts who believe that exploitation by industrialised countries and multinational companies - past and present - is a major factor, other factors being climate, lack of natural resources, and racial and cultural traits.

liabilities   Verbindlichkeiten;
                                                    Passiva

Generally speaking, liabilities represent a firm's financial obligations. In the U.S.A.
and in Austria, liabilities are listed on the credit (or right-hand) side of the balance
sheet. This is in contrast to Britain, where they appear on the debit (or left-hand)
side. For balance sheet purposes, the items listed on the liability side are broadly
grouped into 'current liabilities', 'long-term liabilities', and 'net worth' (see: equity
capital). Strictly speaking, net worth is not a liability, but is shown on the liability
side because it too represents a source of funds. Therefore, 'liabilities' is
increasingly being replaced by 'liabilities and capital' as the proper title for one
side of the balance sheet.

liability insurance   Haftpflichtversicherung

Under liability insurance (also referred to as 'third-party insurance'), the
undertaking of the insurer is to indemnify the insured for sums which the latter
becomes liable to pay to third persons in respect of personal injuries or damage to
their property.

Liability insurance plays an important role, for instance, in motor insurance,
because every motorist is required by law to take out insurance covering his legal
liability for death or personal injury to third parties, as well as his liability for
damage to their property (e.g., to their cars).

Other types of liability insurance which are of particular importance to business
men cover an employer's liability for the acts of his employees and product
liability.

lighter   Leichter(schiff)

A lighter is a boat, usually flat-bottomed, which is used for unloading and loading
ships not brought to wharf (because they may be unable to enter the port) and for
transporting goods in port.

lighterage   Leichtergebühr;
                                                    Kosten für die Leichterung

By lighterage is meant the cost of hiring lighters, as well as the cost of carrying
goods by lighters.

line[1]   Produktlinie (bei Herstellern);
                                                    Warengruppe (bei Händlern)

In a marketing context, line, or product line, refers to a broad group or class of
products.

230

line[2]

Gewerbe,
Sparte,
Branche

Line can also be used as a synonym for 'industry', 'trade', or 'occupation'. It is not normally employed in the case of compound words, where industry and trade are the rule (e.g., chemical industry, tourist trade).

liquidity

Liquidität

In a business context, the term 'liquidity' refers to an organisation's ability to meet its financial obligations - as and when they fall due - without having to sell fixed assets. Liquidity can be measured by relating some or all of the subject organisation's current assets to its current liabilities. For example, (net) working capital (i.e., current assets minus current liabilities) or the current ratio (i.e., current assets to current liabilities) are measures of a firm's liquidity. A commonly used measure of bank liquidity is the ratio of loans to deposits. A firm that lacks liquidity in the sense defined in this entry is said to be insolvent, which does not necessarily mean that its total liabilities exceed its assets.

The term may also be used to describe the ease with which assets can be converted into cash (e.g., marketable securities are more liquid than plant and equipment). In some cases, it even refers to the liquid assets themselves (e.g., cash, marketable securities, accounts receivable).

list price

Listenpreis

The list price is the price which is shown in a price-list, and from which trade and quantity discounts are deducted.

Lloyd's

Lloyd's

Lloyd's is a society of private insurers in London, often called 'Lloyd's of London'. It was incorporated by Act of Parliament in 1871. The Corporation of Lloyd's is not an insurance company, but a leading international insurance market.

The members of Lloyd's are private insurers, known as the 'underwriting members of Lloyd's', 'Lloyd's underwriters', or simply 'underwriters'. These underwriters transact insurance business for their own account, and their liability is unlimited, which means that they are liable to the full extent of their private fortunes to meet their insurance commitments. Lloyd's itself does no underwriting, i.e., it does not accept insurance, nor does it assume liability for the insurance business transacted by its underwriting members (e.g., the fact that a Lloyd's underwriter defaults in the payment of a loss under a Lloyd's policy imposes no liability on Lloyd's itself). Lloyd's offers, therefore, insurance written by individuals, as contrasted with insurance written by companies.

Underwriting membership of Lloyd's is open to men and women of any nationality. To be admitted as a new member, an underwriter has to meet stringent financial requirements, e.g., he/she has to make a substantial deposit.

Today, there are over 20,000 underwriting members, who, because of the complexity of modern insurance transactions and the large sums insured, are formed into some four hundred groups, called 'syndicates', varying in size from a few to more than a thousand members. Each syndicate usually specialises in a particular class of business. The affairs of each syndicate are managed by an underwriting agent, who represents his syndicate at Lloyd's and who conducts the actual underwriting on behalf of all the syndicate members. This, however, does not affect the personal and individual responsibility of each underwriter. The underwriting agent, who is usually, but not necessarily, a member of the syndicate for which he acts, is responsible for appointing a professional underwriter for each main class of business. Thus, the underwriting agents, through appointed underwriters, accept on behalf of the syndicate members the risks brought to Lloyd's. If the insurance is for a relatively large amount, several syndicates may participate, but each member of a syndicate is liable only for a proportionate fraction of the risk accepted by the underwriting agent on his syndicate's behalf.

Insurance at Lloyd's is effected in the underwriting room (usually just called 'The Room'), where the Lloyd's underwriters are to be found. One of the main characteristics of Lloyd's is that a Lloyd's underwriter does not do business with the general public, but only with a broker who is a member of Lloyd's (such a broker is referred to as a 'Lloyd's broker'). The general public are denied access to The Room, and, therefore, a person who wishes to effect an insurance at Lloyd's has to employ the services of such a broker. Lloyd's brokers are key figures in the Lloyd's market, because Lloyd's underwriters have no other contact with the insuring public. They represent their clients, not the underwriters, and it is their duty to negotiate the best available terms for their clients. The Lloyd's broker is not restricted to Lloyd's and can also place business with the insurance companies.

On receiving a request for insurance cover a Lloyd's broker first makes out the 'slip' - a sheet of folded paper with details of the risk. The broker then negotiates a rate of premium with underwriters expert in that particular type of business. He may obtain several quotations before deciding on the best one. When the broker and an underwriter have agreed on the premium, the underwriter accepts the risk on behalf of his syndicate by putting his initials on the slip. If the risk involved is large, the underwriter accepts only part of it, and the broker will have to find other syndicates who are prepared to insure/underwrite the remainder of the risk at the same premium rate. Large risks are usually spread over the whole market, cover being shared by Lloyd's underwriters and the insurance companies. The fully subscribed slip, which is the complete and final contract between the parties, is sent to Lloyd's Policy Signing Office, where the policy is prepared.

Finally, it should be noted that Lloyd's was originally a market exclusively for marine insurance. Today, however, Lloyd's underwriters are willing to insure a wide range of risks, including ships, aircraft, oil rigs, motor cars, fire, personal accident, third-party liability, etc..

lock-out   Aussperrung (von Arbeitern)

If, in an industrial dispute, an employer closes down his firm and prevents his employees from performing their work (and earning their wages), the action is called a 'lock-out'. Lock-outs, which are practically unknown in Austria, are not unusual in West Germany, where employers in a particular industry may retaliate against a partial strike by locking out the workers of the firms not affected by the strike.

logistics

Logistik,
physische Distribution

Logistics, also called 'physical distribution', is the management of the physical flow of products from the producer to the final consumer. It is, therefore, concerned with plant and warehouse location, inventory control, materials handling, methods of transportation, order processing, and related activities.

long-term liabilities

langfristige Verbindlichkeiten

'Long-term liabilities', also referred to as 'long-term debt', is a balance sheet item showing all obligations which will not be payable within approximately one year of the balance sheet date (i.e., all obligations which are not current). In many cases, debts are payable serially or in instalments, a certain amount being payable each year. The amount of the debt to be paid during the ensuing accounting period should be shown as current liability, and the balance of the obligations as long-term liability.

Long-term liabilities are incurred to finance additional plant, equipment, or land; to obtain additional working capital; to meet a current debt; or to pay off another long-term debt.

The most common examples of long-term liabilities are long-term promissory notes (payable to banks or trade creditors), mortgage loans, bonds payable (including mortgage bonds, i.e., bonds secured by mortgages on land, or on land and buildings), and estimated long-term liabilities (see: current liabilities).

loss leader

Lockvogelangebot

Loss leaders, or leader items, are articles sold at lower than regular prices (e.g., at or even below cost) to attract customers. The idea is that customers will come into the shop to buy the advertised loss leader(s) and will stay to buy also other, regularly priced items. Leader pricing is prohibited in a number of U.S. states.

M

magnetic disk   Magnetplatte

Magnetic disks are secondary computer storage devices. Data in the form of magnetised spots is stored on, and retrieved from, them with the help of read-write heads. Magnetic disks are made either of flexible material (flexible or floppy disks) or of hard material (hard disks). They either are attached firmly to the disk drive (rigid disks) or can be replaced (removable disks).

mail order   Versandgeschäft,
                                  Versandhandel

Mail order is a system of retailing where the customer sends orders to the seller by post, and the goods are delivered to the customer's home. Shopping is done from a catalogue produced by the mail-order firm and either sent to prospective customers direct or shown to them by part-time agents. The economic advantages of such a system are quite obvious, as are its disadvantages: it is possible for the mail-order house to use inexpensive premises and unskilled labour, thus reducing its operating costs. For the customer, the main attraction is the convenience of "fireside shopping" and the ease with which he can get credit. Against these advantages one must set the high cost of catalogues and advertising, the need to hold large stocks (which ties up a lot of working capital), the lack of personal contact, and the impossibility of changing prices or the range of goods offered once the catalogue has been printed.

mail room equipment   Postbearbeitungsmaschinen

In a well-equipped mail room, few tasks are left for manual operation. Letters can be folded, inserted into envelopes, addressed, sealed, franked, and tied into bundles quite automatically. These jobs can be performed either by separate machines, such as paper-folding machines, addressing machines, envelope-sealing machines, franking machines (which print postage stamps on envelopes or paper strips), or by an integrated mailing machine, which combines these various functions.

mainframe[1]   Zentraleinheit

Generally, the term 'mainframe' refers to the combination of central processor (arithmetic-logic unit and control unit) and primary memory of a computer system and is, therefore, a synonym for 'central processing unit'.

mainframe[2]

Großrechner,
Großrechenanlage

The term 'mainframe', or 'mainframe computer', may also be used to describe a large computer system.

management[1]

Management,
Geschäftsleitung,
Führungskräfte

The term 'management' refers to the group of persons that control a business, in particular a public limited company or a corporation, and includes the executive directors and the managers ranking below them. Management is traditionally divided into 'top management' and 'middle management'.

Top management is usually led by the chief executive officer and his deputy, who work closely with the board of directors, and includes the heads of the various divisions or departments. Immediately below them is the middle management, to which many of the responsibilities of the highest-ranking officers are delegated. For instance, the production manager and the marketing manager (U.S.: vice-president in charge of production; vice-president in charge of marketing) belong to top management, while the works managers and the sales manager, reporting to them, are members of middle management.

management[2]

Unternehmensführung

Management includes all activities involved in running a business organisation. In particular, managers are concerned with preparing and making decisions and ensuring that they are carried out. The management process can be broken down in various ways, but most books on management list some or all of the following activities as essential ingredients:
1. identifying, formulating, and setting objectives;
2. planning - establishing long-term (i.e., strategic) and short-term (i.e., tactical) plans;
3. establishing, maintaining, and modifying a suitable organisation, involving an organisational structure and organisational procedures;
4. implementing - getting results through other people, which involves delegating, motivating, and commanding;
5. controlling - measuring performance, comparing results with predetermined standards, and taking corrective action if necessary;
6. communicating with the other members of the organisation;
7. establishing and maintaining contacts with the outside world, representing the organisation in negotiations with customers, suppliers, trade unions, government, etc..

It is obvious that some of the above-mentioned activities are not mutually exclusive and that there is a certain amount of overlap. Communicating with the other members of the organisation is obviously an all-pervasive function.

In carrying out the management process managers rely on various management techniques to achieve their goals. Qualitative management techniques include management by objectives, management by results, and management by exception, while network analysis, simulation, linear programming, risk analysis, and decision trees are examples of quantitative techniques, roughly equivalent to operations research.

Another important aspect of the management process is the style of leadership, or management style, used by the executives of an organisation. Management styles range from very authoritarian (little confidence in subordinates; no participation in goal-setting and decision-making; motivation by fear, threats, and punishment) to very co-operative (motivation of subordinates by participation and involvement, complete trust in subordinates). The second style recommends itself not only for humanitarian and solidarity reasons, but, as Likert, an American researcher, has shown, companies with a very co-operative management style are more likely to have a continuous record of high productivity.

manufacturer's agent

Werksvertreter,
selbständiger Vertreter einer
Herstellerfirma

A manufacturer's agent is an agent authorised by a manufacturer to sell part or all of the latter's product range within an exclusive territory. The agent, who is independent and in no way an employee of the manufacturer, has little or no control over the prices and terms of sale. He usually represents several non-competing manufacturers of related products, and he is paid on a commission basis.

manufacturing management

Produktionswirtschaft

Manufacturing management, or production management, is an extremely complex subject, and it should be noted that this short article can provide only the barest outline on the subject.

Manufacturing management, as, in effect, most other areas of management, involves strategic-level (i.e., long-term) and tactical-level (i.e., short-term) decisions. The former are concerned with the design of the production system and, therefore, with the desired level of output, the number and location of production facilities, the plant layout, the methods of production (job-order production, batch production, flow production), the specific plant and equipment to be installed, and with the design of the planning and control systems.

Tactical-level decisions deal with production control (in particular, with work scheduling and allocation of machines to jobs), maintenance, quality control, and, possibly, with inventory management (which may be grouped with purchasing) and control of labour costs (which may be integrated with personnel management).

marginalism

grenztheoretischer Ansatz

Marginalism, or the marginal approach, is a method of economic analysis with wide applications in business administration and economics. The marginal approach focuses attention on what happens at the margin, i.e., on the effects of adding one unit to, or subtracting one unit from, an economic total, such as a given quantity of consumer goods or factor inputs.

Marginal utility, for instance, is the utility derived from consuming one more unit of a good (e.g., drinking one more glass of water), while the marginal product represents the output attributable to the last unit of input added in a production process (e.g., if one more worker is added to a group of agricultural labourers cultivating a given area of land).

The interesting point is that marginal utility or marginal productivity may be higher or lower than average utility or average productivity, depending on whether the last unit is added to a small number or a large number of existing units. The first few glasses of water, to use the same example again, will have a very high marginal utility. The more glasses are consumed by a person, however, the smaller the marginal utility will become, until finally it will disappear and turn negative (disutility).

The marginal approach offers interesting insights into the workings of the economic system. It can be used to explain, for instance, why water, although essential to life, is in most places a free good, while diamonds, whose generic utility is fairly low, are very expensive (the paradox of value). This is because the price of a good is determined by its marginal utility, which is very low in the case of water, because there is so much of it, but which is high in the case of diamonds, because they are very rare.

Other applications of the marginal approach, e.g., the use of the concept of marginal productivity in the theory of income distribution, are more controversial.

| **marine insurance** | G.B.: Seetransportversicherung; U.S.A.: See- und Binnentransportversicherung |

Marine insurance (in the U.S.A. called 'ocean marine insurance') is the oldest branch of the insurance business. In a narrow sense, (ocean) marine insurance covers goods in transit by sea ((ocean) marine cargo insurance) and ocean vessels (marine hull insurance). The term '(ocean) marine insurance', however, is somewhat misleading, because the contract of (ocean) marine insurance can be extended so as to protect the insured against loss of, or damage to, the goods in transit on inland waterways or by land (e.g., by road or by rail) incidental to the sea voyage. In commercial practice, the (ocean) marine insurance policy embodies the 'warehouse-to-warehouse clause'. Goods insured on a warehouse-to-warehouse basis (warehouse-to-warehouse insurance) are covered from the moment they leave the seller's warehouse until they are delivered to the buyer's warehouse at the place of destination.

In general, under a contract of (ocean) marine insurance, the insurer agrees, against payment of a specified premium, to compensate the insured, up to a specified amount, for any loss of, or damage to, the subject-matter insured (ship or cargo) while in transit. The following are some illustrative examples of risks covered: loss or damage due to fire, explosion, stranding or sinking of the vessel, collision, entry of seawater into the vessel or container, overturning or derailment of land conveyance, acts of god (e.g., earthquake, flood, lightning, etc.), theft, etc.. Political risks, such as war and strike risks, are excluded from coverage but may be covered for an extra premium.

One important advantage of (ocean) marine cargo insurance is that in the case of loss of, or damage to, the goods the insurer guarantees immediate payment, even though the carrier may eventually be held liable (under the contract of carriage by sea, the shipowner is liable only if he acts negligently). On payment of the insurance money, the insured must assign to the insurer any claims he may have against the carrier (right of subrogation).

In the United States, the term 'marine insurance' is used in a much broader sense and refers to both ocean transportation and land transportation. Therefore, a distinction is made between 'ocean marine insurance' and 'inland marine insurance', the latter covering goods in transit by land and on inland waterways (goods-in-transit insurance, or transit insurance), the means of transport by which they are carried, and other instrumentalities of transportation, e.g., bridges, tunnels, piers, wharves, docks.

market   Markt

A market, in its general economic sense, is a social institution that brings suppliers and demanders of goods, services, and other objects of value (e.g., securities, foreign exchange) into contact with one another, providing a forum for potential exchanges and for the interplay of supply and demand.

The term may denote a particular place where buying and selling is carried out, as in the case of open-air markets held in market towns or as in the case of highly organised securities markets (stock exchanges), but it does not necessarily imply a specific location. Foreign exchange markets, for instance, typically consist of loose associations of financial institutions physically far from one another but linked by means of telecommunications.

The term may be applied to the economy as a whole, to broad categories of goods and services (e.g., consumer goods market, factor markets), or to individual commodities (e.g., the fruit market). Other classifications are based on geographic, demographic, or life-style criteria (e.g., the French market, the youth market, the gay market).

Finally, it should be noted that the term 'market' may also refer to the aggregate demand of potential buyers for a particular product or service (e.g., "the total footwear market is $3bn a year").

marketing   Marketing,
                                               Absatzpolitik

Originally, marketing simply meant "selling goods in a market (or elsewhere)". Modern marketing, although it still involves selling, is, however, a much more complicated thing. It might be defined as a complex system or programme of business activities designed to plan, price, promote, and distribute products (goods and/or services) with a view to satisfying customer wants and needs, and, of course, to meeting certain organisational goals (such as a minimum return on investment). For mnemotechnical reasons, the main elements of the marketing programme, or marketing mix, are often referred to as the 'four Ps': Product, Price, Promotion, and Place. The first three are more or less self-explanatory and discussed in greater detail under the headings of "product policy", "price policy", and "promotion" elsewhere in the book. 'Place', which was obviously selected more for the fact that it starts with a "P" than for its meaning, denotes 'distribution' and is dealt with under that heading.

Not only is modern marketing a much more complicated activity than selling, it even requires the whole business organisation to be subordinated to the marketing philosophy. Research and development, production, and finance are supposed to take their cues from marketing. This approach is reflected in the increasing importance of marketing departments and marketing managers within the organisation.

As has already been mentioned, in modern marketing, the emphasis is on the satisfaction of consumer wants and needs rather than on products, which are regarded as tools for achieving that end. This may sound like splitting hairs, but from a modern marketing point of view, a company selling drill bits, for instance, is actually in the business of producing holes, for which other products (e.g., laser beams) might be suitable. The realisation that this is so may have important consequences for the company's product policy.

The validity of the marketing concept, as outlined in this entry, has recently been questioned, because it fails to allow for long-run consumer and public welfare, leads to a misallocation of resources, and tends to neglect the social costs involved in concentrating exclusively on short-run consumer wants: quick lunches may satisfy a genuine consumer need but are probably not very wholesome; disposable bottles may be very convenient but represent a waste of resources and a burden on the environment. A marketing concept that tries to avoid these pitfalls is called 'societal marketing' or 'socially responsible marketing'.

Another new development is the application of the marketing concept to non-business organisations, such as governments, political parties, museums, schools and universities, charities, etc. (non-profit marketing). Although the relationship of these organisations with their respective target groups in a modern society may superficially resemble the marketing of ordinary goods and services, many scholars think that more is lost than gained by this extension of the marketing concept, and that it represents an unjustified encroachment on fields that are essentially not amenable to business analysis.

marketing research   Absatzforschung

Marketing research is the employment of scientific methods in the solution of marketing problems, or, in the words of the American Marketing Association, the systematic gathering, recording, and analysing of data about marketing problems. The two definitions show that marketing research is not identical with, but includes, market research. Other types of research included are: advertising research, product research, pricing studies, distribution channels and distribution cost studies, plant and warehouse location studies, etc..

market research   Marktforschung

Market research is the systematic gathering and analysis of market data, such as market size, market potential, market share, market characteristics. The term should not be confused with 'marketing research', which has a wider meaning and includes market research.

market segmentation   Marktsegmentierung

Market segmentation is a marketing strategy which divides a firm's market into a number of smaller sub-markets, each having different characteristics. Market segmentation may be carried out on the basis of age (e.g., "the youth market"), sex (e.g., "the men market"), life-style (e.g., "the gay market"), etc.. The general idea is to provide an alternative to mass marketing, which tries to reach as many customers as possible with one product and one marketing programme. By contrast, a firm employing market segmentation will tailor its products and marketing programmes to relatively small sub-markets. In many cases, this will allow it to make better use of its marketing resources, and may be the only way to survive in an increasingly competitive marketing environment.

market share   Marktanteil

Market share, as the name suggests, is the proportion or percentage of total market sales attributable to a particular firm or group of firms (e.g., to one chemical company or to all Austrian chemical companies). Statements about market share are, however, only meaningful if the market to which they refer is carefully defined. A company producing and selling soap, for instance, may have 20% of the Austrian soap market but only 1 per cent of the world soap market. But this is not the whole story. The sales of this soap company may also be expressed as a percentage of the Austrian or the world toiletries market, in which case the percentage figures will be much lower.

Market share is an important strategic marketing variable. Firms generally pursue a policy of increasing their market share, which may be the only method of increasing sales, namely, in a static (mature) or shrinking market. Market share is sometimes referred to as 'market penetration', a term which is, however, also used to describe the act of increasing one's market share - by definition - at the expense of one's competitors.

From the linguistic point of view, it should be noted that market share is never used in the plural.

marking   Beschriftung,
                                          Markierung

The term 'marking' is applied either to the placing of a mark on a package, or to a mark so placed. There are two principal types of marking which may be found on packages: shipping marks and caution marks.

Shipping marks are intended to identify the individual shipment. They include the consignor's and the consignee's own distinctive marks, the order number, the port of destination, the number of package and total number of packages, weights (gross weight, net weight), measurements, and the country of origin.

Caution marks include special instructions regarding the manner of handling, loading, lifting, etc., and various warnings for the carrier's and the consignee's benefit.

The following are some examples of caution marks:
glass - handle with care: Vorsicht Glas
fragile: zerbrechlich
inflammable, U.S.: flammable: feuergefährlich
keep dry; keep away from moisture: vor Nässe schützen
keep in cool place: kühl aufbewahren
this side up; top: oben
bottom: unten
lift here: hier anheben
use no hooks: keine Haken verwenden
open this end: hier öffnen
do not stack upside down: nicht stürzen

The marks to be shown on a package are usually stipulated in the contract of sale, and the buyer's instructions with regard to marking must be strictly complied with.

markup   Handelsspanne;
                                  Kalkulationszuschlag

The markup is the difference between the selling price and the cost of a particular item. It can be expressed either in terms of some monetary unit (dollars, pounds, etc.) or as a percentage. In the latter case, there are two ways of calculating the markup. It can be expressed as a percentage of the selling price (which is more common) or of the cost of the item. The markup based on selling price should be translated by 'Handelsspanne', the markup based on cost by 'Kalkulationszuschlag'.

materials management   Materialwirtschaft

Materials management refers to the grouping of all materials-related activities, such as procurement, or purchasing, storage, materials handling, transport, and even production control, in one department under a materials manager. This regrouping of activities traditionally assigned to other departments presumably reflects the recognition of the increasing importance of materials for a business organisation. Further details are dealt with under the headings of "procurement (management)" and "inventory management".

merchandise   Ware,
                                 Waren,
                                 Handelswaren

Merchandise (never used in the plural) refers to goods, especially manufactured articles, that are bought for resale without any further processing.

merchant bank   „Merchant Bank"

Typically, the U.K. merchant bank offers some or all of the following highly specialised banking services:

1. Acceptance of bills of exchange, especially in connection with foreign trade. This is the traditional domain of a subgroup of merchant banks referred to as 'acceptance houses'. They lend their first-class names to customers by accepting their documentary drafts (acceptance credits) and arrange for the discount of these acceptances at the finest rates.
2. Export and project finance where long-term credit is required, including international loan syndication.
3. Foreign exchange dealing and advisory services.
4. Investment management on behalf of private and institutional clients.
5. Domestic and international securities underwriting and trading, services which are provided mainly by the 'issuing houses', another important type of merchant bank and the approximate British equivalent of the U.S. 'investment banks'.
6. Corporate finance advice on mergers, acquisitions, and venture capital investment.

In addition to the traditional British acceptance houses and issuing houses, a growing number of subsidiaries of U.K. clearing banks and U.S. commercial banks have started to operate in the profitable field of merchant banking.

merger   Fusion

In British English, the term 'merger' covers three distinct methods of combining business enterprises. Under the first method, a large (or relatively large) enterprise swallows up, or absorbs, a smaller firm, i.e., it acquires the smaller firm, winds it up, extinguishing its identity. The German expression for this method (there is no specific British term) is 'Fusion durch Aufnahme'. The second method is very similar: two or more companies merge into a third company specifically established for this purpose. Here too, the original companies lose their identities. Sometimes the term 'amalgamation' is used for this variety, although it should be noted that none of the terms in this field has a precise legal meaning. Finally, under the third method, one company acquires a majority interest in another firm, effectively making it its subsidiary. This means that the firm taken over by the larger company retains its legal existence, although, economically, it will be controlled by the parent company, just like any other subsidiary. The last variety is sometimes referred to in German management literature as "unechte Fusion".

To avoid confusion, it should be remembered that, in American English, the term 'amalgamation' is normally used to describe varieties one and two (which means it corresponds to the German 'echte Fusion'), while 'merger' is reserved for the first variety only (large company swallows up small firm). For combinations where a new company is established to absorb the other companies (i.e., for variety two) the term 'consolidation' can be used.

method of payment   Zahlungsmethode

In settling an indebtedness the following methods of payment may be used: payment in kind; payment in cash (banknotes and coins); payment by postal order; payment by money order; payment by cheque; payment by bank draft; payment by traveller's cheque; payment by credit card; payment by bill of exchange; payment by promissory note; payment by credit transfer (bank giro and national giro); payment by bank transfer (mail transfer, telegraphic transfer, telex transfer, SWIFT); clean collection; documentary collection ('documents against payment', 'documents against acceptance'); payment by documentary letter of credit.

microdocumentation   Mikrodokumentation

Under this space-saving filing system, letters and other documents are reduced to tiny photographic images, smaller than a postage stamp, while the original documents are usually destroyed. Microdocuments may be stored either on long strips or on sheets of film, the latter being called 'microfiche', 'superfiche', or 'ultrafiche', depending on the number of images mounted on an A6 frame.

The necessary equipment includes a film unit, into which documents are fed for filming, and a reader, which produces a magnified image on a screen. Information can be retrieved automatically by press-button selection of the filing code number, which brings the required frame into view on the reader screen. A further development in microfilming is Computer Output on Microfilm (COM).

micro-economics   Mikroökonomie, Mikroökonomik

Economic theory is conventionally divided into 'micro-economics' and 'macro-economics'. The difference between the two lies in the level of aggregation at which economic phenomena are analysed.

Micro-economics, as the name suggests, deals with the smaller economic units, such as households and business firms, and the way in which their decisions interrelate. The central concept of micro-economics is the market.

Macro-economics, on the other hand, is concerned with broad economic aggregates, such as national income, saving, investment, money supply, etc., and their relationships.

The distinction between the two approaches sounds neat. But, in fact, it involves a number of problems, which have been glossed over by the neoclassical school of economics.

middleman   Absatzmittler

A middleman (also called a 'marketing intermediary') is an independent business concern standing between producers and ultimate household consumers or industrial users. A middleman renders particular services in connection with purchases and/or sales of products as they move from producers to consumers. Middlemen can be classified on the basis of whether they take title to the products involved or not: 'merchants' (the two major groups of merchant middlemen are wholesalers and retailers) actually take title to the goods, 'agents' (examples of agent middlemen are brokers, commercial agents, etc.) and 'employees' (e.g., commercial travellers) do not take title, although they play an active and important role in the transfer of ownership.

minutes   Protokoll

The term 'minutes' refers to the official record of a meeting. Usually, a member other than the person in the chair is responsible for keeping the minutes, i.e., for taking down the relevant details of a meeting, such as the time when the meeting was called to order (i.e., when it was officially opened by the chairman), the names of those attending, the motions tabled and put to the vote, the number of those in favour and those against, the resolutions taken, etc.. Informal discussion is usually not recorded in the minutes, although any member may insist on a particular remark being minuted if he or she considers it important.

After the meeting, the minutes are typed out, signed by the chairman and the person responsible for keeping them, and then circulated to the members. The minutes of a particular meeting are dealt with under item one of the agenda of the next meeting where they may be "taken as read" or where alterations requested by members have to be discussed.

mnemonics   mnemotechnische Abkürzungen

Mnemonics are abbreviations, symbols, or codes chosen to assist human memory. For example, ADD is used for addition, SUB for subtraction, and so on.

modem   Modem

Modem is a contraction of MOdulator-DEModulator. This device enables computer equipment to be connected to communication links (such as "voice grade" telephone lines). It converts digital computer signals into appropriate analogue signals (e.g., frequencies) at a transmission terminal (modulation) and converts them back into digital signals at a receiving terminal (demodulation).

monetary policy   Geld- und Kreditpolitik,
                                      Notenbankpolitik

Monetary policy attempts to achieve, or to assist in achieving, the broad goals of economic policy (full employment, low rate of inflation) by controlling the money supply or the interest rates. Today, there seems to be a tendency to concentrate on the money supply, using interest rates as a policy instrument or allowing them to fluctuate freely. Other policy instruments employed by the monetary authorities include: open-market operations, reserve requirements (in British English called 'special deposits'), and direct controls on the availability of credit. Monetary policy is typically implemented by the central bank of a country (the Bank of England in the U.K., the Federal Reserve System in the United States).

A central bank pursuing a policy of "easy money" may lower interest rates (thus encouraging people and firms to borrow more from the banks, which means that the banks create more money), it may ease reserve requirements (also making it easier for banks to lend more), and it may relax direct controls, if any, on the availability of credit. The opposite is true of a policy of "tight money", particularly of a credit squeeze, or credit crunch.

Monetary policy - and, by implication, monetary theory on which it is based - is a highly controversial subject. Different schools of economic thought hold different views on the relative importance of monetary policy and fiscal policy. Keynesians emphasise changes in taxation and expenditure, while monetarists favour monetary measures as means of controlling economic activity. Moreover, there is a continuing debate on the effectiveness of the various policy instruments in influencing the monetary aggregates.

money   Geld

'Money', not to be confused with 'cash', comprises two elements: legal tender, i.e., banknotes and coins in a specific country's currency, and deposit money, consisting of current account deposits, which are recorded in bank ledgers or, more recently, also on computer storage facilities (electronic money).

Money may function as a medium of exchange, as a measure of value for goods and services, and as a store of value.

money market   Geldmarkt

While the capital market is concerned with the provision of long-term capital (both equity and loan), the money market is a market for short-term credit, i.e., for financial claims with a maturity of less than one year. Its main purpose is to enable the participants to meet their short-term liquidity requirements and to invest their excess liquidity profitably.

The participants of the money market are usually financial intermediaries, such as banks, discount houses (in London), bill brokers, and the like, rather than ultimate borrowers and lenders, i.e., private persons and companies, although dealings in Treasury bills and commercial paper are an exception to this rule. It is for this reason that the money market is often referred to as a 'wholesale market' or an 'interbank market'.

Lending and borrowing in the money market is based on a wide range of financial assets. These include: Treasury bills (promissory notes issued by the government to raise short-term funds), certificates of deposit, call money (interbank sight deposits), overnight money (short-term interbank time deposits), and, in the United States, also Federal Funds (a form of interbank lending) and commercial paper (promissory notes issued by large corporations to raise short-term funds).

money order   Geldanweisung

Money orders are a safe means of remitting money to distant points, both at home and abroad. They are particularly useful to people who do not maintain a current account. When payment is effected by money order, the issuing agency (e.g., a bank or a post office), acting upon the request of the remitting person, and on payment of a small fee, instructs the paying agency (another post office, a bank branch, etc.) to pay a certain sum of money either to bearer or to a specified person, the payee. The instructions for payment may be transmitted direct to the paying agency (either by telegram or by mail), in which case the payee has to be informed separately; or they may take the form of a cheque-like instrument, which the remitting person sends to the payee, who may subsequently cash it at the place of payment indicated on the order.

In the U.K., money orders are issued exclusively by post offices, and inland orders can be sent only by telegram (telegraphic orders). The cheque-like variety is peculiar to the United States, although British post offices offer a similar instrument for the remittance of small sums (up to ten pounds), viz., the postal order.

money supply   Geldmenge

The term 'money supply' denotes the amount of money which exists in an economy at any given time. Narrowly defined, it includes banknotes and coin in circulation (i.e., excluding those held by the banking system) and private sector non-bank current account deposits (i.e., excluding interbank deposits).

In most countries, the current account deposits are by far the most important component of the money supply, accounting for around 70 to 80 per cent of the total. From the point of view of monetary theory, the current account deposits (U.S.: sight deposits) included in the money supply are referred to as 'deposit money'. Money supply, as defined above, is called M1. There also exist wider definitions of the money supply, which include, for instance, time deposits, public sector deposits, and so on (M2, M3). Each country uses a different set of monetary aggregates, geared to the requirements of its monetary policy.

In conclusion, one should not fail to mention that the money supply is notoriously difficult to define and to measure, which may lead to all sorts of difficulties in the implementation of monetary policy.

mortgage   Hypothek

Depending on the legal theory adopted by a particular country or state, a mortgage is either a conditional transfer of property from a debtor to a creditor or an interest in property granted by the former to the latter. The purpose of this legal device is to secure a loan. The debtor is called the 'mortgager' (also spelt 'mortgagor'), the creditor the 'mortgagee'. If the borrower fails to repay a loan secured by a mortgage, the mortgagee is entitled to request a court to 'foreclose', i.e., to vest the title to the property in him, enabling him to sell or otherwise use the property to extinguish the debt.

The most common form of mortgage is the one relating to real property, or real estate, although both British and American law recognise also a chattel mortgage, i.e., an interest in personal property, such as motor cars, furniture, works of art.

most-favoured-nation clause   Meistbegünstigungsklausel

Generally speaking, the most-favoured-nation clause is a provision in a commercial treaty between two countries that protects them against tariff discrimination by each other. It guarantees that the parties to the agreement will mutually grant each other any tariff concession that either may offer to third countries.

Apart from being adopted in bilateral treaties, the MFN clause may also be agreed upon on a multilateral basis. For example, since 1948, all signatories to the General Agreement on Tariffs and Trade (G.A.T.T.) have agreed to abide by the MFN principle; in other words, all member countries of G.A.T.T. undertake to grant each other any tariff reductions which they might offer to other member or non-member countries.

There are, however, several important exceptions to the MFN rule under G.A.T.T.. First, G.A.T.T. specifically exempts from most-favoured-nation obligations those countries which are members of a customs union, e.g., of the European Economic Community (E.E.C., also known as the Common Market). A customs union establishes a free trade regime among its member countries by abolishing all, or major groups of, internal tariffs. But imports from all non-member countries, i.e., also from other G.A.T.T. countries, are subject to a common external tariff. The second exception applies to the member countries of a free trade area, e.g., of the European Free Trade Association (E.F.T.A.), which abolishes all internal tariffs, but permits each member to levy its own tariff on imports from non-member countries. Here, the degree of discrimination against non-member states, including other members of G.A.T.T., depends on the tariff levels of the constituent nations, since no common external tariff is applied.

In all cases of deviation from the MFN clause, the countries involved must seek a G.A.T.T. waiver to the rule. Finally, it should be noted that tariff discrimination has become much less of a problem in the course of time, although outright violations of the MFN principle do occur. Still, the very existence of the rule represents a check on potential discriminatory trade practices.

motor insurance   Kraftfahrversicherung

Motor insurance covers the insured's liability towards other people arising out of the use of a motor vehicle. This third-party cover includes death or personal injury caused to other individuals (i.e., all persons outside and inside the vehicle) and damage to property (for example, to other cars). In addition, motor insurance may also cover the owner of a motor vehicle against loss of, or damage to, the vehicle insured arising from accident, fire, theft, etc..

Strangely enough, there is no separate term for what is called 'Autokaskoversicherung' in Austria and West Germany.

multinational company   multinationale Unternehmung,
                                       multinationaler Konzern,
                                       Multi

A multinational company, also referred to as a 'multinational group', 'multinational corporation', or simply 'multinational', is a company which has subsidiaries in more than one other country, the subsidiaries being incorporated under the laws of the respective host countries. Other terms for this type of organisation are 'international company/corporation' and 'transnational company/corporation'. Commonly, all these terms are used interchangeably, although in specialised publications attempts have been made to differentiate between them.

Multinationals operate from an international (or global) perspective, i.e., they regard the whole world as their field of operation, allocating production and distribution according to local labour costs and skills, taxation (tax rates, capital allowances, tax holidays, and other tax breaks), industrial relations (especially a country's strike record), subsidies, availability of raw materials, etc..

The second half of the 20th century has seen a rapid expansion of such firms, and their effect on the economies of the countries in which they operate has aroused considerable controversy. While hardly anybody would maintain that their influence has been all to the bad - after all, they are an important means of transferring technology and capital, of creating jobs, and of generally encouraging the economic development of the host countries -, there are many who think that the disadvantages outweigh the advantages.

Multinationals have been criticised for developing industries which are not really suited to the needs of the host countries and which may even destroy local industries that are. For instance, the large plantations set up by multinationals produce mostly for export and crowd out local agriculture, making the host country dependent on food imports. Another example are the high-technology, capital-intensive industries, which are preferred by multinationals and have little impact on the host country's economy as a whole. Another criticism is that multinationals exploit the host countries by exporting more capital from them than they import into them. The existence of a large number of foreign-controlled companies may weaken the ability of the host country's government to control its economy, since many decisions on investment, research, product lines, exports, wage policies, etc., are made in the foreign parent companies' headquarters. Foreign-controlled companies may have an unwelcome effect on local cultures, shaping consumer tastes and values away from local traditions and values. Multinationals have even been accused of deliberately meddling in the political affairs of the countries where they operate. There are persistent rumours that ITT helped to bring down Allende in Chile in 1973. Another standard criticism is that multinationals deprive local treasuries of tax revenues by manipulating the prices charged in intra-group transactions, a practice referred to as 'transfer pricing'.

This long, but by no means exhaustive, list of criticisms may serve to illustrate the potential conflict of interest between multinational companies and host countries. However, there are also many instances of mutually beneficial co-operation, and some multinationals have changed their high-handed manner and are showing more understanding for the real needs of the countries in which they operate.

| **multiple store** | Filialunternehmen, Filialist, Ladenkette, Filialkette |

A multiple store, or multiple shop, or corporate chain store in the United States, consists of two or more (according to another definition, of eleven or more) outlets which are centrally owned and operated. The centralised method of operation offers a number of advantages: it permits the standardisation of shop fronts, store layouts, range of goods offered, advertising, displays, etc., as well as the use of highly trained marketing specialists, all of which tends to make for economies and higher productivity. As a result, multiples are frequently able to offer their goods at lower prices than the small independent retailer with only one or two outlets.

There are, however, a number of offsetting disadvantages. Multiple stores are less flexible than unit shops, and less able to react quickly to changes in local demand and to meet price reductions of competitors. It is for this reason that some multiples have begun to give their local managers more discretion in certain areas of management, with a consequent loss of some benefits of centralisation.

multiplier   Multiplikator

The multiplier is primarily used in connection with the theory of income determination, i.e., the theory that tries to explain why there is a particular level of national income in an economy rather than another. The original mutiplier, as developed by Kahn and by Keynes, relates changes in "investment" (the only form of autonomous expenditure in a closed economy without a government sector) to changes in national income. Whenever there is a change in investment, national income will also change. The multiplier indicates what multiple of the original change in investment the change in national income will be. If, for instance, investment is increased by one million dollars and the resulting increase in national income is two million dollars, the multiplier would be two, and so on. The size of the multiplier depends on a constant, to be determined by empirical research, viz., on the marginal propensity to consume, which, in turn, depends on the marginal propensity to save (the two propensities add up to one). The higher the marginal propensity to consume, i.e., the more of the income generated by the change in investment is spent rather than saved, the higher the multiplier will be. Even without any detailed proofs or calculations, it is probably intuitively obvious that the effect of a change in investment will depend on whether a high or a low percentage of the income generated by it is spent on goods and services.

In more complicated models, representing, for instance, an open economy with a government sector, other forms of autonomous expenditure, viz., exports and government expenditure, have to be taken into account. Moreover, it is possible to calculate a separate multiplier for each type of autonomous expenditure, e.g., an export multiplier, relating changes in exports to changes in national income, or a government expenditure multiplier. Furthermore, it should be noted that in a complex, modern economy, the propensity to consume is determined not only by the propensity to save, but also by the propensity to import or the propensity to tax, imports and taxes representing "withdrawals" from the income stream, just as savings do.

Finally, it may be worth mentioning that the multiplier concept has also been found useful in other areas of economic theory, e.g., in monetary theory, where a credit multiplier is used.

N

national income   Volkseinkommen (im engeren und
                                        weiteren Sinn)

Strictly speaking, the term 'national income' refers to the sum of money incomes received by the nationals of a particular country from current economic activity (i.e., it is the sum total of wages, salaries, rents, profits, interest and dividends, etc.). But occasionally it is also loosely applied to related aggregates, such as national expenditure and national output.

National income in the narrower sense of the term can be calculated from gross national product by deducting depreciation and indirect business taxes (e.g., value-added tax) and adding subsidies. National income in this sense is, therefore, synonymous with 'net national product at factor prices'.

nationalised industries   verstaatlichte Industrie

Nationalised industries are composed of enterprises owned and controlled by the state. The actual degree of control exercised by government varies from country to country. In Great Britain, for instance, the nationalised undertakings are kept on a fairly long leash. Although the ministers of the sponsoring departments appoint and dismiss the chairmen and have power to give general directions, and although management are accountable to Parliament in a number of ways, the government does not interfere in day-to-day management.

Nationalised undertakings are usually the result of nationalisation, i.e., the conversion into national property of privately owned enterprises. But they may also be set up by a government from scratch or converted from government departments, as in the case of the British Post Office.

Nationalised industries and nationalisation are highly controversial subjects. Normally, socialist governments are in favour of, while conservative governments are against, nationalisation. The arguments put forward to justify nationalisation include elimination of wasteful competition (especially in the case of natural monopolies, such as railways); provision of essential services; national security; prevention of foreign control; suitability as an instrument of industrial policy; fiscal reasons (raising revenue); and last but not least, ideological arguments, such as the desirability of public ownership in itself, and the idea that key areas of the national economy should be communal property and run for the benefit of the nation as a whole rather than for private profit. The critics of nationalisation, on the other hand, point to lack of efficiency, bureaucracy, inflexibility, and to government interference, especially when plants have to be closed down, workers to be made redundant, or new managers to be appointed.

negotiable instruments begebbare Wertpapiere,
abstrakte Wertpapiere

A negotiable instrument is a special type of legal device that can be used to transfer the rights embodied in it by mere delivery (in the case of instruments made out to bearer) or by indorsement and delivery (in the case of instruments made out to order). The most important negotiable instruments are the bill of exchange, the cheque, the warehouse warrant, and the bill of lading.

If, for instance, a cheque is duly indorsed and delivered, the right to receive a specified sum of money from the drawee bank is automatically transferred from the indorser to the indorsee. Where rights not so embodied are to be transferred, a separate contract is necessary, as in an assignment of accounts receivable.

Moreover, a negotiable instrument enables the holder in due course to acquire an even better title than his predecessor possessed. If, for instance, a bill of exchange obtained by fraud is indorsed to a bona fide holder for value, the indorsee is entitled to all rights arising from the bill and is not affected by the defect in the title of the previous holder.

Some instruments, such as the bill of exchange and the cheque, are negotiable unless their negotiability is explicitly excluded, while the bill of lading is negotiable only if made negotiable by the shipper. The bill of lading differs from the bill of exchange and the cheque in one other important respect: although it can be used to transfer the right to receive the goods covered by the bill from the carrier, the holder of a bill of lading cannot acquire a better title than his predecessor possessed. In other words, it does not offer any protection to the bona fide holder in this respect. In view of this difference, some authorities deny the bill of lading the character of a truly negotiable instrument and classify it as "quasi-negotiable".

network Netzwerk

Networks are digital communication systems linking various pieces of equipment, such as word processors, personal computers, mainframes, computer terminals, facsimile machines, etc., either located in the same office or same area (local area networks) or distributed all over the world (global or long-haul networks).

Data can be transmitted over telephone lines, optical fibres, wideband coaxial cables, or by radio link. Wideband cables are also capable of transmitting television pictures (e.g., for video-conferencing). The link enables the otherwise isolated (stand-alone) pieces of equipment to "talk" to each other to share information resources.

nominal nominell

In economics, the expressions 'nominal' and 'in nominal terms' indicate that a monetary variable (such as sales, wages, income, etc.) has not been corrected for price changes. The statement that sales have risen by 10 per cent in nominal terms, for instance, does not reveal how much of this increase is due to price changes and how much to movements in the underlying physical quantities (i.e., tons, pounds, bushels, the number of units of goods or services sold). Changes in nominal terms can be converted into changes in real terms by using an appropriate price index.

non-cumulative quantity discount   Einzelauftragsrabatt

A non-cumulative quantity discount is based on an individual order.
Examples: A retailer may sell golf balls at £1 each or three for £2.50.
A seller may grant a quantity discount of 3% on any order exceeding £100.

A slightly different approach is represented by the quantity discount schedule, which is used mainly by manufacturers and wholesalers. This form of non-cumulative quantity discount is based on the principle: the larger the quantity per order, the higher the rate of discount. The aim is to encourage the buyer to place as big an order as he can in order to get the highest possible rate of discount. The following example shows a quantity discount schedule used by a manufacturer of adhesives:

boxes purchased on single order	price per box
1 - 5	£12.75
6 - 10	£12.50
11 - 20	£12.25
over 20	£12.00

non-depletable resources   unbegrenzt nutzbare Resourcen (Energieträger)

Resources that are not used up by exploitation are called 'non-depletable' or 'renewable'. Utilising a non-depletable resource, e.g., using the flow of a river to generate electricity, is like living off the interest that accrues from a deposit in the bank. Burning coal or splitting uranium, on the other hand, is like drawing on the principal (i.e., the capital deposited) itself.

In general, the use of renewable resources is less damaging to the environment than is the exploitation of deposits of depletable (or non-renewable) resources. Renewable resource exploitation may, however, become a burden on the environment if the scale is too large. Cases in point are solar satellites and large river dam projects, such as Assuan and Hainburg.

non-tariff trade barrier   nichttarifäres Handelshemmnis

The term 'non-tariff trade barriers' is a collective term for all obstacles, other than tariffs, which restrict the free flow of trade. The most important non-tariff barriers are the quantitative restrictions in the form of import quotas. "Voluntary" export quotas, which are sometimes required by buyer countries from low-price supplier countries, have the same effect as quantitative restrictions on imports. An exporting country may, perhaps for fear of retaliatory measures by the importing country, "voluntarily" agree to export not more than a fixed amount of a certain commodity to that importing country, as is the case, for example, with Japanese car exports to the U.S.A..

Other non-tariff trade restrictions include, for example, discriminatory customs valuation methods; health, veterinary, and sanitary regulations; safety standards;

labelling requirements for various products; food and drug laws which discriminate against foreign products or are applied in a discriminatory manner; discrimination in favour of domestic suppliers in connection with government procurement (e.g., failure to put a government contract out to international tender).

In pursuing its main goal, i.e., an equal, non-discriminatory treatment for all trading nations, the General Agreement on Tariffs and Trade (G.A.T.T.) makes every effort to reduce, or even eliminate, all non-tariff trade barriers (e.g., in the Tokyo Round).

notes payable
Schuldwechsel,
Wechselverbindlichkeiten

Generally speaking, a note payable is a promissory note with reference to its maker. In accounting, 'notes payable' is the name of a ledger account or balance sheet item showing separately or in one amount those liabilities to trade creditors (i.e., suppliers of goods and/or services), banks, and other creditors which are evidenced by promissory notes. Notes payable issued to banks for current loans are often listed as bank loans.

It is important to note that bills of exchange are often - justifiably - included in notes payable, since these instruments, when accepted, represent - in the same way as promissory notes do - written promises to pay and can, therefore, be treated similarly for accounting purposes. This is the reason why the terms 'notes payable' and 'bills payable' are usually used interchangeably.

In Great Britain, the corresponding balance sheet caption would be 'bills payable', since British firms hardly ever use promissory notes in connection with the sale of goods and services.

For more complete analytical purposes, notes payable should be classified on the balance sheet as follows: notes payable - trade (referred to as 'trade notes payable' and 'bills payable' are usually used interchangeably.
employees; notes payable - partners; notes payable - miscellaneous.

notes receivable
Besitzwechsel,
Wechselforderungen

In general, a note receivable is a promissory note in the possession of the payee or an indorsee (i.e., somebody to whom the note has been transferred). For example, a business firm may receive promissory notes from trade debtors (i.e., buyers of goods and/or services), from employees, partners, shareholders, affiliated companies, and others for loans granted to them, etc.. Promissory notes received for goods and/or services offer a business firm more security than accounts receivable, because the former represent written evidences of indebtedness, a characteristic that improves their enforceability in court.

In accounting, 'notes receivable' is the name of a ledger account or balance sheet item. In many firms, the Notes Receivable account includes only trade notes receivable (i.e., promissory notes received from trade debtors), whereas all other notes receivable are reported separately. Therefore, the term 'notes receivable' is normally taken to mean 'trade notes receivable'.

Finally, one should bear in mind that it is common practice to report not only promissory notes but also bills of exchange under the caption of "notes receivable". The reason for this is that these instruments have basically the same characteristics and can, therefore, be treated similarly from the accounting point of view. Consequently, the terms 'notes receivable' and 'bills receivable' are usually used interchangeably. In G.B., where promissory notes are rare, the caption of the relevant account is "bills receivable".

NOW account   kombiniertes Spar- und Scheckkonto

Technically, a NOW account is an interest-bearing savings account which enables the depositor to make payments to third parties by means of Negotiable Orders of Withdrawal. These instruments are similar to checks drawn against regular checking account balances.

NOW accounts can be held only by individuals and non-profit organisations, and are offered by U.S. savings banks, savings and loan associations, and U.S. commercial banks.

NOW accounts, which were introduced in 1981, are in effect interest-bearing checking accounts, which enable U.S. banks and other financial institutions to avoid the prohibition of interest payments on demand deposits.

nuclear power   Atomkraft,
                                     Kernkraft

Atomic fission of nuclear fuels (uranium, etc.) produces heat which can be used to generate electricity in the same way as heat produced by fossil fuels. Of all the advantages claimed for nuclear power by its advocates, at least three cannot be denied even by its opponents:
1. Nuclear power-stations do not have a visible plume, and are therefore less of an eyesore than comparable fossil fuel plants.
2. Nuclear fuel requires only a tiny fraction of the space taken by comparable fossil fuels: yearly fuel requirements of a nuclear plant the size of Zwentendorf are 20 tonnes of UO_2 fuel. A fossil fuel-fired plant of comparable performance would burn 1.1 million tonnes of oil or 1.5 million tonnes of coal, and need a constant supply. Fuel supplies for a nuclear plant lasting several years could thus theoretically be stored on site. In practice, this is hardly ever done for financial reasons.
3. Nuclear power-plants need to be recharged only once a year. In a couple of severe U.S. winters in the late 1970s, nuclear power-plants proved more reliable than coal-fired plants, some of which were put out of action as barges and trains with coal supplies got stuck in ice and snow.
All the other advantages claimed for nuclear power are seriously questioned by sceptics.

When President Eisenhower launched his "Atoms for Peace" programme in 1953, the peaceful use of atomic fission promised relief from the psychological trauma the U.S. public and politicians had been suffering since the U.S. military had exploded two nuclear devices over Japan in 1945. The general notion was that nuclear power would be clean, safe, and "too cheap to meter" (= too cheap to measure). At least the latter assumption has turned out to be wrong, and the other two are now being doubted by many. In this article, ecological concerns about the use of nuclear power will not be considered, *) but emphasis will be laid on the economic aspects as exemplified by recent developments in the U.S.A..

At the dawn of the nuclear age, reluctant private U.S. utilities had to be persuaded to buy nuclear power-stations by being offered extremely favourable terms on the first dozen or so nuclear plants. These "loss leaders" have turned out to be, from the point of view of the utilities, very good bargains and thus cheap producers of electricity. When prices of the plants had to be raised to realistic levels to cover the costs of the construction firms, and when additional safety regulations had to be complied with, costs soared, and nuclear power suddenly looked economically much less attractive. Today, the nuclear industry is fighting a losing battle in the United States. Since 1978, not a single new nuclear plant has been ordered by U.S. utilities, and while a few older projects are completed and switched on each year, dozens of planned or half-finished U.S. "nukes" have been cancelled, and a number of almost completed ones have, like Zwentendorf, never been able to go on line.

In Europe, with the exception of the French nuclear programme, nuclear projects have also been cut severely.

In some third-world countries, governments are still strongly interested in nuclear power, partly because they hope to obtain some know-how to apply to nuclear weapons manufacture. The first ldc (less developed country) to demonstrate that an entirely "peaceful" application of nuclear reactors could, in spite of all inspection measures and international treaties, be converted for military purposes was India, which exploded a nuclear device on the basis of entirely peaceful equipment supplied by Canada.

---

*) interested readers are referred to Walt Patterson, Nuclear Power, Penguin, London, 1978, and Peter Weish, Radioaktivität und Umwelt, Vienna, 1981.

O

(ocean) marine insurance policy   Seetransportversicherungspolizze

An (ocean) marine insurance policy is written evidence of the contract of (ocean) marine insurance. (Ocean) marine insurance policies may be classified according to the subject-matter insured into 'hull policies' (covering the ship) and 'ocean cargo policies', the latter being subdivided into 'voyage policies', 'time policies', 'mixed policies', 'floating policies', and policies in the form of 'open cover'. All these types of ocean cargo policy may be classified according to the scope of coverage into 'f.p.a. policies', 'w.a. policies', and 'all-risks policies'.

A policy based on f.p.a. can be obtained at a lower rate of premium than a w.a. policy, but does not provide such comprehensive insurance cover as the latter; the w.a. policy, in turn, provides less extensive cover than the more expensive all-risks policy. In modern practice, the choice of an exporter is often between the f.p.a. policy and the all-risks policy; the w.a. policy is less frequently used. It is worth mentioning that f.p.a., w.a., and all-risks clauses were abolished in Great Britain in 1983. They were replaced by three new types of insurance coverage, referred to as 'Cover A', 'Cover B', and 'Cover C', A being similar to the former all-risks coverage, B falling between f.p.a. and w.a., and C offering the insured less protection than f.p.a..

offer[1]   Antrag

A prerequisite for the conclusion of a contract is that two or more persons must arrive at a mutual understanding with one another on the object of the contract. Generally, this is accomplished by one party making a proposal, and the other party accepting this proposal. This proposal made by one party to the other is referred to as the 'offer', the party making the offer is the 'offeror', and the party to whom the offer is made is the 'offeree'. The offeree may either accept the offer (acceptance) or reject it (non-acceptance). Acceptance of the offer by the offeree results in a contract.

An offer must be strictly distinguished from an 'invitation to treat', which is frequently referred to as an 'offer' in commercial practice (e.g., offer without engagement), but which – from the legal point of view – is merely an invitation to make offers and, therefore, does not result in a contract if taken up.

When an offeror makes an offer, he thereby confers on the offeree the power to enter into a contract by accepting the offer. The offer, however, is not valid for an indefinite period. It may be terminated in the following ways:

1. Provisions in the offer: the offeror often fixes a time limit for acceptance, e.g., "This offer must be accepted or rejected within ten days". The time does not start to run until the offer is received. Acceptance of the offer after the time limit has expired does not result in a contract, but is, in legal effect, a new offer to contract on the terms of the original offer. This new offer may be accepted by the original offeror, this acceptance resulting in a contract.

2. Expiry of time: if no time for acceptance is stated, the offer terminates on the expiry of a reasonable time. The length of time which is reasonable depends on the circumstances.
3. Revocation of the offer: as a general rule, the offeror may revoke his offer at any time before acceptance. This holds even if a time limit for acceptance has been stipulated. The revocation is not effective until it is received by the offeree, which means that the offeree is entitled to accept the offer, creating a binding contract, until he actually receives the revocation. In contrast to British and American law, in Austria, the offeror cannot change or revoke his offer after it has been received by the offeree, unless, of course, the latter concurs. This applies also to offers with a fixed time limit for acceptance. In other words, in Austria, the offer is binding on the offeror during the time limit for acceptance.
4. Rejection of the offer: if the offeree rejects an offer, it is terminated, and any subsequent attempt to accept it is inoperative. If the offeree replies to the offeror by making a qualified acceptance (also called a conditional acceptance), the offer is terminated. A qualified acceptance is a statement by the offeree that he will accept the offer only if certain changes are made in the terms of the offer. A qualified acceptance, therefore, constitutes a rejection of the offer combined with a counter-offer, which is, in effect, a new offer by the offeree.

offer[2] (of goods)

Anbot,
Angebot,
Offerte (betreffend Waren)

By submitting an offer (also referred to as a 'quotation') the seller declares his willingness to sell certain goods at certain prices and on certain terms.

Offers can be made orally or in writing. Verbal or telegraphic offers should be confirmed by letter. Frequently, offers are prepared on printed forms (quotation forms), which are mailed either with or without a covering letter.

Offers may be submitted in response to an inquiry (solicited offers), or without an inquiry having been made (unsolicited or voluntary offers).

A complete offer should cover the following points:
1. nature and quality of the goods offered;
2. quantity;
3. prices and any discounts;
4. delivery period;
5. terms of delivery;
6. terms of payment.

As has already been mentioned, many communications that are called 'offers' in commercial practice (e.g., offers without engagement) are not 'offers' in the legal sense of the word. (see: offer[1])

offer[3]

Briefkurs

The term 'offer' may also refer to the rate of exchange, either spot or forward, at which a bank/foreign exchange dealer agrees to sell a foreign currency, i.e., it is synonymous with 'selling rate' or 'offered rate'.

offer without engagement

freibleibendes Angebot,
unverbindliches Angebot

An offer without engagement (also referred to as an 'offer subject to confirmation') is an offer which is not binding on the seller. If the seller does not want to be bound, he makes an offer subject to certain conditions. For instance, he may stipulate:
1. Prices are subject to change without notice.
2. Subject to price ruling at time of dispatch.
3. Subject to prior sale. / Subject to being unsold. / Subject unsold. / This offer is made subject to the goods being unsold when the order is received. /
4. Goods ordered can be supplied only until our stocks run out / are depleted / are exhausted /.

Frequently, sellers, when making an offer, only stipulate "This offer is subject to confirmation" or "This offer is without engagement".

An 'offer without engagement' is not an 'offer' within the meaning of the law of contract, but merely an 'invitation to treat'. Consequently, an order placed by the buyer against the seller's offer without engagement does not result in a contract. From the legal point of view, this order is an offer, which may be accepted or rejected by the seller.

office personnel

Büropersonal

The constitution of the office personnel must, obviously, vary considerably with the size of the office, the number of staff employed, and the degree of functionalisation. In most offices, however, the following staff can be found: there will be an office manager – usually not a member of the top management team –, who is in charge of the whole office and responsible for planning a suitable organisational structure for his department, for defining the duties and responsibilities of his staff, for checking performance against plans, and for supervising the work in his department. One or several senior clerks will assist him in the general administration of the office. Clerks of various grades will be required to perform specific clerical functions, such as filing (filing clerks), mail handling (post-room staff), and typing (shorthand typists and/or audio typists, frequently centralised in a typing pool).

officer

etwa: Mitglied der Gesellschaftsleitung
(einer Kapitalgesellschaft)

The term 'officer' is mainly used in American English, although it also exists in British English, where it has a slightly different meaning.

In the U.S.A., officers (also referred to as 'corporate officers') are full-time agents of the corporation who work under a contract of employment and are in charge of the corporation's day-to-day affairs. They are appointed by the board of directors and can be removed by them, with or without cause, at any time. They derive their power and authority from the provisions of the charter or the bylaws, or from resolutions of the board.

The Model Business Corporation Act provides that the officers of a corporation shall be the president, one or more vice-presidents, the secretary, and the treasurer. The statutes of some states require fewer officers and most allow more, if desired. In addition, it is becoming increasingly common for a corporation to establish the office of chairman of the board.

In most corporations, the president, the equivalent of the British managing director, acts as general manager, or chief executive officer. He has broad managerial functions and presides at all meetings of the stockholders, of the board of directors, and of the executive committee, provided the office of chairman does not exist. In corporations where the position of chairman of the board is provided for in the articles of incorporation or in the bylaws, it is generally a position of great authority, in some cases greater than that of the president. The usual division of authority between the president and the chairman allots the active administration of the corporation and the supervision of other officers and employees to the former. The chairman of the board, on the other hand, tends to play more of a role in the formulation of general policies and also acts in an advisory capacity to the president and to the board.

The original purpose of the office of vice-president was, as the name of the office indicates, to provide someone to succeed the president if and when his position became vacant, and to serve as acting president during the president's temporary absence or disability. But the modern tendency is to regard the vice-president merely as an officer inferior in rank to the president, performing such duties as the president or the board may direct. In some cases, the heads of the various departments are made vice-presidents under such titles as 'vice-president in charge of marketing', 'vice-president in charge of procurement', etc..

Every company in the U.K. or corporation in the U.S.A. must have a company secretary, who is responsible for ensuring that the company observes the statutory and its own internal provisions. He has to convene meetings as directed by the board, attend meetings of members and of directors, take minutes thereof, keep the statutory books and registers, deal with transfers of shares, etc.; in American corporations, he also has custody of the corporate seal. A director may act as secretary unless he is the sole director. The secretary of a public limited company must be a professionally qualified person. In smaller companies, the secretary is the finance director (U.S.: treasurer) at the same time.

The treasurer has custody of the funds of the corporation. He is the proper officer to receive payments to the corporation and to disburse corporate funds for authorised purposes.

off-line

off-line,
rechnerunabhängig

Off-line means "not connected to, or not under the direct control of, the central processing unit". A magnetic tape in a library may be considered as an example of off-line storage. Off-line processing refers to processing activities on equipment not directly connected to the CPU and thus not under program control. Off-line is contrasted with 'on-line'.

on-line

This term is normally used in connection with peripheral equipment which is under the control of, and in direct communication with, the central processing unit. For instance, an on-line file is a file of data which is held on an on-line storage device and can be used in real-time applications as a continually available data source. On-line is contrasted with 'off-line'.

open account
offene Rechnung

'Open account' is a form of payment under which a buyer who makes regular purchases from the same supplier does not pay for each purchase separately, but monthly, quarterly, or at any other predetermined interval, and on agreed terms (e.g., payment has to be effected by the tenth of the succeeding month). The amount of credit extended on open account is usually limited, the upper limit depending on the customer's creditworthiness.

Under open account terms, the supplier charges all invoices sent out to his customer to the latter's account, and, at the end of the period agreed upon, sends him a statement of account, showing the amount payable. Payment is usually effected by cheque, by credit transfer, or, in foreign trade, by banker's draft or by telegraphic transfer.

The essential feature of open account terms is that the buyer's obligation to pay is not evidenced by a negotiable instrument, such as by a B/E drawn by the seller on the buyer or by a promissory note issued by the buyer to the seller. Since there is no evidence of debt, serious collection problems may arise if the buyer defaults. Therefore, when granting open account terms, the seller must have absolute trust that the buyer can, and will, pay at the agreed time. As a result, open account sales are only made to a buyer with whom the seller has had favourable business relations for a long time, or, in foreign trade, to a branch or subsidiary of the supplier.

open cover
Pauschaldeckung

The open cover has become the most common form of cargo insurance. It is a method of effecting insurance for recurring shipments, the details of which are unknown when the insurance is taken out. Under this arrangement, the insurer agrees to cover all goods transported during a certain period of time, usually 12 months. In many respects, the open cover resembles the floating policy; in particular, the insured is likewise bound to declare all individual shipments to the insurer. It differs from the latter mainly in that it covers all shipments effected during a certain period instead of up to a fixed sum, which means that there is no limit to the number and total value of shipments insured during the policy period. There is also no lump sum premium payable in advance. The premium is generally paid monthly and is based on the value of the shipments declared during the preceding month.

Declarations of shipments under both open covers and floating policies are made by the insured to the insurer in a prescribed form, usually on printed certificates.

These 'certificates of insurance' are provided by the insurer in triplicate or quadruplicate. The insured must complete each certificate by inserting details of the relevant shipment, e.g., the value insured, the packing, marks, numbers, and other particulars of the goods. A copy of the certificate is then sent to the insurer, whilst the insured uses the remaining copies as evidence of the existence of insurance. Briefly, a certificate of insurance is proof of insurance for an individual consignment insured under an open cover or a floating policy, and it takes the place of the policy in respect of the consignment to which it refers.

open-market operation   Offen-Markt-Operation

By open-market operations we understand the buying and selling of government securities by the central bank with a view to controlling the money supply (in particular M1 and M2) and/or interest rates.

If the central bank wants to increase the money supply, it buys government securities from the private sector. A decrease in the money supply can be brought about by the central bank selling government securities to the private sector. In the first case, public sector sight deposits are used to pay for the government securities and will, therefore, flow from the public sector into the private sector, increasing the money supply. In the second case, however, private sector sight deposits will be shifted into the public sector, thus reducing the money supply.

Strictly speaking, the above definition is too narrow since open-market operations are not necessarily restricted to central banks. They can be used to control the supply of, and the demand for, (and therefore the price of) any commodity. For example, they are employed to stabilise the prices of certain primary commodities (buffer stocks) and exchange rates.

opportunity cost   Opportunitätskosten

The term 'opportunity cost' denotes the benefits sacrificed or forgone by taking one course of action instead of another. The opportunity cost of building a shopping centre, for instance, is the profits that can be expected from, or might have been made by, building an office block or a private residential development. From the example it can be seen that opportunity cost is an important tool in making investment decisions and in allocating resources in general.

optical character recognition   optische Zeichenerkennung

By optical character recognition (OCR) we understand the identification of characters by a machine through the use of light-sensitive devices. Scanning devices are used in point-of-sale systems (to read price information), but also by banks (to read documents).

The most sophisticated device is a machine developed by Kurzweil (the Kurzweil Data Entry Machine or KDEM), which is able to read any type of printed material (such as books, newspapers, documents), even if different types of fount are used on the same page.

option   (Wertpapier-)Option

On the stock exchange, an option is the right, or privilege, acquired for a consideration (the premium), either to buy or to sell a certain number of shares or other securities within a designated period of time at an agreed price.

There are four parties to an option: the writer, or maker, of the option, the buyer, or holder, of the option, the broker arranging the transaction, and the indorser, i.e., a stock exchange member firm which guarantees that the maker will honour his undertaking.

Options come in two varieties: 'calls', which give holders the right to buy the underlying security, and 'puts', which give holders the right to sell the underlying security in accordance with the provisions of the option contract. Options are not, however, obligations. Holders can let their positions expire unused if the price of the underlying security does not move favourably during the life of the option.

The holder of a put will exercise his option if the price of the underlying security falls. Puts are, therefore, defensive in nature, and the premium, or option fee, represents a kind of insurance premium. The holder of a call, on the other hand, will exercise his option when the price of the underlying security has risen sufficiently, for then he will be able to resell it in the open market at the prevailing higher price and thus make a profit.

Apart from exercising the option or letting it expire, there is in some countries (e.g., in the United States and in Great Britain) a third possibility: the option may be sold on an options exchange, i.e., an institution specialising in trading options.

order bill   (Order-)Wechsel

An order bill is a bill of exchange which is payable to, or to the order of, a specified person. A bill is deemed to be an order bill if it is made payable to a specified person, without any further words prohibiting transfer, e.g., "Pay Mr. Brown" or "Pay Mr. Brown or order". (A bill, however, which is payable to "Mr. Brown only" or to "Mr. Brown but not to his order" or is marked "not negotiable" is not an order bill and, in fact, is not a negotiable instrument. Such a bill is known as a 'non-negotiable bill of exchange' or a 'not-negotiable bill of exchange'.)

An order bill is transferred simply by indorsement and delivery of the bill. In the case of an indorsement in blank, i.e., the indorser signs his name only without adding that of the indorsee, the order bill becomes a bearer bill. On the other hand, a bearer bill can be transformed into an order bill by simply indorsing it to a named indorsee or his order.

order book   Auftragsbestand,
                                                  Bestand an unerledigten Aufträgen

Originally, an order book was – as the name suggests – a book into which orders were entered as they arrived. Today, order books are frequently files holding the actual order documents received. But if used in business journals or textbooks, the term usually refers to the 'total amount of orders on hand', or, in U.S.

terminology, to the 'backlog of unfilled orders'. This can be measured either in terms of money (e.g., three million pounds worth of orders), in terms of some physical unit (e.g., orders for 60,000 metric tons), or in terms of work weeks.

From the above definition it should be clear that order book is a stock concept – it relates to a point of time. The size of the order book is determined by the rate of incoming orders (order intake) and by the rate of deliveries, or shipments. The aggregate order book of an industry or of the economy as a whole is an important leading indicator.

order cheque   Namensscheck

An order cheque – which is the most common kind of cheque in Great Britain – is a cheque made payable to a particular person, or his order (e.g., "Pay John Brown or order £50").

Like all other instruments payable to order, the order cheque is transferable by indorsement and delivery. Banks require indorsements in the following cases:
1. where the payee (or indorsee) requests payment in cash over the counter, which is possible only if the cheque is uncrossed, i.e., open. Banks, however, do not require the payee (or indorsee) of a cheque to indorse it when the amount is to be paid into his account;
2. where the payee transfers the cheque to another person (indorsee).

If the drawer of an order cheque wants to draw cash from his account, he makes the cheque payable to himself by writing "Self" or "Cash" in the appropriate space of the order cheque form. He may cash a cheque drawn to "Self or Order" also at a bank other than the drawee bank by showing his cheque card.

order (for goods)   Auftrag,
                                          Bestellung (über Waren)

An order may be defined as a request by a prospective customer to a seller to supply goods.

Orders are placed either in response to an offer or on the buyer's own initiative, without a preceding offer. In the latter case, the buyer declares his willingness to buy certain goods if the seller can supply them at the prices and on the terms stated.

Orders can be placed orally or in writing. Orders placed by telephone should be confirmed in writing to avoid misunderstandings.

A complete order should cover the same points as an offer, e.g., quantity, quality, colour, packing, and price of the goods; terms of payment and delivery; mode of transport; etc..

From the legal point of view, it should be noted that an order placed against a firm offer results in a contract, provided it is placed on time (i.e., within the time limit for acceptance) and constitutes an unqualified acceptance of the offer. By contrast, an order following an offer without engagement does not result in a contract until it has been accepted by the seller in the form of a confirmation of order.

order intake
Auftragseingang

The expression 'order intake', or 'new orders', refers to the amount of orders (measured in terms of money, some physical unit, or in terms of work weeks) received by an enterprise during a specified period of time. In contrast to order book, order intake is a flow concept, since it refers to a period of time.

The aggregate order intake, just as the aggregate order book, is an important leading indicator. A high rate of incoming orders obviously points to an increase in economic activity.

organic farming
biologischer Landbau

In contrast to agribusiness, organic farming does not, except in emergencies, use herbicides, pesticides, or other poisons, or artificial fertilisers. Organic farming is more labour-intensive than are the current methods of agribusiness. This was regarded as a grave disadvantage in the past, but current unemployment figures may teach us to see this aspect in a new light. Yields per hectare are almost the same as on ordinary farms. Energy input is much lower, because heavy machinery (which would compress the soil) and artificial fertiliser (which would contribute to the pollution of the rivers, and is very energy-intensive in its manufacture) are not used.

Organic food sometimes still contains traces of environmental poisons, because organic farmers cannot seal their farms off from neighbouring traditional farms and from industrial pollution.

Organic farming is most bitterly opposed by the chemical industry, which relies heavily on agricultural chemicals and on artificial fertiliser for its profits.

organisation
Organisation

One of the more important meanings of this elusive term is the 'organisational structure' of social or socio-technical systems, such as business enterprises. Organisational structures can be described either in terms of the basic organisational units into which a business organisation is divided, or in terms of the formal relationships between these units.

In the case of a 'functional organisation', each basic organisational unit (called department) represents a specialist activity, or function. Thus, a functionally organised multi-product industrial enterprise will have a purchasing department, a production department, a marketing department, etc., each of which is then subdivided into units (e.g., sections) concerned with a particular product or group of products. If the same enterprise is organised on divisional lines ('divisional organisation'), the basic unit of organisation will be the division, each division being concerned with a particular product or group of products and subdivided into functional units. Thus, a chemical group may have a plastics division, a pharmaceutical division, a pesticide division, etc., and each of these divisions will be subdivided into organisational units dealing with research and development, production, marketing, etc..

The distinction between 'line organisation' and 'staff-and-line organisation' is based on two important types of relationship between the organisational units of an enterprise. A line relationship between two units implies that one (the superior unit) has authority to give commands to the other (the subordinate unit). Thus, in the case of a line organisation, there is a chain of command (or rather a number of chains) from the top to the bottom of the organisation. Each unit (with the exception of the highest and the lowest) receives commands only from the one above it and gives commands only to the one below it. In an organisation chart, this chain of command could be represented by a line starting, for instance, with the president and running down through the vice-president of production, the works manager, the foreman, to the machine operator. Hence the name line organisation.

Staff relationships are of an advisory or a service nature. The marketing manager of an organisation, a line manager, may, for instance, be assisted by a marketing research unit reporting to him but having no line authority, i.e., no authority to give commands to other units. An enterprise having both line and staff relationships between its units is appropriately referred to as having a line-and-staff organisation.

Functional, divisional, line, and staff-and-line organisations are only the most basic types of structure to be found in business enterprises. In reality, there is a much greater variety of organisational arrangements. Modern books on the theory of organisation also list matrix organisation, profit centres, project teams, working parties, and intrapreneurial units. Some of these are obviously only temporary organisational structures and reflect the greater flexibility observable of late in this field.

Generally speaking, it is probably safe to say that the older hierarchical and centralised types of arrangement are gradually being replaced with organisational structures that put a greater emphasis on co-operation and decentralisation.

A discussion of the principal types of organisational structure, however brief, would be incomplete without a mention being made of organisational procedures, i.e., the formal rules governing the interaction of the organisational units, and of the great variety of informal relationships between these units. Failure to pay enough attention to the latter type of relationship has often led to great difficulties in otherwise efficiently organised enterprises.

overdraft   Kontoüberziehung,
                                              Kontokorrentkredit,
                                              Überziehungskredit

The term 'overdraft' has two slightly different meanings: on the one hand, it refers to the extent to which a current account at a bank is overdrawn by its holder; on the other hand, it denotes a very common type of short-term loan. In the latter case, a bank simply permits its customer to overdraw his current account up to a specified amount, the credit line. This is in contrast to an ordinary loan, where a separate loan account is opened, from which the money is withdrawn and into which repayments are made. The customer can draw on his credit line at any time during the agreed period. If part or all of the overdraft is repaid before this period has expired (e.g., when customers make payments into the borrower's account), he is allowed to borrow again, provided that the credit line is not exceeded. This means that the overdraft is a type of revolving credit.

Interest is charged on the amount overdrawn at the end of each day, i.e., on the balance outstanding from time to time and on a daily basis, but the bank usually levies an additional charge (the commitment fee) for agreeing to the stand-by arrangement. The commercial rationale of the commitment fee, which is a small percentage either of the total credit line or of the unused portion of the credit line, is that, although the borrower may not make use of the overdraft facility at any given time, the bank must nevertheless have sufficient funds ready against a possible call on its resources. The bank may also insist that the customer should deposit easily saleable shares or other property as security for the repayment of the overdraft.

Overdrafts are suited extremely well to business firms, as the problem of co-ordinating outflows (e.g., payment of wages and salaries, settlement of invoices from suppliers, etc.) and inflows of funds (from sales) is, to some extent, solved automatically.

P

package

Packung,
Packstück,
Frachtstück,
Kollo (Plural: Kolli);
Verpackung

The term 'package' is applied to goods and the wrapping or container in which they have been packed, e.g., package of cigarettes, package of fruits and vegetables. Occasionally, the term is applied to the wrapping or container only.

packaging

Aufmachung,
Packungsgestaltung

Packaging is a marketing term and may be defined as the general group of activities which involve designing and producing the container or wrapping for a product.

The main packaging objectives are to give the package an appealing appearance, thereby attracting the attention of customers, and to protect the product. Therefore, packaging is an important promotional device, particularly in connection with modern retailing methods (self-service) where many products would be difficult to sell without attractive and distinctive packaging. Cosmetic articles and toiletries are a case in point. Other packaging objectives are to make the product available in proper amounts or sizes, identify branded products, make effective displays, etc.. The component elements of packaging are size, shape, materials, colour, and text, and each packaging element must be developed in harmony with the other elements.

packet switching

Paketvermittlungstechnik

Under the packet switching method, data is transferred over a communication link not in a continuous stream, but in the form of packets. In this way, the transmission capacity of the system is used more efficiently.

packing

Verpackung

Packing goods, i.e., wrapping them or putting them in suitable containers, serves at least three distinct purposes: the first is to protect the goods from damage or theft while they are in transit. Eggs with their delicate shells would hardly survive even a short journey if they were not placed in special trays and stacked in cartons.

Secondly, packing in many cases greatly facilitates handling. There are many goods that would be difficult to distribute in loose form or in bulk without great inconvenience to all concerned. Liquids are an obvious case in point.

Thirdly, packing, or packaging, as it is often called in this context, helps to identify branded products and to give them a pleasing appearance. This is particularly important for goods sold by the self-service system. It would be difficult to distinguish, let us say, between the chocolates of two competing manufacturers if it were not for the distinctive wrappings in which they are sold.

The type of packing selected depends to a large extent on the goods involved and the method and duration of transport. Liquids require leakproof containers, such as tanks, vats, barrels, demijohns, or bottles, while for vegetables and fruit, crates, which admit air freely because they are not fully enclosed, are perfectly suitable. Eggs must be given more protection than potatoes, which can be shipped in coarse sacks. Goods transported by sea need to be protected more carefully than those sent a short distance overland. Cases may have to be tin-lined or hermetically sealed to keep out sea water or ship's sweat, thus providing a really seaworthy packing. The choice of packing materials or containers depends not only on the method of transport and the nature of the goods, but also on their value. Goods with a high value per unit of weight or volume justify a much greater expenditure on packing than cheap goods. Here, too, the business man is faced with a trade-off situation and has to find an acceptable compromise.

Any discussion of packing, however sketchy, would be incomplete without a mention being made of the environmental issues involved. Packing, especially the packing of consumer goods, has to be disposed of after use and represents a heavy burden on the environment. This is particularly true of plastic materials which are not biodegradable, i.e., cannot be broken down by the forces of nature. The problem has become acute because the volume of packing has grown much faster than the volume of goods sold. Pressure is being put on firms by environmental organisations and by governments to reduce packing to the absolute minimum and to use more environmentally benign materials. Sorting of solid household wastes at the points of collection and recycling are other steps that might help solve the environmental problems connected with packing.

packing list   Packliste

A packing list is a list of the articles contained in a particular package or container. A detailed packing list may help a buyer to identify specific items, and it facilitates customs clearance in foreign trade.

pallet   Palette

A pallet is a portable platform of wood, metal, or other material, designed for handling by fork-lift trucks or other mechanical lifting and carrying devices, and is mainly used for the carriage and storage of goods. It usually accompanies the consignment throughout the transit from the factory premises to the retailer.

Palletisation is a form of unitisation. Under this method, the goods are bound together if necessary, placed on a standard-size pallet, and loaded on to the transport vehicle, loaded pallets frequently being stacked on top of one another.

Basically, the fact that many pallets are built to internationally standardised dimensions means that freight handling can be fully mechanised by using standard equipment, thus reducing the time and cost of many operations. In addition, palletisation reduces packing and facilitates stowage.

paper clip   Büroklammer

A paper clip is a device consisting of a length of wire bent into flat loops that can be separated by a slight pressure to clasp several sheets of paper together.

particular average   Partikularhavarie,
                                       besondere Havarie

Particular average, a term used in (ocean) marine insurance, can be defined as partial loss of, or damage to, the insured subject-matter caused by a peril insured against, provided the loss or damage is not due to a general average act. Some examples of particular average are: damage to the vessel or cargo by fire; damage to the vessel by heavy seas, stranding, or collision; impairment of the quality of cargo by seawater, etc..

The law treats every loss that is not total as partial loss. Total loss is either 'actual total loss' or 'constructive total loss'. Actual total loss occurs where the subject-matter insured is destroyed (e.g., total destruction of the goods by fire, sinking of the ship in deep water, etc.), or where the subject-matter has been so badly damaged that it has lost its commercial nature (for example, if a consignment of foodstuffs damaged by seawater can then only be used as fertiliser). A constructive total loss, as far as goods are concerned, occurs if the costs of repairing the damage and forwarding the goods to their destination would exceed their value on arrival.

partnership   Personengesellschaft

A partnership is an association of two or more persons (maximum of twenty) who, as co-owners, carry on a business for the purpose of making a profit. Unlike a company, it has no separate legal existence independent of its members. Although a partnership may be formed by tacit agreement, it is highly desirable that a "tailor-made" formal partnership agreement (also known as 'articles of partnership') is drawn up, in which are set out the rights, powers, and duties of the partners. The contents of the partnership agreement will vary with the nature of the partnership and the business concerned, but are likely to include the following:
1. The name of the firm and the names and addresses of the partners.
2. The nature of the business.
3. The capital of the firm and the contribution to be made by each partner (either in cash or in the form of assets and/or services, that is, in kind).
4. The extent to which the partners are to take part in the management of the business.
5. The proportion in which profits are to be shared and losses borne.
6. The amounts that partners may withdraw for their personal use.

7. The interest payable on loans and drawings.
8. The duration of the partnership and the conditions under which it may be brought to an end.
9. Provisions for the dissolution of the partnership.

Partnerships may be classified into 'general partnerships' and 'limited partnerships'. The most important characteristic of a general partnership is that all members – referred to as 'general partners' – have unlimited liability, which means that they are fully liable for all debts and obligations of the firm, and that even their private fortune can be called upon to meet any business debts. This is true of both the 'active' (or 'managing') partners, who take a full part in the running of the business, and the 'silent' (or 'sleeping'/'dormant') partners, if any, who agree to contribute capital and to share in the profits or losses, but to take no part in the management. From the above it is clear that the 'silent partner' in British general partnerships is not the exact equivalent of the 'stille Gesellschafter' in an Austrian 'stille Gesellschaft', the main difference being that the 'stille Gesellschafter' has only limited liability, whereas the silent partner in a general partnership is fully liable. To avoid confusion, it is suggested to render 'stiller Gesellschafter' as 'undisclosed partner (with limited liability)'.

The limited partnership, which is very rare in G.B. and the U.S.A., has two different types of partner: 'general partners', with unlimited liability, and 'limited partners', whose liability is limited to the amount of their agreed capital contribution. Each partnership which is registered as a limited partnership must have at least one general partner. In contrast to the general partner, the limited partner may not share in the management.

The two main advantages of a partnership – compared with a sole trader – are its ability to raise additional capital to expand the business, and the sharing of the duties and losses among the partners. On the other hand, the most obvious disadvantages are the unlimited liability of the general partners and the sharing of profits.

pattern
(Stoff-)Muster

A pattern is a sample, especially a small cutting of textile material, to show quality, colour, and design.

payables
Verbindlichkeiten (einschließlich Schuldwechsel), hauptsächlich aufgrund von Warenlieferungen und Leistungen

Generally speaking, the term 'payables' refers to the total of accounts payable and notes or bills payable. This shows that a payable may be either an account payable or a note payable. In accounting practice, however, 'payables' is frequently used in a narrower sense, viz., as a synonym for either 'trade payables' (i.e., trade accounts payable plus trade notes payable) or 'trade accounts payable'.

payee (of a bill of exchange)

(Wechsel-)Begünstigter,
(Wechsel-)Nehmer,
(Wechsel-)Remittent

The payee of a bill is the person in whose favour the bill is made payable. He can transfer the bill by indorsement and delivery, thus becoming the first indorser. In the case of a bill to one's own order, the payee is identical with the drawer.

payee (of a cheque)

(Scheck-)Empfänger,
(Scheck-)Nehmer,
(Scheck-)Remittent

The payee of a cheque is the person to whom the cheque is made payable.

payment in advance

Vorauszahlung

A 'payment in advance', also known as an 'advance payment' or a 'prepayment', may be defined as a payment received for goods or services prior to delivery or performance. Receiving cash prior to performing services or delivering goods creates a legal obligation on the part of the seller to perform the services or to deliver the goods in the future. This means that the buyer bears the risk of the seller defaulting on his obligation.

payment (of a bill of exchange)   Zahlung (eines Wechsels)

The law requires the holder of the bill to present it for payment within reasonable time (in Austria, within one year from the date of issue) if it is payable at sight, or on the day payment falls due (date of maturity, or due date) if it is a time bill. If the date of maturity is a non-business day, the bill must be presented on the succeeding business day. If the holder fails to present the bill on time, the drawer and indorsers are discharged from their liability. This leaves only the acceptor liable, and the benefit of having all the parties jointly and severally liable is lost.

In the absence of any indication to the contrary, a bill is payable at the drawee's office or residence (Holschuld). But the drawer may specify the place of payment on the bill. Should he fail to do so, the drawee is entitled to specify it when accepting the bill. In commercial practice, a bill is usually payable at a bank (domiciled bill) rather than at the drawee's office or residence.

payment on receipt of goods   Zahlung bei Erhalt der Waren

When payment is to be made on receipt of the goods, the goods are delivered to the buyer, who is expected to pay for them promptly. By contrast, under 'cash on delivery' terms, a third party (e.g., the post office, the railway, or a forwarding agent) is entrusted with the collection of the purchase price, the goods being released to the buyer only after payment has been made.

payment on receipt of invoice   Zahlung bei Erhalt der Rechnung

'Payment on receipt of invoice', or 'payment on invoice', means that the buyer has to pay for the goods and/or services as soon as he receives the invoice.

penetration pricing   Penetrationspreisstrategie

In this pricing strategy, a low initial price is set for a new product in order to reach the mass market immediately and to achieve maximum market penetration.

performance bond   Liefer- oder Leistungsgarantie, Erfüllungsgarantie

A performance bond is a guarantee[2] by which the issuer (usually a bank) undertakes to protect a buyer (referred to as the 'beneficiary') against the failure of the supplier or contractor to perform the contract. If the supplier or contractor does not perform the contract, the buyer can call the bond, which means that the buyer can require the bond issuer to pay the guaranteed amount, usually 10 per cent of the contract price.

performance of the contract (of sale)   (Kauf-)Vertragserfüllung

Performance of the contract means the fulfilment of the contractual obligations by the contracting parties. Under a contract of sale, it is the duty of the seller to deliver the goods in conformity with the contract, and of the buyer to accept the goods and pay for them.

peripherals   periphere Einheiten, die Peripherie

Peripherals, or peripheral devices, are hardware units that work in conjunction with the computer, but are not part of the computer itself. They include storage units (e.g., disk drives), input devices (e.g., magnetic tape readers, optical scanners, keyboard terminals), and output devices (e.g., printers, plotters, VDUs in the narrower sense of the word).

In practice, input and output devices are frequently combined (input/output devices) to allow an interactive mode of operation. A VDU is normally combined with a keyboard in a single unit.

personal computer   Personalcomputer, PC

A personal computer (PC) is a general-purpose microcomputer. In contrast to mainframes and minicomputers, which usually have more than one terminal and can therefore be used by more than one person at the same time, personal computers are single-user machines, designed to be operated by one person at a time. Personal computers should also be distinguished from home computers. The latter are cheap domestic hobby machines with limited storage capacity, while the term 'personal computer' is reserved for sophisticated units with powerful processors, large-capacity disk storage, high-resolution colour graphics, and many other options. Personal computers can be used as stand-alone units, or, if connected to other computers, either as "intelligent" terminals or as elements in a network configuration.

The most common type of personal computer is the desk-top model, which, as the name indicates, fits on a desk – screen, keyboard, disk drive, printer, and all. But at the time of writing, portables are becoming more and more important. Portables come in three different sizes: notebook, briefcase, and transportable. The last variety is not really a portable since it can be lugged around only with difficulty.

personal selling   persönlicher Verkauf

Personal selling is the most important promotional activity. This is reflected by the fact that in the United States, for instance, expenditure on personal selling amounts to between 8 and 15 per cent of net sales, the corresponding figure for advertising being 1 to 3 per cent. Personal selling has great advantages over the other promotional activities. Since it involves face-to-face contact with the prospective customer, it permits the salesman to use customer feedback and to modify his presentation in mid-course. Moreover, personal selling is the only form of promotion that may lead directly to a sale. In many cases, the salesman will not only arouse interest but will actually sell the product involved. Personal selling may be carried out behind the counter, or in the field by people collectively referred to as the 'sales force'.

personnel management   Personalwirtschaft

Personnel management, or personnel administration, the term preferred in the United States, is the application of the management process to the human element in an organisation. More specifically, it is the management function responsible for recruiting, selecting, training, placing, promoting, rewarding, motivating, and, yes, dismissing employees with a view to achieving the overall goals of a particular organisation.

Personnel management is an all-pervasive function, i.e., it is performed not only by specialists but by anybody managing people in an organisation. It therefore exists in the small firm, which employs only a few people, as well as in the large organisation, which has a personnel manager, who exercises some, but not all, functions of personnel management. In large companies, a works manager, sales manager, office manager, and foreman still continue to influence and, perhaps, control the recruitment, training, promotion, and pay of those who work for them, although they will be assisted, advised, guided, and, to some extent, controlled by the personnel manager in doing this.

Personnel management is influenced by certain explicit or implicit assumptions about human behaviour in organisations. Taylorism, or scientific management, with its heavy emphasis on work measurement (time and motion studies) and purely monetary incentives, is based on a mechanistic view of human behaviour and regards employees simply as a specialised form of input. Other management philosophies, such as the Human Relations movement and the social systems model, show more respect for the employees as human beings, setting a greater store by motivation, job satisfaction, conflict solution, co-operation, and worker participation.

photovoltaic conversion photovoltaische Umwandlung

Photovoltaic conversion is the direct conversion of (sun)light into electricity by means of photovoltaic cells (solar cells). Discovered 150 years ago, photovoltaic conversion was until the 1950s only used in tiny selenium cells for photographic exposure metres. With the chance discovery of the photovoltaic qualities of silicon in 1954, a much more efficient and much cheaper material was available. Silicon converts around 10 per cent of the sunlight into electricity (selenium converts 1 per cent), and is the world's second most abundant element, covering 28 per cent of the earth's crust.

Solar electricity is probably the electricity source of the future. It is safe and remarkably clean and could be applied in both centralised and decentralised systems. Additional space requirements would not be too much of a problem, since photovoltaic tiles can be put upon roof-tops.

Although research and development still account for much of the solar cell industry, practical use of the technology is growing quickly. All communications satellites are powered by photovoltaic cells, and in remote areas telephones often rely on photovoltaics. On a more limited basis, solar cells provide power for water pumping, desalination, and lighting. There are now over 10,000 residences in the world powered by solar electricity, mainly in rural areas without access to utility power lines. A solar-powered experimental car crossed Australia in 20 days in 1983, and a solar aeroplane crossed the British Channel a year earlier.

The main obstacle preventing immediate large-scale application is the high cost. However, cost per peak watt went down from $30 to $10 between 1975 and 1982 alone, while production has risen a hundredfold since 1970. Optimists predict a breakthrough within the next few years, hoping that the photovoltaic cell will emulate the history of the transistor, which is also a silicon-based device, and which has experienced enormous cost reductions since its invention in 1949.

piggyback service Huckepack-Verkehr

Piggyback is a combination of road and rail transport. Under this method, loaded road vehicles (e.g., lorries, trailer units, articulated lorries, trailers, and semi-trailers) are driven from the shipper's premises to the rail terminal, moved on to flat waggons, and transported to the agreed terminal, where they are loaded off the waggons and driven to their final destination.

The piggyback method combines the advantages of cheaper rail service for long hauls and cheaper and more convenient road service for local collection and delivery of the goods. Other benefits are: reduced handling of the actual goods and packages, resulting in lower freight rates and faster service; low risk of damage and pilferage, because neither marshalling of waggons nor rehandling of individual packages is required; fast delivery due to the relatively high average speed of piggyback trains.

planned obsolescence

geplante Produktveralterung

Planned obsolescence is a product strategy that tries to make a product out-of-date before it is physically worn out, the idea being to increase the replacement demand. This may be achieved by making frequent changes in superficial product characteristics (style), supported by advertising and other promotional activities. The term may also be applied to the strategy of deliberately building a product so that it does not last as long as it could.

Both strategies involve a waste of resources and are criticised by environmentally-minded people and organisations, although it may be difficult to determine the amount of waste with any degree of precision. The reason for this is that it is impossible to know when the consumer durables in question would have been abandoned spontaneously in favour of new models or fashions in the absence of planned obsolescence.

plotter

Kurvenschreiber,
Kurvendrucker,
Plotter

A plotter is an output device capable of converting the electrical impulses transmitted by the CPU into line drawings of varying complexity, e.g., diagrams, charts, graphs, as well as full-sized manufacturing patterns.

ploughback

Selbstfinanzierung,
Gewinnthesaurierung

Ploughback (U.S.: plowback), also known as 'self-financing', refers to a company's practice of not distributing all its profits, but retaining a portion to be used either for investment in current and fixed assets or for the retirement of debt (compare: dividend). Although there is no explicit cost for the use of the company's internally generated funds, ploughback does not come free. By reinvesting its own profits the company obviously foregoes other investment opportunities. In other words, there is an opportunity cost in the form of 'imputed interest', which should be allowed for in the company's cost accounts.

Ploughback is a very convenient form of financing, and, since costs, as has already been mentioned, are not explicit, there is a danger that internally generated funds will be used less wisely, because management might be tempted to apply less stringent criteria than in the case of funds raised externally. However that may be, ploughback is an extremely important method of financing, especially in the United States, where creditors' funds are relatively scarce and, therefore, relatively expensive.

point of sale system

POS-System

A point of sale system, or POS system, is a computer application in retailing. The basic idea is to capture the sales data at the checkout counter and to use it for stock control, ordering, and similar purposes. The checkout person enters product, price, and volume data into a cash-register type computer terminal, either manually or with the help of a scanning device, capable of reading information pre-recorded on the products or packages. In addition to printing the sales slip, the terminal passes on the data to a central computer that is programmed to update stock records, and to print orders for the central warehouse or for outside suppliers when the stock of a particular item has fallen below a predetermined level. Moreover, the system may be used to analyse sales data from various angles, e.g., to identify fast-moving and slow-moving items as an aid to the organisation's product policy.

Sophisticated POS systems provide a link with the banking system and enable a customer to pay his bills through a separate nearby terminal. All a customer has to do is insert a plastic card and key in his PIN code and the amount payable, thus directly debiting his own account and crediting the retail organisation's account. The payee benefits through the immediate availability of funds, and the customer is spared the expense and trouble of writing out a cheque. In spite of these obvious advantages, consumer acceptance of this combined system, referred to as EFTPOS (also spelt: eftpos) has so far been less than enthusiastic.

pollution   (Umwelt-)Verschmutzung

Pollution is the poisoning of our environment by pollutants from natural or man-made sources. In accordance with the three elements of the ecosphere, the main types of pollution are soil pollution, water pollution, and air pollution. Where solid, liquid, or gaseous pollutants are involved, pollution is measured in p.p.m. (parts per million). Pollution by radioactive substances is measured in rem (roentgen equivalent man). Noise pollution is the deterioration of the quality of life caused by background noise from machinery, vehicles, or aircraft, while thermal pollution is the heating up of rivers, etc., for example, by the waste heat of power-stations.

Local pollution of the environment has been a problem since the beginning of civilisation, whereas global environmental pollution is a feature of the last few decades.

postal order   „Postbon",
                                             „Postanweisung" (für kleine Beträge)

Postal orders represent a safe method of making small payments by post. Postal orders are issued by British post offices for certain fixed values, ranging from 10p to £10. The value of the order may be increased to some small extent by adding postage stamps.

The sender buys the postal order, paying a small extra fee, and sends it to the payee, who can cash it at any post office in Great Britain and in certain other countries. The sender can guard against the risk of the postal order being stolen by filling in the name of the payee and the post office at which it can be cashed; or, better still, by filling in the payee's name and then crossing the order, i.e., drawing two parallel lines across the face of it. In that case, the postal order cannot be cashed at a post office, but must be paid into a bank account.

preference share   Vorzugsaktie

Preference shares (U.S.: preferred stock) are shares that carry some preferential right vis-a-vis ordinary shares. Although they may be treated preferentially in many ways, most of them are preferred as to dividend and as to return of capital in a winding up. Preference as to dividend usually means that preference shareholders are entitled to receive a dividend before ordinary shareholders get theirs, so that in a year with little profit they might get a dividend, while the ordinary dividend may be passed. This arrangement requires a fixed percentage of dividend, which makes preference shares similar to debentures. The company is, however, not obliged to pay a dividend on preference shares in years with no or only little profit, while the interest on debentures has to be paid, no matter whether there is a profit or a loss.

In the U.K., preference shares are legally deemed to be 'cumulative' (cumulative preference shares) unless the company's articles of association specifically make them 'non-cumulative'. This means that if there is no dividend in a particular year, the right to that dividend is not lost, but dividend arrears have to be paid in later years when there is again sufficient profit, the right to dividend arrears being limited to five years.

The voting power of preference shareholders is usually restricted by providing that they shall have no right to attend general meetings or vote there, unless their dividend is six months in arrear. But other arrangements concerning voting power are possible: some companies have preference shares with multiple voting rights, which may be very important when a take-over bid for the company is made.

Apart from the standard type of preference share, there are 'redeemable preference shares', which have to be repaid like debentures, and 'participating preference shares', which, in addition to their fixed-rate dividend, may get a variable dividend if there are sufficient profits to pay the ordinary shareholders a pre-arranged rate of dividend.

premium[1]   Versicherungsprämie

In insurance, premium (also 'insurance premium') is the consideration which the insurer receives from the policyholder for his undertaking to pay the sum insured if the event insured against occurs.

premium[2]   Report

In the foreign exchange market, the term 'premium' refers to the difference between the higher forward rate and the lower spot rate. This means that the foreign currency concerned is more expensive in the forward market than in the spot market. (see: forward rate)

premium[3]   Agio

In an investment context, premium is the amount by which a share or bond stands above its nominal (or par) value. Where shares are issued at par, they may go to a premium right away if the issue price has been set too low. As in the case of discount[3], a premium may be related not to the par value but to some other point of reference. For instance, the shares of an investment trust may stand at a premium to (i.e., be higher than) the asset or portfolio value per share.

premium[4]

Werbegeschenk,
kleine Zugabe

One of the many applications of the term 'premium' is in marketing, where it may refer to a small item given away with the main purchase either free or at a favourable price (usually at cost). The small plastic toys that can be found in the packages of breakfast cereals are called 'premiums', as are the slightly more valuable toys that can be obtained from the seller of a particular article by sending in a coupon attached to the main product package.

premium[5]

Spitzen- (z.B. Spitzenqualität),
Qualitäts- (z.B. Qualitätswein),
Prestige- (z.B. Prestigepreis)

Another marketing application of the term 'premium' is in compound words, like 'premium price', 'premium quality', 'premium brand'. In all these examples it is used to indicate that the price (and, by implication, the quality) of the product involved is above the usual average (however vaguely defined), and that the article is, therefore, clothed in an aura of prestige. Especially if the quality is not that much higher, premium brands have to be supported by heavy advertising and other promotional activities to create and sustain a prestige image.

price

Preis,
Kurs

In economics, the term 'price' denotes the consideration in cash (or in kind) for the transfer of something valuable, such as goods, services, currencies, securities, the use of money or property for a limited period of time, etc.. In commercial practice, however, it is normally restricted to the amount of money payable for goods, services, and securities. In other applications, the word 'rate' is preferred. Interest rate is the price for the temporary use of somebody else's money, exchange rate is the price of one currency in terms of another.

Price may refer either to one unit of a commodity (unit price) or to the amount of money payable for a specified number of units or for something where units are not applicable, e.g., for five tons of coal (total price) or for a specific painting by Rembrandt.

Prices may be either free to respond to changes in supply and demand or controlled by the government or some other (usually large) organisation.

price-list

Preisliste

A price-list is a printed list showing the prices which are either charged by the seller to the buyer or recommended to him for resale.

price policy

Preis- und Konditionenpolitik

Pricing products is an extremely complex and, at the same time, extremely important marketing activity: complex, because so many variables are involved; important, because, in the long run, the success and even the survival of a firm will depend on the prices it charges for its products.

First, it should be quite clear what the price of a product really refers to. It may be the naked physical product to be picked up and paid for immediately by the buyer (cash-and-carry price) or the product plus any number of additional services (e.g., delivery, modification, installation, credit). Moreover, since it is the price actually paid by the customer that counts, discounts and similar allowances also form part of what is referred to as 'price policy'.

A seller's price policy will be determined by the type of market he operates in. Under pure (or perfect) competition, with many sellers and buyers, sellers are simply price-takers, i.e., they have to sell at market prices. A monopolist, on the other hand, has discretionary power over prices (and output), since there are no competitors. Oligopolistic markets, dominated by a few large firms, are characterised by mutually recognised interdependence of the rival sellers' price policies.

Moreover, price policies cannot be conceived and implemented independently of the other elements and goals of a firm's business policy, especially of the other elements of its marketing mix. The use of skilful advertising, for instance putting across a product as a luxury brand, may enable a firm to charge higher (i.e., premium) prices. Pricing strategies will depend on whether a firm wants to maximise profits in the short run and skim the market (skim-the-cream pricing) or to secure a large market share in the long run (penetration pricing), or whether it wants to secure a minimum return on investment or eliminate a few upstart competitors.

Costs (and therefore the determinants of costs, such as raw material prices, wages, volume, capacity utilisation) have an important influence on price, since no firm will be able to sell below cost in the long run.

Finally, both suppliers and governments may restrict a seller's room for manoeuvre. When resale price maintenance was still permitted in the U.K., it was quite common for suppliers to blacklist resellers that did not adhere to the prices set by the suppliers; and government may use its powers to control prices in various ways (incomes policy).

primary market

Primärmarkt,
Emissionsmarkt

The term is usually applied to the market for new issues of securities, that is, to the market whose main function is the raising of fresh capital. Primary securities markets are much less tightly organised than secondary markets (stock exchanges). They are not normally housed in separate buildings, but consist of loose associations of specialised banks (issuing houses in London, investment banks in the United States) representing the ultimate issuers, and private and institutional investors.

Securities may be issued in a number of ways, for instance, by direct invitation to the public, by an offer for sale, or by a rights issue. Under the first method, the company will normally use the services of an issuing house to handle the details and to arrange for the issue to be underwritten. (This is to ensure that the whole issue is actually sold.) Under the second method, an issuing house (or a broker) will buy the whole issue outright and sell it at a slightly higher price for its own account. Rights issues are issues of new shares to existing shareholders.

principal[1]

Kreditsumme,
Darlehenssumme,
Kapital (im Gegensatz zu den damit verbundenen Zinsen)

The term 'principal' may be used to describe an amount lent (or borrowed), exclusive of the interest payable on it. The term is frequently used in conjunction with 'interest', as in "the repayment of principal and the payment of interest are secured by a mortgage".

principal[2]

Geschäftsherr,
vertretene Firma,
vertretene Person

The term 'principal' may also refer to a legal or natural person who authorises another legal or natural person (the agent) to act on his behalf (i.e., for his account and usually in his name), e.g., to represent him in some business transaction. (For further details see: agent)

principal[3]

Akkreditivsteller

In connection with a letter of credit, the term 'principal' denotes an importer who instructs his bank to open a letter of credit in favour of the exporter. It is, therefore, synonymous with 'applicant for the credit'.

principal[4]

Hauptschuldner

In legal and in banking contexts, the term 'principal', or 'principal debtor', may refer to a natural or legal person primarily liable on an obligation, as distinguished from a guarantor. A principal in this sense is, therefore, a person who owes a debt which another person is liable to pay in the case of his (i.e., the principal's) default in paying it.

printer

Drucker

The printer is easily the most important hard-copy output device. Some devices print characters using a mechanical process, such as striking the surface of the paper with a type hammer, while others are based on thermal, chemical, photographic, or laser processes. Both types can print characters in one of three ways: character by character, line by line, or page by page. It is obvious that the last method is the fastest (approximately 8,500 pages, or 750,000 lines, per hour).

procurement (management) Beschaffung(-swirtschaft)

In the widest sense of the term, procurement refers to the process of obtaining all the inputs required by a business organisation to achieve its objectives. This means that it includes not only the purchase of materials (i.e., raw materials, components, and services), merchandise, and capital equipment, but also the raising of capital, the recruiting and hiring of personnel, and the obtaining of information. In practice, the meaning of the term is normally restricted to the obtaining of materials, merchandise, and items of capital equipment, and even the latter are sometimes excluded. In this case, the function is normally referred to as 'purchasing'.

Manufacturing organisations typically spend more than half of their sales revenue on the purchase of materials in the supply markets. In the case of retail organisations, this percentage is even higher. Therefore, management always has, or at least should have, devoted a great deal of time and energy to organising the procurement function efficiently.

The main objectives of purchasing management are to make sure that the materials of the type and quality required for production and/or sale are available in sufficient quantities when needed, and at the lowest possible cost to the organisation. Planning material requirements (material requirement planning, or MRP), selecting and evaluating suppliers (sourcing and vendor rating), and, in the case of components, deciding whether to produce them in-house or obtain them from outside sources (make-or-buy decision), all play an important role in achieving these objectives. As in many other areas of management, there are trade-offs between the goals, which must not be overlooked: giving priority to cutting costs may jeopardise the security of supplies, and, of course, quality, as always, has its price.

In recent years, it has been the planning aspect of purchasing management that has attracted special attention. Ad hoc, hand-to-mouth purchasing has increasingly been replaced with policies giving more weight to strategic (i.e., long-term) considerations. Another fairly recent development – this time in the field of organisation – has been the integration of purchasing with inventory management (see: materials management), which seems quite logical in view of the many links between these two functions.

Another important aspect of purchasing management is concerned with the nitty-gritty details of the purchasing procedure: purchases are initiated by the production department, the marketing department, or any other operating department, and the purchasing department acts on their behalf. The purchasing department will receive requisitions (either specific or blanket) from these other departments, it will check the specifications, select a suitable supplier or suitable suppliers (on the basis of either inquiries and quotations, invitations to tender and tenders, or buyer records), it will negotiate the contract(s), place the order(s) or award the contract(s), progress the order(s), receive the goods, inspect the goods, and place them in stock, where applicable.

producer goods Produktionsgüter

Producer goods are goods used in the production of other goods. Examples include: machine tools, extrusion presses, process-control computers, blast furnaces, continuous casters, etc.. Since producer goods are not required for their own sake, the demand for them is a derived demand, based on their usefulness in ultimately producing consumer goods.

Just as in the case of consumer goods, producer goods may be classified into a durable and a non-durable variety. 'Durable producer goods', also called 'capital goods', 'investment goods', or 'hard (producer) goods', can be used more often than once, they give off a stream of services during their useful lives, are subject to wear and tear (and possibly to obsolescence), and are, therefore, used up only gradually. 'Non-durable producer goods', also called 'soft (producer) goods', include factory supplies (e.g., chemicals) and fuel and are used up in the process of production.

product   Produkt

In modern marketing, the term 'product' is not restricted to tangible (or physical) goods, but includes anything that is capable of satisfying consumer wants and needs. Therefore, it obviously includes also services (e.g., a hair cut, a specific type of loan, an overdraft facility), but even in the case of tangible goods, the emphasis is on the benefits provided by them rather than on their physical attributes.

Products may be classified in any number of ways. A typical marketing (i.e., consumer-oriented) classification is the one into convenience and shopping goods. 'Convenience goods' are consumer goods bought frequently in small quantities with a minimum of deliberation, e.g., candy, cigarettes, chewing gum. 'Shopping goods', on the other hand, are purchased only after "shopping around", i.e., after careful consideration of competing products (e.g., furniture, motor cars).

product differentiation   Produktdifferenzierung

Product differentiation is a marketing strategy which involves creating and promoting an awareness of (frequently artificial) differences between the products of a particular firm and basically similar products offered by its competitors. This can be achieved by skilful advertising, the use of brand names, and attractive packaging and design. If the strategy is successful, consumers will not regard competing products as perfect substitutes, and the firm will thus be insulated from price competition. If, in fact, a product has established itself in the public mind, it may command a premium price.

product innovation   Produktinnovation

Product innovation is an extremely important element in a firm's business policy. The very existence of a company may depend on its ability to come up with attractive new products at the right time, i.e., right from the point of view of the consumer and right in terms of the company's sales and profits. Large firms do not leave such an important area to chance. They use carefully planned procedures to make sure that they will not have to rely for ever on their old troupers, which may already have entered the stage of decline in their life cycles.

Product innovation involves the generation of new product ideas (by research departments, private inventors, sales people), screening (weeding out the non-starters), business analysis (in terms of market demand, profitability, product features), product development (converting the ideas into a physical product), test marketing, and commercialisation (development of full-scale production and marketing programmes, and the launching of the product).

However, in spite of such careful planning, heavy expenditure on research and development, and the setting up of independent venture groups within large organisations, the attrition rate, i.e., the proportion of new products that fail to make it to the market-place and turn out to be flops, is still very high. It is unlikely that the element of chance can ever be eliminated completely from what is essentially a creative process.

production   Produktion (im weiteren Sinn)

In economics, the term 'production' has a wider meaning than in everyday usage. It includes not only the conversion of raw materials into manufactured or semi-manufactured goods, but also the extraction of natural resources, as well as activities that do not result in tangible products, i.e., services.

From the foregoing it can be seen that production in this wider sense is coextensive with the creation of utilities or value added.

productivity   Produktivität

Productivity is generally defined as the ratio of output to input. The ratio is calculated by dividing a given output by the number of input units required to produce that output. In other words, it tells us how many units of output are produced from one unit of input.

The best-known variant of the concept of productivity is 'labour productivity', which relates a given output to the labour input required to produce it, disregarding all other inputs (capital and/or land). Since labour input is usually measured in man-hours, labour productivity can be defined as output per man-hour. An increase in labour productivity leads to higher output if input remains constant, or to a reduction in labour input if output is to remain constant. In the latter case, there will be redundancies unless working hours are reduced.

product life cycle   Produktlebenszyklus

The expression denotes the development of the sales volume and the profits generated by a particular product over its span of life. The cycle is generally divided into six stages: introduction (launch), growth, maturity, saturation, decline, and abandonment. There are, however, a number of exceptions. For one, a firm may decide to revive a declining brand by "re-launching" it; or, in special cases, the product involved is never really abandoned, but sales and/or profits are allowed to stagnate at a low level (petrification).

product line　　　　　　　　　　Produktlinie (bei Herstellern);
　　　　　　　　　　　　　　　　　Warengruppe (bei Händlern)

A product line is a broad group, or class, of products which possess similar physical characteristics and are intended for broadly similar uses. The depth of a product line is determined by the number of different items, colours, models, etc., it comprises (e.g., a line of shoes may consist of only one or two types, such as men's shoes and women's shoes, or of many different types, such as men's shoes, women's shoes, ski boots, tennis shoes, slippers, etc.). A firm may decide to carry only one line or several lines. In the former case, the product line would be coextensive with the firm's product range, or product mix. A department store, for instance, generally carries a large number of lines (roughly corresponding to the number of departments), while stockists often carry only one line (e.g., photographic supplies or electrical appliances).

product manager　　　　　　　Produktmanager

One method of overcoming the lack of co-ordination between the various departments or sections of a firm (production, purchasing, finance, advertising, selling, etc.), especially in connection with the development of new products, is to give a product manager or brand manager overall responsibility for one product or a group of products. Product managers typically report to a top marketing executive, have no line authority, and are expected to co-ordinate the activities of the various departments or sections concerned with a particular product or particular products. They do so by organising and planning new product development, setting marketing goals, preparing sales and profit budgets as well as advertising and selling plans. Since they have little authority, their effectiveness depends on their ability to persuade other managers.

product mix　　　　　　　　　Produktionsprogramm (bei Herstellern);
　　　　　　　　　　　　　　　　Leistungsprogramm (bei Anbietern von
　　　　　　　　　　　　　　　　Dienstleistungen);
　　　　　　　　　　　　　　　　Sortiment, Verkaufsprogramm (bei
　　　　　　　　　　　　　　　　Händlern)

The product mix represents the full range of products (i.e., of goods and/or services) offered by a particular firm. Its structure is determined by the number of different lines carried (breadth of the range) and by the number of items, models, etc., in each line (depth of the range). The terms 'product mix' and 'product range' have basically the same meaning. The latter, however, is purely descriptive, while the former emphasises the strategic aspect. It is essential for a firm to get as close as possible to an "optimum" product mix in terms of profit, growth, and risk. Decisions relating to the product mix are part of the wider field of product policy.

product policy　　　　　　　　Produktpolitik

Product policy – a key element in the marketing mix – is the sum total of all decisions relating to the offering of a firm. The first problem in this field is to determine what product or products to buy/produce and sell.

A decision has to be made whether to concentrate on one product or offer a wider range of goods and/or services. Then it may be necessary to decide whether to expand or to simplify an existing product range (diversification versus simplification). New products have to be identified and developed that fit a firm's range in terms of profit, growth, and risk. Product innovation is an extremely important area because a firm's survival may depend on its ability to come up with new products when the existing items have reached maturity. Other decisions are concerned with the quality of the product, with branding, packaging, and related aspects. A firm may decide to go up-market (trading up) or down-market (trading down), which is obviously the opposite strategy; it may decide to use one brand for all its products, or a separate brand for each important line; it may decide to drop brands altogether and to concentrate on generic items. This list of product decisions could be extended considerably, but it is sufficient to give a rough idea of what is involved in this important aspect of the marketing mix.

product positioning   Produktpositionierung

One important aim of promotion is to create, maintain, or change the consumers' perception of the benefits of a product in comparison with competing products, in short, to "position" the product. A particular product may be cast as "expensive but reliable", "good value for money", or as "socially responsible". Correctly positioning a product is an important determinant of company profits.

profit-sharing   Gewinnbeteiligung (der Arbeitnehmer)

Profit-sharing is an arrangement by which employees receive, in addition to their wages or salaries, a share of the profits of the business organisation they work for. It usually takes the form of an agreement to pay annually (or in instalments) a fixed proportion of the profits made during the preceding year. There are, however, also deferred profit-sharing plans, under which the profit due to an employee is paid into a trust fund and released on the occurrence of specified events (severance of employment, death, retirement, etc.).

Profit-sharing plans may include either all employees (provided they meet specific requirements as to length of service, etc.) or only a limited number of employees (e.g., only top management may be eligible). Another aspect of profit-sharing plans is the definition of the profit on which they are based. There is a tendency to exclude extraordinary items, such as proceeds from the sale of a subsidiary company, from the definition.

The case for profit-sharing can be summarised in three words: equity, involvement, and incentive. Since employees have contributed to the profits by their labour, it is only fair, or equitable, that they should receive a share of them. If employees benefit directly from the success of the enterprise, measured by its profitability, they can be expected to be concerned for its success and to work harder. It should be noted, however, that these principles are not generally accepted. For one thing, profit-sharing seems to provide only little direct incentive to most employees, because payments are too far removed from today's work and probably too small to have any influence on it. Secondly, there is a body of opinion that opposes all forms of profit-sharing as an attempt to gloss over the conflict of interests between employees and employers and as a threat to trade-unionism.

pro forma invoice   Proformarechnung

A pro forma invoice is a special form of invoice, which differs from an ordinary invoice only in being marked 'Pro forma'. It is used in a number of special circumstances, e.g.,
1. as a formal quotation to show the customer what he would have to pay if he decided to buy the goods;
2. as a polite request for payment in advance for goods ordered by an unknown or unreliable customer;
3. if the goods are sent 'on approval' or on similar terms;
4. if the goods are sent 'on consignment', i.e., if the goods are sent to a consignee for sale on commission.

In addition, importers may need a pro forma invoice to be able to apply for an import licence and/or a foreign exchange permit. In cases where payment has to be made by documentary letter of credit, the pro forma invoice is frequently used to inform the importer of the amount for which the letter of credit has to be opened.

programming language   Programmiersprache

A programming language is an artificial language (i.e., a set of symbols and rules regulating their use) that can be used to formulate instructions for a data processing system. There are two main types of language. First, machine languages, or machine codes, which are used to write object programs in binary form and can be understood by the computer directly. Second, higher-level languages, also referred to as problem-oriented languages, which enable the programmers to write source programs. Since the computer only understands and executes object programs (i.e., machine language programs), these source programs have to be translated into object programs by a special operating software program (compiler).

Assembly languages are an in-between variety. Basically, they are machine codes with certain characteristics of higher-level languages (e.g., mnemonic notation). The source programs written in assembly language have to be translated into object programs with the help of a special program, called an 'assembler'. It should also be noted that both machine languages and assembly languages are machine-oriented languages.

The best-known higher-level languages are COBOL (Common Business-Oriented Language), BASIC (Beginner's All-purpose Symbolic Instruction Code), FORTRAN (Formula Translation), ALGOL (Algorithmic Language), APL (A Programming Language), and PL1 (Programming Language One).

progressive taxation   progressive Besteuerung

From a technical point of view, progressive taxation involves the application of ever higher tax rates to successive slices of the tax base, e.g., of income or capital. For example, in the U.K., the first slice of income, or income bracket, (i.e., the first £12,800) currently attracts a rate of 30 per cent (basic rate), the second slice (i.e., the next £2,300) one of 40 per cent, and so on, until a maximum rate of 60 per cent on the slice of income exceeding £31,500 is reached. By contrast, under a system of proportional taxation, a uniform rate, or flat rate, is applied to total income.

Under a progressive tax system, the rate applied to the top tax bracket (i.e., to the last slice of income) of a particular taxpayer is referred to as the 'marginal tax rate', which must be distinguished from the 'average tax rate'. The latter is calculated by dividing the total tax burden, resulting from the application of the progressive rate, by one per cent of total taxable income. The marginal tax rate plays an important role when taxpayers have to decide whether to earn more or less. High marginal tax rates are said to have a disincentive effect, i.e., they are supposed to act as a drag on people's efforts. There is, however, also a counter-argument, viz., that a steeply progressive tax will induce people to work harder to achieve a planned increase in after-tax income.

Since low-income earners pay a smaller portion of their incomes in tax than high-income earners, progressive taxes are a means of redistributing income. Advocates of this system also adduce the diminishing marginal utility of money as a justification for progressive taxation.

One problem arising in connection with a progressive tax in an inflationary situation is bracket creep, or fiscal drag. Inflation pushes taxpayers up into higher tax brackets, although there may be no increase in real income. To avoid this, it would be necessary to index tax brackets and tax allowances.

promissory note — eigener Wechsel, Solawechsel

A promissory note is "an unconditional promise in writing, made by one person to another, signed by the maker, engaging to pay on demand or at a fixed or determinable future time a sum certain in money to, or to the order of, a specified person, or to bearer".

With necessary modifications, the rules which apply to bills of exchange apply also to promissory notes. A promissory note differs from a bill of exchange in two main respects:
1. In contrast to a bill of exchange, a promissory note is not an "order to pay", but a "promise to pay". Consequently, there are only two parties to a promissory note: the one who makes the promise and makes out the note – the 'maker', and the one to whom payment is to be made – the 'payee'.
2. Promissory notes do not require acceptance, which would be meaningless since it would have to be given by the person promising to pay. The maker of the note, like the acceptor of a bill, is the party primarily liable on it. Thus, a promissory note has more or less the same function as an accepted bill.

Promissory notes usually bear an interest clause, indicating the rate at which interest is to be paid until maturity (e.g., "On June 15, 1985, I promise to pay to Mr. Smith, or order, the sum of £230, together with interest at 9% p.a.").

Promissory notes, which, like bills of exchange, are negotiable instruments transferable by indorsement and delivery, are comparatively rare in Great Britain. In the United States, however, they are very common in banking and finance (e.g., most banks require borrowers to make out a note, promising to repay the principal amount of credit plus interest), and also in mercantile transactions (e.g., a seller of goods may insist on the buyer making out a note, promising to pay the purchase price of the goods on the date agreed upon). In cases where loans have to be repaid in instalments, or where goods are bought on the instalment plan, the notes even include the schedule of payments, stating the exact dates when the instalments have to be paid.

Typical examples of promissory notes are Treasury bills and commercial paper, two important money market instruments.

promotion   Kommunikationspolitik

A firm's promotional efforts constitute a subsystem of its total marketing effort. Promotion is an exercise in persuasive communication, the idea being to inform, persuade, and influence the consumer with a view to shifting the demand curve for the firm's products to the right – in other words, with a view to increasing the demand without having to lower the price. Promotion – which should not be confused with sales promotion – includes advertising, personal selling, public relations, and sales promotion.

promotional mix   Kommunikations-Mix,
                                                kommunikationspolitischer Mix

The promotional mix is the combination of promotional tools (advertising, public relations, personal selling, sales promotion) used by a firm to inform, persuade, and influence the target group it has selected. The structure of the promotional mix, i.e., the weight assigned to each of the promotional tools, is determined, among other things, by the size of the promotional budget, the nature of the market, and the nature of the product. Some firms spend most of the money available for promotional activities on advertising, while others rely mainly on their sales force to reach the chosen target group.

property[1]   Eigentum

In its legal, abstract sense, property, or ownership, is a right, viz., the right to use something more or less without restriction. The ownership of movables is referred to as 'personal property', the ownership of land and buildings as 'real property'.

Property may be private or public. In the former case, the things are owned by private individuals or organisations, while in the latter case, the state represented by the government of the day is the owner.

property[2]   Immobilien,
                                                Realitäten

The term 'property' has, however, also a more concrete meaning. In many contexts, it refers not to the abstract right but to the physical thing(s) actually owned, in particular to land and buildings, i.e., to real property or what the Americans call 'real estate'. Property companies buy and sell property in the property market, and, if they are large, their shares, referred to as 'property shares', are quoted on the stock exchange.

In this more specialised sense, property may be classified into 'residential property' (dwellings, blocks of flats, etc.), 'commercial property' (office blocks and stores), and 'industrial property' (factories, workshops, etc.).

property tax   Vermögenssteuer (in den U.S.A.)

Generally, property tax is a direct tax levied by state and local governments in the United States on the assessed value of real and personal property. Real property includes farm land and farm buildings, residential land and homes, commercial land and business buildings, forest, etc.. Personal property may further be categorised into 'tangible' (e.g., livestock, farm machinery, furniture, jewelry, inventories, motor vehicles) and 'intangible' (e.g., stocks, bonds, mortgages, money, bank deposits).

The property tax object varies from state to state. In a small number of states, property tax is a real estate tax, i.e., personal property is legally exempted from tax. In the majority of states, real estate accounts for a high percentage of the tax base, but, in addition, varying combinations of tangible and intangible personal property are included. Most of these states exempt specific items of tangible personal property (e.g., household goods) and all intangible personal property from the property tax, although in a few states selected intangible items are subject to property tax at low rates.

Since property tax is imposed by both state governments and several types of local government units, such as counties, municipalities, townships, school districts, special assessment districts, etc., the owner of property pays a number of different property taxes on the same tax base. The amount of property tax payable by a taxpayer to each unit of government is computed by multiplying the assessed value of property (i.e., the value of property determined by local assessors as the basis for computing property tax) by the appropriate tax rate. This rate is fixed by each unit of government on the basis of its projected financial needs and is usually expressed as so many dollars of tax per $100 or per $1,000 of assessed value.

Whereas the U.S. property tax is a tax levied by state and local governments mainly on real property, regardless of any liens or debts (and is, therefore, comparable to the 'Grundsteuer' in Austria and the 'rates' in the United Kingdom), the Austrian 'Vermögenssteuer' is imposed by the federal government on all kinds of property, both real and personal, the taxpayer being entitled to deduct all his debts when computing the amount subject to tax. It is for these reasons that the Austrian 'Vermögenssteuer' should be translated by 'net wealth tax'.

prospect[1]   potentieller Kunde,
                                                   (Kauf-)Interessent

The term 'prospect' is a synonym for 'prospective customer', i.e., a potential buyer of goods and/or services of a particular supplier.

It is one of the main tasks of marketing to identify prospects and, by the skilful use of promotion (advertising, personal selling, public relations, sales promotion), to convert them into actual customers.

prospect[2]   Aussicht

The word 'prospect' also means 'expectation', 'future outlook', as, for example, in: "There is a prospect of a large order from Saudi Arabia"; "We see little prospect of making a profit this year"; "There are no prospects of success for this advertising campaign".

prospective customer   potentieller Kunde, (Kauf-)Interessent

A prospective customer (also called a 'prospect') is a potential buyer (a firm or a person) of goods and/or services of a particular supplier.

protective tariff   Schutzzoll

Protective tariffs, or protective duties, are levied by the government for the purpose of protecting certain domestic industries, in particular infant (or new) industries, from foreign competition. Consequently, protective tariffs are applied to a wide range of manufactured goods.

An extreme form of protective tariff is the 'prohibitive tariff', or 'prohibitive duty', where the rate is so high that imports of a certain commodity are decreased to a very low level or prevented altogether. Therefore, it yields no or only little revenue for the government.

Prohibitive duties are usually imposed to protect domestic producers against ruinous foreign competition, or to retaliate against similar action by another country.

provision   Wertberichtigung, Abschreibungsaufwand; Rückstellung

In British accounting usage, the term 'provision' refers to any amount charged to revenue either to reflect a reduction in the value of an asset or to provide for some known liability the amount of which cannot be determined with substantial accuracy. In contrast to reserves, which represent appropriations of profits, provisions are charges against income and, therefore, reduce the amount of profits available for distribution or transfer to reserves.

Provisions for depreciation in respect of tangible fixed assets or provisions for bad debts are examples of the first variety, reflecting a loss of value. These provisions are roughly equivalent to valuation allowances (formerly known as 'valuation reserves'), used in U.S. accounts.

A provision for an estimated liability may be set up in connection with an action for damages pending while the accounts are being drawn up.

public corporation

wirtschaftliche Unternehmung der öffentlichen Hand

In contrast to privately held companies, public corporations are undertakings owned and run by government. The term must not be mixed up with 'public limited company', nor with 'publicly held corporation', an American term referring to a privately owned corporation with a large number of members.

In Britain, the public corporation is the form of business organisation used for public utilities (providing essential services, such as gas, electricity, broadcasting, and passenger transport) and nationalised industries. Well-known examples are the British Gas Corporation, the Electricity Council and the Central Electricity Generating Board, the British Broadcasting Corporation (BBC), the British Railways Board, British Airways, the British Steel Corporation, The National Coal Board, etc..

A public corporation is brought into being by an Act of Parliament. Any powers it possesses, or assets it controls, are conferred on it by statute. It operates under independent management, but control is exercised by a board appointed by the appropriate Minister. This board acts like the board of directors of a (limited) company, but has wider responsibilities and less freedom of action.

public relations

Public Relations,
P.R.,
Öffentlichkeitsarbeit

Public relations is the deliberate effort to establish and maintain mutual confidence between an organisation and its public. In the case of a business organisation, this would include the general public, the firm's employees, customers, shareholders, etc.. Public relations involves, first of all, ascertaining and evaluating public opinion, i.e., trying to find out what the public think and feel about the firm and its products; secondly, advising the firm's managers on how to deal with public opinion as it exists; and finally, trying to influence public opinion with the help of various communication techniques.

Public relations departments, which are usually corporate staff units reporting to top-level management, or outside public relations consultants carry out a great variety of activities. They will, for instance, supply the media with interesting information about the firm in the hope that they will disseminate it free of charge (publicity), they will organise press conferences, sponsor cultural events, handle important customer complaints, organise lobbying efforts – all with a view to creating goodwill and projecting a positive corporate image.

punch

Locher

A punch is a small device for cutting holes into paper, card, or some other material. The variety used in the office is often referred to as a 'paper punch'. It is mainly used to cut holes into letters and other documents to be stored in arch board files.

purchasing power   Kaufkraft

Purchasing power denotes the amount of goods and services that a monetary unit, such as a dollar, a pound sterling, or an Austrian schilling, can buy. In contrast to the nominal value of money (i.e., the denominations shown on coins and banknotes), the purchasing power of money is not stable, but changes in an inverse proportion to prices. When prices rise, purchasing power falls, and vice versa. Changes in purchasing power are usually measured by means of a consumer price index, based on a representative sample of goods and services (shopping basket).

The term is also frequently used to describe the amount of cash and credit available to consumers for the purchase of goods and services. In this sense, an increase in purchasing power, for example, simply means that consumers have more money to buy goods and services.

In terms of economic policy, the first type of purchasing power can be influenced by controlling prices, while, in the second case, disposable income is the decisive factor.

Q

quantity discount   Mengenrabatt

A quantity discount (U.S.: 'bulk discount') is a reduction on the list price granted to buyers and is based on the quantity purchased. Where the discount is determined by the quantity purchased at a given time, it is known as 'non-cumulative quantity discount'. Where it is based on the quantity purchased over a period of time, regardless of the size and number of individual orders, it is referred to as 'cumulative quantity discount'.

Quantity discounts are justified on the basis of economies of scale. Orders for large quantities can lead to lower-cost production runs and to a reduction in selling, packing, transporting, and collecting costs.

R

rack jobber
Regal-Großhändler

A rack jobber is a special type of wholesaler performing many functions that would normally be performed by the retailer. The retailer (usually a supermarket or large food store) provides the necessary space for the proper display of the goods, while the rack jobber supplies the goods (typically non-food items, such as books, toys, stationery, records), sets up the display racks, and keeps them filled.

radio pager
Radio Pager (Piepserl)

A radio pager, also referred to as a 'bleeper', is a small portable communication device. It enables the person carrying it to be contacted by telephone callers. When somebody calls, the radio pager sounds, i.e., it gives off bleeps, warning the user that somebody is trying to reach him. The user can then call his office. Varying degrees of sophistication are offered. There are bleepers with memories, so that the user can choose not to be disturbed during meetings, for instance.

random access memory
Direktzugriffsspeicher, Randomspeicher

A random access memory is a storage device in which the access time is effectively independent of the location of the data. The term is frequently abbreviated to RAM. (see: storage device)

rates
Gemeindesteuern im Vereinigten Königreich

Rates are taxes levied by local authorities (local taxes) in the United Kingdom on the rateable value of (real) property (e.g., houses, commercial and industrial premises, and non-agricultural land), as assessed by valuation officers of the Board of Inland Revenue. Thus, rates are comparable to the U.S. 'property tax' and the 'Grundsteuer' in Austria and West Germany. The rateable value of a property is assessed periodically and is broadly equivalent to its annual rental value, i.e., the rent at which it may reasonably be let in the open market.

The person required by law to pay the rates is generally the occupier of the property (i.e., either the owner-occupier or the tenant). However, in the case of small properties rented on a weekly basis, it is common practice for landlords to pay the rates and include the cost in the rents they charge. The rating authority may also levy rates on empty properties at any percentage up to the full amount, in which case the rates are payable by the owner of the property.

The amount of rates payable by each ratepayer is determined by multiplying the rateable value of the property by the rate poundage – an amount per £ of rateable value, fixed annually by the local authority according to its projected financial needs. For example, if the rateable value is £10,000 and the rate poundage 40p, the occupier has to pay £4,000 in rates. The rate poundage varies considerably from one local authority to another and is usually much higher for commercial and industrial rates (non-domestic rates) than for domestic rates.

It is worth mentioning that householders with low incomes may apply for rebates of rates, which are computed by reference to a ratepayer's income, family commitments, and rates due.

rationalisation   Rationalisierung

Rationalisation includes all efforts to make business units or industries more efficient and productive. These efforts involve the economical use of resources, the elimination of waste and duplication, and the standardisation and concentration of business activity to achieve economies of scale through the introduction of specialised machinery and mass-production techniques. Rationalisation, however desirable in itself, inevitably leads to redundancies if not accompanied by an increase in demand and sales.

rationing   Rationierung

Rationing is a method of allocating scarce supplies. In cases where demand exceeds supply and where it would be undesirable or unfair to allow prices to rise to restore equilibrium, rationing may be used to ensure that all in need will get at least some of the goods or services in question.

In the absence of rationing, prices may rise to such an extent that the commodities involved are effectively put out of the reach of a large number of people. If prices are controlled, queues will form, which is not a particularly fair method of allocation either.

Rationing is used by governments in exceptional circumstances, such as in wars, when there are severe shortages of essential commodities. It may, however, also be used by suppliers, who will put customers on allocation (i.e., satisfy only part of their requirements) if, for one reason or another, they do not want to raise prices to reduce demand.

real   real

If used in connection with a monetary variable (such as sales, income, interest, return), the expressions 'real' and 'in real terms' indicate that the variable in question has been corrected for price changes to provide an estimate of the underlying physical quantities (amount of goods and services). The economic significance, let us say, of a 10 per cent rise in sales depends, of course, a lot on the behaviour of prices over the same period. The increase will be more than 10 per cent in real terms if there has been a fall in prices; it will be less than 10 per cent if prices have risen. Only in the absence of any price change will the increase in real terms be equal to the increase in nominal terms. Changes in nominal terms can be converted into real terms by using an appropriate price index.

real-time processing   Echtzeitverarbeitung

A modern industrial process control system is a typical example of real-time data processing. Input data (e.g., a temperature reading) is processed quickly enough for the result to be used as feedback information (e.g., to increase or decrease the flow of fuel). Airline booking systems represent another real-time application. Here, each booking must be processed immediately for a completely up-to-date picture of the state of affairs to be maintained by the computer. Real-time processing is contrasted with 'batch processing'.

rebate   (im nachhinein gewährter) Preisnachlaß

The term 'rebate' is used when part of the payment for goods and/or services is returned to the buyer, for example as a reward for buying exclusively from a particular seller over a period of time (loyalty rebate). Strictly speaking, therefore, a rebate differs from a discount, which is deducted in advance, although the two terms are often used interchangeably in practice.

receivables   Forderungen;
Forderungen (einschließlich Besitzwechsel)
aufgrund von Warenlieferungen und
Leistungen

In general, the term 'receivables' refers to the total of accounts receivable and notes or bills receivable. A receivable, therefore, may be either an account receivable or a note receivable. In accounting practice, however, 'receivables' is frequently used in a narrower sense, viz., as a synonym for either 'trade receivables' (i.e., trade accounts receivable plus trade notes receivable) or 'trade accounts receivable'.

received bill of lading   Übernahmekonnossement

A received bill of lading (also called a 'received for shipment bill of lading') is a document stating that the goods have been delivered into the shipowner's custody for subsequent shipment, in which case they might be stored in a ship or warehouse under his control. A received bill does not provide evidence of the actual shipment and is, therefore, less valuable than a shipped bill of lading. For example, under a c.i.f. contract, the buyer need not accept a received bill as part of the shipping documents, but may insist on a shipped bill, unless the contrary is expressly agreed upon by the parties to the contract of sale.

After the goods have been loaded on board the carrying vessel, the received bill may be converted into a shipped bill by means of a notation, dated and signed by the shipowner or his agent (e.g., the master of the ship).

recycling   Abfallverwertung,
Recycling

The unintended by-products of production and consumption can (and should) be reused or recycled instead of being thrown away. Reusing is the repeated use of objects and materials, as in the case of returnable glass bottles which are washed and refilled. Recycling implies some change, as in the case of non-returnable glass bottles which may be collected, melted down, and made into new glass bottles.

As the wastes of our affluent life-style may soon be too much of a burden for our planet, many demand a rapid transition from our present "throw-away society" to a "recycling society", which would cause much less pollution, and would need much less energy and much fewer resources to keep it going.

redundancy   Abbau (von Arbeitskräften)

In a labour context, redundancy refers to the dismissal of an employee or a group of employees because there is no longer any work for him/them. Redundancies may be caused by falling demand or by rationalisation and should not be confused with dismissals for other reasons, e.g., for protracted absenteeism, theft, or unfitness for a particular job. The term is used in this sense only in the U.K., where the Redundancy Payments Act 1965 requires an employer either to show that a dismissal is not due to redundancy or to pay compensation (redundancy payment) to the employee if it is.

reflation   Reflation;
                                             Aufschwungphase;
                                             expansive Konjunkturpolitik,
                                             Konjunkturbelebungsmaßnahmen

Originally, the term referred to a recovery of prices to a previous (desirable) level after a fall caused by a slump or recession. It was contrasted with 'inflation', denoting any further rise in prices.

Today, the main emphasis is not on price movements, but rather on the increase in aggregate demand and in the level of economic activity. Reflation is used to describe the first phase in the recovery of an economy from a slump before the stage of full employment (with rising prices) is reached.

Even more frequently, it refers to the stimulatory government policy adopted to achieve this. Reflationary measures include fiscal policies, such as tax cuts or higher government expenditure, and/or monetary policies, e.g., lower interest rates or easier money.

In most cases, recovery from a slump – characterised by idle machines, high stocks of unsold goods, and high unemployment – requires stimulatory action by the government, because private initiative is not sufficient. Once the recovery has started, the economy tends to grow, extra spending creating extra employment and incomes, which, in turn, leads to more spending. Previously unemployed resources are drawn into production to meet rising demand. At first, because each round of extra spending is matched by an increased supply of goods and services, there is little rise in prices. Eventually, when all the slack has been taken up, i.e., when all resources are fully employed, no further increases in output will be possible. If demand continues to increase, prices will rise.

regional policy

Regionalpolitik

In very general terms, regional policy aims at altering the spatial distribution, or regional pattern, of economic activity and economic performance. In most cases, this means improving the economic situation in areas of a country that suffer from low growth and income levels and chronically high unemployment. Typical regional development policies include: direct government grants to improve the infrastructure, investment incentives to encourage firms to move to the areas concerned, provision of low-cost loans, development corporations, etc..

regulation of promotional activities

Regelmentierung kommunikations-politischer Aktivitäten

It is not surprising that promotional activities should be subject to a variety of controls and regulations, both mandatory (i.e., established by the government) and voluntary (i.e., sponsored by trade associations or similar bodies). Since promotion is designed to attract attention, abuses are quickly noted, and demands arise to do something about them. Advertising is a particularly sensitive area. In many countries, false or deceptive advertising is prohibited. In the United States, for instance, the Federal Trade Commission, which administers the relevant laws, may ask a firm to substantiate doubtful advertising claims and may compel it to run corrective advertisements. In Austria, comparative advertising, particularly the use of knocking copy, is prohibited, i.e., an advertiser is not allowed to claim that his product is better than his competitors', let alone mention these competitors by name. This latter practice is allowed in the United States, although the advertising industry's trade association discourages "improper disparagement of other products or industries". T.V. advertising of cigarettes is prohibited in the United States, in Great Britain, and in Austria. In the former two countries, manufacturers are even required to label cigarettes as being dangerous to health.

The main purpose of the regulation of promotional activities, which the above examples are intended to illustrate, is to protect the consumer. It should be regarded, together with controls on other aspects of marketing (e.g., labelling, pricing, packaging), as an important element of the consumer movement.

rejection (of goods)

Annahmeverweigerung (von Waren)

The buyer is entitled to reject the goods, thus repudiating the contract, if the seller has broken important terms of the contract of sale, e.g., if the goods delivered are not in accordance with their description in the contract; if they are unsuitable for the particular purpose for which, with the knowledge of the seller, they are bought; if, in the case of a sale by sample, the goods do not conform to the sample.

A buyer who wishes to reject the goods has to intimate to the seller that he refuses to accept them. This notice may be given verbally or in writing, and the buyer should make certain that it reaches the seller, otherwise it is ineffective. The buyer who rejects the goods is not bound to return them to the seller unless this is agreed upon.

reminder (concerning payment)   Zahlungserinnerung

In business life, a reminder (concerning payment) may be a letter, a copy of the invoice or statement of account, or a printed notice, etc., sent by a supplier to the buyer if the latter has not paid for the goods and/or services on time. The purpose of sending a reminder is to bring the amount overdue to the customer's attention. When sending copies of invoices or statements as reminders, many firms add a rubber-stamped notation (e.g., "account overdue – please remit"), a printed card, etc.. Sometimes a reminder is included in an offer or sales letter sent to a customer (hidden reminder).

If the reminder does not produce any results, it is usually followed by more severely worded 'collection letters'. In each letter that is written the request for payment becomes more insistent and urgent than in the previous one. In the final collection letter, the supplier demands payment and warns the customer that drastic steps will be taken unless payment is made immediately. Such steps may be, for example, drawing a sight draft for collection through the customer's bank, or turning the account over to a collection agency or a lawyer.

The number of reminders and collection letters sent to a customer before action is taken varies according to circumstances.

remittance   der übermittelte Betrag; die Zahlungsübermittlung

The term 'remittance' is applied to a sum of money sent to a person or firm at another place, in the form of cash (banknotes and coins), cheque, bank draft, postal order, money order, credit transfer, bank transfer, etc..

In addition, the term 'remittance' is also applied to the act of sending the money.

repeat order   Nachbestellung

A repeat order, or re-order, is an order for goods which have been previously bought from the same supplier at the same prices and on the same terms.

replacement   Ersatz(lieferung)

If the goods sent by a supplier to a buyer have been lost, destroyed, or badly damaged in transit, the supplier may send a replacement, which means that he sends exactly the same contract goods again. In other words, the term 'replacement' is applied to goods which have exactly the same quality, colour, etc., as the goods which they replace.

Substitutes, by contrast, are offered or sent if, for example, the precise quality is temporarily out of stock or no longer produced, or cannot be supplied for any other reason. Thus, the term 'substitute' refers to goods which are only similar as to quality, colour, etc., to the goods instead of which they are offered or sent.

representative   Vertreter

The term 'representative' is used very loosely in commercial practice. In general, it seems to cover sales representatives, and all agents, distributors, and dealers with exclusive territorial rights. The main feature of a representative is that he works on a continuing basis with his principal (that is why a broker is not called a representative).

resale price maintenance   Preisbindung zweiter Hand, vertikale Preisbindung

Resale price maintenance is a method by which manufacturers and wholesalers control, or at least try to control, the prices at which retailers resell their products. Usually, it is the manufacturer who sets a minimum price below which retailers must not sell. Should a retailer fail to honour a resale price maintenance agreement, the manufacturers might stop supplying him. The object of the whole exercise is, of course, to prevent (cut-throat?) price competition and possible negative effects on the image of branded articles. Since resale price maintenance – euphemistically called 'fair trade' in the U.S.A. – is prohibited by both British and American laws (in G.B. by the Resale Prices Act 1964, in the United States by the Consumer Goods Pricing Act 1975), manufacturers and wholesalers have had to resort to 'recommended' (or 'suggested') retail prices – a toothless form of price control.

rescheduling (of debts)   Umschuldung

If a debtor (either a sovereign country or a large company) is unable to repay a loan on time, it will approach the lender (usually a syndicate of banks) with a request for rescheduling, i.e., it will ask the lender to extend the maturity of the loan. The banks will normally agree to this, and, if necessary, will even grant the borrower a fresh loan to enable him to meet his interest payments. They are usually prepared to do so because, in most cases, the alternative would be the borrower's default, which would have rather unpleasant consequences for the banks' balance sheets.

Strictly speaking, rescheduling means "changing the repayment schedule of a loan", but since in practice this always involves a stretching of the term of the loan, the expression has become a euphemism for an extension of maturity.

reserve   Rücklage

In British accounting usage, the term 'reserve' describes an amount set aside out of profits in a public or private limited company. Reserves are created by debiting the appropriation account and crediting a reserve account, used to accumulate the annual transfers, or allocations, from profits. This procedure is necessary because the share capital of companies is fixed and can be changed only by special resolution of the general meeting. In a partnership, for instance, these amounts would simply be credited to the capital account. The term 'reserve' tends to suggest that an equivalent amount of cash or resources easily convertible into cash has been stashed away. But this is not so. Reserves are simply a subdivision of shareholders' funds, or equity capital, and the cash which they once represented will have long been spent in some way or other.

Reserves are frequently subdivided into 'revenue reserves', or 'general reserves', and 'capital reserves'. The main difference between the two types is that revenue reserves may at any time be transferred back to the appropriation account, for instance, to top up a meagre dividend, while capital reserves may not be so released. Both revenue reserves and capital reserves may, however, be capitalised, i.e., converted into share capital by an issue of bonus shares. This is often done to bring the share capital of a company into line with the funds actually used.

All this refers to 'open reserves', i.e., to reserves shown as such in the balance sheet. It is also possible to set up 'hidden reserves', or 'secret reserves', e.g., by undervaluing assets or overvaluing liabilities. It should be noted that these practices reduce the profit before tax, or pre-tax profit, while open reserves are appropriations of the net profit after tax.

In American accounting usage, there is a general tendency to avoid the term 'reserve'. The reason for this is, to quote Finney, an American accounting authority, that "probably no other term appears to have been accorded greater variation of meanings and use in accounting than the word 'reserve'". Originally, the term was used to describe, among other things, an appropriation of profit (a net worth reserve), or an estimated liability (a liability reserve), or a deduction from the value of an asset (a valuation reserve). Today, such terms as 'retained earnings' (for net worth reserves) and 'allowances' (for valuation reserves) are used.

retail banking

Mengengeschäft der Banken, Bankleistungen für Lohn- und Gehaltsempfänger und gewerbliche Kleinkunden

Retail banking services are standardised banking services, including personal loans, small-scale savings and checking accounts, and funds transfers. These services are offered mainly to private individuals, but also to commercial and other small business enterprises through the retail branch office networks of the commercial banks.

retailer

Einzelhändler, Detaillist

Retailers, i.e., firms that specialise in catering to the final consumer, are the last link in the chain of distribution, starting with the manufacturer. Retailing is not, however, the exclusive domain of retailers. In fact, any firm that sells to the final consumer is making retail sales. A manufacturer distributing cosmetics door-to-door is engaging in retailing, and so is the farmer selling apples from a road-side stand. Retailing proper is a vast industry with millions of outlets, catering for every conceivable need, and sales running into hundreds of billions of dollars. Since retail outlets must be close to the final consumer, only a limited amount of centralisation (e.g., in shopping centres) is possible, which explains the large number of shops.

Retail shops may be classified according to a number of criteria: size (e.g., supermarkets, neighbourhood stores), type of goods sold (e.g., hardware stores), selling method (e.g., mail-order houses), or ownership (e.g., independent retailers, chain stores).

retail price   Einzelhandelspreis

Retail price is the price charged to the ultimate consumer, either by the manufacturer, wholesaler, or retailer.

Retail Price Index   Verbraucherpreisindex

The British Retail Price Index, or Index of Retail Prices, is not, as the name would suggest, an index of prices charged in retail shops, but measures the monthly changes in the prices of the much wider range of goods and services typically purchased by the final consumer. The shopping basket, i.e., the selection of goods and services covered by the index, is divided into ten groups: food, alcoholic drinks, tobacco, housing, fuel and light, durable household goods, clothing and footwear, transport and vehicles, and miscellaneous goods and services. The Retail Price Index is a weighted index, with the weights intended to reflect the consumption and spending pattern of British households. Weights, which are derived from the Family Expenditure Survey, have to be changed frequently in order to bring the index up to date. In 1914, when the index was published for the first time, food, for example, accounted for 60 per cent of total expenditure, while the corresponding figure for 1962 was around 32 per cent.

Since the way in which individuals or households divide their expenditure may differ considerably from the spending pattern used by the Retail Price Index, it is obvious that it cannot give a precise description of the changes in the cost of living as they affect the various people and households. In spite of this shortcoming, the Retail Price Index, which is compiled by the Department of Employment, is the most important measure of inflation used in Great Britain. Its American counterpart is the Consumer Price Index (CPI).

retrieval   Retrieval,
                                               Informationsrückgewinnung,
                                               Datenabruf

Retrieval, in a data processing context, refers to the recovering of stored data from a storage device.

return[1]   (amtlicher) Bericht,
                                               Erklärung,
                                               Aufstellung

A return is a formal report compiled and submitted by order. The revenue authorities, for example, require taxpayers to file a variety of returns, the most common being the income-tax return and the V.A.T. return. The authorities need the returns to make a final assessment of the tax concerned.

return[2]

Ertrag,
Rendite

Return is a ratio used to measure the profitability of some economic activity, i.e., it relates the results of an activity to some or all of the inputs required to produce these results.

In 'diminishing returns' and 'returns to scale', the expression refers to the physical output derived from a combination of fixed and/or variable inputs.

It is most commonly used, however, to describe the profit of some form of investment (whether real or financial) expressed as a proportion or percentage of the capital outlay. ROI (Return On Investment), which can be found not only in English but also in German management literature, relates profits, sales, and capital invested, and may be used to measure the profitability of enterprises as a whole, of establishments, product lines, or individual products.

In the field of financial investment, return is often used as a synonym for 'yield', e.g., for the dividend yield, expressing the dividend of a share as a percentage of its market price.

return[3] (pl.)

Retourware

If used in the plural, the term 'return' refers to goods which a buyer sends back to the seller, either for a refund, in exchange for other goods, or for credit towards a future purchase. To determine net sales, returns must be deducted from gross sales.

revaluation (of a currency)

Aufwertung (einer Währung)

The term 'revaluation', or 'upvaluation', is used where a country with a fixed rate of exchange officially increases the value of its home currency in terms of other currencies.

By contrast, under a system of floating rates, a rise in the exchange rate is known as an 'appreciation'. But since in practice the prevailing system is "dirty floating" (i.e., a system of floating rates of exchange with government/central bank intervention on a discretionary basis), the distinction between 'revaluation' and 'appreciation' has become blurred.

Revaluations are typical of countries with "hard" currencies, i.e., strong currencies, which are the result of balance-of-payments surpluses.

Revaluation means that a larger amount of foreign currency is needed to buy the home currency, and a smaller amount of home currency to buy the same amount of foreign currency. Consequently, the major effect of a revaluation is that, on the one hand, it makes exports of goods and services more expensive for foreign buyers (this means that domestic goods and services become less competitive in foreign markets) and discourages capital imports, while, on the other hand, it makes visible and invisible imports cheaper for domestic buyers and encourages the outflow of capital. Therefore, revaluing the domestic currency is a suitable method of reducing a country's balance-of-payments surplus. This may be desirable since it would do a country no good to go on piling up foreign exchange reserves indefinitely. Furthermore, as a revaluation cheapens imported commodities, it helps the government to bring inflation under control.

A revaluation-prone currency may well give rise to speculative activity by bulls, who try to make a profit by buying that currency and selling it after the expected revaluation at the more favourable rate of exchange. For the purpose of avoiding speculative pressure against the currency, any consideration of revaluing a currency is usually kept secret by the government/central bank.

revenue
Ertrag,
Erlös

According to the American Institute of Certified Public Accountants (AICPA), revenue, or income, is a gross increase in assets (i.e., an inflow of assets in the form of cash, receivables, or other property from customers) or a gross decrease in liabilities, and is derived from three general activities: (i) selling goods, (ii) rendering services and permitting others to use resources of the enterprise (which results in interest, dividends, rents, royalties, fees, and the like), and (iii) disposing of resources other than goods – for example, plant and equipment, or investments in other business firms. Revenue does not include receipt of assets purchased, proceeds of borrowing, investments by owners, etc..

Revenues may be classified into 'operating revenues', 'non-operating revenues', and 'extraordinary revenues'. Operating revenues may be defined as revenues from ordinary sales (sales revenue, i.e., the gross proceeds resulting from the transfer of goods or services to buyers) or from other transactions in the ordinary course of business. In other words, operating revenues are revenues derived from a firm's principal operating activities (i.e., from the normal and recurring primary operations of a business firm).

Non-operating revenues, also known as 'other revenues', 'other income', or 'non-operating income', encompass a wide range of recurring items which are not directly related to a firm's principal operations, and which, therefore, cannot be classified as operating revenues. Examples of non-operating revenues are: dividends earned, interest earned, rent earned, royalties earned, fees earned, gains from foreign exchange fluctuations, gains from the sale of securities, etc..

Extraordinary revenues differ from non-operating revenues by their unusual nature and infrequency of occurrence. Two typical examples of unusual and infrequently occurring items are gains arising from the expropriation of plant by a foreign government, and damages received in a lawsuit.

revenue tariff
Finanzzoll

Revenue tariffs, or revenue duties, as the name suggests, are levied by the government for the purpose of raising revenue. While, of course, protective duties – in addition to protecting domestic industries from foreign competition – also raise revenue, a tariff levied on a commodity not produced domestically (e.g., in Austria, the import duty on passenger cars, coffee, tea, etc.) exists purely for revenue-raising purposes.

revocable (documentary) letter of credit

widerrufliches Dokumentenakkreditiv

A revocable credit is a form of letter of credit which, in contrast to an irrevocable L/C, may be cancelled or amended by the issuing bank or the applicant/buyer at any moment without prior notice to the beneficiary, i.e., without the beneficiary's approval. Therefore, it is not the practice of the advising bank to confirm a revocable L/C.

Under a revocable L/C, it is quite common for the issuing bank to authorise the advising bank to act as paying bank. However, it follows from the nature of a revocable credit that it conveys no engagement or obligation on the part of the advising bank or the issuing bank. Even if the beneficiary has been informed that the advising bank has been authorised by the issuing bank to honour his draft on presentation of the shipping documents, the credit does not say that the advising bank will definitely pay or accept the draft. It may be that the advising bank realises that for economic or political reasons (e.g., measures taken by the importer's government to prohibit the transfer of foreign exchange to the exporter's country) it would be unable to obtain any reimbursement from the issuing bank for any money paid to the beneficiary, and, therefore, would not honour the draft even if the documents conform to the terms of the credit. If, on the other hand, the advising bank has honoured a draft under a revocable credit prior to receiving notice of cancellation or amendment, the issuing bank must reimburse it. This means that a revocable L/C can be cancelled without the approval of the beneficiary only before presentation of the draft together with the shipping documents to the advising/paying bank.

From what has been said so far it should be clear that, from the exporter's point of view, a revocable L/C is the least favourable type of credit, providing him with much less security than an irrevocable credit, the danger being that the contract goods may be shipped and the credit revoked before the draft is honoured by the advising/paying bank. A revocable L/C may be considered merely a means of arranging payment, thus being a guidance for the exporter in preparing his draft and documents. Nowadays, it is only used in transactions with reliable customers and subsidiaries.

rights issue

Emission von jungen Aktien (Bezugsaktien), Aktienemission auf Bezugsrechtsbasis

A rights issue is an issue of new shares to existing shareholders, usually at favourable prices. A company wishing to increase its capital will frequently use this method, because it is cheaper and administratively simpler than other ways of issuing shares. New shares are offered to existing shareholders on a pro-rata basis, e.g., one new share for every three shares held. Shareholders that are not interested in the new issue may sell their 'rights'.

roll-on/roll-off

Roll-on/Roll-off Verkehr, Ro-ro-Verkehr

Roll-on/roll-off (Ro-Ro), in the United states referred to as 'fishyback service', is a combination of road and sea transport. Under the Ro-Ro method, loaded road vehicles are driven on to a ferry or ship (roll-on/roll-off ship) at the port of shipment and off at the port of destination. The ferry or ship is thus used as a moving bridge. Road vehicles so transported include delivery vans; lorries; trailer units, consisting of a tractor and one or more trailers; articulated lorries, consisting of a tractor and a semi-trailer; trailers; and semi-trailers.

In many cases, the tractors, or tractive units, of trailer units and of articulated lorries are not transported together with the trailers and semi-trailers. The latter are disconnected at the port of loading and pulled by motor vehicles over a ramp into the ship's hold. At the port of destination, they are taken over by compatible tractive units and driven to their final destination. This method has several advantages over the transport of driver-accompanied vehicles. The main drawback of the latter method is that the shipping charges are higher, because the tractive unit has to be carried to and fro, and that overhead costs are increased owing to an expensive tractor and a driver being idle during sea transport.

Briefly, the major benefits of Ro-Ro are: reduced handling of the actual goods and packages; competitive costs for unit loads; scheduled services.

S

sale by sample
Kauf nach Probe

When a sale is by sample, it is understood that the goods to be delivered must correspond to the sample agreed on by the two parties to the contract of sale. The buyer must have reasonable opportunity to compare the goods delivered with the sample. If the goods are not up to sample, the buyer is entitled to reject them, which means that he has to return them immediately, otherwise he will be presumed to have accepted them. Where only part of the goods are not up to sample, the buyer must accept or reject the lot (unless the contract is severable, i.e., unless part deliveries are allowed, in which case each part delivery may be treated separately). Mere display of a sample during negotiations does not make the contract a sale by sample. There must be a definite agreement to this effect.

sale on approval
Kauf auf Probe

If goods are delivered to a buyer under an agreement that he may test or use the goods for the purpose of determining whether or not he wishes to buy them, the sale is a sale on approval. The buyer may return the goods without payment within the agreed period of time (approval period) or, if no such period has been stated, within reasonable time. What a 'reasonable time' is depends on the circumstances. In Austria, the approval period, unless otherwise stipulated, is three days for personal property and one year for real property.

In a sale on approval, unless otherwise agreed, the risk of loss of, and the title to, the goods do not pass to the buyer until acceptance. A buyer who retains the goods beyond the approval period is regarded as having accepted (bought) them and cannot afterwards compel the supplier to take them back. A return of the goods after the expiry of the approval period is only possible if the buyer has informed the supplier within the period that he does not want to keep them. The return of the goods, if any, is at the seller's risk and expense.

sale on deferred terms
Zielkauf

A sale on deferred terms, or credit sale, is a transaction under which a supplier sells goods to a buyer on credit (i.e., on deferred terms), which means that the supplier grants a supplier credit to the buyer. The supplier specifies the period of time allowed for payment. For example, the terms "net 30" indicate that the invoice must be paid within 30 days. In addition to extending credit, the seller may grant a cash discount if the invoice is paid during the early part of the credit period.

sales[1]   Umsatz

In accounting, the term 'sales' refers to the total revenue received by a firm from selling goods and services in the normal course of buiness. Gross sales include returns, discounts, and value-added tax, if any, while net sales exclude these items. Sales are always related to a specific period of time, i.e., they represent a flow concept.

sales[2]   Absatz

The term 'sales' may also refer to the quantity sold, as in 'unit sales', that is, the number of items sold.

sales force   Vertreterorganisation,
                                    Mitarbeiter im Außendienst

Sales force is a collective term denoting the employees of a firm engaged in selling the firm's product(s). Although, strictly speaking, it can be applied to both the staff taking orders behind the counter and to those actually calling on prospects and customers, it normally refers only to the people selling in the field, variously called 'sales representatives', 'sales reps', 'commercial travellers', 'field executives', 'sales engineers', etc..

Managing the sales force is a complex task, usually entrusted to the sales manager. It involves, among other things, selecting and training the sales force, assigning particular territories to them, fixing sales quotas, developing the call policy, collecting and digesting the information passed on by them, fixing the compensation for the sales people, and, finally, evaluating their performance in the light of the foregoing.

sales letter   Werbebrief

The sales letter is the most selective of all forms of advertising. Unlike press and poster advertising, it aims to sell particular kinds of goods or services to selected types of customers, e.g., office equipment to business firms, etc..

A sales letter is either a form of unsolicited offer or it is intended to produce inquiries (e.g., a supplier promises to send catalogues, price-lists, patterns, samples, etc., on return of a detachable form or card, usually prepaid). A sales letter is sent as a personal letter, i.e., handwritten, typed, or printed, with the addressee being mentioned personally. Frequently, printed advertising material is enclosed.

sales literature   Verkaufsliteratur,
                                    Werbeliteratur

Sales literature is an all-inclusive term for any printed material that is intended to give prospective buyers detailed information about goods with the ultimate aim of increasing sales. Sales literature includes catalogues, leaflets, brochures, etc..

sales promotion

Verkaufsförderung

According to Kotler, sales promotion is a collection of promotional tools not formally classifiable as advertising, personal selling, or public relations. It can be subdivided into consumer promotion (e.g., free samples, coupons, premiums, contests), trade promotion (e.g., dealer sales contests), and sales-force promotion (e.g., bonuses, contests, etc.). Consumer promotion is basically geared to the point of sale.

sales tax

allgemein: Umsatzsteuer;
U.S.: Einphasenumsatzsteuer

On a theoretical level, sales tax is defined as a tax levied on the sales of a firm. It may be imposed either at each stage in the production and distribution of goods and services (multi-stage sales tax, e.g., value-added tax, turnover tax) or at only one stage (single-stage sales tax), usually at the retail level. A multi-stage sales tax is, therefore, imposed not only on retail prices but also on the prices charged by manufacturers and wholesalers.

The sales tax in force in the U.S.A. is a retail sales tax, which means that it is levied only at the retail level. It is a broad-based tax, chargeable on a wide range of goods and services, both essential and non-essential, and is, therefore, sometimes referred to as 'general sales tax'. By contrast, sales taxes imposed only on a limited range of commodities are known as 'narrow-based sales taxes', or 'excise taxes'.

The U.S. sales tax is levied by the state and local governments (state and local sales taxes), and not by the federal government. The tax rates may differ from state to state, and even from county to county within a state. For example, the tax rate in New York State ranges from 4% to 8.25%, the 8.25% rate being charged in New York City. In the District of Columbia, the normal sales tax rate is 6%, but certain goods and services are subject to special rates (e.g., food sold by vending machines is taxed at 2%, food sold in restaurants, hotels, and snack-bars at 8%). It should be noted that the prices for goods and services quoted to the ultimate customer (e.g., on price tickets and menus) are net prices, which means that he has to add the amount of sales tax to arrive at the actual amount to be paid.

sample[1]

Muster,
Probe

In a commercial context, sample refers to a small portion or one unit of a larger quantity of goods. Since a sample is meant to display the same characteristics as the bulk from which it is taken/drawn, it is a convenient method of showing the prospective customer what the goods offered to him are like. Samples are often sent to the prospective customer to enable him to test them carefully and to decide whether or not to make the purchase. Samples are also distributed free of charge, as by sales representatives or as a promotion in retail establishments.

A contract of sale that is explicitly based on a sample is called a 'sale by sample' or a 'sale according to sample'.

The term 'sample' may be used for raw materials (such as wool, tobacco, cotton) or for finished goods (e.g., tooth-brushes, combs, etc.). Small cuttings of textiles intended to show what the whole piece is like are usually called 'patterns'.

sample[2]

Stichprobe,
statistische Teilmenge

In statistics, a sample is a set of units chosen to represent a larger set, called the 'population' or 'universe'. There are many effective methods of selecting samples. A sample may be selected from the universe as a whole or from certain parts or strata of the universe. In either case, selection may be at random (random sample), according to somebody's judgement, or by other methods.

Sample surveys are used because they are cheaper and less time-consuming than full counts, or censuses, (where each item of the universe is enumerated) and give, for all practical purposes, the same results if blown up correctly.

saving

Sparen,
Spartätigkeit

Saving occurs when current income exceeds current expenditure, or, in the case of companies, when part of the profit is retained and not distributed to the shareholders. The money not spent or distributed can be held in liquid form (a wad of banknotes stashed away under the famous mattress) or in the form of financial claims of varying maturity and marketability: current account deposits, time deposits, Treasury bills, bonds, shares, life insurance policies, pension schemes, etc.. Corporate savings are usually ploughed back, i.e., reinvested in the business enterprise.

People and organisations save to provide for future contingencies ("putting aside money for a rainy day"), to accumulate the purchase price of a major durable item (e.g., a car or a machine tool), to make a return, or for a variety of psychological reasons, e.g., because they simply hate spending money.

The total volume of savings in an economy depends on the size of the income, the propensity to save (i.e., the savings rate), and, to a lesser degree, on the rate of interest.

Saving is an extremely important economic activity since it provides funds for productive investment. For instance, the money deposited in a bank account by a private person may be on-lent by the bank to a business enterprise to enable it to buy machines or other items of capital equipment.

savings account

Sparkonto

A savings account represents a special type of interest-bearing time deposit. Savings deposits differ from ordinary time deposits in that they are subject to certain legal restrictions, e.g., with regard to the notice of withdrawal and the type of holder. In the U.S.A., for instance, only individuals and certain non-profit organisations are permitted to hold savings accounts.

Depositors typically use their savings accounts to gradually accumulate funds from their earnings, or income.

Deposits may be withdrawn only upon presentation of the passbook, in which deposit and withdrawal entries are made, with banks frequently waiving the statutory period of notice.

savings bank   Sparkasse

Both in the U.K. and the U.S.A., a savings bank is a non-profit organisation set up to receive interest-bearing savings deposits from people of moderate means.

In Great Britain, the 'trustee savings banks', first established during the Industrial Revolution, are legally required to pay all deposits received into the Bank of England to the credit of the National Debt Commissioner. This means that the deposits are covered by a government guarantee, but interest rates are lower than those offered by commercial banks.

Trustee savings banks operate under the control of a board of honorary trustees, but are run by salaried managers. In contrast to many other countries, British savings banks do not extend home loans. Since 1964, they have been authorised to offer current account services (including cheques and standing orders), personal loans, travellers' cheques, etc.. These services are not available for business purposes, but can only be used by private individuals and non-profit organisations.

The 'National Savings Bank', originally called the 'Post Office Savings Bank', offers similar services (including national giro) on a nation-wide basis, using most post offices as its branch network.

U.S. savings banks invest the funds of small savers in high-grade bonds and real estate mortgages, both under strict public supervision. Most of these institutions, which can be classified as 'mutual savings banks', headed by a board of trustees, and 'stock savings banks', are authorised to offer NOW accounts.

Although U.S. savings banks are not permitted to offer the complete range of banking services performed by commercial banks, they have broader competitive powers than the savings and loan associations.

savings rate   Sparquote

The personal savings rate (there is also a national variant, which takes into account corporate savings) is calculated by dividing the disposable income of a given period into the savings of that period, multiplying by one hundred. The savings rate, therefore, shows the percentage of disposable income that is not spent but saved.

The savings rate plays an important role in determining the level of national income. The higher the savings rate, the less effective, for example, a given tax cut will be in stimulating economic activity. On the other hand, a low savings rate may mean that not enough money is being set aside for productive investment.

seasonal adjustment   saisonale Bereinigung

Seasonal adjustment is a procedure by which seasonal influences are removed from statistical time series, the most important method used being the calculation of moving averages. The main purpose of the exercise is to render the series more realistic by making them reflect the underlying trend more accurately. Seasonally adjusted time series include labour force, employment, price, and volume statistics. If, for example, the seasonal increase in the labour force in the summer months due to the inflow of student workers were not corrected, the relevant series might present a misleading picture of what is actually happening to the labour force.

seasonal discount   Saisonrabatt

A seasonal discount is a price reduction of a certain percentage which is given to a customer who places an order during the slack season. An illustrative example is the tourist industry, which offers its services at lower prices during the off-season. Seasonal discounts, however, are not limited to service industries. They are often offered by manufacturers, because off-season orders enable them to make better use of their production facilities (for example, manufacturers of air conditioners). Retailers also grant seasonal discounts in order to clear residual stocks of seasonal goods. Prices for sports articles are adjusted this way.

sectors of the economy   Wirtschaftssektoren

One method of sectoring an economy is to divide it into a 'primary', a 'secondary', and a 'tertiary' sector.

The primary sector includes all extractive industries, i.e., mining, fishing, agriculture, forestry, quarrying, and related activities. It is therefore concerned with obtaining raw materials.

The secondary sector, also called 'manufacturing' or 'manufacturing industry', is then concerned with converting these raw materials into finished (manufactured) goods, frequently using semi-manufactured goods in the process. It is a moot point whether industries mainly concerned with assembling products from components (e.g, the motor industry) should be included in the manufacturing industry or assigned to a special category, which might be called 'construction'.

The tertiary sector comprises the service industries, i.e., industries that produce intangible "goods", where production and consumption coincide. Insurance companies, banks, road haulage companies, hair dressers, and business consultants are some examples of firms operating in the tertiary sector.

The relative importance of the three sectors varies from country to country. Less developed countries typically have large primary sectors, with a lot of people working in agriculture. Mature economies, like the United States or Great Britain, are characterised by large and growing tertiary sectors.

The economy may, however, also be divided into a 'public sector' and into a 'private sector', with some modern economists (e.g., Weisbrod) adding a "third", viz., the 'voluntary sector'. The public sector includes central and local governments, the nationalised industries, and other public corporations, like the Post Office Corporation and the central bank. The private sector, on the other hand, is composed of all the private profit-making concerns, e.g., manufacturing companies, banks, insurance companies, publishing houses, and so on. The voluntary sector is more difficult to describe and is dealt with under a separate heading.

312

securities   Wertpapiere

Securities – the term is nearly always used in the plural – are transferable certificates of ownership or indebtedness. Although this definition theoretically includes also bills of exchange and other negotiable or quasi-negotiable instruments, in practice the use of the term is restricted to securities dealt in on the stock exchange, such as shares, bonds, debentures, etc..

From the legal point of view, it should be noted that securities are not mere acknowledgements, but rather embodiments, of the rights to which they relate. In other words, the rights, e.g., a claim to the payment of a certain sum of money, can only be exercised in connection with the instrument.

From the above definition it can be seen that there are two basic types of securities, viz., 'equity securities', representing what is commonly referred to as "ownership rights", and 'debt securities', representing creditorship rights. Shares, issued by companies, are typical examples of the former, and bonds, issued by governments or companies, typical examples of the latter variety. For a more detailed interpretation of "ownership rights" see "equity securities".

security (for a loan)   (Kredit-)Sicherung

Since a lender has to bear the risk of the borrower's default, he may wish to provide himself with a second line of defence, on which to fall back should the borrower fail to meet his obligations. The lender may, therefore, insist on some kind of security for the (re)payment of principal and interest, additional to the personal liability of the borrower.

Securities for loans include guarantees (where a third party undertakes to be secondarily liable for the debt), pledges (where shares, bonds, warehouse warrants, or even goods are delivered into the custody of the lender for the term of the loan), and, finally, arrangements where the lender retains an interest, or a lien, in real or personal property, which the borrower may go on using as long as he meets his obligations. The most important variety of the last arrangement is the real estate mortgage.

The term 'collateral security', which is often used in connection with lending, may refer either to any security additional (i.e., collateral) to the personal liability of the borrower or, more commonly, to the shares, bonds, etc., pledged as security.

sellers' market   Verkäufermarkt

Sellers' market refers to a situation where market conditions are favourable to sellers because demand is running ahead of supply. The immediate post-war period, when most goods were in short supply, is a typical example of a sellers' market.

selling rate   Briefkurs

The selling rate (also referred to as the 'offered rate' or 'offer') is the rate of exchange, either spot or forward, at which a bank/foreign exchange dealer agrees to sell a foreign currency. If a customer wants to buy a certain amount of foreign currency from a bank, he can do so only at the bank's selling rate.

The Concise Oxford Dictionary defines a share as "one of the equal parts into which a company's capital is divided entitling holder to proportion of profits", and, one must add, giving him certain other rights, e.g., the right to vote at the general meetings of the company and to share in the proceeds of a voluntary winding up.

There are many different types of shares, and the rights of the shareholder depend, to some extent, on the type of share involved. 'Ordinary shares', also known as 'equity shares' or 'equities', represent the risk capital of the company (see: equity securities). 'Preference shares' carry certain "privileges", which may, in fact, not represent true advantages (see: preference share). 'Deferred shares' are a special class of share on which a dividend can be paid only after all other kinds of shares (e.g., ordinary and preference shares) have received theirs. Deferred shares are usually held by founders, promoters, or managers.

Ordinary shares are, as a rule, voting shares, but some companies also issue non-voting ordinary shares, called 'class 'A' shares' (the voting variety being referred to as 'class 'B' shares'). Preference shares are usually non-voting, although there are certain exceptions (see: preference share).

A share normally has a nominal value (also referred to as the 'face value' or 'par value'), which means that a certain sum of money (e.g., £1, 50p) is shown on the face of the instrument. (By the way, nominal values in West Germany and in Austria are much higher than in G.B.). This does not necessarily imply that shares have to be issued at par. Many companies issue shares above par (i.e., at a premium) or below par (i.e., at a discount) to allow for last-minute changes in market conditions. Issues below par are prohibited under Austrian law. In the United States and in Canada, companies are permitted to issue no-par value shares, which, as the name suggests, have no face value. They simply represent a given fraction (let us say, one tenthousandth) of the capital of the company involved, which means, among other things, that dividends have to be expressed as a fixed amount of money per share.

Shares may be issued to bearer, i.e., not to any named person, in which case they are referred to as 'bearer shares' and can be passed on simply by delivery. 'Registered shares' are registered in the books of the company in the name of the owner. They are transferred by indorsement and delivery or by assignment.

'Bonus shares' are additional shares issued free of charge to shareholders in proportion to the shares they already hold. Although there is no payment for bonus shares, they do not represent a gift, since they are the result of a capitalisation of reserves and do not change the equity position of the shareholders.

Shares may be classified in many other ways. There are, for instance, 'quoted shares' and 'unquoted shares', 'fully-paid shares' and 'partly-paid shares', 'industrial shares' (industrials), 'property shares' (properties), and many others.

In the United States, shares are often collectively referred to as 'stock'. Thus, ordinary shares are called 'common stock', preference shares 'preferred stock', voting shares 'voting stock', and so on.

shareholder

The members of a company are called 'shareholders'. Membership of a company coincides exactly with the legal ownership of the shares thereof. The normal method of becoming a member is either by "subscribing" the memorandum of association (the subscribers become the first members), by application for an allotment of shares, or by having shares transferred from an existing member.

While each member enjoys certain individual rights vis-a-vis the company (e.g., right to receive dividends, voting rights), the power to influence and control company policy is vested in the members collectively. This power is exercised at company meetings, officially referred to as 'general meetings'. Normally, company meetings are not well attended, and the few members with large holdings are usually able to dominate and control the proceedings.

Every company must hold an annual general meeting (AGM) in every calendar year to provide its members with the opportunity to express their collective will. The ordinary business of an AGM usually comprises the declaration of a dividend, the consideration of the accounts and of the directors' report, the election of directors, and the appointment and remuneration of the auditors.

Any general meeting which is not an AGM is an extraordinary general meeting. Such meetings may be convened at any time by the directors, but also a qualified minority of shareholders may requisition such a meeting, in which case the directors must call it.

The first general meeting of a company has, under the terms of the Companies Acts, to be convened immediately after the company has commenced business. This meeting is called the 'statutory meeting'.

Normally, meetings of members are convened by the directors by giving 21 days' notice to anyone who has a right to be present. The proceedings are under the control of the chairman. The articles of association usually stipulate that the chairman of the board of directors shall act as chairman at company meetings. Failing such a provision, the members present appoint their own chairman. The chairman has a second (i.e., casting) vote if this is provided for in the articles. No business may be conducted unless a specified minimum number of members (quorum) are personally present. In the absence of any special provision in the articles, this minimum number is two. Each member is entitled to attend a general meeting in person or may designate a proxy, who need not himself be a member of the company. Both the written authority to vote and the person designated to vote for the shareholder are called 'proxy'. When it comes to voting, each member or proxy generally has one vote per voting share on a poll (written vote), or only one vote if a show of hands has been agreed upon. Normally, resolutions are passed by a simple majority of votes. The chairman may adjourn a meeting with the consent of the members and proxies attending. Minutes must be kept of all general meetings and these must be signed by the chairman. The minute book has to be kept at the registered office and has to be available for inspection by the members.

The legal situation concerning the members of an American corporation is substantially the same, although the terminology is different: shareholders are called 'shareholders' or 'stockholders', the annual general meeting is referred to as the 'annual meeting of shareholders' or the 'annual meeting of stockholders', while the American term for the extraordinary general meeting is 'special shareholder meeting' or 'special stockholder meeting'.

shipped bill of lading   Bordkonnossement

A shipped bill of lading (also known as an 'on-board bill of lading', particularly in the U.S.A.) is a document in which the shipowner acknowledges that the goods have actually been loaded on board the carrying vessel.

The consignees are usually anxious to ensure that the goods they have ordered are actually on their way to them at the time when the documents are presented under a documentary letter of credit or a documentary collection. Consequently, most contracts of sale call for a 'shipped bill', and not a 'received bill', as the latter does not signify that the goods are actually on board ship.

shipper

(allgemein) Absender, Versender;
(im Seefrachtgeschäft) Befrachter,
Verschiffer, Ablader

The term 'shipper' refers to the party concluding the contract of carriage with a carrier. Depending on the specific circumstances, the shipper may be the consignor, the consignee (e.g., in the case of f.a.s. or f.o.b. contracts), or a forwarding agent, who enters into the contract of carriage in his own name and for the account of his client (i.e., the consignor or the consignee).

shipping documents   Versanddokumente

Shipping documents are documents relating to an export shipment. The most important shipping documents are: bill of lading, consignment note, air waybill, commercial invoice, customs invoice, consular invoice, insurance policy (ocean cargo policy, transit insurance policy, air cargo policy) and insurance certificate, warehouse warrant, and certificate of origin. In addition, other documents may be needed, such as packing lists, showing the contents of the individual packages, weight certificates, blacklist certificates (e.g., required by Arab countries to exclude firms doing business with Israel), health, veterinary, or sanitary certificates (sometimes required in connection with purchases of foodstuffs, hides, and livestock), etc..

Most of these documents are needed by the importer to take delivery of the goods, to arrange for the clearance of the goods through customs, and to claim payment from the insurance company in the event of loss of, or damage to, the goods. From the exporter's point of view, they play an important role in the case of payment by 'cash against documents', 'documents against payment', 'documents against acceptance', or by 'documentary letter of credit'.

short selling   Leerverkauf

A short sale is the sale of shares (stock), bonds, commodities, foreign currencies, etc., which the seller does not own at the time of the sale. Technically, this can be done either by borrowing the assets to be sold and effecting immediate delivery or by postponing delivery to an agreed date. In the latter case, payment of the purchase price, which is fixed at the time of the sale, is also postponed. The borrowing method is used on the New York Stock Exchange, while the second approach is typical of the London Stock Exchange.

Whichever method is used, the short seller will eventually have to cover himself, i.e., to buy the shares, currencies, etc., either to return them to the lender or to deliver them to the buyer. Selling short (or "taking a short position", in investment jargon) is a common speculative strategy used by operators when they expect prices to fall and hope to make a profit by covering themselves at the lower levels. Short selling is a typical bear strategy.

sight bill   Sichtwechsel

A sight bill, also known as a 'sight draft', is a bill of exchange (i) which is stated to be payable on demand, or at sight, or on presentation; or (ii) in which no time for payment has been stated. (Examples: "On demand pay Mr. Brown or order 300 pounds"; "At sight pay to me or my order the sum of 300 pounds".).

Since a sight bill is payable as soon as it is presented to the drawee, it need not be presented for acceptance. The holder of the sight bill (payee, indorsee, or bearer of the bill) must present it for payment within reasonable time (in Austria, within one year from the date of issue).

simplification of the product mix   Sortimentsbereinigung

Product mix simplification is a product strategy that involves the removal of certain items from a product line and/or the elimination of a whole line. The general idea is usually to weed out slow-moving, unprofitable items and to concentrate on the fast sellers.

skim-the-cream pricing   Abschöpfungspreisstrategie

The skimming strategy involves setting a high initial price for a new product to appeal to the high-income segment of a particular market. The idea is usually to lower the price later on when competitors have moved in or when it is desired to tap the lower end of the market.

slump   starker Rückgang (z.B., Preiseinbruch, Kurssturz); Konjunktureinbruch, starke Rezession, Wirtschaftskrise

The Concise Oxford Dictionary defines 'slump' as a "sudden or rapid or great fall". The term may be applied to practically any economic variable. Share prices as well as property values may experience a slump. If used alone without any qualifying word, it frequently refers to a sharp fall in economic activity and is, therefore, synonymous with 'severe recession' or 'depression'.

social costs   soziale Kosten

Social costs, or negative externalities, are costs which have to be borne by the public in general rather than by the producer or consumer of an article. For example, the pollution of the environment caused by a production process has traditionally had no reflection at all in the cost structure of the article produced.

In his book, The Social Costs of Private Enterprise, Harvard, 1950, William Kapp was the first person to cover the field of social costs in general and to trace the causal relationship between business activities and such expensive social outlays as the impairment of human health through occupational diseases, air and water pollution, the depletion and destruction of animal species, the premature exhaustion of energy resources, soil erosion and depletion, deforestation, etc.. While Kapp used the concept of social costs to criticise private capitalism, it is now clear that social costs arise under any political system. For example, it is little comfort to the inhabitants of the Czech Giant Mountains that the factories and power-stations responsible for the smoke emissions which have killed their forests are not in private but in public ownership.

social security tax   Sozialversicherungsbeitrag

Social security taxes, or national insurance contributions, as they are called in the U.K., differ from other taxes in that they are more directly linked to the benefits received by the taxpayers, or contributors. In the United States, as well as in Austria, the United Kingdom, and the Federal Republic of Germany, these taxes do not flow into the general pool of tax revenues, but are used exclusively to pay social security benefits and to meet the administrative costs of the social security systems. Thus, they are more in the nature of insurance premiums, although the revenue raised through them falls short of what is actually needed and has to be supplemented with funds from general taxation. Another departure from the insurance principle are the benefits paid to people who have not themselves paid any taxes. Supplementary benefits in the United Kingdom would be a case in point.

Social security taxes are levied on both employers and employees. They are used to finance a wide range of social security benefits, such as sickness benefits, unemployment benefits, retirement pensions, and disablement benefits, or whatever they are called in the various national systems.

Social security taxes and benefits are sensitive political issues: on the one hand, they are associated with the fundamental human need for security and protection from the vicissitudes of life, on the other hand, they involve huge financial flows and are closely connected with the general problems of tax resistance and of financing public expenditure. In view of what economists have dubbed the "fiscal crisis of the modern state", many governments are trying to cut back social security benefits or, since across the board cuts would hit the poorest section of the population hardest, to make them more selective.

soft copy   Softcopy

In contrast to hard-copy output devices, soft-copy devices generate only a temporary image of the data output. Examples of soft copies are the light images on a VDU screen or audible sounds. The term is contrasted with 'hard copy'.

318

soft energy path   sanfte Energiepolitik

The soft path scenario that has been most thoroughly investigated is the one concerning mankind's energy future (cf. Amory Lovins, Soft Energy Paths, Pelican, London, 1977). While traditional (i.e., hard path) energy philosophy postulates that energy needs will go on rising forever (or at least for a very long period to come), and that the gap will have to be filled by increasingly exotic energy sources, such as power from nuclear fission and fusion, advocates of the soft path contend that in fact we are not using too little but too much energy, wasting quite a large portion, as is the case with domestic heating in badly insulated homes.

As all energy production involves some burden on the environment, overall energy consumption could and should be lowered rather than increased. That this is feasible is borne out by the fact that in Austria and in other countries energy consumption has been going down in recent years without a corresponding decrease in gnp – a "de-coupling" effect which was thought impossible only a few years ago.

Since, by now, a kilowatt saved by conservation is much cheaper than any additional kilowatt produced, and as the positive effects of conservation and energy production are the same (e.g., a comfortably warm room), most of the limited amount of money that can be invested in the energy field should not be invested in new energy-generating capacity, but in technology which improves energy efficiency and thus the utilisation of already existing generating capacity. Additional conservation can be brought about by educational measures which lead to changes in life-style.

It should also be noted that soft path alternatives in other fields (e.g., organic farming) are regularly less energy-intensive than are traditional hard paths.

No matter how much energy can be saved by a combination of changes in technology and life-style, energy will still be needed to maintain an adequate standard of living. Advocates of the soft path contend that this remaining need for energy can, after allowing for a certain period of transition, be satisfied exclusively by soft energy technology.

soft energy technology   sanfte Energietechnologie

Soft energy technologies exploit energy sources that can be regarded as clean alternatives to the present-day hard energy path. Such technologies include some well-established ones, such as hydro-electric schemes, some very modern ones that are under development (e.g., photovoltaic cells), and modernised versions of very old ones (e.g., modern wind converters, which are the successors to the classical windmill).

The most promising aspects of soft energy technologies are solar power and its derivatives. Solar power can be tapped with collectors to heat water, or with photovoltaic cells for direct conversion into electricity. The power of running water is used in water-mills and hydro-electric power-stations, wind power is harnessed by windmills and wind converters, and in wind farms (i.e., large arrays of wind converters, as in California). Wave power can be harnessed by means of wave power-stations (now under experimental development at Edinburgh University).

Biogas converters extract combustible methane from biomass (e.g., agricultural waste, etc.) for domestic heating or electricity generation, reducing the biomass to a very fine fertiliser. Tidal power-plants (as the one in operation at St. Malo, France, and the one under consideration for the Severn estuary, G.B.) do not, as the soft energy technologies previously mentioned, use direct or indirect solar energy, but exploit what might be called 'lunar energy', because the tides are mainly caused by the gravitational pull of the moon.

soft loan   weiches Darlehen

Originally, a soft loan was a hard currency loan to a less developed country repayable in the ldc's soft currency. Today, the term denotes any loan to an ldc granted on concessionary – i.e., more favourable than commercial – terms. Ordinary commercial loans are referred to as 'hard loans'. A typical soft loan would carry a very low interest rate, have a long repayment period and, quite possibly, a period of grace during which no repayments or only interest payments have to be made. The benefit accruing to the less developed country from the difference between commercial and concessionary terms is referred to as the 'grant element' of the loan.

Soft loans are granted by individual countries on a bilateral basis or by international organisations, such as the International Development Association (I.D.A., the soft loan arm of the World Bank), on a multilateral basis.

soft path   sanfter Weg

As much of our present-day technology follows a hard path, which entails large-scale destruction of our natural life-support systems, concerned scientists in many fields are searching for more modern (or, in some cases, rediscovering older) techniques which are environmentally benign and could, together with some change in our wasteful life-style, stop the destruction of our biosphere before it is too late. This alternative approach is what environmentalists call the 'soft path'.

In agriculture, for example, the soft alternative to present-day agribusiness is organic farming. Likewise, soft approaches to chemistry, cosmetics, etc., are currently being explored (cf. Hans-Werner Mackwitz, Zeitbombe Chemie, Vienna, 1983). The area in which soft alternatives have been most thoroughly explored is the energy field (see: hard energy path; soft energy path).

software   Software

Software denotes the programs and routines (i.e., parts of programs) and associated documentation needed to operate a data processing system. The term is frequently restricted to the set of standard programs offered by a manufacturer or software specialist for a particular machine.

Software includes operating software (or systems software), which controls the execution of computer programs and performs related functions, and applications software, designed for the execution of specific tasks (e.g., word processing and accounting programs, electronic spread sheets, but also computer games).

solar (energy) satellite   Energiesatellit

The biggest and most ambitious application of solar power presently envisaged is a large solar satellite with an area of several square miles. Such satellites would receive a continuous supply of solar energy and beam it to receivers on the earth via microwaves.

Solar satellite systems would draw considerable opposition from the advocates of a soft energy path, because they would contribute to the centralisation and concentration of power in a few hands, and also to the entropy (heating up) of our planet. Also, aberrations of the microwave beams could have devastating effects.

solar power   Sonnenenergie

Solar power, or solar energy, is one of the most promising and attractive forms of renewable energy. With one exception (solar satellites), its applications are clean and safe and do not contribute to the entropy (i.e., heating up) of the earth.

Solar energy can be harnessed by means of black solar collectors and used to heat up water for swimming pools and for domestic purposes. A more fascinating application is direct conversion into electricity by means of solar cells, which may, within a few decades, completely revolutionise the field of electricity generation throughout the world. Neither application requires much additional space, since installations can be made on currently unused roof-tops.

sole agent   Alleinvertreter,
Gebiets- oder Bezirksvertreter

A sole agent (also referred to as an 'exclusive agent') is an agent who has the exclusive trading rights with respect to the principal's goods in a particular territory. He is frequently prohibited from handling directly competitive products. Under a sole agency (also called an 'exclusive agency'), the agent is usually paid a commission on all sales emanating from his territory, no matter whether they have been procured by his efforts or not. As a rule, he undertakes to promote systematically in the territory reserved to him the distribution of the principal's goods by an organisation of subagents, by advertisements, or by other means.

The main difference between the sole agent and the sole distributor is that the former concludes contracts with customers on behalf of his principal, who then enters into a direct contractual relationship with the third parties (customers), while the sole distributor buys and resells the goods for his own account, and no contractual relationship is established between principal and third party.

sole trader   Einzelkaufmann,
Einzelunternehmung

The simplest form of business undertaking is that run by one person: the sole trader, one-man firm, or, in American English, the sole proprietorship. The sole trader (U.S.: 'sole proprietor') provides the capital – some of which he may borrow –, makes his own decisions, and bears the risk. The profit he makes is his own. It includes elements of salary for his own services (earnings of management) and interest on the capital he has invested. He has unlimited liability, i.e., if his business fails, his private fortune can be called upon to meet his business debts.

The one-man firm is suitable for small businesses in the retail trade and crafts, or, more generally, wherever the element of personal service is important and little capital is required for the operation. The advantages are flexibility, quick decisions and initiative in management, and that no legal formalities are necessary. On the other hand, it is difficult for the sole trader to raise additional capital to expand his business, and to be his own buyer, sales manager, accountant, etc., all in one.

special inquiry   bestimmte Anfrage

In a special inquiry (also referred to as a 'specific inquiry'), a prospective customer asks a supplier to submit a detailed offer, including the price and terms of payment and delivery. In addition to this, if he has a special problem – for example, if he wants to obtain a special price for regular orders, or exclusive selling rights for a particular area – , his inquiry must specify full details of his requirements.

specific duty   spezifischer Zoll

Specific duties are charged at rates based not on the value of the goods, as in the case of ad valorem duties, but on some measure of quantity. The basis of assessment may be either weight (e.g., for salt), length (e.g., for films), surface area (e.g., for floor coverings), or number of units (e.g., for livestock).

In the majority of European countries, including Austria, specific duties are much less important than ad valorem duties, the former being used only for a limited range of commodities.

speculation   Spekulation

Speculation is an (economic?) activity where an operator tries to exploit short-term price fluctuations, basically by buying low and selling high (usually in the same market). Anything of value and subject to price fluctuations may become an object of speculation – commodities, property, securities, currencies, works of art, jewels, and what have you.

A speculator is, therefore, not interested in the current income (dividends, interest, etc.) to be derived from long-term investments, but he concentrates on quick capital gains. In doing so he obviously has to assume risks. If his forecast of price fluctuations turns out to be wrong, he will make a capital loss. Also the long-term investor has to assume risks, but in his case they are incidental to the enterprise, while they are the very essence of speculation. Speculation, therefore, is very close to gambling, the main difference being that in gambling risks are artificially created, while in speculation they still arise from some underlying economic activity. But the two activities are sufficiently similar for a number of gambling terms to have found their way into stock exchange terminology. 'Blue chips' would be a case in point.

While the person principally concerned by the success or failure of speculation (which may "make or break him") is the speculator himself, the social costs and benefits involved should not be left out of account. It is argued that speculators, by assuming risks, benefit the ultimate buyers and sellers, who may be less-experienced risk-takers, and help to even out price fluctuations by buying when prices are low and selling when they are high. But it should not be forgotten that speculators are not immune from irrational waves of optimism or pessimism, and that ill-judged speculation may magnify price fluctuations to the detriment of the economy as a whole. Third-world countries dependent on one or two commodities for their export earnings and monetary authorities trying to fight a run on a currency will be hard to convince that speculation is ultimately all to the good.

spot rate (of exchange)   (Devisen-)Kassakurs

The spot rate is the rate of exchange quoted for spot transactions, i.e., for purchases and sales of a foreign currency for immediate delivery and payment.

In commercial practice, spot transactions (apart from those between bank and customer which are carried out the same day) have to be settled on the second business day following the agreement to buy and sell, the delay allowing completion of the necessary paperwork. A typical spot transaction in the interbank market may involve a U.S. bank arranging for the transfer of £1m to a London bank. Assuming a spot rate of $1.9195/£, the U.S. bank would transfer £1m to the London bank, which, in turn, would transfer $1,919,500 to the U.S. bank.

The spot rate is also the rate on the basis of which the forward rates are calculated.

staff[1]   Belegschaft, Belegschaftsmitglieder, Personal (in Dienstleistungsbetrieben)

Staff, or personnel, refers to a body of persons carrying out work under common management. There is a tendency to use the term for the employees of service businesses, e.g., insurance companies, newspapers, and the like. By contrast, the employees of steelworks and similar establishments are, as a rule, collectively referred to as 'work-force'.

It should be noted that the word frequently takes the verb in the plural, as in "five staff were dismissed".

staff[2]   Stab, Stabstelle

In a narrower sense, staff is used to describe a unit or group of people in a large organisation who are not in the direct line of command, but provide advice and assistance to line units instead of carrying out operational tasks. Public relations and marketing research departments are typical examples of staff units, the former frequently reporting to the managing director/president, and the latter to the marketing manager.

stag   Konzertzeichner

This British term refers to a bull in the new issue market. A stag will apply for an allotment of shares in a new issue with the intention of selling them at a profit as quickly as possible, preferably before he himself has had to pay for them in full. If stags are successful, this is an indication that the issue price of the share involved was pitched too low and that the proceeds for the issuing company could have been higher. Stagging can be avoided by making a tender issue, under which investors interested in a new issue have to submit offers (tenders) and the issue price is determined by the market.

standing order   Dauerauftrag

A standing order is an arrangement between a buyer and a supplier according to which the supplier delivers goods in specified quantities at certain intervals until further notice.

As applied in banking, a standing order is a written instruction by a customer to his bank to pay a stated sum of money from his current account to a named party at certain stated dates (usually at regular intervals) until further notice or until the date indicated. It is a convenient arrangement for payment of regularly recurring items of fixed amount, such as instalments, rents, insurance premiums, subscriptions, etc.. The only thing the customer has to do is complete the bank's standing order form; he has to state the payee's name, the amount to be paid at stated intervals, and the duration of the order.

stapler   Heftmaschine

A stapler (also referred to as a 'stapling machine') is a small, usually hand-operated, device for joining papers together. Both ends of a small U-shaped wire (the staple) are driven through the papers and clinched to hold them together.

statement of account   Aufstellung der offenen Posten,
                                            Kontoauszug

Customers who have an account, i.e., a regular business relationship, with a supplier receive statements of account at regular intervals, for example, once a month or once every quarter.

A statement of account is a summary of the transactions between the buyer and the seller during the period it covers. It shows at a given date the state of affairs between the supplier and his customer. The statement is, in effect, a copy of the customer's account since it was last balanced. It starts with the balance, if any, owing at the beginning of the period, to which are added the amounts, but not the details, of invoices and debit notes issued, and from which are deducted the amounts of any credit notes issued to the buyer and any payments made by him. The closing balance shows the amount still owing at the date of the statement, which, unlike the preceding invoices, is a demand for payment. Statements, as a rule, bear an indication of the terms of payment, e.g., 2% 15 days. Any balance remaining unpaid at the end of the period covered by the statement would be carried forward to the statement for the next period.

A statement of account enables the customer to compare the account kept by the supplier with his own records, and, in addition, acts as a reminder that payment is due.

Finally, it should be noted that a supplier usually includes the clause E.&O.E. (errors and omissions excepted) in statements as well as in invoices, which means that he reserves the right to correct any errors and omissions that may be contained in the document.

stationery

Bürobedarf,
Büromaterial,
Büroartikel

The term 'stationery' (mind the spelling and do not confuse with 'stationary') has the same meaning as 'office supplies'. In other words, it includes everything that can be obtained from a stationer's shop: typing paper in various sizes (foolscap, corresponding to A4, or quarto, corresponding to A5), forms, envelopes, postcards, files and folders, adhesive tapes, duplicator supplies, carbon paper, typewriter ribbons, punches, staplers, appointment calendars, notepaper, memo pads (note pads, copy blocks), ballpoint pens, felt pens, correction fluid, pencil-sharpeners, erasers, markers, transparencies, rocker blotters, index cards, metal tabs, etc..

stock[1]

Lager,
Lagerbestand,
Vorratsvermögen

see: inventory

stock[2]

Aktienkapital,
Grundkapital,
Stammkapital

Stock, or capital stock, is the legal capital of an American corporation divided into shares (of stock). The term may also be applied to the shares themselves, although not to an individual share (i.e., not to the actual document).

stock[3]

Wertpapier(e)

In colloquial and journalistic usage, the plural 'stocks' is used to describe both ordinary shares (equities) and gilt-edged securities (government stocks). This means that, for all practical purposes, the term has become synonymous with 'securities'.

stockbroker

Börsenmakler

Stockbrokers have, in fact, a number of functions, such as to advise their clients on the selection and management of their investments or to arrange the listing of securities. But their main function is, no doubt, to act as agents in buying and selling securities. They buy and sell securities for their clients' account, who, as members of the public, are not allowed to enter the stock exchange premises. In the United States, brokers may also deal for their own account, i.e., buy and sell as principals, risking their own money. In this case, they are called 'specialists', because, with their own money at stake, they concentrate on certain types of security which they know really well. On the London Stock Exchange, 'single capacity' is still the rule, which means that brokers can only deal for their clients' account, while there is a separate category of stock exchange member, the jobber, who is allowed to act as principal – but not as agent. At the time of writing, plans are afoot to change the British system, and dual capacity may be introduced in the near future.

Another change affecting the London stock market concerns brokers' commissions. Brokers are rewarded for their main service in the form of a commission, calculated as a percentage of the value of the transaction involved. Brokers' commissions in London used to be fixed, i.e., all the brokers charged the same percentage. At the time of writing, fixed commissions are being phased out and gradually replaced by negotiated commissions. This means that brokers are beginning to have to compete on price.

Under both the New York and the London Stock Exchange rules, brokers are not allowed to trade as individuals, but must form partnerships or (in the United States) also corporations.

stock concept   Bestandsgröße, Zeitpunktgröße

A stock concept is an economic variable whose quantity or value is measured at a particular point of time. Order books (the total amount of orders on hand at a given point of time), the money supply (the total amount of money existing in an economy at any given time), and also the assets and liabilities of an economic unit (e.g., as shown in the balance sheet on the accounting date) are examples of stock concepts, which should be carefully distinguished from flow concepts.

stock exchange   Effektenbörse

The stock exchange is a market for securities, such as for shares and debentures (U.S.: corporate bonds), issued by private companies, as well as for government bonds, or government stocks.

The stock exchange is a tightly organised market, which means that, in contrast to ordinary markets, where ultimate buyers and sellers meet, only members (brokers; in London, brokers and jobbers) are allowed to take part in the dealings. If private persons or institutions want to buy certain shares, they have to instruct a broker, who will carry out the transaction on their behalf.

The stock exchange is, moreover, mainly a secondary market, i.e., it is concerned less with issuing new securities than with buying and selling securities that have already been issued. The market for new issues (primary market) is less tightly organised and is a loose association of specialised banks (issuing houses in London, investment banks in the United States) and private and institutional investors.

Although, therefore, the stock market plays only a subordinate role in the raising of fresh capital, it has a strong indirect influence on the primary market. New issues would be much more difficult if investors did not know that they could sell their newly acquired securities in a well-organised market whenever they should think it fit to do so.

The two best known stock exchanges in the English-speaking countries are the New York Stock Exchange (NYSE, Wall Street) and the London Stock Exchange. Also worth mentioning are the American Stock Exchange (AMEX) and the recently founded Unlisted Securities Market in London (USM), both of which specialise in the shares of new and smaller companies, which would be unable to meet the stringent listing requirements of the two main exchanges.

stock exchange indices   Börsenindizes

In the stock exchange, like in any other market, people are interested not only in individual price movements, but also in general trends. Since trends can best be measured by index figures, there exist a number of stock exchange indices to meet this information need.

Stock exchange indices may be narrowly based, like the FT industrial ordinary index and the Dow-Jones industrial average, each comprising the ordinary shares/common stocks of 30 important industrial companies/corporations, or they may be broadly based, like Standard & Poor's index, which covers 500 widely held common stocks. In between fall sectoral indices (e.g., the FT actuaries gold mine index).

Stock exchange indices may be simple unweighted averages, measuring crude price movements (both the Dow-Jones industrial average and the FT ordinary fall into this category). More sophisticated indices weight the prices of the securities/issues included, either on the basis of the number of securities outstanding or on the basis of their market capitalisation. (Standard & Poor's is an example of the former, the FT actuaries for oil companies an example of the latter variety).

In addition to giving a general impression of price movements, stock exchange indices may also be used as yardsticks for measuring investment performance (capital gains). An investment fund, for instance, whose performance falls below some well-known market average will have a difficult time justifying its existence to the investing community.

The two best-known stock exchange indices are certainly the Dow-Jones industrial average (New York Stock Exchange) and the FT ordinary (London Stock Exchange). The former was named in honour of Messrs. Dow and Jones, who founded an investors' service and did some pioneering work in measuring stock price movements. The latter is published by the Financial Times, a British daily which devotes a lot of its space to the coverage of investment news.

stock exchange quotation   Börsennotierung

Before an issue of securities can be dealt in on a stock exchange, it is necessary to obtain a stock exchange quotation, or listing, i.e., to have it included in the list of securities in which trading on a particular exchange is permitted. Applications for a listing must be made through a broker and are subjected to close scrutiny by the competent stock exchange department (Department of Stock Lists at the New York Stock Exchange, Quotations Department of the London Stock Exchange). Issues are only approved for listing if a number of stringent requirements are met (e.g., provision of detailed financial information, likelihood of an active market in the issue involved). In the United States, an issue must additionally be registered with the Securities & Exchange Commission (S.E.C.) before it is admitted to dealings, i.e., before actual trading begins on the floor of the exchange.

stockist
Fachhändler, Fachgeschäft

Stockists, or limited-line stores, are retail outlets, either independently owned or belonging to a larger organisation (e.g., a chain), which carry a restricted range of goods. Usually, they specialise in one particular line of products, e.g., electrical appliances, shoes, consumer electronics, furs, men's fashions, etc.. Their appeal to the consumer is based on a carefully selected range of high-quality products, personal service, expert advice, and after-sales service. These advantages help to offset the somewhat higher prices due to the relatively low volume (especially in comparison with discount stores).

stockjobber
Effekteneigenhändler

Stockjobbers can be found only on the London Stock Exchange. They are the members that buy and sell securities for their own account, risking their own money. This is in contrast to the brokers, who only carry out orders for their clients and do not take title to the securities involved. Jobbers are basically wholesalers, i.e., they buy from, and sell to , other jobbers and brokers, and have, again in contrast to the brokers, no direct contact with the investing public. Jobbers, since their own money is at stake, specialise in certain types of security (e.g., oil shares, tobacco shares, gilt-edged securities) which they know really well. They act as market makers, i.e., they try to maintain an orderly market in their particular security, even if outside demand should at the moment not be sufficient.

The strict separation between members allowed to deal for their own account and those merely acting as agents is typical of the London Stock Exchange. The technical word for this situation is 'single capacity'. 'Dual capacity' prevails in the United States, and at the time of writing discussions are going on whether this system should be introduced in London too.

A corollary to this is that jobbers do not earn a commission, but make a profit (loss), just like any other dealer operating for his own account. The jobber's margin, by the way, is called the 'jobber's turn'.

storage
Lagerhaltung, Lagerung

Since production and consumption frequently do not coincide, it is essential for the goods to be held and preserved against the time when they are actually required by the final consumer. This is where storage, or warehousing, comes in, whose main function it is to bridge the period between production and consumption and to adjust supply and demand with regard to time. Storage, which is part of logistics, or physical distribution, is carried out by manufacturers, wholesalers, retailers, carriers, public warehouses, etc.. Storage by the final consumer, however, is excluded by definition.

The actual storage facilities used depend to some extent on the type of product involved: gravel can be stored in open yards, as there is no need to protect it from the inclemency of the weather; meat, fish, fruit, and other perishables require refrigerated facilities, otherwise they would deteriorate and go bad quickly.

As in many other fields, efficiency in warehousing can be improved by computers and automation. Modern warehouses may feature automatic computer-controlled equipment which enables replenishing, picking (i.e., selection), and assembling operations to be carried out without the intervention of human staff.

storage device   Speichergerät

Computers have to store large amounts of data and retrieve it if directed to do so. The data may be stored either in the CPU itself (internal or primary storage) or in peripheral storage devices, located outside the computer (external or secondary storage). A computer's internal memory is usually not very large and is only used to hold the instructions and data necessary for a processing activity currently being handled by the computer. External memory devices can have a much larger storage capacity. Magnetic cores and semiconductor storage devices (chips) are used for primary storage, while magnetic tapes and disks (hard disks, flexible or floppy disks) are typical external storage devices.

Storage devices can be classified according to the access method used. Data stored on magnetic tape has to be accessed sequentially. This means that in order to locate a specific item of data, the computer has to read through all data from the beginning. Random access (storage) devices, such as magnetic disks, magnetic drums, or semiconductor devices, enable the computer to find data with the help of addresses, without there being any need to search through each item in the file concerned. Random access (or direct access) devices are, therefore, much faster than sequential access (storage) devices.

strike   Streik

A strike is a concerted stoppage of work as a protest by workers against wages, working conditions, redundancies, plant closures, or some other cause of dissatisfaction. A strike may continue until the demands of the workers have been satisfied or the other side to the dispute agrees to have formal discussions or negotiations. A strike that has been ordered or condoned by the appropriate trade union is called an 'official strike', while one that has not been so endorsed is termed 'unofficial ' or 'wildcat'. A strike, or walk-out, as it is sometimes called, is labour's most powerful weapon in an industrial dispute.

One aspect of strikes that has attracted a lot of attention lately is picketing. Pickets are workers stationed outside a place of business during an industrial dispute to inform the public and to dissuade workers from entering. Secondary picketing, i.e., picketing by people not directly involved in the strike, has been outlawed in the U.K..

subrogation

Subrogation,
Eintritt des Versicherers in die Rechte
des Versicherten

In insurance, the term 'subrogation' means the right of the insurer to any remedies which the insured may have against third parties who are wholly or partly responsible for the loss or damage in respect of which a claim has been paid. Under subrogation rights, the insurer is entitled to any recovery obtained by the insured and any recovery which he himself may obtain in the insured's name. The maximum amount to which the insurer is entitled under his subrogation rights is the amount of the claim paid. Any amount in excess of the claim which the insurer may recover must be paid to the insured.

The purpose of subrogation is to prevent the insured from recovering more than once for the same loss or damage. In a case, for instance, where goods are damaged owing to collision, the insured cannot claim the insurance money from the insurer and then sue the owners of the ship that negligently caused the collision. Under subrogation, the right to sue the owners of the ship passes from the insured to the insurer on payment of the claim.

subsidy

Subvention

Subsidies are payments made by the government to whole industries, individual business firms, or other organisations to achieve certain goals which the government considers to be important. These goals include: low prices to consumers (e.g., food subsidies), low rents (housing subsidies), job creation and preservation, maintenance of farm incomes (agricultural subsidies), promotion of exports (export subsidies, e.g., interest subsidies on export credits), etc..

supermarket

Supermarkt

Although there is no universally accepted definition of a supermarket, the term is generally taken to mean a large-scale, departmentalised self-service store (according to Gartside, not less than 2,000 square feet of selling space) selling a wide variety of goods, with the main emphasis on food and other consumer staples. Smaller retail establishments operating on the same or a similar principle are called 'self-service stores', larger ones 'hypermarkets'.

The main attractions of a supermarket are convenience of shopping, lower prices (made possible by a minimum of service), automation (warehousing and check-out operations), high turnover, and bulk buying.

supplier

Lieferant,
Lieferer,
Anbieter

A supplier is usually a firm selling goods and/or services to other firms, private individuals, government agencies, etc..

supplier credit

Lieferkredit,
Lieferantenkredit

Supplier credit (in British English known as 'trade credit') is a form of short-term financing (i.e., up to one year). Most buyers are not required to pay for goods and/or services on delivery, but are allowed a stated period of time before payment is due. During this period, the seller of the goods and/or services extends credit to the buyer. In other words, a supplier credit involves the extension of deferred payment terms by the seller to the buyer. Credit can be extended on an open account basis (primarily in sales to branches and subsidiaries or well-established customers), through the use of time drafts, or through promissory notes issued by the buyer to the seller.

supply[1]

Angebot (im volkswirtschaftlichen Sinn)

In economic theory, the term 'supply' denotes the amount of a commodity or service offered for sale at a given price. Just as in the case of demand, supply is determined also by factors other than price, the most important being the cost of production and the period of time allowed to supply to adjust to a change in prices. In economic analysis, these other factors are frequently assumed to be constant (the 'ceteris paribus' or 'all other things being equal' condition). This assumption enables supply and price to be related in what is called the 'supply function' (with price as the independent and supply as the dependent variable) and to be graphed in the supply curve.

supply[2]

Vorrat

Supply, in everyday usage, refers to the stock, store, or amount of something provided, available, or accessible. A firm, for instance, may have a supply of fuel, which is gradually used up and will be in danger of giving out unless replenished, or topped up. Certain commodities may be in short, others in abundant, supply. In the first case, the amount available is too small, in the second, more than enough, to satisfy present requirements.

If used in the plural, the term refers to the collection of things necessary for a particular purpose. Factory supplies, for example, are the supplementary materials (other than raw materials) required to carry on a manufacturing process, and might include small tools, nails, screws and other consumables, as well as fuel and lubricants.

supply curve

Angebotskurve

The supply curve is the graphical representation of the supply function, i.e., of the relationship between price and supply. It shows us how many units of a particular commodity or service would be offered for sale at various prices, assuming that all other factors (such as the cost of production, the period of time involved) remain constant. The supply curve normally slopes upwards from left to right. This indicates that, other things being equal, more is offered for sale at higher prices. There are, however, exceptions. For example, where goods are in fixed supply, the supply curve would be a straight vertical line (such as in the case of paintings by Rembrandt). Another exception is the case where a fall in prices calls forth a larger supply because suppliers fear that prices might fall still further, and where, therefore, the supply curve actually slopes downwards. If changes in the other factors are allowed, this would be reflected not in a movement along the curve, but in a shift of the whole curve.

survey

Erhebung,
Studie,
Untersuchung

Surveys are conducted to obtain information about a specific universe, or population, i.e., about a number of defined events, objects, or people. A survey may, for instance, be carried out to determine how many people in a particular geographical area have heard of a particular brand (brand awareness). Although it may be perfectly feasible to ask every single person living in the specified area, it is much more common to collect the information only from a sample of the complete universe. This is done because censuses, or full counts, are much more expensive than sample surveys and really unnecessary. If the sample is selected according to statistical principles – in many cases a random sample is used – and if the correct methods of statistical estimation are applied, the results will, for all practical purposes, be the same as if a full count had been carried out. As indicated in the above example, surveys may be based on personal or telephone interviews. It is, however, also possible to use questionnaires or the observational method (e.g., counting the number of people entering a supermarket).

Surveys – sometimes referred to as 'field research' – are an important source of primary data, i.e., data collected specifically for the project in hand. (The other source would be experiments.)

The method employed to collect secondary data, i.e., data originally collected for some other purpose, is called 'desk research'. For example, income data collected originally by revenue authorities for tax purposes may be used as secondary data in an investigation of distribution of income.

surveyor

Havariekommissar,
Schadensachverständiger

When used in insurance, the term 'surveyor' refers to a competent person with the knowledge and skill to carry out a survey on the damage to insured property, such as ships and their cargoes, planes, buildings and machinery, etc.. After a close examination of the damage, he makes out a survey report, which gives details of the cause and extent of the damage, and which the insured needs together with the policy, and possibly other documents, to support his insurance claim.

T

take-home pay

effektiv ausbezahlter Lohn

Take-home pay is the net amount of money that an employee finds in his pay-packet (if he is paid in cash) or that is credited to his account (if payment is made by credit transfer). The amount in question is figured out (i.e., computed) by the firm's pay-roll section by adding up the regular wage or salary, pay for overtime, bonuses, benefits, if any, and deducting P.A.Y.E. tax (withholding tax in American usage), the employee's national insurance contribution (social security tax in the U.S.A.), and union dues where applicable.

take-over bid

(öffentliches) Übernahmeangebot

Take-over bids (U.S.: 'tender offers') are a distinctive feature of British and American business life, as even a short glance at the business pages of the Financial Times or the Herald Tribune will show. Companies are constantly trying to take over other companies either to add them to their portfolio of subsidiaries or, maybe, to strip them of their assets, i.e., to break them up and sell off the valuable bits.

A company wishing to take over another company may either agree the bid with the "victim's" board (friendly or agreed take-over bid) or it may go over their heads and appeal to the shareholders direct (unfriendly or contested take-over bid). In the latter case, the victim's management is likely to fight back, for instance, by making optimistic profit forecasts and generally trying to convince the shareholders that they would be better off with the present management in charge. Or, they may even call in a third, more acceptable, company (the famous "white knight") to fend off the unwelcome suitor.

In any case, the bidder will have to offer the shareholders an attractive price, possibly well in excess of what they can currently get at the stock exchange. Payment for the shares can be in cash (cash bid), in the form of securities of the company making the bid (paper bid), or some combination of the two.

target group

Zielgruppe

The target group, or target audience, is the people who an advertiser wants to reach by using a given medium or set of media. The main problem is to choose the medium or combination of media that will reach as many members of the target audience and as few people outside the target group as possible.

tax allowance

Steuerfreibetrag

A tax allowance (U.S.: 'tax deduction') may be defined as a specified sum of money which a taxpayer can deduct from his assessable income/profit (i.e., total or gross income/profit). A tax allowance differs from a tax credit in that it is subtracted from the income subject to tax, whereas a credit is deducted after the total tax liability has been calculated. Thus, a tax allowance of a given amount is less valuable to the taxpayer than a credit of the same amount. The value of a tax allowance for the taxpayer depends on his level of income/profit. The higher the income/profit, the higher his marginal tax rate, and, consequently, the greater the value of his tax allowance. In the case of a tax credit, however, the value is the same to all recipients, since it is deducted from their tax bills.

To mention only one example, in Great Britain, an individual is entitled to deduct what is called 'personal allowances', the amount deductible depending on the marital status of the taxpayer and on the number and age of his children. Personal allowances also include such items as the blind person's allowance and the age allowance.

taxation   Besteuerung

Taxes are compulsory levies imposed by local and/or central governments on a regular basis and usually not designated for a special purpose. They are regarded as a contribution to the general revenue pool, from which most government expenditure is financed. The majority of taxes are unrequited, i.e., they are not paid in exchange for a specific object, right, or service provided by government. Although taxes are presumably collected for the general welfare of the taxpayers, the tax liability of the individual taxpayer is independent of any benefit received.

There are, however, several exceptions to this broad rule: certain types of stamp duty, for instance, are levied in return for a particular service rendered by the authorities (e.g., legalising documents, issuing passports). It should be noted that neither in British nor in American English is there a parallel to the precise terminological distinction between 'Abgaben', 'Steuern', 'Gebühren', and 'Beiträge' in Austrian and German usage. The terms 'levy', 'tax', and 'duty' are often used interchangeably, and their distribution is based on idiomatic rather than on conceptual grounds. Moreover, there are differences between British and American usage: the American equivalent of the British 'national insurance contribution' is the 'social security (payroll) tax'. The British levy on a person's estate passing at death was called 'estate duty' (before it was replaced by capital transfer tax), a very similar levy in the United States is referred to as 'estate tax'.

The following basic concepts should prove useful in any discussion on taxation: 'tax object', 'tax base', 'tax rate', 'revenue authorities'.

The tax object is the thing, transaction, or sum of money subject to tax. In the long history of taxation, governments have shown great ingenuity in identifying potential sources of revenue, and have imposed taxes on a wide variety of objects: there are (or at least were) taxes on personal income (income tax), on profits (e.g., corporation tax), on capital gains (capital gains tax), on documents (stamp duties), on lifetime gifts and estates passing at death (capital transfer tax), on sales or expenditure (sales tax, V.A.T., turnover tax), on windows facing the street, on the people living in a household, and so on, so that the famous song by the Beatles ("The Taxman") is only a slight exaggeration of the actual situation:

IF YOU DRIVE A CAR, I'LL TAX THE STREET.
IF YOU TRY TO SIT, I'LL TAX YOUR SEAT.
IF YOU GET TOO COLD, I'LL TAX THE HEAT.
IF YOU TAKE A WALK, I'LL TAX YOUR FEET.

The tax base is the physical unit or, more commonly, the monetary amount to which the tax rate is applied. For example, a tax on motor cars (the tax object) may use the horsepower of the car, the cubic capacity of its engine, or its price as a tax base.

The tax rate is the percentage by which the tax base has to be multiplied to arrive at the tax liability, or tax burden, i.e., the amount of tax to be paid. In the case of proportional taxes, or flat rate taxes, the tax rate is the same for all levels of the tax base, which means that the tax burden rises in line with the tax base. Progressive taxes are based on the principle: the higher the tax base, the higher the tax rate, which leads to a more than proportionate rise in the tax burden relative to the tax base. In the case of regressive taxes, the tax rate falls as the tax base rises, the tax burden growing more slowly than the tax base. But this is not the whole story: taxes that are nominally proportional (e.g., a tax on cigarettes and a tax on sugar) turn out to be decidedly regressive in practice (i.e., if related not to their formal tax bases, but to the income of the taxpayer), because the share of personal income spent on cigarettes and sugar declines as the level of personal income rises. Poll taxes, levied as a fixed amount per capita, are obviously regressive for the same reason.

Revenue authorities are the government departments or agencies responsible for tax matters. In the United Kingdom, taxation is the concern of the Treasury, the Board of Inland Revenue (for direct taxes), and the Board of Customs and Excise (for indirect taxes, such as V.A.T. and customs duties). In the United States, it is the concern of the Treasury and the Internal Revenue Service.

Taxes are considered to have three functions: (i) fiscal or budgetary, to raise funds to meet government expenditure; (ii) economic, to promote such general goals as full employment, monetary stability, a satisfactory rate of growth; and (iii) social or redistributive, to lessen inequalities in the distribution of income and wealth, especially by means of progressive taxation. Since these three functions are interrelated, there are bound to be conflicts among them. Thus, the level or composition of taxes considered necessary for budgetary reasons may tend to hold back the rate of economic growth.

Aside from its main functions, taxation serves many lesser purposes. It may be used, for instance, to discourage the consumption of alcoholic beverages and cigarettes, considered undesirable on the grounds of public health, but also to induce people to save energy.

Taxation is a very sensitive issue: on the one hand, taxes are absolutely necessary to finance government activities, control the economy, and achieve greater equality of incomes and wealth; on the other hand, they represent one of the most visible and painful forms of government interference in the private sphere. Even otherwise quite publicly-minded people resent having to pay large portions of what they earn or own over to the revenue authorities. A high tax burden, whether due to a large number of taxes or high (progressive) tax rates, is likely to arouse tax resistance and lead to tax evasion, or even emigration, thus defeating the very purpose of taxation. In view of this, governments should move carefully in this field. If outright tax reductions are not possible, they should, at least, try to protect people from bracket creep, or fiscal drag, i.e., from automatic hidden tax increases caused by taxpayers moving into higher tax brackets solely as a result of inflation. This could be done by indexing tax brackets and tax allowances. Another suggestion would be to avoid taxes that are difficult to administer and where the cost of collection eats up a large portion of the gross revenue raised. Finally, people would probably show less resistance to high taxes if they felt that their money was being used carefully and for reasonable purposes.

tax avoidance
Steuervermeidung,
Steuerumgehung

In general, tax avoidance refers to the reduction of a person's tax liability to the lowest possible level by legal means. It involves, for example, arranging one's financial affairs in such a way as to take advantage of legally permissible alternative tax rates or alternative methods of reporting and assessing income/profit. A taxpayer may try to minimise his tax liability by utilising all possible tax reliefs (e.g., tax credits and tax allowances), or by fully exploiting the discrepancies and loopholes in the tax laws. Tax loopholes are provisions in tax laws which have the unintentional side-effect of permitting a person's or a firm's income or profit, etc., to go untaxed or to be taxed at a lower rate. Their full exploitation requires detailed knowledge of the relevant tax laws. In addition, tax avoidance may also take the form of refraining from taxable actions, e.g., smoking.

tax credit
Steuerabsetzbetrag

A tax credit is defined as a specified sum of money a taxpayer can deduct from his tax liability, the latter being calculated by multiplying the taxable income/profit by the applicable tax rate.

A tax credit differs from a tax allowance in the following essential respect: it is subtracted after the total tax liability has been calculated, whereas a tax allowance is deducted from a person's/company's assessable income/profit (i.e., total or gross income/profit), thus leading to a reduction in the taxable income/profit. This shows that a tax credit of a given amount is more valuable to a taxpayer than a tax allowance of the same amount. For example, a taxpayer who is in the 50% income tax bracket reduces his total tax burden by £100 if he is allowed a £100 tax credit, but his total burden is reduced by only £50 if he is given a £100 allowance.

Among the most important examples of tax credits are the 'foreign tax credit', the 'investment tax credit' in the U.S.A., and the 'sole earner's credit' in Austria. The foreign tax credit, designed to alleviate the problem of double taxation, allows the taxpayer to deduct from his tax liability any tax paid by him in a foreign country (foreign tax) on income arising there. The investment tax credit, the main purpose of which is to encourage investment by businesses, enables the taxpayer to credit against his tax liability a given percentage of investment spending (capital expenditure) incurred during the period of assessment. The sole earner's credit, as the term implies, may be claimed by the taxpayer if his/her spouse is not gainfully employed.

tax evasion
Steuerhinterziehung

Tax evasion, in contrast to tax avoidance, is illegal. A taxpayer is said to evade taxes if he either performs an act prohibited, or fails to perform an act prescribed, by tax laws, with the intention or effect of reducing or completely eliminating his tax liability. A person or firm may, for instance, defraud the revenue authorities by failing to report or by underreporting income, sales, or assets for tax assessment.

Tax evasion, like any other offence or crime, is subject to penalties, whose severity usually depends on the amount of tax defrauded/evaded.

tax haven   Steuerparadies, Steueroase

The term 'tax haven' is generally used to refer to any country or locality
1. which levies no taxes; or
2. which levies taxes only on domestic income/profit, whereas foreign-source income/profit is liable to no or only little tax; or
3. which grants special tax privileges to certain types of taxable persons, mainly to foreign companies.

It is for these tax advantages that many companies and wealthy individuals choose to base themselves in a tax haven. In addition, foreign enterprises may set up letter-box companies (brass-plate companies) in a tax haven to avoid payment of taxes in their own country, where tax rates are much higher. For example, a company exporting from country A to country B may be able, on paper, to export its products to a subsidiary in a tax haven at a low price and re-export them from the tax haven to country B at a high price. Thus, it would earn little, if any, profit on the transaction in country A, where it would be subject to normal corporation tax, and a high profit in the tax haven, where it would pay little or no tax.

The number of tax havens is legion; prominent examples are the Bahamas, Bermuda, the Cayman Islands, Switzerland, Liechtenstein, and Luxembourg.

tax liability[1]   Steuerpflicht

In general, the term 'tax liability' means a taxpayer's basic obligation to pay taxes. For example, the Austrian income tax system makes a clear distinction between 'unlimited' tax liability and 'limited' tax liability. An individual having his place of residence or his customary place of abode in Austria is subject to unlimited income tax liability, i.e., he has to pay income tax on his total income, no matter where it originates (world-wide income). If an individual has neither his place of residence nor his customary place of abode in Austria, he may be subject to limited tax liability, i.e., he has to pay income tax only on his income arising in Austria.

tax liability[2]   Steuerschuld

The term 'tax liability' may also refer to the actual amount of tax to be paid by a taxpayer. For instance, the income tax liability is calculated by multiplying a taxpayer's taxable income by the applicable tax rate, V.A.T. liability by deducting input tax from output tax.

telephone   Telefon

The telephone is easily the most popular telecommunications device. In the United States, for instance, there are 64 telephones to every 100 people.

There is probably no need to describe an ordinary telephone in great detail. The most important parts you should remember are the dial for dialling the number of the person or firm you want to speak to, and the receiver (consisting of an earpiece and a mouthpiece), which can be lifted from, and put back on, the rest.

Originally, trunk (or long-distance) calls had to be connected by the exchange operator; today, subscriber-dialled trunk calls are possible to nearly anywhere in the world. Since it would be wasteful and unnecessary to have a separate line for each telephone, most organisations have a manual or automatic private branch exchange (PBX) with dozens, or even hundreds, of extensions.

Of course, modern technological developments have not bypassed the telephone: dials have been replaced with keyboards (keyphones, where numbers are no longer dialled but keyed in), digital transmission and optical fibres are being tested, teleconferencing facilities (which enable up to ten people located in different parts of the world to confer over the phone) are becoming more and more popular, as is the viewphone (which enables the participants to see each other). Moreover, a host of new devices to be used in conjunction with the telephone are on sale, including automatic diallers, telephone answering machines, radio pagers, and modems (acoustic couplers).

telephone answering machine   (automatischer)
                                        Telefonanrufbeantworter

A telephone answering machine is used to cover the period when a telephone is left unattended. Similar to a tape-recorder and attached to a telephone, it is capable of answering incoming calls automatically. It will give the caller a tape-recorded message, and record any statement made by him in reply. A caller might, for instance, wish to place an order or request the visit of a sales rep or serviceman. The recorded message can then be played back at any time.

telephone call   Telefonanruf

When making a (tele)phone call, you first have to lift the receiver, then you dial (or, in the case of a push-button telephone, or keyphone, key in) the number. If it is a 'local call', you dial the relevant local telephone number, which you may obtain from a telephone directory or from Directory Inquiries, unless it is an unlisted (or ex-directory) number. In the case of a 'trunk call', or 'long-distance call', you either have to ring up the operator and ask him or her to connect your call or, which is more usual now, you simply dial the appropriate city or area code before the local number of the subscriber you are calling. In international telephone calls, the city or area code has to be preceded by the country code, or by the international access code plus the country code if the person or firm called is located in another continent. 'Subscriber trunk dialling' (S.T.D.), or 'direct dialling', as it is being increasingly called even in Great Britain, is now available practically everywhere.

Normally, a telephone call is paid for by the subscriber from whose telephone the call is being made, but there are several exceptions. It is possible to reverse the charges, i.e., to arrange for a call to be paid for at the receiving end ('reverse charge call', or 'collect call'). In this case, the call has, of course, to go through the operator. Another exception is the 'free-phone system' ('toll-free system' in the United states), under which firms arrange with the Post Office or telephone company to pay for any calls to a specified number. Firms use this arrangement, for instance, to encourage inquiries.

Teletex

Teletex,
öffentlicher Bürofernschreibdienst

Teletex (not to be confused with Teletext) is a public system of conveying text via data transmission, for instance from one word processor to another. The text must already be held in a computer-type memory in standard computer-coded form.

Teletext

Teletext

Teletext (not to be confused with Teletex) is one of the many home or office information retrieval systems covered by the generic term 'videotex'. It uses one-way broadcast signals as a link between the providers of information and the users' T.V. sets. The term 'Teletext' is used in Austria and corresponds to 'Videotext' in West Germany and 'Broadcast Videotex' in Great Britain.

telex

Fernschreibdienst

In simple terms, a telex machine is a combination of a typewriter and a telephone, which can be used to send and receive messages to, or from respectively, almost everywhere in the world. By dialling or keying in a number the telex operator can connect his telex machine with his correspondent's machine (either direct or via an exchange operator) and can then proceed to type a message, which is transmitted almost instantaneously. Modern telex equipment features punched tape, magnetic tape, or even floppy disk devices and can be used to originate, correct, edit, and store messages to be sent later on – at a much greater speed than could be managed by an operator. This makes telex communications even more efficient and economical, putting it far ahead of telephone calls and telegrams. By adding a VDU screen to a modern telex machine it is possible to upgrade it to an electronic mail terminal.

The style of telex communications is simple, terse, and characterised by the use of abbreviations, obviously to save time and money (e.g., RYT for REFERENCE YOUR TELEX, OCC for YOUR CORRESPONDENT'S NUMBER IS OCCUPIED). Some firms use special codes to make messages even shorter and more economical (e.g., the ABC Code, where "Idrofano" stands for the message "What were the imports last week?").

Strictly speaking, the word 'Telex' refers to the national system, or network, which connects the individual subscribers, the machine itself should be called a 'teleprinter' (U.S.: 'teletypewriter').

339

temporary importation of goods   Eingangsvormerkverkehr

Basically, goods being imported into a customs territory are subject to import duty. Most countries, however, have adopted a special procedure for goods which are imported only for a certain period of time and are then re-exported. Under this procedure, for example, certain goods may be imported into a country free of duty if they are subsequently re-exported in the same state – usually within a period of six months. Goods which are imported only temporarily include foreign samples used by commercial travellers; foreign exhibition goods; foreign goods for repair; foreign road vehicles imported by non-residents (e.g., a lorry carrying imported goods); etc..

tender   Submissionsangebot; Ausschreibung(sverfahren)

Strictly speaking, a tender is an offer submitted in response to an invitation to tender. But the term may also be applied loosely to the whole process of selecting suppliers on a competitive basis, which consists of the invitation to tender, the submission of the tenders, and the awarding of the contract.

The tender system is used in many fields – even in the securities markets – but by far its most common application is where a government agency or public body wants to make sure that it will receive a large number of competitive offers for whatever project it has in hand (e.g., building a road or a bridge, or buying a fleet of vehicles). Many countries have legal rules which determine when a public body or government agency has to put a contract out to tender, and many have acceded to the GATT convention on public procurement, dealing with international tenders.

In open tendering, the tender-inviting party will run a tender notice in one or more widely-read papers or journals, inviting all competent firms to submit their offers. Under selective tendering procedures, the invitation will go out only to a selected number of firms which have met the agency's prequalification standards.

Prospective tenderers obtain the necessary tender documents, or specification documents, from the inviting party or from its agent against payment of a fee, prepare their tenders, and file them, in many cases, in a plain and sealed envelope on or before the closing date specified in the tender documents. All this is intended to safeguard competition, and in many countries, collusion, i.e., secret collaboration between tenderers, and other practices restricting competition in this field are prohibited by law.

At an appointed date after the expiry of the period fixed for the submission of tenders, the tenders received by the inviting party are opened and examined carefully. As a rule, the contract is awarded to the tenderer offering the most favourable prices and terms. This implies that the contract need not go to the lowest tenderer.

To make sure that only bona fide tenderers put in offers, the tender-inviting party often requires tenderers to post a tender bond, i.e., to provide a bank guarantee which can be called by the tender-inviting party should the successful tenderer refuse to accept the contract. Moreover, the successful tenderer may be asked to post a performance bond to guarantee the faithful performance of the contract.

This brief description of tendering procedures is based on British terminology. In the United States, 'bid', 'bidder', and 'bidding' are used for 'tender', 'tenderer', and 'tendering', and 'advertisement for bids' is used instead of 'invitation to tender', or 'invitation for tenders'. Moreover, the expression 'letting the contract' (i.e., awarding the contract) seems to be more common in the United States than in Great Britain.

tender bond

Bietungsgarantie,
Ausschreibungsgarantie

A tender bond (also known as a 'tender guarantee', 'bid bond', or 'bid guarantee') is a guarantee[2] by which the issuer (usually a bank) undertakes to protect the tender-inviting party against the failure of the tenderer to enter into a contract if his tender is accepted. In this case, the tender-inviting party can call the bond, and the issuer must pay the amount guaranteed, which usually does not exceed 10 per cent of the bid price.

term[1]

Laufzeit

In commercial English, the word 'term' is frequently taken to mean a "limited period of time", as, for example, in 'term of an insurance policy' (i.e., the period during which the policy is in force) or in 'term of a bill of exchange/promissory note' (i.e., the period until the bill of exchange/promissory note matures). The 'term of a patent' is the period during which the patent right may be exercised. The 'term of payment', or 'payment term', refers to the period within which the customer has to pay for the goods and/or services, while 'term of credit' is used to describe the period for which the lender grants a credit. 'Term of office' is the period during which a person is in office, e.g., the term of office of the U.S. President is four years.

term[2]

Bedingung,
Klausel

The word 'term' is also used as a synonym for 'condition', 'clause', 'stipulation', as in the case of 'trade terms', 'terms of payment', 'terms of delivery', 'terms to the trade' (i.e., terms granted to resellers), etc..

In colloquial English, it may also be used for 'price' (e.g., "his terms are £15 a lesson"; "what are your terms?").

terminal

Datenendgerät,
Terminal

In a data processing context, terminal – in its widest sense – refers to any point at which data may be input to, or output from, a data communications system. In other words, it is applied to any input and/or output device.

In practice, 'terminal' is most frequently used to describe a visual display unit, including a keyboard for interactive communication.

terms of delivery   Lieferbedingungen

The terms of delivery specify the time, place, and mode of delivery of the goods. In international trade, the place and mode of delivery are usually specified by standardised trade terms, e.g., by the INCOTERMS.

The following are a few examples of terms of delivery as they may be found in a business letter:

1. At present our time of delivery is two to three weeks. (Gegenwärtig beträgt unsere Lieferzeit zwei bis drei Wochen.)
2. Delivery will be effected f.o.b. Hamburg. (Lieferung erfolgt f.o.b. Hamburg.)
3. Delivery is to be made not later than Oct. 10. (Lieferung muß bis spätestens 10. Oktober erfolgen.)
4. Delivery can be effected in Vienna within four weeks after receipt of order. / ... within four weeks of order. / ... within four weeks from (of) receiving order. / (Lieferung kann in Wien innerhalb von vier Wochen nach Auftragseingang erfolgen.)
5. Please arrange for the goods to be sent by air. (Bitte veranlassen Sie, daß die Waren per Luftfracht versendet werden.)

terms of payment   Zahlungsbedingungen

The terms of payment specify the time of payment, the method of payment, and discounts, if any.

The terms of payment are negotiable between the contracting parties and may be laid down explicitly and in great detail in the contract. However, there are also "quasi-standardised" terms, which normally specify only certain aspects, e.g., 'payment in advance', 'cash with order', 'documents against payment', 'documents against acceptance'.

The U.N. and other international organisations are engaged in drawing up standardised terms of payment (PAYTERMS), which – in contrast to the INCOTERMS, dealing with the costs and risks of delivery – have not yet been widely accepted.

terms of trade   (reales) außenwirtschaftliches
                                     Austauschverhältnis

The terms of trade are the ratio of export prices to import prices, or, more precisely, of an index of export prices to an index of import prices. With the help of this ratio it is possible to measure changes in the purchasing power of exports in terms of imports. If export prices rise relative to import prices, the terms of trade are said to improve, because more imports can be bought for the same amount of exports, or the same amount of imports can be bought with a smaller amount of exports. If, on the other hand, export prices fall relatively speaking, the terms of trade deteriorate, i.e., they move against the country concerned. These changes must, however, be interpreted with care. An improvement in the terms of trade refers to prices only and tells us nothing about possible effects on volume. A sharp increase in export prices relative to import prices may well reduce export volume and, therefore, harm the country's balance of payments.

Many economists believe that the terms of trade of the less developed countries have deteriorated and those of the industrialised countries have improved in the course of this century, because prices of industrial goods have risen more sharply than commodity prices. Other economists have cast doubts on this theory, pointing out that the situation looks quite different if the current-account terms of trade (based on the prices of goods and services) are used instead of the commodity terms of trade (which exclude services).

through bill of lading   Durchkonnossement

A through bill of lading is a shipping document issued where the carriage by sea forms only part of the complete transit and the goods have to be transported also by land and/or air carriers. Through bills of lading are also issued where the first sea carrier does not call at the port of destination and a second sea carrier has to be used for the remaining part of the voyage. Obviously, it is much more convenient for the shipper to take out a through bill than to contract with the various carriers who have to carry the goods at the consecutive stages of the transit.

The shipper who takes out a through bill has only to deal with the carrier who signs the bill. This carrier undertakes to arrange the transshipment(s) of the goods with the oncarrier(s). The goods are delivered by the last oncarrier to the consignee only upon presentation of one of the originals of the through bill.

A special form of through bill is the through bill of lading covering oncarriage by air. This type is used where the goods, after having been unloaded at the port of discharge, are carried to their ultimate inland destination by air.

time bill   etwa: Zielwechsel (umfaßt Tagwechsel, Nachsichtwechsel und Datowechsel)

A time bill, also referred to as a 'time draft', is a bill of exchange which is payable
1. at a fixed date (e.g., "On April 1, 1985, pay to me or my order 300 U.S. dollars"); or
2. a specified period of time after sight (e.g., "90 days after sight pay ...". In practice, "90 days after sight" means "90 days after acceptance", because acceptance is taken as sight.); or
3. a specified period of time after the date of issue (e.g., "30 days after date pay ...").

It should be noted that in Austria there is no exact equivalent of the term 'time bill'. A time bill payable at a fixed date is equivalent to 'Tagwechsel', one payable a specified period of time after sight equivalent to 'Nachsichtwechsel', and one payable a specified period of time after date equivalent to 'Datowechsel'.

time of payment   Zahlungszeitpunkt

The time of payment is an extremely important element in contracts of sale and similar contracts since it affects a variety of costs and risks (e.g., interest costs and the time value of money, the risk of non-payment, the transfer risk).

In most cases, the time of payment is defined with reference to the delivery of the goods, although it may also be determined by the date or receipt of invoice (e.g., 'payment on receipt of invoice', 'payment within 60 days from date of invoice'). Moreover, it is also possible for payment to be stipulated for a fixed date.

Under the first method, payment may be effected either before delivery (e.g., 'payment in advance', 'cash with order', 'down payment'), on delivery (e.g., 'cash on delivery', 'payment on receipt of goods', 'down payment', and, especially in international trade, 'cash against documents', 'documents against payment', 'documentary letter of credit available against a sight draft'), or after delivery (i.e., where goods are sold on credit, e.g., '30 days net', 'two months' credit', '2/10, net 30', 'against three months' acceptance', 'open account terms', and, especially in international trade, 'documents against acceptance', 'documentary letter of credit available against a time draft').

trade¹   Handel (im engeren Sinne)

Trade, in its narrowest sense, refers to the buying and selling of goods, including barter, i.e., the exchange of goods for other goods and/or services.

In the case of 'domestic trade', the parties involved are residents of the same country, while 'foreign trade' (also referred to as 'external trade' or 'overseas trade') crosses the border and involves buyers and sellers in different countries.

If contrasted with commerce, trade is normally taken to mean the transfer of title to goods and of the corresponding consideration (payment), while commerce, in addition, includes a variety of auxiliary services that help to implement and facilitate the transfer of title. The most important of these services are: transport (physical transfer), warehousing, insurance, banking, and marketing.

trade²   Gewerbe,
                                             Sparte,
                                             Branche

Trade may also denote a mechanical or mercantile occupation carried on as a means of livelihood or profit (as in "he is a carpenter by trade"), or an industry (as in 'motor trade', 'building trade', 'textile trade', or 'trade press').

trade³   Geschäft(e),
                                             Geschäftstätigkeit

In British English, the term 'trade' refers not only to the buying and selling of commodities, but also to dealings in services and to business activity in general. This is why the profit/loss derived from the regular business activity of a firm is called 'trading profit'/'trading loss' (U.S.: 'operating profit'/'operating loss') and why the British say 'trade cycle' instead of 'business cycle'. The same consideration applies to the term 'sole trader', who is called 'sole proprietor' in the United States.

trade association   Fachverband

A trade association is an organisation set up by firms in a particular industry. It is formed for the purpose of protecting the interests of its members, and to represent them, e.g., in negotiations with the government, with trade unions, or with other trade associations.

trade cycle   Konjunkturzyklus

The term 'trade cycle' (U.S.: 'business cycle') refers to the more or less periodic fluctuations in the level of economic activity (as measured by the gnp) around what is called the trend line. The trade cycle may be divided into two stages, or phases (expansion and contraction), or, more usually, into four stages (boom, recession, depression, recovery).

The 'boom' is characterised by fast economic growth, full employment, high demand, and rising prices. Eventually, every boom will peak out, i.e., real gnp will begin to fall, and the cycle will enter the second stage, referred to as the 'recession' (according to American practice, a decline in real gnp for at least two consecutive quarters). A prolonged and severe recession is called a 'depression', e.g., the Great Depression from 1929 to 1932. The economy may, however, bottom out, i.e., real gnp may start rising again, before depression is reached. The period following a recession or depression is the 'recovery', or 'revival', which, if the upward trend is strong enough and maintained for some time, develops into a boom, although it may be aborted earlier.

Trade cycle theory is a highly controversial subject, and there are many different explanations of why the economy behaves in such a way. They range from the sun-spot theory (sun spots influence crops, and crops influence general economic activity) to complicated models combining the accelerator and the multiplier. Marxist economists attribute the cyclical fluctuations to defects inherent in the capitalist system. Whatever the true explanation, the cyclical behaviour of economic systems involves great hardship (e.g., unemployment in times of recession and depression) and a waste of resources in general (underutilisation of capacity). It is for this reason that governments, by deploying counter-cyclical policies, try to eliminate, or at least to mitigate, them as far as possible.

trade discount   Handelsrabatt,
Wiederverkäuferrabatt,
Stufenrabatt

A trade discount is a reduction in the price – usually a percentage of the list price – which is granted to a specific class of buyers, such as wholesalers or retailers, to compensate them for the performance of particular marketing functions. The size of the trade discount is ideally proportional to the costs incurred in reselling the product. Retailers have the highest operating cost per unit of sales; therefore, they enjoy the largest trade discounts on the product's retail price. For example, a manufacturer may quote a retail list price of £100 with trade discounts of 40 per cent and 15 per cent. The ultimate consumer pays the retailer £100, the retailer pays the wholesaler £60 (£100 less 40%), and the wholesaler pays the manufacturer £51 (£60 less 15%). The wholesaler is given the 40 and the 15 per cent discount and, in selling to the retailer, retains the 15 per cent to cover the costs of the wholesaling functions and passes on the 40 per cent to the retailer. It should be noted that the 40 and 15 per cent do not constitute a total discount of 55 per cent off the list price. Each discount percentage in the chain of discounts is computed on the amount remaining after the preceding percentage has been deducted.

Quoting retail prices and allowing trade discounts to different classes of buyers enables a manufacturer to use only one price list and, what is more important, to exercise a certain degree of control over the pricing policy in the channel of distribution.

trade policy   (Außen-)Handelspolitik

Trade policy comprises all measures taken by a government to control exports and imports of goods and services. Generally speaking, governments tend to promote exports because they provide foreign exchange, and to impose controls on imports.

In promoting exports, governments use both direct and indirect measures. Indirect export promotion comprises the services rendered to exporters by the country's diplomatic and consular missions, the provision of export information by government sources, government participation in foreign fairs and exhibitions, and other promotional efforts undertaken by the government abroad. In addition, indirect measures also include the granting of tax advantages to exporters (e.g., zero-rating of exports) and monetary measures, such as devaluing the domestic currency.

Direct export promotion includes the payment of export subsidies (in the form of straight cash payments by the government to exporters or in the form of interest subsidies on export credits), government export financing (e.g., the granting of buyer credits to foreign buyers, or of refinancing loans to exporters to finance their claims arising from supplier credits), and export credit insurance in the form of export credit guarantees (i.e., government-insurance facilities covering political and commercial risks which are peculiar to export transactions, but are not normally covered by commercial insurance).

Import controls comprise import duties and various non-tariff trade barriers. Import duties, like any other form of protectionism, or trade barrier, tend to reduce imports (which may help domestic industries and the balance of payments), but, on the other hand, they increase the cost of living, reduce international competitiveness, and invite other countries to retaliate by increasing their import duties.

trade reference   "Firmenreferenz"

When a customer places an order with a supplier with whom he has not previously done business, it is common practice for him to furnish the supplier with trade references. These are the names of persons or firms with whom the customer has had business contacts and to whom the supplier may refer for information about his financial standing and reputation. (For example, a customer may supply the following trade reference: "The following firms will be glad to furnish information as to our financial standing and reputation:

B. Kisby & Co.Ltd., 28 – 30 Lytham Square,
Liverpool;
The TELSTAR Manufacturing Co. plc, Century House,
Bristol.")

It should be mentioned that the customer may, alternatively or in addition, give the name and address of his banker.

trade terms   Handelsklauseln

Contracts of sale providing for the shipment of goods to foreign countries usually contain clauses relating to the delivery of the goods (methods, costs, risks, etc.) which are not customary in home trade. These trade terms are expressions that set out the rights and obligations of each party when it comes to transporting the goods. The main purpose of trade terms is to determine at what point the seller has fulfilled his obligations so that the goods, in a legal sense, can be said to have been delivered to the buyer.

These clauses have been developed by international mercantile custom to simplify the sale of goods abroad. Their meaning may be modified by agreement of the parties, the custom of a particular trade or in a particular port, etc., and they are sometimes interpreted differently in various countries. These differences may lead to misunderstandings and disputes among those engaged in international trade. To avoid this, frequent attempts have been made to standardise the terms, as, for example, in the INCOTERMS, published by the International Chamber of Commerce, or in the REVISED AMERICAN FOREIGN TRADE DEFINITIONS 1941.

trade union   Gewerkschaft

Trade unions (called 'labor unions' in the United States) are voluntary associations of employees formed for the purpose of protecting their interests, especially vis-a-vis their employers, in such areas as wage rates, working hours, working conditions, redundancies, etc..They try to achieve their goals by negotiating with individual employers or employers' organisations, but also by taking industrial action, if necessary (e.g., organising strikes, go-slows, etc.). Many trade unions, however, also engage in other activities. They may, for instance, provide educational and welfare services to their members (vocational training, strike pay, holiday homes, etc.) or support individual politicians and political parties to further their cause on the parliamentary level.

Today, we take the right of workers to form and join trade unions for granted. It is often forgotten that this right of combination had to be fought for. In Great Britain, for instance, some 40 acts prohibiting the formation of unions in various trades were not repealed until 1824.

Trade unions can be formed by combining workers in a particular craft (craft union), in a particular industry (industrial union), or on some other principle (e.g., white-collar union).

The individual unions are usually affiliated to some national federation or umbrella organisation (such as the Trades Union Congress – T.U.C. – in the U.K. or the American Federation of Labor and Congress of Industrial Organizations – A.F.L.-C.I.O. – in the United States) to discuss and solve problems common to all unions.

An objective assessment of the trade union movement is difficult, if not impossible, since unions, by nature, have to take sides. So we can offer only a personal view. It is probably safe to say that many of the basic rights enjoyed by working people would not exist but for the trade unions. On the other hand, trade unions have lately shown a tendency to become rigid, inflexible, and undemocratic, qualities which are particularly unfortunate in view of the rapid structural change which our economies are undergoing at the moment. This does not mean that the unions should be abolished. It means that they should be reformed, preferably from within, and should change their strategy. It is probably wrong and counter-productive to try to protect jobs in declining industries. Trade unions should rather insist on the creation of new jobs, and on retraining and removal grants for their members. But this is easier said than done, especially if an industry is suddenly threatened with a large number of redundancies.

trade-weighted value (of a currency)

außenhandelsgewichteter Außenwert (einer Währung)

The question of how much a particular currency is worth abroad can be answered in different ways. First, it is possible to express its value in terms of a large number of different currencies. This means that the currency concerned will have not only one but many different external values, which, moreover, may behave quite differently. For example, the value of the pound may fall vis-a-vis the yen, but rise vis-a-vis the dollar, and so on. If a single figure measuring the external value of a currency is required, it is necessary to use an index comprising the most important foreign currencies. The average of all external values of a particular currency is set equal to 100, and changes are expressed as percentages. If, for example, the value of the pound expressed in terms of a currency index is 112, this means that it has increased by 12 per cent on the base period. The increase is, as has already been explained, an average and may mask sharper rises in terms of several currencies, which are offset by falls or smaller rises in other currencies.

To make the currency index more realistic, normally a weighted version is used to reflect the relative importance of the component currencies. A very common method of determining the weights is to calculate them on the basis of the percentage shares of external trade denominated in a particular foreign currency in the total value of foreign trade of the country whose currency is being measured. Hence the name 'trade-weighted value'. In the currency index used to measure the external value of the pound, for instance, the Italian lira is assigned a lower weight than the D-mark or the U.S. dollar, since less of Britain's trade is denominated in Italian lire than in D-marks or U.S. dollars.

trading down

Umstellung auf ein weniger hochwertiges Sortiment, Trading-Down

Trading down – the opposite of trading up – involves the addition of lower-priced items to a line of high-priced prestige items, or the eventual elimination of the higher-priced items. The idea is, of course, to attract lower-income or more budget-minded customers and thus to broaden the customer base. This strategy may, however, backfire if the addition of cheaper products tarnishes the image of the higher-priced items and drives away the old customers.

trading stamp   Rabattmarke

Trading stamps are paper stamps which retailers, mainly supermarkets, give their customers in proportion to the value of their purchases as a kind of discount in order to encourage sales. The customer collects the stamps in a special book (stamp book), which, when full, he can exchange for money or for goods, either at the retailer's where he obtained the stamps (which is more usual in Austria) or at a special trading stamp centre (which is common practice in Great Britain). Stamps typically cost the retailers two to three per cent of sales. (They pay £2 to £3 for a thousand stamps, and give one stamp for every 10 pence worth of purchases.).

trading up   Sortimentsaufwertung,
                                     Trading-Up

Trading up is a product strategy by which a manufacturer or dealer adds high-priced prestige products to his line of low-priced products, or even completely replaces the latter with the former. The aim of this move is to attract a new class of customers and to benefit from the usually higher profit margins on higher-priced prestige products. Whether such a strategy is really successful depends on the individual circumstances. There is always a danger, however, that the firm will be unable to shed its image of being a seller of "cheap" goods.

trailer   Anhänger

A trailer is a wheeled road vehicle drawn by some other vehicle (tractive unit, or tractor) and specifically used for carrying goods.

By contrast, a semi-trailer has wheels only at the back, and its front is supported by the rear of its tractive unit when attached.

transfer of technology   Technologietransfer

The term is usually used in a restricted sense and refers to the fact that technology (i.e., the knowledge concerned with the application of science to the production of goods and services) developed in industrial countries is made available to less developed countries.

Technology may take many forms and may be transferred in many ways. It may be represented by patents, know-how, trade marks, and other forms of industrial property, or it may be embodied in plant and equipment and in what some economists call "human capital" (i.e., trained personnel).

The transfer may be effected by contracts of sale, licensing agreements, by means of training programmes, or by seconding qualified personnel. The transfer of technology may involve government agencies, international organisations, private institutions, independent commercial firms, parent and subsidiary companies of multinational groups, and parties to co-operation agreements ("joint ventures"). Technology may be transferred on commercial or on concessionary terms, i.e., it may be sold at market prices, below market prices, or it may be given away free of charge (technical aid).

Although there can be no doubt that less developed countries need new technologies, the question is whether the technologies developed by the industrialised countries are always suitable for third-world countries.

transfer price   (konzerninterner) Verrechnungspreis

Transfer prices are the prices charged and paid on intra-group transactions, i.e., on the sale of goods and/or services by one group company (either the parent or one of the subsidiaries) to another group company. Since buyers and sellers in intra-group transactions do not deal at arm's length with one another (i.e., they are not independent of one another), it is possible for transfer prices to differ considerably from market prices charged to independent customers. The ability to manipulate prices in this way gives a large multinational group considerable scope in allocating the profits on such transactions to countries with low tax rates. For example, a group company in a high-tax country might under-invoice goods or services supplied to another group company in a low-tax country, thus reducing its own profits while increasing the profits of its trading partner. Where the seller operates from a low-tax country, the opposite strategy (viz., over-invoicing) would be required to minimise the group's overall tax liability.

In recent years, such practices have become much more difficult to carry out because revenue and customs authorities have adopted tougher rules on transfer pricing. One method used is to require the exporting company to submit a document (e.g., a consular invoice or a customs invoice) on which the domestic (market) price of the export goods has to be stated.

transfer risk   Konvertierungs- und Transferrisiko

Transfer risk is defined as the risk of an imposition of exchange controls by the importer's country or of a shortage of foreign currency. This means that the importer's local currency deposit in payment for goods and/or services cannot be converted into the appropriate foreign currency and transferred to the exporter's country.

transport   Transport

In its most general sense, transport means the physical transfer of goods from one place to another, as opposed to the legal transfer of title from the seller to the buyer.

An efficient transport system is essential to the individual manufacturer or trade, as well as to the domestic and the international economy as a whole. Transport plays a vital role in the distribution of goods from producers to ultimate consumers and is, therefore, an important element in the whole marketing process. Efficient transport lowers distribution costs, which enables firms to open up new markets and, consequently, increase production. By facilitating the movement of goods transport offers industrial firms a wider choice of locations, allowing them to select regions which give the best balance of economic advantages. From an overall point of view, transport has, among other things, a positive impact on the standard of living by making it possible for countries to import a wide range of commodities they cannot produce themselves.

Economic and legal aspects as well as advantages and disadvantages of the various modes of transport are dealt with under the headings of "carriage of goods by air", "carriage of goods on inland waterways", "carriage of goods by rail", "carriage of goods by road", and "carriage of goods by sea".

transportation insurance   Transportversicherung

'Transportation insurance', which is only used in American English, is an all-inclusive term for ocean marine insurance, inland marine insurance, and aviation insurance.

traveller's cheque   Reisescheck

Travellers' cheques are cheque-like instruments drawn by a bank or a similar financial institution on itself and sold to persons wishing to have a safe means of payment when travelling abroad. Travellers' cheques can be cashed at practically any bank throughout the world. They are obtainable in nearly all important currencies and are issued in fixed denominations (e.g., denominations for U.S. $-cheques: $10, $20, $50, and $100). The most important institutions issuing and selling travellers' cheques are: Bank of America, First National City Bank, American Express Company, Barclays, etc.. Travellers' cheques are, however, also sold by many other banks on a commission basis.

The following is a practical example of how to use travellers' cheques: a person wishing to travel to, say, the U.S.A. may buy $-travellers' cheques from his bank at a price equal to the face value plus a bank commission (e.g., in Austria, the commission is usually 1 per cent). When purchasing travellers' cheques, the buyer must sign each of them on the front in the space provided. Together with the cheques, the customer gets a receipt, which he should keep separate from his cheques. In the case of loss or theft, this receipt is needed as evidence of the purchase. If the customer needs cash during his stay in the U.S.A., he presents the cheques to a U.S. bank, signs them once again in the presence of a bank officer, and gets U.S. dollars. Apart from being cashed at banks, travellers' cheques are also accepted by hotels, shops, restaurants, etc.. The countersignature serves as a safeguard against dishonest finders or thieves. Only if the signature and the countersignature correspond, will the cheque be honoured. It is obvious that travellers' cheques should never be countersigned except in the presence of the person who agrees to accept them. Finally, it should be noted that the customer may also use his $-travellers' cheques in countries other than the U.S.A..

One major advantage of travellers' cheques is that the owner of lost or stolen cheques is reimbursed by the issuing institution, provided he has not countersigned them. The numbers and amounts of lost or stolen cheques should be reported without delay to the issuing institution.

Unused cheques are redeemable at face value by the issuing institution.

trial order   Probeauftrag,
                                    Kauf zur Probe

A trial order is an order for a small quantity of goods for testing purposes. It may be followed by a larger order if the buyer is satisfied with the quality of the goods, or if he finds that there is a market for them.

trust[1]   Treuhand(verhältnis)

In legal usage, a trust is an arrangement under which a person or a corporation (the trustee) holds and administers property for the benefit of another person or other persons (the beneficiary/beneficiaries). Trusts are created by transferring the nominal ownership of property to a trustee, enjoining him to use it only for the benefit of a specified person or specified persons.

Trusts are very common in the management of private affairs (e.g., a father may create a trust for his children in his will), but they can also be found in the commercial field. In the second half of the 19th century, before holding companies were permitted in the United States, trusts were used to create monopolies by combining the most important firms in a particular industry (Massachusetts trusts). Other examples of commercial applications are the British unit trusts (see: investment fund) and the trust companies in the United States.

trust[2]   wettbewerbshemmender
                                    Unternehmenszusammenschluß

In commercial usage, a trust is a combination of firms formed with the intention or effect of restricting competition. Trusts may be created in a number of ways, e.g., by forming a trust in the narrower sense of the word (see: trust[1]), by setting up a holding company, or by entering into an explicit or implicit contract to restrain competition. From this definition it can be seen that the term 'trust' covers the historical Massachusetts trust, groups of companies dominating the market, and certain types of cartels.

tug   Schlepper

A tug, or tugboat, is a small and very powerful motor vessel specially built for towing (pulling along) other, usually much larger, ships.

turnover[1]   Umschlagshäufigkeit

By turnover is meant the number of times a set of items is replaced within a given period of time, normally a year. The term usually refers to the turnover of stock, or inventory (stock turnover, stockturn, inventory turnover). In this case, turnover is calculated by dividing average stock (average inventory) into annual sales, both valued either at cost or at selling prices. The result of this calculation indicates how often the stock (inventory) has been 'turned over'. By the way, average stock (average inventory) is computed by adding up opening stock (beginning inventory) and closing stock (ending inventory), dividing by two.

Different lines have different rates of turnover. A fishmonger will have a very high rate of turnover since he sells his entire stock almost daily, while a bookseller will have a much lower rate of turnover because he turns over his stock only twice or three times a year.

turnover[2]   Umsatz

In British usage, turnover refers also to the total revenue received by a firm from selling goods and services in the ordinary course of business, i.e., it is synonymous with 'sales[1]'.

turnover[3]   Fluktuation

see: labour turnover

turnover tax   Bruttoallphasenumsatzsteuer

The turnover tax is a multi-stage sales tax, i.e., it is levied at each stage in the production and distribution of goods and services. Since the tax burden can usually be shifted forward by including the tax paid in the selling price of the commodity, the disadvantage of this tax is that the value taxed at each stage includes the tax paid at earlier stages, which means that tax is paid on tax, and, the more stages there are, the more expensive the final product must be. This shows that the turnover tax is a cumulative, multi-stage tax, also known as 'cascade tax'. The disadvantage of multiple taxation is avoided by V.A.T., under which each seller in the chain of distribution is allowed to deduct the input tax he has paid to his suppliers from his overall V.A.T. liability.

In Austria, turnover tax was replaced by V.A.T. in 1972.

typewriter   Schreibmaschine

The typewriter, which is one of the oldest office machines, started out as a fairly simple mechanical device, which was – and still is – operated by hitting keys marked with letters and other characters. This activates a separate lever for each character and brings an embossed printing element into contact with the back of a coloured ribbon, thus marking the paper, which is fed into the machine and secured there by means of a platen.

In electric typewriters, the type bars are replaced with a golf-ball typing element, activated by an electric motor, with the keys establishing the necessary electric contact when pressed. The electric motor also operates the carriage return. Many electric typewriters include a correction feature, which does away with the rather messy correction process by means of a fluid.

The next stage was the electronic typewriter with a daisy-wheel printing element, a small electronic memory, a line display (up to forty characters), and an advanced automatic correction feature, which simplifies the correction of mistakes if they occur in the line just being typed. Advanced models enable the typist to type a line into the machine's memory, correct it, and have it printed while typing the next line.

A number of producers offer components which can be added to electronic typewriters, converting them into fully-fledged word processing systems.

typing pool
zentrales Schreibbüro,
zentrale Schreibstelle

Typing pools are large rooms devoted exclusively to typing chores. They provide a centralised typing service in large firms. Dozens of audio typists transcribe material from recordings either distributed to them by a supervisor or made on their own dictating machines direct from the dictator's office through the PBX (private branch exchange).

U

**unconfirmed irrevocable
(documentary) letter of credit**

unbestätigtes, unwiderrufliches
Dokumentenakkreditiv

An unconfirmed irrevocable L/C differs from a confirmed irrevocable L/C in that
the advising bank, after having received the irrevocable L/C from the issuing bank,
merely advises/informs the beneficiary of the terms of the credit without
confirming it, i.e., without adding its undertaking to pay to that of the issuing bank.
Therefore, an unconfirmed L/C does not convey any engagement on the part of
the advising bank.

Under an unconfirmed irrevocable L/C, the beneficiary may draw a sight draft or
time draft on the issuing bank and present it together with the shipping documents
to the advising bank, which, in turn, may forward them to the issuing bank for
payment or acceptance. However, it is much more common for the issuing bank to
authorise the advising bank to honour a draft drawn on it by the exporter under the
L/C. The advising/paying bank will nearly always pay the beneficiary of such a
credit if the documents conform to the terms of the credit. But it should be clearly
understood that this is voluntary, and that the advising bank is under no obligation
to honour such a draft. For example, the advising bank would refuse to honour the
draft in cases where it may have reason to believe that it would not obtain
reimbursement from the issuing bank for any amount paid to the beneficiary (e.g.,
when there is a danger that exchange controls might be imposed by the importer's
country).

From the foregoing it can be seen that selling against an unconfirmed irrevocable
L/C is safe if the credit is issued by a reliable bank, and the political situation in the
country concerned is stable.

underground economy

Schattenwirtschaft

The underground economy, also known as the 'shadow economy' or 'black
economy', comprises all economic activities which are not recorded in the national
income statistics, either because they are illegal or, although legal, are not
reported, mainly to evade taxes. Illegal activities include drug dealing, prostitution,
bribery, fraud, theft and burglary, etc., while unreported income may stem from
self-employment, dependent employment, investment activities, and so on. The
incomes of moonlighters and unlicensed workers are of special importance in this
context.

It is difficult, if not impossible, to determine the size of the underground economy
with any degree of precision. Experts estimate the U.S. underground income for
1981 at $420 billion, equal to about 14 per cent of official gnp. The corresponding
figure for Italy should be as high as 25 per cent.

The existence of an underground economy not only distorts national income
statistics, but also unemployment figures. According to one estimate, official
figures overstate unemployment by as much as two per cent. The main problem,

however, is the loss of tax revenue for the government, although it must not be forgotten that much of the underground economic activity might never take place if taxes had to be paid on it.

underwriter[1]

Versicherer

In insurance, the term 'underwriter' is applied to a company or individual prepared to accept insurance risks. In this sense, therefore, every insurer, whether a company or an individual, is an underwriter. In practice, however, the term is more commonly applied to insurers who are individuals, e.g., to Lloyd's underwriters. These individual underwriters are usually formed into groups, called 'underwriting syndicates', or 'syndicates of underwriters', which normally specialise in a particular class of business.

underwriter[2]

Emissionsgarant,
Emissionsmittler

An underwriter in the investment field is an issuing house, a broker, or an investment bank engaged in underwriting.

underwriting

G.B.: Emissionsgarantie, Underwriting
U.S.A.: Fremdemission,
Emissionsgeschäft

When used in an investment context, the term 'underwriting' refers to the services offered by specialised financial institutions to companies wishing to raise capital by issuing securities. There is, however, a difference between British and American usage in so far as in Great Britain the term is used in a narrower sense than in the United States. In Great Britain, underwriting denotes only the guarantee offered by an issuing house or a broker to take up any part of a new issue that is not taken up by the public. In the United States, this is referred to as 'pure underwriting' and represents only one variant of underwriting in general. There is also 'commitment underwriting', where an American investment bank buys the whole issue outright, selling it at a slightly higher price for its own account. In Great Britain, the latter method is called an 'offer for sale' and is not regarded as underwriting.

unemployment

Arbeitslosigkeit

The generally accepted meaning of unemployment is the inability of people who are able and willing to work to find employment at the going wage rate. Alternatively, the term may also refer to the number of unemployed. From this definition it can be seen that only involuntary joblessness (an American term) is regarded as unemployment in the proper sense of the word, while voluntary forms (rentiers, housewives) are excluded. It must be admitted that the distinction between involuntary and voluntary unemployment is not as clear as may appear from the above definition, and it may be incorrect as well as unfair to classify a housewife that has given up looking for a job as "voluntarily unemployed" ("discouraged workers").

In view of the complexity of the economic system, it is not surprising that there should always be some unemployment, even though the number of vacancies may actually exceed the number of job-seekers. "Friction" (i.e., the imperfections of the labour market, such as the time lost between two jobs, lack of information) is responsible for this type of unemployment. Anything that speeds up the search process will obviously reduce 'frictional unemployment' (e.g., more and better information, jobcentres, placement agencies).

'Seasonal unemployment' is due to the seasonal pattern of work in some industries, most markedly in tourism, agriculture, and construction. It is extremely difficult, if not impossible, to eliminate seasonal unemployment, although careful planning of work in the building industry and, where feasible, the encouragement of a second "season" in tourism may help to mitigate the problem.

Frictional and seasonal unemployment, although involving a considerable waste of resources and much hardship, are not the real problem. This cannot be said of short-term 'cyclical' and long-term 'growth-gap' unemployment, which are both caused by a deficiency of demand. To illustrate the dimension of the problem involved, it may be sufficient to mention that 23% of the British labour force and 26% of the Austrian labour force were unemployed during the Great Depression, and that, at the time of writing, unemployment (how much cyclical and how much growth-gap?) in the O.E.C.D. countries is still a staggering 9 per cent, or 32 million out of work. Reflationary policies would be a suitable remedy for cyclical unemployment. In the case of growth-gap unemployment, there is a more fundamental discrepancy between the supply of, and the demand for, labour, a discrepancy that may require unorthodox methods (e.g., shorter working week, job sharing) if it is either impossible or undesirable to encourage growth rates that would absorb the surplus labour.

'Structural unemployment' is not due to any lack of jobs, but to a mismatch between the type and/or location of jobs offered and the qualifications and/or location of the job-seekers. Some economists regard the geographical element of structural unemployment, and some even structural unemployment as a whole, as a special variety of frictional unemployment. Whatever classification is used, structural unemployment is characteristic of periods with rapid and profound structural changes in the economy. Suggested remedies are: retraining, increased geographical mobility (retraining and relocation grants), short-term and medium-term labour market forecasts, information campaigns on job opportunities, etc..

'Technological unemployment' results from the replacement of workers by labour-saving machines, computers, microprocessors, etc., or, to use the appropriate economic jargon, from an increase in the capital-labour ratio. Here again, economic growth will probably not be sufficient to absorb the redundant workers, and a shorter working week may be the only solution. The main fears in connection with this measure are that it will push up costs or reduce aggregate demand. This need not happen if the reduction in working hours does not exceed productivity gains, and real wages are neither increased nor decreased.

unemployment rate   Arbeitslosenrate

The unemployment rate is calculated by dividing the number of unemployed into the labour force, multiplying by one hundred. In other words, it expresses the number of unemployed as a percentage of the labour resources available at given wage rates. Apart from economic and institutional factors (e.g., school-leaving age, retirement age), the rate is also influenced by the definition of "unemployed people". (see: labour force)

unilateral transfers

Übertragungsbilanz,
Bilanz der Transferleistungen,
Bilanz der unentgeltlichen Leistungen

Unilateral transfers form part of the balance of payments on current account and include all transfers – in the form of commodities, services, or money – made to, or received from, non-residents without any consideration. In other words, a person or government transfers commodities, services, or money to some other person or government in a foreign country, but receives nothing in exchange.

Unilateral transfers typically include private (personal and institutional) transfers (e.g., private donations by charitable institutions, like OXFAM; remittances by migrant workers to their families) and official transfers (e.g., pensions, economic aid, military aid). It should be remembered that transfers made to foreign countries have a negative impact on the current account, just as have visible and/or invisible imports, whereas the opposite is true of transfers received.

unitisation

Bildung von Einheitsladungen

Unitisation means the creation of unit loads. A 'unit load', or 'unitised load', is a single item or a number of items packed or arranged in a specified manner and capable of being handled as a unit. Unitisation may be accomplished by placing the item or items in a container (containerisation) or by stacking it or them on a pallet (palletisation).

When unit loads are transported, the movement of goods no longer involves passing individual packages from hand to hand during transport. Instead, the handling equipment at the different stages of the transport process can be adapted to the standard sizes of the unit loads, thus enabling freight handling to be fully mechanised. Other advantages of unitisation are:
1. Unit loads can easily be transferred between the various modes of transport, e.g., from road to rail, rail to ship, etc., without constant rehandling of the individual items contained in them.
2. Low risk of damage and pilferage, leading to a reduction in insurance premiums.
3. Savings in packing costs.

unit pricing

Grundpreisauszeichnung

This has been standard practice in wholesale transactions for a long time. It simply involves stating the price for one unit (e.g., one ounce, one pound) of the product in question. The new development is its extension to retail selling, where it is intended to facilitate price comparisons. A jar of jam would then be marked not only with the price for the whole jar, but also with the price for one ounce.

unit shop   Einzelgeschäft

A typical unit shop is a small, independent, owner-operated retail establishment. The term emphasises the fact that, in contrast to the multiple store, there is only one outlet. Unit shops, which can be found in many different lines (groceries, hardware, electrical appliances, etc.), are facing heavy competition from the large retail concerns, especially from supermarkets and discount stores. In spite of this, many are able to hold their own and at least to eke out an existence, because they enjoy certain advantages inherent in small-scale operations. These include: flexibility, the absence of red tape, personal interest of the owner and his family (reflected in the term 'mom-and-pop store'), friendly atmosphere, personal service, convenient location (reflected in the terms 'neighbourhood store' and 'corner shop'), low overheads, etc.. The disadvantages are equally obvious: low volume, higher prices (inability to obtain quantity discounts), small catchment area, small number of customers, limited range of goods, low profits and low return on capital invested, especially if struck after allowing for what the owner-operator would earn as an employee in a comparable job (i.e., the earnings of management).

unsolicited offer   unverlangtes Angebot

An unsolicited offer (also called a 'voluntary offer') is an offer sent to a prospective customer without an inquiry having been made. This type of offer may be sent to an individual person or firm or a small number of persons or firms and is frequently made in the form of sales letters.

Unsolicited offers are often sent to regular customers to inform them of a special opportunity (e.g., goods at particularly favourable prices), or to customers who have not sent orders for a long time. To create new business, firms may send unsolicited offers to a carefully chosen list of potential customers.

V

valuation account   Wertberichtigungskonto

A valuation account is an account which partly or wholly offsets one or more other accounts. For example, Accumulated Depreciation is a valuation account related to specified depreciable assets, and Allowance for Bad Debts is a valuation account related to accounts receivable.

value-added tax   Mehrwertsteuer (MWST)

Value-added tax (V.A.T.) is a multi-stage, comprehensive, non-cumulative sales tax. 'Multi-stage' means that the tax is levied at each stage in the production and distribution process whenever goods are imported or change hands or services are rendered. The term 'comprehensive', or 'broad-based', indicates that, in contrast to excise duties, V.A.T. is basically chargeable on all goods and services, although the system provides for certain exceptions. 'Non-cumulative' means that the tax paid at one stage is not included in the tax base for the next stage. This is in contrast to the turnover tax, or cascade tax.

Under the V.A.T. system, a trader (i.e., a seller of goods and/or services) charges his customers a certain percentage of the sales price (there may be different rates for different types of transactions, or supplies, in V.A.T. jargon), which he pays over to the fiscal authorities (in the U.K., to the Board of Customs and Excise). In doing so he is allowed to deduct any value-added tax that he has had to pay to his suppliers (i.e., his input tax). This means that the tax payable at any particular stage is levied only on the difference between the selling price and the cost of the goods and services obtained by the trader from his suppliers, in other words, on the value added by the former. Hence the name 'value-added tax'. It will be clear from the foregoing that, although paid by the firms involved in the production and distribution of the goods or services concerned, V.A.T. is ultimately borne by the final consumer, who is unable to shift the tax. (see: indirect tax)

As has already been mentioned, different transactions may be chargeable at different rates, the idea being to tax essentials at lower rates and luxury goods at higher rates. Some types of transactions may be zero-rated. This means that they are completely relieved from V.A.T., although the trader involved is allowed to deduct the input tax he has paid to his suppliers from his overall V.A.T. liability, which, in certain cases, may result in a refund. In all countries that have adopted this system (the most important are the members of the E.E.C. and Austria), exports are zero-rated, and exporters do not charge V.A.T. to their customers. (In the U.K., also food is relieved from V.A.T.). Imports, on the other hand, are subject to import V.A.T., as well as to customs duties, if any.

Another method of relief from V.A.T. is exemption, under which a trader does not charge V.A.T. to his customers, but, in contrast to zero-rating, he is <u>not</u> allowed to deduct the input tax paid to his suppliers.

videotex

Videotex

At the time of writing, videotex is emerging as the generic label applied to electronic information retrieval systems, whatever the telecommunications technology on which they are based. The term, therefore, covers systems using telephone lines, cables, or broadcast signals, such as Teletext, Videotext, Bildschirmtext, Prestel, Teledata, etc..

Videotex information retrieval systems enable private or business users to call up on their video screens (either special VDUs or modified T.V. sets) news on any selected topic and a variety of continuously updated information on various subjects, such as airline schedules, stock and commodity prices.

visual display unit

optische Datenanzeige,
Datensichtgerät,
Terminal

Visual display units (VDUs, also referred to as 'video display terminals') are output devices for making computer-processed data available to users. Many of these units, or terminals, include a cathode-ray tube (CRT) with a screen to display information either in digital form (figures, characters) or in graphic form (lines, curves, etc.). Smaller displays are often based on liquid crystal technology (LCD, liquid-crystal display). In practice, a visual display unit also incorporates a keyboard to enable inquiries to be made (interactive mode of operation).

voluntary sector

„dritter" Sektor

Traditionally, the economy has been divided into a private sector and a public sector, with the former including the private profit-making firms, and the latter the government agencies, nationalised industries, and other public corporations. Recently, however, economists – with the American economist Weisbrod foremost among them – have identified a "third" sector, which comprises voluntary, non-profit organisations, such as fire brigades, the Red Cross, worker co-operatives, neighbourhood associations, agricultural communes, local food co-operatives, self-help groups, etc..

These organisations, which typically are small, flexible, and neighbourhood-oriented, have developed in response to the failure of the other two sectors to supply certain essential needs, for such reasons as lack of vision, lack of funds, bureaucratic inefficiency, absence of profits, etc.. More positively, the voluntary sector owes its existence to a desire for active social involvement and more direct forms of democracy.

It is difficult to assess the purely economic importance of the voluntary sector. According to American estimates, the gross product attributable to it in the United States in 1974 was around $70 billion, or roughly 5 per cent of the American gnp.

voyage policy   Reisepolizze,
                                               Einzelpolizze

A voyage policy (also referred to as a 'special policy', 'specific policy', or 'individual policy') is a kind of (ocean) marine insurance policy, under which the subject-matter (ship or cargo) is insured for one specified trip from one point to another. This means that both hull policies and ocean cargo policies may be written as voyage policies.

In contrast to a voyage policy, a 'time policy' covers the subject-matter for a stipulated period of time. A 'mixed policy', which is frequently used in commercial practice, is one which covers both a voyage and a period of time (e.g., "from London to Cadiz for two months").

W

w.a.   w.a.

W.a., standing for 'with average', is a type of insurance cover for goods in (ocean) marine insurance. W.a. means that, incontrast to an f.p.a. policy, the insurer is not only liable for total loss/damage and general average, but also for particular average loss (i.e., partial loss of, or damage to, the goods not due to a general average act).

In detail, a w.a. policy covers
1. total loss of, or damage to, the goods due to major sea perils, such as stranding, sinking, fire, explosion, collision, heavy weather, etc.;
2. total loss of, or damage to, any package during loading, transshipment, or discharge;
3. general average loss/damage and contribution; and
4. partial loss of, or damage to, the goods
   (i) if the ship is stranded, sunk, or burnt, or
   (ii) if the loss or damage is attributable to fire, explosion, collision or contact of the vessel with any external object (ice included).
Partial loss or damage by other sea perils (in particular, heavy weather damage) is fully recoverable provided the loss or damage exceeds a certain percentage of the sum insured stated in the policy (in the case of most cargoes, three per cent). This percentage, known as the 'franchise', is intended to eliminate the expense of handling numerous small claims.

In practice, the only difference in cover between w.a. and f.p.a. occurs when partial loss is caused by heavy weather and the vessel has not been stranded, sunk, or burnt during the voyage. Under a w.a. policy, the loss would be recoverable subject to the franchise, but under an f.p.a. policy, it is not recoverable at all.

wage   Lohn

In its wider sense, the term 'wage' refers to the income derived from dependent employment. At this level, it is contrasted with other factor incomes, such as profit and rent. In a narrower sense, the term is applied to the income of blue-collar employees and should be contrasted with salary – the income of white-collar (or salaried) employees.

Another useful distinction is the one between wage(s) and earnings. The term 'wage(s)' is usually restricted to the remuneration received for a standard working week (or any other unit of time chosen as a basis for paying wages), while earnings include wages in this sense and, in addition, also overtime pay and fringe benefits.

It is also important to distinguish between nominal wages and real wages. Nominal wages are expressed in monetary terms, while real wages refer to the amount of goods and services that can be bought for a given nominal wage.

Wages play an extremely important role in the economic life of a country because they represent, on the one hand, the main source of income for the majority of the working population, and, on the other hand, an important cost element for the business organisations. The level of wages directly affects the standard of living of employees and, since it is a major determinant of profits, also the standard of living of employers and the level of investment. Thus, inevitably, there is a constant tug-of-war between employees and employers, with the former trying to push up wages and the latter trying to keep them down. The actual level of wages at any given time is, therefore, determined by the balance of power in the struggle, the outcome being decided by such factors as the demand for, and the supply of, labour, the economic situation, profit margins, trade union power and policy, negotiation skills, etc.. In most countries, the government is also a force to be reckoned with. Most governments pursue some kind of incomes policy, e.g., setting minimum wages, imposing wage freezes or compulsory arbitration.

wage systems   Lohnformen

Wages are paid in two main ways: by time (time rates) or by piece, i.e., output (piece rates). Time rates are usually in the form of hourly, shift, or weekly rates for a specified number of hours. Time rates are suitable for precision work and dangerous work, where a wage-induced increase in speed may lead to lower quality and a higher rejection rate or to more accidents respectively. But this method is also used for work involving a large number of different activities, where output is difficult to measure (e.g., repair work or materials handling). In some cases, time rates are combined with a bonus element (bonus system). Ideally, time rates induce employees to work more carefully, but, at worst, they may encourage loitering and idleness if the employer does not use other (non-monetary) incentives or disincentives to maintain a reasonable level of output.

In the case of piece rates, the remuneration paid to the worker depends on the output produced within a given period of time by him or by a group of workers of which he is a member. This is the least sophisticated version of piece rates. Most firms use slightly more complicated methods, for instance, the task system of pay, which is based on a standard time allowance for a particular job or task. Under this system, an employee working very quickly during an eight-hour working day may, for instance, be paid for 10 hours. In a variant of this system, a bonus is paid for the time saved on the time allowance. Piece rates and the bonus system are often referred to as 'payment by results' or 'incentive payments', since their main purpose is to induce employees to work harder. The piece-rate system is a controversial method of payment. On the one hand, it may enable an efficient worker to earn more, but, on the other hand, it may become a dehumanising form of exploitation. (Witness the reports by Walraff on piece work in German industry.)

warehouse warrant   Orderlagerschein

When goods are deposited in a public warehouse, the depositor receives from the warehouse keeper either a warehouse warrant (in the U.S. called a 'negotiable warehouse receipt') or a warehouse receipt (in the U.S. known as a 'non-negotiable warehouse receipt'). The warehouse warrant is issued to the depositor or his order and, consequently, can be transferred by indorsement and delivery.

From the legal point of view, it serves as a receipt for the goods and, like the bill of lading, is also a document of title to the goods, giving the holder of the document (i.e., either the depositor, or any other person to whom it may have been transferred) the right to claim delivery of the goods from the warehouse keeper. Being a document of title, the warehouse warrant is a symbol of the goods in storage represented by the document, and a transfer of the warehouse warrant is deemed to be a symbolic transfer of the ownership and/or possession of the goods. When the time comes for the holder of the warehouse warrant to withdraw the goods from the warehouse, he must produce the document.

The practical value of the warehouse warrant is to enable the holder to dispose of the goods while they are in storage. They may be sold merely by indorsing and delivering the warehouse warrant to the indorsee.

In contrast to the warehouse warrant, the warehouse receipt is only a receipt for the goods, in which the warehouse keeper undertakes to deliver the goods to the depositor. Such a receipt is not a document of title, and the warehouse keeper will release the goods to the depositor even though the latter does not produce or surrender the receipt, since no one other than the depositor is entitled to demand delivery of the goods.

war risks insurance   Kriegsversicherung

War risks insurance may be described in general terms as a kind of insurance covering loss of, or damage to, the insured subject-matter caused by war, civil war, revolution, rebellion, insurrection, etc..

The various war risks are, however, always excluded from a policy in the ordinary form, but may be specifically insured against for an extra premium. In cargo insurance, for example, it is usual to reinstate the war risks into the policy and to incorporate, in addition, any hostile act, mines, and torpedoes.

wharfage   Kaigebühren;
                                Kailagergeld

Wharfage means the charge one has to pay for the use of a wharf for freight handling, as well as the charge for storing goods at a wharf.

wholesale banking   (kommerzielles) Großgeschäft der
                                Banken,
                                Großgeschäft der Banken mit
                                „geldmarktfähigen" Kunden

In the United States, where the term originated, wholesale banking means providing loans and other banking services to major corporations and governmental and financial institutions, as well as catering for the investment and related needs of wealthy individuals.

In Britain, the term 'wholesale bank' refers to banking institutions (such as merchant banks, London-based subsidiaries of U.S. and other foreign banks, and other money market banks) that deal mainly in large sums of money, and on behalf of companies rather than private individuals.

wholesaler

Großhändler, Grossist

Typically, a wholesaler buys in large quantities from manufacturers to sell to retailers in smaller quantities. But strictly speaking, wholesale transactions need not be carried out by wholesalers, nor need the quantities involved be large. Any sale to a business customer or institution (government, hospitals, etc.) of goods and services not intended for personal use, i.e., any sale to any customer that is not an ultimate one, represents a wholesale transaction. This means that also retailers (e.g., when selling to restaurants) or manufacturers (e.g., when selling to other manufacturers or retailers) can engage in wholesaling. The term 'wholesaler', however, is normally reserved to firms that are primarily engaged in wholesaling. Another distinction that should be observed is the one between wholesalers and wholesaling middlemen. Wholesalers buy and sell for their own account, taking title to the goods, while wholesaling middlemen (such as brokers) act for their principal's (e.g., a manufacturer's) account.

Wholesalers, in the United States also referred to as 'distributors' or 'jobbers', provide marketing services that are essential in the process of moving goods from the manufacturer to the consumer, services that would have to be provided by somebody else (e.g., the manufacturer or retailer) if the wholesaler did not exist. Being specialists, wholesalers are, however, more likely to provide these services efficiently and at a low cost. A simple example should serve to highlight the potential economies involved in wholesaling. Six manufacturers selling to four retailers would result in 24 transactions. By using the services of one wholesaler the number of transactions can be reduced to 10.

The specialised services offered by the wholesaler to the manufacturer or retailer, or both, include: delivery, storage, credit, market information, personal selling, assembling and dividing, and related matters.

Wholesalers may be classified either on the basis of the range of goods offered or on the basis of the services provided by them. Accordingly, there are general-line wholesalers (e.g., food wholesalers) and specialty wholesalers (e.g., frozen food wholesalers); full-service and limited-service wholesalers (e.g., cash-and-carry wholesalers). The rack jobber is a special type of full-service wholesaler (actually, he offers more services than the regular full-service unit), specialising in a particular line of goods (e.g., books).

word processing

(automatisierte) Textverarbeitung

Word processing involves the manipulation of words, sentences, and paragraphs for the purpose of originating, revising, editing, reformating, and reproducing letters, reports, and other texts. Typically, the term is applied to these activities only if they are carried out with the help of sophisticated equipment, such as mainframe computers, personal computers, or special word processors. What does this mean in practical terms? The words are typed on a keyboard, stored in the word processor's memory (usually a floppy disk), and displayed on a visual display unit. By pressing a few keys mistakes can be corrected quickly. Standard phrases (e.g., "We enclose our price list") are kept in the word processor's memory, and a personal touch (e.g., "You may be specially interested by item 4") can be quickly inserted. Once the corrections have been keyed in, the typing or printing is done at great speed. If the machine is linked to a telephone line or a network, letters can be sent electronically to other word processors, thus saving postal costs.

worker co-operative   Produktivgenossenschaft

A worker co-operative, or workers' productive society, is an enterprise controlled – and in many cases owned – jointly by all or some employees. The employee-members are paid wages and salaries, and the surplus remaining after all current business expenses have been met and some of it has been set aside for investment is either shared among the members in the form of a bonus or may be used for charitable purposes. There are no profits in the ordinary sense of the word.

Ideally, the worker co-operative is a more egalitarian form of business organisation than the sole trader, the partnership, and the company, since it is run by the workers themselves on the principle of "one man – one vote". Worker co-operatives are an attempt to eliminate the separation between labour and capital and the consequent alienation of workers typical of the traditional forms of enterprise. Workers that own, or at least control, the organisation they work for can be expected to show greater involvement and job satisfaction than their colleagues working for a traditional entrepreneur. This does not mean that worker co-operatives have no problems. Setting aside sufficient funds for investment purposes, for instance, might be more difficult than in a traditional firm, and making workers redundant is likely to be even more of a problem.

Worker co-operatives are usually quite small and often form part of the counter-culture. Not only do they produce a distinct range of products (whole foods, alternative furniture), but the way things are done is at least as important as the articles produced.

Worker co-operatives can be found in most countries of the world, although there are large variations in numbers. There are very few co-operatives of this type in Great Britain and Austria, where until recently the labour movement and the trade unions were opposed, or at least indifferent, to worker co-operatives and considered nationalisation a more efficient method of breaking the "capitalist stranglehold" on the economy. Worker co-operatives are definitely more popular in France, Italy, and in Spain where the Mondragon co-operatives, started in the inter-war period, have been very successful and have become an important factor in the Spanish (more precisely, in the Basque) economy.

Generally speaking, this type of co-operative seems to be experiencing an upswing. Many new co-operatives are being formed, some of them by workers buying out a bankrupt firm to protect their jobs.

worker participation   Arbeitnehmermitbestimmung

Worker (or employee) participation is based on the idea that working people should be informed about, consulted about, and help decide about their working lives instead of simply carrying out commands which are passed down to them from the higher levels of management and which they may not even fully understand.

Worker participation may be implemented at various levels in a business organisation. Shop-floor participation, for instance, involves the workers engaged in the actual production and/or distribution of goods and basically means that they are given greater freedom to organise their work. In the case of boardroom participation, the workers, through their representatives, take part in the consultation and decision-making of the board of directors, laying down the fundamental objects of the company, reviewing and approving corporate plans, deciding about mergers, take-overs, aquisitions, and divestitures, etc.. Worker directors, as these representatives are called, are rare in Great Britain, since worker representation on company boards is optional. In West Germany and Austria, by contrast, the law requires one third (and in some German industries, even half) of the members of the supervisory board of large companies to be workers' representatives.

Worker participation may be regarded as part of a wider movement seeking to apply the principles of political democracy to other fields of life, and, from that point of view, is often referred to as 'industrial democracy'.

working capital   Nettoumlaufvermögen

The most widely accepted definition of working capital is "current assets minus current liabilities". There are, however, some authors who distinguish between 'gross working capital' (equal to current assets) and 'net working capital' (equal to the difference between current assets and current liabilities).

Working capital can be regarded as a measure of liquidity, although it suffers from the same limitations as the current ratio (which is calculated by dividing current assets by current liabilities), because it includes the relatively illiquid inventories.

Apart from being used as a measure of liquidity, working capital may also serve as a basis for statements of changes in financial position. Statements of changes in financial position on a working capital basis show the sources and uses of working capital and the change (increase or decrease) in working capital between two balance sheet dates. They are an alternative to statements of changes in financial position on a cash basis (cash-flow statements).

work station   Bildschirmarbeitsplatz

In data processing and office systems, a work station would normally consist of a visual display unit and a keyboard, enabling an operator to perform his or her task.

work-to-rule   Dienst nach Vorschrift,
                                      Aktion „Vorschrift"

Work-to-rule is a form of industrial action in which the employees remain at work, but slow down operations by observing the regulations relating to their work strictly and literally. In contrast to a go-slow, work-to-rule does not constitute a breach of the contract of employment, and is, therefore, a safe and efficient measure of putting pressure on an employer.

Y

yield

Rendite,
Effektivverzinsung

Yield is the income derived from a financial investment expressed as a percentage of the value of that investment. The term is used in connection with dividends from shares, interest from bonds, rent from property, etc..

In the case of shares, we have to distinguish between 'dividend yield', i.e., the last dividend expressed as a percentage of the current share price, and 'earnings yield', in which case earnings per share (i.e., both distributed and retained profits per share) are used as the basis for the calculation. The price-earnings ratio, or price-earnings multiple, provides the same information as the earnings yield, but presents it in a slightly different way. It is calculated by dividing earnings per share into the current share price. A price-earnings ratio (p/e) of, say, 5 indicates that the current price is five times the earnings per share and would correspond to an earnings yield of 20%.

In the case of bonds, the current yield has to be contrasted with the yield to redemption, which allows for such elements as issue price and redemption price, maturity, time of interest payments (e.g., whether interest is paid annually or semi-annually), etc..